New Concise Webster's Dictionary

A comprehensive guide
to the English language
for home, office, and school.

MODERN PUBLISHING
A Division of Unisystems, Inc.
New York, New York 10022

• • •

• • •

Printed in U.S.A.

This version of the Longman New Pocket Dictionary is published by arrangement with Longman UK Limited, London.

CONTENTS

PAGE

Guide to the dictionary

spelling — **°conversation** /kon″ vər sā′ shən/ *noun*
a talk: *I had a long* **conversation** *with your teacher.*

see exercise 1 on page 6 for more information on how to find words in the dictionary

meaning — **°clinic** /klin′ ik/ *noun*
a place where people go to see a doctor

all the definitions are written using only 1,600 common words
° before a word means that it is used in definitions

more than one meaning — **diet** /dī′ ət/ *noun*
1 what you eat
2 special food eaten by people who want to get thinner, or people who are ill: *She is* **on a diet.**

the most common meaning is shown first

examples — **°foot** /fo͝ot/ *noun*
(*plural* **feet** /fēt/)
1 the part of your leg that you stand on: *We decided to go* **on foot** (=walking).
2 the bottom of something: *the* **foot** of a hill
3 a measure of length equal to twelve inches: *The man was six* **foot/feet** *two (inches).*

the examples show how the word is used with other words in a sentence
see exercise 2 on page 6

part of speech — **import[1]** /im pôrt′/ *verb*
to bring into a country for use there: *We* **import** *many automobiles in our country.*

import[2] /im′ pôrt/ *noun*
something that is imported: *Cocoa is one of our* **imports.**

[1] and [2] show different grammatical uses of words which are spelled the same
see exercise 3 on page 7

difficult past tense — **°know** /nō/ *verb*
(*past tense* **knew** /no͞o/, *past participle* **known** /nōn/)
1 to have in the mind; have learned: *Do you* **know** *what happened? I* **know** *how to swim.*

this is shown when a verb does not add *-ed* to form the past tense
see exercise 4 on page 7

rain[2] *noun (no plural)*
water falling from the sky: *There was* **rain** *in the night.*

related words — **rainbow** /rān′ bō/ *noun* an arch of colors in the sky, especially after rain
raincoat *noun* a coat that keeps out the rain

words made from the main word are listed below it
examples are usually given to illustrate or explain the words

difficult plurals — **reply**[2] *noun* (*plural* **replies**)
an answer: *His* **reply** *was, "I'm very well, thank you."*

plurals are shown for all nouns which do not just add *-s*
see exercise 5 on page 8

no plural — **sap** /sap/ *noun (no plural)*
the liquid inside a plant which feeds the plant

nouns marked *(no plural)* do not have a plural form and are not used with *a* or *an*
see exercise 6 on page 8

°**shame** /shām/ *noun*
the feeling you have when you have done something wrong or silly: *When his teacher told his parents about his behavior, he felt great* **shame. What a shame** (=I'm sorry) *that you can't go home.*

idioms — common idioms and phrases are shown in heavy type

°**shut** /shut/ *verb (present participle* **shutting,** *past* **shut**)
to move something so that it is not open; close: *Please, will you* **shut** *the door? He decided to* **shut down** (=close for ever) *the shop.* **Shut up!** (=a rather rude way of saying Be quiet!)

verb phrases — verb phrases, which have a special meaning, are shown in heavy type, with explanations

pronunciation and stress — **technology** /tek nol′ə jē/ *noun (no plural)*
using the knowledge we get through science to make things in factories, build things, etc.

the dictionary shows full pronunciation and stress
see Pronunciation Guide for the symbols used

a b c d e f g h i j k l m n o p q r s t u v w x y z

1

Alphabetical order: how to find a word in the dictionary quickly

The words in the dictionary are listed in alphabetical order. Above is the alphabet.

A word which begins with **b,** like **book,** will be near the front of the dictionary, but one which begins with **t,** like **table,** will be near the back, and one which begins with **m,** like **make,** will be near the middle of the dictionary.

First practice putting these words into alphabetical order, without using the dictionary:

road	far	see
ask	house	turn
box	zoo	careful

Now look at these words:

and	August	asleep
about	agree	aim
atom	allow	address

All these words start with the letter **a,** so to put them into alphabetical order you must look at the second letter of the word. **b** comes before **n,** so you will find **about** before **and** in the dictionary. Now put the other words above into alphabetical order.

If the first two letters of the words are the same, you have to look at the third letters, and so on.

To help you to find the words quickly, the first or last word on each page is shown at the top of the page.

2

Using the examples

The examples tell you more about what a word means and how it is used in a sentence. For example, look at:

°**foot** /fŏŏt/ *noun*
(*plural* **feet** /fēt/)
1 the part of your leg that you stand on: *We decided to go* **on foot** (= walking).
2 the bottom of something: *the* **foot** *of a hill*
3 a measure of length equal to twelve inches: *The man was six* **foot/feet** *two (inches).*

From the examples we see that **on foot** means "walking", that the bottom of a hill is called the **foot** of a hill, and that when foot means "a measure of length" the plural can be **foot** or **feet.**

Now look at these entries in the dictionary, read the examples, then write different sentences yourself using the words:

usual	imagine	regret
give	quite	what
job	accident	before

example: **usual**

Peter went to school at the **usual** *time today.*

3

Noun, verb, adjective

When you hear or read a new word, you need to know what sort of word it is before you can use it in a sentence. Look at the words below and see which sentence you can use them in:

table	new	small
eat	red	teacher
goat	sleep	work

1. *I can see the...*
2. *I...at home.*
3. *My house is...*

example: **table**

I can see the **table.**

The words which can be used in the first sentence are all names of a person, place, animal, or thing: they are **nouns.** The words which can be used in the second sentence all tell us what someone or something does or is: they are **verbs.** The words which can be used in the third sentence all describe something: they are **adjectives.**

Now look at these words in the dictionary. Write them in three lists: nouns, verbs, and adjectives. Then use each one in a sentence:

sell	grow	make
door	lovely	river
common	want	work

example: **sell**

We **sell** *lemonade.*

4

Verb endings

Most verbs add **-ing** to form the present participle, and **-ed** to form the simple past tense and the past participle.

For example: **walk**

Peter **is walking** *home from school.*
He **walked** *home from school yesterday.*
He **has walked** *home from school every day this week.*

Some verbs change their endings, or have completely different forms in the past tenses.

For example: **drive**

Peter's father **is driving** *home from work.*
He **drove** *home from work yesterday.*
He **has driven** *home from work every day this week.*

Now look at these verbs in the dictionary and make sentences with them, like the ones above:

eat	fly	swim
drop	leave	take
catch	read	teach

example: **eat**

Anna **is eating** *a banana.*
She **ate** *a banana yesterday.*
She **has eaten** *a banana every day this week.*

5

Plural forms of nouns

Most nouns add **-s** to form their plurals (like **dog:** a **dog,** some **dogs**). Some have different plural forms (like **man:** a **man,** some **men**). This dictionary tells you when you do not just add **-s** to form the plural.

For example:

sheep /shēp/ *noun*
(*plural* **sheep**)

Look at the entries in the dictionary for the nouns listed below. Write sentences with the words, using the plural form:

child	foot	shelf
box	leaf	thief
enemy	mouse	zebra

example: **child**

There are thirty **children** *in my class.*

6

Uncountable nouns

Some nouns do not have a plural form (like **water**). This means that they are never used with **a** or **an**. This dictionary tells you when a noun does not have a plural form.

For example:

traffic /traf′ ik/ *noun*
(no plural)

Look at the entries in the dictionary for the nouns listed below. Then decide if they fit in sentence 1 or sentence 2:

cup	bread	spoon
milk	flour	tea
bottle	mango	yam

1. *I bought three. . .s from the shop.*
2. *I bought some. . .from the shop.*

examples: **cup, milk**

I bought three **cups** *from the shop.*
I bought some **milk** *from the shop.*

PRONUNCIATION GUIDE

Accents

Symbol	Usage
[ʹ]	primary stress
[ʺ]	secondary stress

Sounds

Symbol	Key Word
a	hat
ā	hay
â	air, hare
ä	harm, balm
b	bit
ch	church
d	dip
e	bet
ē	be
f	few, phony, tough
g	gap
h	hat
hw	white, somewhere

Sounds

Symbol	Key Word
i	bit
ī	bite
j	jury, budge
k	kin, cat, clique
l	lip, puddle
m	me, him, hymn
n	nut, tin
ng	sing
o	hot, top
ō	over, coat, toe
ô	sought, tall, lawn
oi	noise, boy
o͝o	cook
ou	bout, cow
o͞o	tool, choose

PRONUNCIATION GUIDE

Sounds Symbol	Key Word	*Sounds* Symbol	Key Word
p	pot, sheep	v	void, ever
r	red	w	win, always
s	simmer, cent, lass	y	yes, buyer
sh	shell, mission, dish	z	zero, clothes
t	tip, stopped	zh	pleasure
th	thin, swath	ə	a in about
TH	them, either, soothe		e in system
u	up		i in stencil
u̇	pull, wood, would		o in lemon
ū	use		u in circus

Aa

°**a** /ə *or* ā/
1 one; any: *I gave him* **a** *pencil.* **A** *bird has two legs.*
2 for each; in each: *The candy costs 10 cents* **a** *bag; three times* **a** *year*
an /an/ is used instead of **a** before a word that starts with the sound of a, e, i, o, or u: **an** *apple and* **an** *orange*

abandon /ə ban′ dən/ *verb*
to leave or give up completely: *The baby was* **abandoned** *by its mother. We* **abandoned** *our vacation plans because we had no money.*

abbreviation /ə brē″ vē a′ shan/ *noun*
a short way of writing a word or name: *Mr. is the* **abbreviation** *for Mister.*

°**ability** /ə bil′ ə tē/ *noun*
the power or knowledge to do something: *She has the* **ability** *to do it, but she is lazy.*

°**able** /ā′ bəl/ *adjective*
having the power or the knowledge to do something: *Is he* **able to** *swim?*

aboard /ə bôrd′/ *preposition, adverb*
on or onto a ship or airplane: "*Are all the passengers* **aboard?**" *asked the captain.*

abolish /ə bäl′ ish/ *verb*
to stop (something that is happening); get rid of completely: *The new government* **abolished** *the tax on clothing.*
abolition /a″ bə lish′ ən/ *noun (no plural)*

°**about** /ə bout′/ *preposition, adverb*
1 concerning; of: *What are you talking* **about?**; *a book* **about** *birds*
2 a little more or less than: *Come (at)* **about** *six o'clock.*
3 here and there: *The children were kicking a ball* **about.** *They walked* **about** *the town.*

°**above** /ə buv′/ *adverb, preposition*
at a higher place; higher than; over: *The lamp hangs* **above** *the table. We watched the birds in the sky* **above. Above all** (= more than anything else) *I like learning English.*

°**abroad** /ə brôd′/ *adverb*
in or to a foreign country: *My brother is studying* **abroad.**

abrupt /ə brupt′/ *adjective*
1 sudden: *an* **abrupt** *knock at the door*
2 not polite: *an* **abrupt** *answer to his question*
abruptly *adverb*

°**absent** /ab′ sənt/ *adjective*
not there; not present: *He was* **absent** *from work last Tuesday.*
absence *noun: Her* **absence** *was noticed by the teacher.*
absentminded *adjective* forgetful

absolute /ab′ sə lo͞ot″/ *adjective*
complete: *Are you telling me the* **absolute** *truth?*
absolutely *adverb*

absorb /əb sôrb′ *or* əb zôrb′/ *verb*
1 to take in liquid slowly: *The cloth* **absorbed** *the water in the bowl.*
2 to learn thoroughly: *I haven't really* **absorbed** *all the rules yet.*
absorbent *adjective* able to take in liquid
absorbing *adjective* very interesting: *an* **absorbing** *book*

absurd /ab surd′ *or* ab zurd′/ *adjective*
very silly: *The story was so* **absurd** *that no one believed it.*
absurdly *adverb*

abuse[1] /ə būz′/ *verb* (*present participle* **abusing,** *past* **abused)**
1 to speak rudely to: *Don't* **abuse** *that old man, he can't help walking slowly.*
2 to treat badly or use wrongly: *The teacher* **abused** *his power: he made his students work in his garden after school.*

abuse[2] /ə būs′/ *noun*
1 rude things said to someone: *The taxi driver was shouting* **abuse** *at the slow cyclists.*
2 bad treatment or wrong use: *The pupil who tore the cover of his book was scolded for* **abuse** *of school property.*

accent[1] /ak′ sent/ *noun*
1 the way a person from a certain place speaks: *Mr. Singh speaks English with an Indian* **accent.**
2 greater weight given to one part of a word when it is said: *In "garden", the* **accent** *is on "gar".*

accent[2] *verb*
to give strength to a word or part of a word: *In the word "garden", "gar" is* **accented.**

°**accept** /ak sept′/ *verb*
1 to receive or take: *James* **accepted** *the apple I offered him.*
2 to agree to do something: *David asked three friends to his party, and they all* **accepted.**
acceptable *adjective* of good enough quality: *Your work is not* **acceptable,** *please do it again.*

access /ak′ ses/ *noun*
a way to get to a place, a person, or something: *There is no* **access** *to the street through that door. Students need* **access** *to books.*

°**accident** /ak′ sə dənt/ *noun*
something, often bad, that happens by chance: *John's had an* **accident:** *he's been knocked down by a car. I'm sorry I broke the cup: it was an* **accident.** *I met Jacob* **by accident** (= by chance) *in the market.*

accident

accidental /ak″ sə dənt′ əl/ *adjective: I didn't mean to break it: it was* **accidental.**
accidentally *adverb*

accommodate /ə kom′ ə dāt″/ *verb* (*present participle* **accommodating,** *past* **accommodated)**
1 to give someone a place to live or stay: *One apartment can* **accommodate** *a family of five.*
2 to have space for: *You could* **accommodate** *another four children in your class.*
accommodation *noun* somewhere to live or stay: *to look for* **accommodation**

accompany /ə kum′ pə nē/ *verb* (*present participle* **accompanying,** *past* **accompanied)**
1 to go with someone: *He* **accompanied** *me to the doctor's.*
2 to play music while someone else is singing or playing another instrument: *Maria sang and I* **accompanied** *her on the piano.*

accomplish /ə kom′ plish/ *verb*
to do or finish satisfactorily: *I*

accomplished *two hours' work before dinner.*

°**according to** /ə kôr′ ding/ *preposition*
from what is said or written: **According to** *him, sugar is bad for you.*

account[1] /ə kount′/ *noun*
1 a story or description: *an exciting* **account** *of the match*
2 a list of payments owed to someone
3 an amount of money kept in a bank: *He paid the money into his* **bank account.**
accountant *noun* a person whose job is to keep accounts for people or companies
accounts *plural noun* lists of money spent and money earned

account[2] *verb*
to give the reason for: *I can't* **account for** *Peter's unhappiness.*

accurate /ak′ ya rət/ *adjective*
right; correct: *Is this watch* **accurate?**
accurately *adverb*

accuse /ə kūz′/ *verb* (*present participle* **accusing,** *past* **accused)**
to say that someone has done something wrong: *The teacher* **accused** *Jacob of hiding the book.*
accusation /ak″ yə za′ shən/ *noun*

accustom /ə kus′ təm/ *verb*
to make someone used to something: *She is* **accustomed** *to studying every day.*

°**ache**[1] /āk/ *verb* (*present participle* **aching,** *past* **ached)**
to be painful; hurt: *Her head* **ached** *all night.*

°**ache**[2] *noun*
a continuing pain: *a stomach* **ache**

achieve /ə chēv′/ *verb* (*present participle* **achieving,** *past* **achieved)**
to do or get successfully by working: *He* **achieved** *top marks in the examination.*
achievement *noun* something that you have worked hard for

acid /as′ əd/ *noun*
a powerful liquid that can burn things

acknowledge /ak näl′ ij/ *verb* (*present participle* **acknowledging,** *past* **acknowledged)**
1 to agree that something is true: *Do you* **acknowledge** *that you've been wrong?*
2 to write that you have received something: *Please* **acknowledge** *my letter.*
acknowledgment *noun*

acquaintance /ə kwānt′ əns/ *noun*
a person you know, but who isn't a friend

acquire /ə kwīre′/ *verb* (*present participle* **acquiring,** *past* **acquired)**
to get or buy: *How did you* **acquire** *this money?*

acre /a′ kər/ *noun*
a measure of land; 43,560 square feet

°**across** /ə krôs/ *adverb, preposition*
from one side of a place to the other; on the other side of something: *They swam* **across** *the river. The house is* **across** *the street.*

°**act**[1] /akt/ *verb*
1 to do or behave: *The children* **acted** *very badly at school.*
2 to pretend to be someone else, in a play or film
action /ak′ shən/ *noun* something done: *The government's* **action** *will prevent war.*

°**act²** *noun*
1 an action; something done: *an* **act** *of bravery*
2 something pretended: *When Jane said she hated him, it was an* **act.** *She likes him really.*
3 a part of a play

°**active¹** /ak′ tiv/ *adjective*
always doing things: *He is an* **active** *member of the club, and loves arranging things for people to do.*
actively *adverb*
activity /ak tiv′ ə tē/ *noun* 1 (*plural* **activities**) something we do, especially as an amusement: *Dancing is her favorite* **activity.**
2 *(no plural)* being active: *The classroom was full of* **activity;** *every child was busy.*

active² *adjective*
doing the action: *In the sentence "John kicked the ball", "kicked" is an* **active** *verb.*
The opposite of **active** is **passive.**

actor /ak′ tər/ *noun*
a man who acts in plays or films

actress /ak′ tris/ *noun* (*plural* **actresses**)
a woman who acts in plays or films

actual /ak′ cho͞o əl/ *adjective*
real and clear: *We think he stole the money, but we have no* **actual** *proof.*
actually *adverb* really; in fact

A.D. /ā dē/
abbreviation of Latin *Anno Domini* used in dating time after the birth of Christ (used in dates)

adapt /ə dapt′/ *verb*
to change; make more suitable: *Have you* **adapted** *to living in a different country?*
adaptable *adjective* (of a person) able to adapt easily

°**add** /ad/ *verb*
1 to put together with something else: *James had seven eggs. I* **added** *three, so now they all* **add up to** *ten.* **Add** *these numbers* **up** *in your book.*
2 to say something more
addition /ə dish′ ən/ *noun* 1 adding 2 something added: *Our baby brother is an* **addition** *to our family.*

adder /ad′ dər/ *or* **viper** *noun*
a snake with a dangerous bite

°**address¹** /ə dres′ *or* ad′ res/ *noun* (*plural* **addresses**)
the name of the place where you live

°**address²** *verb*
1 to write an address on: *She* **addressed** *the letter.*
2 to speak to: *The football captain* **addressed** *his team.*

adequate /ad′ ə kwit/ *adjective*
enough: *There is* **adequate** *food for everyone.*

°**adjective** /ad′ jə tiv/ *noun*
a word that describes something: *In the phrase "a beautiful song", "beautiful" is an* **adjective.**

adjust /ə just′/ *verb*
to make a small change in something to make it better: *Joseph* **adjusted** *the bicycle seat so that his feet reached the ground.*

administer /ad min′ əs tər/ *verb*
to govern; look after the running of: *The government* **administers** *the country.*
administration /ad min″ əs trā′ shən/ *noun: The principal's job is the* **administration** *of the school.*

admiral /ad′ mə rəl/ *noun*
the most important officer in the navy (see)

°**admire** /ad mīr′/ *verb* (*present participle* **admiring,** *past* **admired**)
to think a person or thing is very good, nice to look at, etc.
admiration /ad′ mə rā′ shən/ *noun: Maria looked at the skirt with* **admiration.**

°**admit** /ad mit′/ *verb* (*present participle* **admitting,** *past* **admitted**)
1 to agree that something unpleasant about yourself is true: *She* **admitted** *she was lazy.*
2 to let in: *This ticket* **admits** *two people to the football game.*
admission /ad mish′ ən/ *noun* **1** something, such as a crime, admitted **2** permission to go in: **Admission** *was free for children.*

adolescent /ad″ ə les′ ənt/ *noun*
someone between about 13 and 19 years old

adopt /ə dopt′/ *verb*
1 to take a child into your family and treat him or her as your own
2 to agree to use: *We* **adopted** *Paul's plan.*

adore /ə dôr′/ *verb* (*present participle* **adoring,** *past* **adored**)
to like or love very much: *She* **adored** *her son. I* **adore** *chocolate.*

adult /ə dult′ *or* ad′ult/ *noun*
a grown-up person

advance /ad vans′/ *verb* (*present participle* **advancing,** *past* **advanced**)
to move forward: *The army* **advanced** *toward the town.*
advanced *adjective:* **advanced** (= more difficult) *lessons*

°**advantage** /ad van′ tij/ *noun*
something that helps a person: *Anna speaks good English, but she has an* **advantage** *because her mother is English.*

°**adventure** /ad ven′ chər/ *noun*
an exciting thing that happens to someone: *He wrote a book about his* **adventures** *as a soldier.*
adventurous *adjective* liking a life full of adventures

°**adverb** /ad′ vurb″/ *noun*
a word which tells us how, when, or where something is done: *In the sentence "She sang a song beautifully today", "beautifully" and "today" are both* **adverbs.**

°**advertise** /ad′ vər tīz″/ *verb* (*present participle* **advertising,** *past* **advertised**)
to put notices where a lot of people will see them: *The company* **advertised** *for a new secretary.*
advertisement /ad′ vər tīz″ mənt/ *noun: The wall was covered with* **advertisements.**

°**advise** /ad vīz′/ *verb* (*present participle* **advising,** *past* **advised**)
to tell (someone) what you think he or she should do: *She* **advised** *me to wear my best clothes.*
advice /ad vīs′/ *noun (no plural): He never* **takes my advice** (= does what I tell him).

affair /ə fâr′/ *noun*
1 work or business: *He put his business* **affairs** *in order.*
2 an event: *The party was a very noisy* **affair.**

affect /ə fekt′/ *verb*
to make a difference to: *The great heat* **affected** *his health* (= he became ill).

affectionate /ə fek′ shə nit/ *adjective*
feeling or showing love
affectionately *adverb*

°**afford** /ə fôrd′/ *verb*
to be able to pay for: *We can't*

afford *a car.*

°**afraid** /ə frād′/ *adjective*
frightened: *James says he's not* **afraid** *of lions!*

°**after** /af′ tər/ *preposition*
1 later than: *Tomorrow is the day* **after** *today.*
2 behind: *The child ran* **after** *her dog. I wanted to go out, but I decided to stay at home and work* **after all** (= considering everything).

°**afternoon** /af″ tər no͞on′/ *noun*
the time between midday and evening

°**afterward** /af′ tər wərd/ *adverb*
later: *We saw the film and* **afterward** *walked home together.*

°**again** /ə gen′/ *adverb*
one more time; once more: *Come and see us* **again** *soon. My aunt visits us* **now and again** (= sometimes).

°**against** /ə genst′ *or* ə ginst′/ *preposition*
1 on the other side from; not agreeing with: *We won our match* **against** *that team. He is* **against** *hunting animals for their skins.*
2 close to; touching: *The ladder is leaning* **against** *the wall.*

°**age** /āj/ *noun*
1 the amount of time someone has lived or something has been: *What is the* **age** *of that church? Mary is eight years* **of age.**
2 a period of time in history: *the* **Iron Age**
aged *adjective* being of the age of: *He was* **aged** *ten.*

agent /ā′ jənt/ *noun*
a person who looks after business for someone else: *A travel* **agent** *arranges transportation.*

°**ago** /ə gō′/ *adverb*
in the past: *We came to live here six years* **ago.**

agony /ag′ ə nē/ *noun*
very bad pain or trouble: *The wounded man was* **in agony.**

°**agree** /ə grē′/ *verb* (*present participle* **agreeing,** *past* **agreed**)
to think the same as someone else: *I* **agree** *with you. He* **agreed to** (= said yes to) *the plan.*
agreement *noun: They have made an* **agreement** *about the plan. They are all* **in agreement.**

agriculture /ag′ rə kul″ chər/ *noun*
the science of growing crops and raising animals; farming
agricultural *adjective*

°**ahead** /ə hed′/ *adverb*
in front; forward: *Walk straight* **ahead** *until you reach the river.*

aid[1] /ād/ *noun*
a help: *A dictionary is an* **aid** *to learning English.*

aid[2] *verb*
to help: *He* **aided** *the criminal.*

°**aim**[1] /ām/ *verb*
1 to point or get ready to throw something toward something else: *He* **aimed** *(the gun) at the lion.*
2 to want to be or do: *He* **aimed** *to swim a mile.*

°**aim**[2] *noun*
1 pointing at or getting ready to throw something
2 something you want to do: *His* **aim** *was to swim a mile.*

°**air**[1] /âr/ *noun*
1 what we breathe: *He came* **by air** (= in an aircraft).
2 an appearance: *an* **air** *of excitement*

aircraft *noun* (*plural* **aircraft**) a flying machine

helicopter

glider

aircraft

airfield *noun* a place where airplanes land

air force *noun* a group of soldiers who use aircraft for fighting

airline *noun* a company which carries people or goods by airplane

airmail *noun* letters and parcels sent by aircraft

airport *noun* a place where aircraft land and take off, and are kept

°**air**[2] *verb*
to make (rooms or clothes) fresh by letting air into them

airplane /ār′ plān″/ *noun*
an engine-driven aircraft heavier than air

alarm[1] /ə lärm′/ *noun*
1 a feeling of fear or danger
2 something that warns of danger: *They heard the fire* **alarm** (= bell).
3 a clock that rings a bell at the time you want to wake up

alarm[2] *verb*
to worry or frighten: *My mother was* **alarmed** *when I fell over.*

album /al′ bəm/ *noun*
a book with empty pages on which you can put photographs, stamps, etc.

°**alcohol** /al′ kə hol/ *noun*
a strong liquid, in beer and other drinks, which makes you feel drunk
alcoholic *adjective: Beer is an* **alcoholic** *drink.*

alert[1] /ə lurt′/ *adjective*
awake and ready to act, study, etc.: *You must keep* **alert** *in class.*

alert[2] *noun*
a signal that someone is in danger

algebra /al′ jə brə/ *noun*
a kind of number work in which you use letters in place of numbers that you do not know

alight[1] /ə līt′/ *verb*
1 to step down from a train, bus, etc.
2 to land: *The bird* **alighted** *on the branch.*

alight[2] *adjective*
burning; on fire: *He set the dry leaves* **alight.**

°**alike** /ə līk′/ *adjective, adverb*
the same in some way: *They were all dressed* **alike** *in white dresses.*

°**alive** /ə līv′/ *adjective*
living; not dead: *Is his grandfather still* **alive?**

°**all** /ôl/ *adjective, adverb*
1 the whole amount of; every one of: *Don't eat* **all** *that bread!*
2 completely: *He was dressed* **all** *in black.*
3 **at all** (used to make "not" stronger): *I'm not* **at all** *sorry I came; I'm glad!*

alley /al′ lē/ *noun*
a narrow road

°**allow** /ə lou′/ *verb*
to let someone do something: *He* **allowed** *me to borrow his hammer.*

°**all right** /ôl rīt/ *or* **alright** *adjective, adverb*
1 well; unhurt: *The car turned over but the driver was* **all right.**
2 good enough; well enough: *Don't shut the door, it's* **all right** *as it is.*
3 yes; I agree: *Shall we go to town?*

All right, *let's go now.*

ally[1] /al′ ī *or* ə lī′/ *noun* (*plural* **allies**)
someone who helps you fight against someone else: *France and England were* **allies** *in the war.*

ally[2] *verb* (*present participle* **allying,** *past* **allied**)
to be an ally of: *England* **allied** *with France.*
alliance *noun: The two countries made an* **alliance.**

°**almost** /ôl′ mōst/ *adverb*
nearly: *Hurry up — it's* **almost** *time for school.*

°**alone** /ə lōn′/ *adverb*
1 without others: *I was* **alone** *all day with no one to talk to.*
2 only: *This key* **alone** *will open the door.*
3 (used in some phrases): **Leave** *the dog* **alone** (= don't touch it or trouble it)!

°**along** /ə lông′/ *preposition, adverb*
1 following the length of; from end to end of: *We walked* **along** *the road.*
2 on; forward: *Move* **along** *please!*
3 with (someone): *Can I bring my friend* **along?**

alongside /ə lông′ sīd′/ *preposition, adverb*
by the side of: *Put your chair* **alongside** *mine.*

°**aloud** /ə loud′/ *adjective*
in a voice that is easy to hear: *She read the story* **aloud** *to her brother.*

°**alphabet** /al′ fə bet/ *noun*
the letters of a language in a special order: *Our* **alphabet** *begins with A and ends with Z.*
alphabetical *adjective: These names are in* **alphabetical order:** *Joseph, Michael, Peter.*

°**already** /ôl red′ ē/ *adverb*
1 before this or that time: *He has seen that film twice* **already.**
2 by now; by this or that time: *It was* **already** *raining when we started our journey.*

°**also** /ôl′ sō/ *adverb*
as well; too: *Rose wasn't the only girl there; Sarah was there* **also.**

altar /ôl′ tər/ *noun*
a raised table in a religious place where things are offered to God

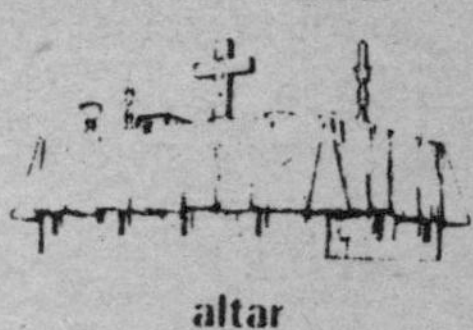
altar

alter /ôl′ tər/ *verb*
to change: *She* **altered** *her plans.*
alteration *noun*

alternate /ôl′ tər nit/ *adjective*
first one, then another: *He works on* **alternate** *Saturdays* (= he works one Saturday, does not work the next, and so on).

alternative[1] /ôl tur′ nə tiv/ *noun*
something you can do or use instead: *I wanted to go out, but I had no money; I had no* **alternative** *to staying at home.*

alternative[2] *adjective*
other; different: *The way was blocked, so we went by an* **alternative** *road.*

°**although** /ôl THō′/
even if; in spite of something: **Although** *they are poor, they are happy.*

altogether /ôl″ tə geTH′ ər/ *adverb*
counting everyone or everything; completely: **Altogether** *there were 12 people in the bus. He's not* **altogether** *sure what to do.*

°**always** /ôl′ wāz/ *adverb*
1 at all times: *The world is* **always** *turning.*
2 for ever: I shall **always** *remember my first day at school.*

am /am/ *verb*
the part of the verb **be** that we use with **I: Am I** *late for dinner?* **I'm** (= I am) *very late,* **aren't I?**

a.m. /ā em/
in the morning: *I got up at 8* **a.m.**

amaze /ə māz′/ *verb* (*present participle* **amazing,** *past* **amazed**)
to surprise very much: *I was* **amazed** *when I found money in the old box.*
amazing *adjective*
amazement *noun: I stopped in* **amazement** *at the strange sight.*

ambassador /am bas′ ə dər/ *noun*
an important person who represents his or her country in another country

ambition /am bish′ ən/ *noun*
1 a strong wish to be successful
2 something wished for: *Her* **ambition** *was to be a famous singer.*
ambitious *adjective*

ambulance /am′ byə ləns/ *noun*
a special car for carrying ill or wounded people

ammunition /am″ yə nish′ ən/ *noun*
something that you can throw or shoot from a weapon to hurt someone or damage something

°**among** /ə mung′/ *preposition*
in the middle of; between: *Share the fruit* **among** *your friends; houses* **among** *the trees*
amongst is another word for **among**

°**amount** /ə mount′/ *noun*
a sum (of money) or a quantity: *a large* **amount** *of gold*

ampere /am′ pēr/ *noun*
a measure of electricity

°**amuse** /ə mūse′/ *verb* (*present participle* **amusing,** *past* **amused**)
to make someone laugh or smile: *The children* **amused** *the old man.*
amusement *noun* **1** enjoyment **2** an enjoyable thing to do: *There were* **amusements** *at the party.*
amusing *adjective*

°**an** /an *or* ən/ see **a**

analyze /an′ ə līz″/ *verb* (*present participle* **analyzing,** *past* **analyzed**)
to find out exactly what something is made of: *The scientist* **analyzed** *the milk and found it contained too much water.*
analysis *noun* (*plural* **analyses**): *an* **analysis** *of the milk*

ancestor /an′ ses″ tər/ *noun*
a person in your family who lived before you did

anchor /ang′ kər/ *noun*
a heavy weight put down from a ship to the bottom of the sea to stop it from moving

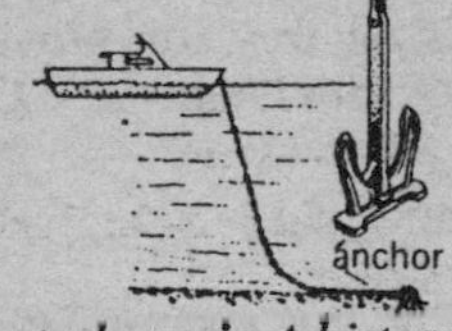

°**ancient** /ān′ shənt/ *adjective*
very old: *to study* **ancient** *history*

°**and** /and *or* ənd *or* ən/
a joining word: *James* **and** *Peter were singing* **and** *dancing.*

angel /ān′ jel/ *noun*
a messenger of God, who is sent from Heaven
angelic *adjective*

°**anger** /ang′ gər/ *noun*
the fierce feeling of wanting to harm or fight other people

°**angle** /ang′ gəl/ *noun*
the shape made when two lines meet each other; a corner

°**angry** /ang′ grē/ *adjective* (**angrier, angriest**)
feeling anger: *I came home late and my mother was* **angry** *(with me).*
angrily *adverb*

°**animal** /an′ ə məl/ *noun*
something alive that is not a plant: *Dogs, goats, and lions are* **animals.**

°**ankle** /ang′ kəl/ *noun*
the part of the leg just above the foot, which can bend

anniversary /an″ ə vur′ sə rē/ *noun* (*plural* **anniversaries**)
the same date each year that something important happened in the past: *We were married on April 7, 1973, so every year we have a party on our* **anniversary** (= April 7th).

announce /ə nouns′/ *verb* (*present participle* **announcing,** *past* **announced**)
to say in public: *The captain* **announced** *that the plane was going to land.*
announcement *noun: The principal read an* **announcement** *to the pupils.*
announcer *noun: The radio* **announcer** *read out the news.*

°**annoy** /ə noi′/ *verb*
to make someone a little angry; trouble someone: *I was* **annoyed** *because I missed the bus and was late for school.*

annual /an′ ū əl/ *adjective*
happening every year: *an* **annual** *event*

°**another** /ə nuth′ ər/
1 one more: *Would you like* **another** *orange?*
2 a different one: *One boy was reading;* **another** *was writing.*

°**answer**[1] /an′ sər/ *verb*
to say or write something after you have been asked a question: "*Did you do it?*" "*No, I didn't,*" *she* **answered.**

°**answer**[2] *noun*
1 what we say or write when we are asked a question: *I asked her the time but she gave no* **answer.**
2 something we are asked to find out: *The* **answer** *is wrong.*

°**ant** /ant/ *noun*
a small insect that lives in large groups

ant

antelope /ant′ ə lōp/ *noun* (*plural* **antelope** *or* **antelopes**)
any of the wild animals which run fast and usually have horns on their heads

°**anxious** /ang′ shəs/ *adjective*
worried
anxiety *noun: Her face was showing her* **anxiety.**

°**any** /en′ ē/ *adjective*
1 no matter what or which: *You can buy sugar at* **any** *big store.*
2 (used in sentences like these to mean **some**): *Have you* **any** *coffee? There isn't* **any** *in the pantry.*

°**anybody** /en′ ē bud″ ē/ *or* **anyone**
any person: *Has* **anybody** *seen my pen?*

anyhow /en′ ē hou″/ *adverb*
see **anyway**

anyone /en′ ē wun″/ see **anybody**

°**anything** /en′ ē thing″/
some thing; no matter what thing: *Did you say* **anything?** *If you want*

anything *to eat, please tell me.*

anyway /en′ ē wā″/ *or* **anyhow** *adverb*
1 no matter what happens: *The dress cost a lot of money, but I bought it* **anyway.**
2 in any way: *You can do the job* **anyway** *you like, but finish it.*

°**anywhere** /en′ ē hwâr″/ *adverb*
in, at, or to any place: *I can't find my key* **anywhere.**

apart /ə pärt′/ *adverb*
separately; away from another, or others: *The two villages are 6 miles* **apart.**

apartment /ə pärt′ mənt/ *noun*
a part of a building, on one floor, where someone lives

ape /āp/ *noun*
a large animal like a monkey, but with a very short tail or no tail: *The gorilla is an* **ape.**

apologize /ə pol′ ə jīz″/ *verb* (*present participle* **apologizing,** *past* **apologized)**
to say you are sorry for something you have done: *You should* **apologize** *to your mother.*
apology *noun* (*plural* **apologies**): *I gave him an* **apology.**

apostrophe /ə pos′ trə fe/ *noun*
the sign ' (used in writing to show that letters have been left out, as in *can't* for *cannot*, or with *s* to show that someone owns something, as in *Sarah's book* or *ladies' hats*)

°**apparatus** /ap″ ə rat′ əs/ *noun*
tools or other things needed for a special purpose: *There is sports apparatus in the gym.*

apparent /ə par′ ənt/ *adjective*
clearly seen or understood: *It was* **apparent** *that he knew nothing about how to repair cars.*
apparently *adverb:* **Apparently,** *you have done a lot of work.*

appeal[1] /ə pēl′/ *verb*
1 to ask for strongly; beg for: *The pupil* **appealed** *for another day to finish his work.*
2 to be pleasing: *The new toy* **appealed to** *the child.*
appealing *adjective* pleasing; *sweet: an* **appealing** *smile*

appeal[2] *noun*
asking for something: *The teacher listened to his* **appeal.**

°**appear** /ə pēr′/ *verb*
1 to seem: *She* **appears** *to be unhappy.*
2 to come into sight suddenly: *Her head* **appeared** *around the door.*
appearance *noun: His sudden* **appearance** *surprised her. She had a sad* **appearance** (= she looked sad).

appetite /ap′ i tīt″/ *noun*
the wish for food: *Anna has a good* **appetite;** *she ate all her dinner.*

applaud /ə plôd′/ *verb*
to strike the hands together or shout, to show pleasure at something: *Everyone* **applauded** *when the play ended.*
applause *noun*

°**apple** /ap′ əl/ *noun*
a round, hard, juicy fruit

appliance /ə plī′ əns/ *noun*
an instrument for doing something useful: *kitchen* **appliances** (= cooking tools)

apply /ə plī′/ *verb* (*present participle* **applying,** *past* **applied)**
1 to ask for: *I want to* **apply for** *the job.*
2 to be about or important to: *The*

school rules **apply to** *us all.*
3 to put on: *The doctor* **applied** *some medicine to the wound.*
application *noun* a written paper asking for something: *an* **application** *for a job*

appoint /ə point′/ *verb*
to give a job to: *I* **appointed** *her as my secretary.*
appointment *noun* **1** a time arranged for seeing someone: *I made an* **appointment** *to see the doctor.*
2 a job

appreciate /ə prē′ shē āt″/ *verb* (*present participle* **appreciating,** *past* **appreciated)**
to be grateful for: *I* **appreciate** *your help.*
appreciation *noun: He gave me a present to show his* **appreciation.**

apprentice /ə pren′ tis/ *noun*
someone who is learning a job

approach /ə prōch′/ *verb*
to come near: *The soldier asked the boy to* **approach** *(him).*

appropriate /ə prō′ prē it/ *adjective*
right; suitable: *A dirty face is not* **appropriate** *for the school photograph.*

°**approve** /ə prōv′/ *verb* (*present participle* **approving,** *past* **approved)**
to say that something is good: *My parents don't* **approve of** *my cigarette smoking.*
approval *noun (no plural): He showed his* **approval** *by smiling.*

approximate /ə prok′ sə mit/ *adjective*
not exact: *The* **approximate** *time is two o'clock.* (= it might be just before or just after two.)
approximately *adverb*

apricot /ap′ ri kät *or* ā prə kät/ *noun*
a round, soft, yellow fruit

°**April** /ā′ prəl/ *noun*
the fourth month of the year

apron /ā′ prən/ *noun*
a protective covering you can put on top of your other clothes to keep them clean

apt /apt/ *adjective*
suitable: *an* **apt** *choice of words*

aquarium /ə kwar′ ē əm/ *noun*
1 a large glass box where live fish are kept
2 a building where there are lots of these boxes for people to look at

°**arch** /ärch/ *noun* (*plural* **arches)**
a curved part of a roof, door, window or bridge

archaeology /är″ kē ol′ ō jē/ *noun*
the study of very old things, especially things made by man
archaeologist *noun*

archbishop /ärch″ bish′ əp/ *noun*
an important Christian leader; a chief bishop (see)

architect /är′ kə tekt/ *noun*
someone who plans buildings
architecture *noun: He studies* **architecture.** *The* **architecture** *of this church is very fine.*

are /är/ *verb*
the part of the verb **be** *that we use with* **we, you** *and* **they:** *Who* **are** *you?* **We're** (= we are) *Jane's friends. They* **aren't** *very tall,* **are they?**

°**area** /âr′ e ə/ *noun*
1 a piece of land or sea: *We are going to build a school in this* **area.**
2 the measure of a surface: *The*

square has an **area** *of nine square inches.*

°**argue** /är′ gū/ *verb* (*present participle* **arguing,** *past* **argued)**
to disagree in words

argument /är′ gyə mənt/ *noun*
a disagreement; quarrel

arise /ə rīz/ *verb* (*present participle* **arising,** *past tense* **arose,** *past participle* **arisen)**
1 to happen: *That question did not* **arise.**
2 to get up: *I* **arose** *early in the morning.*

arithmetic /ə rith′ mə tic/ *noun*
science and art of computing positive, real numbers

°**arm** /ärm/ *noun*
the part of the body between the shoulder and the hand
armchair *noun* a chair with supports on which to rest one's arms
arms *plural noun* weapons like guns and bombs: *The* **armed forces** *of a country are its army, navy, and air force.*

armor /är′ mər/ *noun*
a covering of metal worn by soldiers in old times to protect them: *An* **armored car** *is a special car protected by heavy metal.*

°**army** /är′ me/ *noun* (*plural* **armies)**
a large number of soldiers training for war on land

°**around** /ə round′/ *preposition, adverb*
1 on all sides of something: *There was a fence* **around** *the yard.*
2 in different places; about: *They walked* **around** *(the town).*

°**arrange** /ə rānj′/ *verb* (*present participle* **arranging,** *past* **arranged)**
1 to put in order: *He* **arranged** *the books on the shelf.*
2 to make plans for: *I have* **arranged** *a party.*
arrangement *noun: to make arrangements for a party*

arrest¹ /ə rest′/ *verb*
to make someone a prisoner: *The criminal was* **arrested** *yesterday.*

arrest² *noun*
an act of arresting: *The police made three* **arrests** *yesterday.*

°**arrive** /ə rīv′/ *verb* (*present participle* **arriving,** *past* **arrived)**
to get to the place you were going to: *At last she* **arrived** *(at the village).*
arrival *noun: The* **arrival** *of the train was delayed.*

°**arrow** /âr′ ō/ *noun*
1 a pointed stick that is shot from a bow (see)

arrows

2 a mark shaped like an arrow which shows direction

°**art** /ärt/ *noun*
1 drawing and painting: *He's very good at* **art.**
2 the ability to do certain things: the **art** *of cooking*

artery /är′ tə rē/ *noun* (*plural* **arteries)**
one of the tubes in the body that carry blood from the heart around the body

°**article¹** /är′ ti kəl/ *noun*
1 a thing: **articles** *of clothing*
2 a piece of writing in a newspaper: *an* **article** *about ships*

article² *noun*
the words "a" or "an" **(indefinite article)** or "the" **(definite article)**

artificial /är″ tə fish′ əl/ *adjective*
not real: **artificial** *flowers*

artist /är′ tist/ *noun*
someone who is good at dancing, painting, playing music, or something skillful like this
artistic *adjective*

°**as** /az/
1 when; while: *We sang* **as** *we walked along the road.*
2 in such a way; like: *Do* **as** *your mother says.*
3 because: *She did not hear us come in* **as** *she was asleep.*
4 (used in some phrases): *I am nearly* **as** *tall* **as** *my father. I'll cook the meal* **as long as** (= if) *you wash the pans afterwards. The man looked* **as if/as though** *he were lost.*

°**ash** /ash/ *noun* (*plural* **ashes**)
gray powder left after something has burned

°**ashamed** /ə shāmd′/ *adjective*
feeling bad about something you have done wrong: *I behaved badly yesterday and I am* **ashamed** *(of myself) now.*

ashore /ə shôr′/ *adverb*
onto the land: *Pull the boat* **ashore!**

°**aside** /ə sīd′/ *adverb*
to or toward one side; away: *We had to move* **aside** *to let the car pass us.*

°**ask** /ask/ *verb*
1 to say a question: *"Who are you?" she* **asked.**
2 to try and get something from someone: *They* **asked** *me the time.*

°**asleep** /ə slēp′/ *adjective*
sleeping: *Is the baby still* **asleep?**

aspirin /as′ prin *or* as′ pər in/ *noun*
a medicine that helps relieve pain

ass /as/ *noun* (*plural* **asses**)
an animal like a small horse with long ears: **Ass** *is another word for* **donkey.**

assemble /ə sem′ bəl/ *verb* (*present participle* **assembling,** *past* **assembled**)
to gather together: *All the people* **assembled** *at Mary's house.*
assembly *noun* (*plural* **assemblies**) a group of people gathered together for a special purpose or meeting

assist /ə sist′/ *verb*
to help: *We all* **assisted** *in mending the roof.*
assistance *noun* help
assistant *noun* a person who helps

associate /ə sō′ shē āt″/ *verb* (*present participle* **associating,** *past* **associated**)
to think of something being with something else: *We* **associate** *blackboards and chalk with school.*
association *noun* a group of people joined together for one purpose

assume /ə so͞om′/ *verb* (*present participle* **assuming,** *past* **assumed**)
to think something is true when no one has said so: *I* **assume** *you always get up at the same time.*

assure /ə sho͝or′/ *verb* (*present participle* **assuring,** *past* **assured**)
to tell someone very firmly: *He* **assured** *me that he had finished.*

asterisk /as′ tə risk/ *noun*
the sign *

astonish /ə ston′ ish/ *verb*
to surprise greatly: *I was* **astonished** *when I heard the school had burned down.*
astonishment *noun*

astronaut /as′ trə nôt″/ *noun*
a person who travels in space

astronomy /as tron′ ə me/ *noun*
the study of the sun, moon, and stars
astronomer *noun* a person who studies the stars

°**at** /at *or* ət/ *preposition*
1 (showing where): *He left his bag* **at** *the station.*
2 (showing when): *It gets cold* **at** *night.*
3 (showing what people are doing or what is happening): *She is* **at** *work. The two armies are* **at** *war.*
4 (used in sentences like these): *I bought two pens* **at** *20 cents each. I am surprised* **at** *what you say. He is good* **at** *football.*

ate /āt/ see **eat**

athlete /ath′ lēt/ *noun*
someone who is good at running, jumping and throwing: **Athletes** *are good at* **athletics** /ath′ let iks/.

atlas /at′ ləs/ *noun* (*plural* **atlases**)
a book of maps

atmosphere /at′ məs fēr″/ *noun*
1 the air surrounding the earth
2 a feeling that a place or group of people give you: *the exciting* **atmosphere** *of a football match*

atom /at′ əm/ *noun*
the smallest part of a substance: **Atomic power** *is power made up from the forces within an* **atom.**

attach /ə tach′/ *verb*
1 to fix something to something else
2 to like very much: *Mary* **was attached to** *her brother.*

°**attack**[1] /ə tak′/ *verb*
to go and fight against or harm someone: *The newspaper* **attacked** (= wrote things against) *the new tax.*

°**attack**[2] *noun*
fighting; trying to harm someone: *an* **attack** *on the soldiers*

attempt[1] /ə tempt′/ *verb*
to try: *She* **attempted** *to cook the dinner.*

attempt[2] *noun*
a try: *She made an* **attempt** *to cook the dinner.*

°**attend** /ə tend′/ *verb*
1 to be present at: *I* **attended** *his birthday party.*
2 to listen to: *Will you* **attend** *to what I'm saying?*
3 to look after: *The doctor* **attended** *me when I had a fever.*
attendance *noun: He sometimes comes to school, and sometimes stays at home: his* **attendance** *at school is not regular.*
attendant *noun: The* **attendant** *takes the money and tells people where to park.*

°**attention** /ə ten′ shən/ *noun*
looking at and listening to someone or some event: *Margaret is not* **paying attention** (= listening) *to what I'm saying.*

attitude /at′ ə to͞od″/ *noun*
the way you think or feel about something: *What is your* **attitude** *about school?*

attract /ə trakt′/ *verb*
to be pleasing to; make someone notice: *Does this job* **attract** *you?*
attractive *adjective* pleasing, especially to look at

audience /ô′ dē əns/ *noun*
all the people watching a play, listening to music, etc.

°**August** /ô′ gəst/ *noun*
the eighth month of the year

°**aunt** /ant *or* änt/ *noun*
the sister of one of your parents, or the wife of the brother of one of your parents

author /ô′ thər/ *noun*
a person who writes a book

authority /ô thôr′ ə tē/ *noun*
1 the power to make people do what you want: *The teacher has* **authority** *to punish any pupil.*
2 (*plural* **authorities**) a person or group who runs or governs something

automatic /ô″ tə mat′ ik/ *adjective*
working by itself: *The* **automatic** *cooker never gets too hot. The heat is turned off* **automatically.**

autumn /ô′ təm/ *noun, adjective*
the season before winter in cool countries, when the leaves fall off the trees

available /ə vāl′ ə bəl/ *adjective*
able to be seen, used, etc.: *Is the manager* **available?**

avenue /av′ ə nū″/ *noun*
a road, especially a main road

°**average** /av′ rij/ *adjective*
1 usual; ordinary: *The* **average** *child enjoys listening to stories.*
2 a word used in arithmetic: *Anne had three candies, Richard had four, and Maria had five: the* **average** *number of candies was four* (3 + 4 + 5 = 12, divided between 3 children = 4 each).

°**avoid** /ə void′/ *verb*
to get or keep away from: *Are you trying to* **avoid** *me?*

°**awake** /ə wāk′/ *adjective*
not sleeping: *The baby is* **awake.**

°**award**[1] /ə wôrd′/ *noun*
a prize, especially for work or courage

award[2] *verb*
to give as an award: *The school* **awarded** *Marie a prize (for her good work).*

aware /ə wâr′/ *adjective*
knowing: *I was not* **aware** *of the fire.*

°**away** /ə wā′/ *adverb*
1 at or to another place; not here: *"Do you live* **far away?**" *"No, quite near."*
2 all the time: *He hammered* **away** *until he made a hole in the wall.*
3 (used in some phrases): *Don't* **throw away** *those boxes; we can use them. Yes, I'll do that* **right away** (= now).

awful /ô′ fəl/ *adjective*
1 very bad or frightening: *an* **awful** *accident*
2 not pleasing; not liked: *That's an* **awful** *book.*
awfully *adverb* very: *She's* **awfully** *clever.*

°**awkward** /ôk′ wərd/ *adjective*
1 not skillful in handling things; not moving in an easy way: *He's very* **awkward**, *he keeps dropping things.*
2 not easy to handle: *The pan is an* **awkward** *shape.*
3 making you feel uncomfortable: *There was an* **awkward** *silence, when no one knew what to say.*
awkwardly *adverb*

°**ax or axe** /aks/ *noun*
a metal blade fixed onto a handle, used for cutting down trees, etc.

axe

Bb

°**baby** /bā′ bē/ *noun (plural* **babies)**
a very young child

bachelor /bach′ lər/ *noun*
a man who is not married

back[1] /bak/ *noun*
1 the part of the body from the neck to the legs: *The* **backbone** *runs down the* **back** *from the neck to the middle of the body. You shouldn't talk about Agnes* **behind her back** (= when she's not here).
2 the part that is furthest from the front; at or near the end: *Write this exercise at the* **back** *of your book. There's a hut* **at the back of** (= behind) *the house.*

°**back**[2] *adverb*
1 at or toward the back part; away from the front: *She tied her long hair* **back** *with a band. Stand* **back** *from the fire; it's very hot.*
2 to or in a place where something or someone was before: *Put the book* **back** *on the shelf when you've finished it.*
3 in return or in reply: *I wrote to her, and she wrote* **back** *(to me) the next day.*
backward /bak′ wərd/ *adverb* **1** toward the back: *He looked* **backward** *to see who was following him.* **2** with the back part in front: *You've put your hat on* **backwards. 3** starting at the end: "*Can you count* **backwards** *from 5?*" "*Yes, 5,4,3,2,1.*"

back[3] *verb*
to move or make something move backward: *She* **backed** *the car out of the narrow road.*

background /bak′ ground″/ *noun*
what is behind something: *This is a photo of Mary, with our house in the* **background.**

bacon /bā′ kən/ *noun (no plural)*
meat from the back or sides of a pig, with salt added

°**bad** /bad/ *adjective*
(worse /wurs/, **worst** /wurst/)
1 not good: *I am* **bad** *at English, but Joe is* **worse** *— he got the* **worst** (= lowest) *marks in the class.*
2 severe: *a* **bad** *cut on his leg*
badly *adverb: His foot was* **badly** *hurt.*

badge /baj/ *noun*
a small sign that we wear to show what we do or have done: *The policeman wears a* **badge** *on his coat.*

badminton /bad′ mit ən/ *noun (no plural)*
a game like tennis played with rackets and shuttlecocks

°**bag** /bag/ *noun*
a container made of soft material (cloth, paper, plastic, leather), which opens at the top

baggage /bag′ ij/ *or* **luggage** *noun (no plural)*
the bags and other containers that a traveler takes with him

bait /bāt/ *noun (no plural)*
food that is used for catching fish or animals

bake /bāk/ *verb (present participle* **baking,** *past* **baked)**
to cook in an oven
baker *noun* someone who owns or works in a bakery

bakery *noun* (*plural* **bakeries**) a place where bread and cakes are baked to be sold

°**balance**[1] /bal′ ən s/ *verb* (*present participle* **balancing,** *past* **balanced**) to keep oneself or something else steady, especially in a difficult position: *Can you* **balance** *a ball on your nose?*

°**balance**[2] *noun*
1 a machine for weighing
2 *(no plural)* steadiness: *The child couldn't* **keep his balance** (= stay steady) *on his new bicycle.*

balcony /bal′ kə ne/ *noun* (*plural* **balconies**) a place like a shelf with sides, on the outside of a building above the ground

balcony

bald /bôld/ *adjective*
with no hair: *a* **bald** *old man*

bale /bāl/ *noun*
a large quantity of goods or material tied tightly together: **bales** *of cotton on the factory floor*

°**ball** /bôl/ *noun*
1 a round object used in games; anything of this shape: *a* **ball** *of wool*
2 a large party for dancing

ballet /bə lā′ *or* bal′ ā/ *noun*
a play without speech, in which the story is told through dance

balloon /bə loon′/ *noun*
a rubber bag that can be blown up with air or gas

ballot /bal′ ət/ *noun*
a way of marking a piece of paper to choose someone: *The club members held a secret* **ballot** *to choose the chairperson.*

ballpoint /bôl′ point″/ *noun*
a pen with a metal ball at the point

ban[1] /ban/ *verb* (*present participle* **banning,** *past* **banned**)
not to allow something: *Smoking is* **banned** *in school.*

ban[2] *noun*
an order not allowing something: *There is a* **ban** *on smoking.*

°**banana** /bə nan′ ə/ *noun*
a long yellow fruit

°**band** /band/ *noun*
1 a narrow piece of material used for holding things together: *Put a* **rubber band** *round these books.*
2 a group of people collected for some purpose
3 a group of people who play music together

bandage[1] /ban′ dij/ *noun*
a long piece of cloth used for covering a wound

bandage[2] *verb* (*present participle* **bandaging,** *past* **bandaged**)
to tie a bandage on

bandit /ban′ dit/ *noun*
a robber, usually armed and one of a group

°**bang** /bang/ *noun*
a loud noise: *There was a* **bang** *as the gun was fired.*
bang *verb*

bangle /bang′ gl/ *noun*
a metal band or chain worn around the arm or ankle

banish /ban′ ish/ *verb*
to send away, usually out of the country, as a punishment

banister /ban′ is tər/ *noun*
a fence that guards the outer edge of stairs

°**bank**[1] /bangk/ *noun*
1 land along the side of a river, lake, etc.
2 a long heap of earth raised above the ground

°**bank**[2] *noun*
a place where money is kept and paid out when we want it
banker *noun* a person who owns or controls a bank
banknote *or* **note** *noun* a piece of paper money

baptize /bap' tīz"/ *verb* (*present participle* **baptizing,** *past* **baptized**)
to put holy water on someone and give him a Christian name: *The baby was* **baptized** *Maria.*
baptism /bap' tizm"/ *noun*

°**bar**[1] /bär/ *noun*
1 a long piece of wood or metal
2 a piece of material such as soap or chocolate

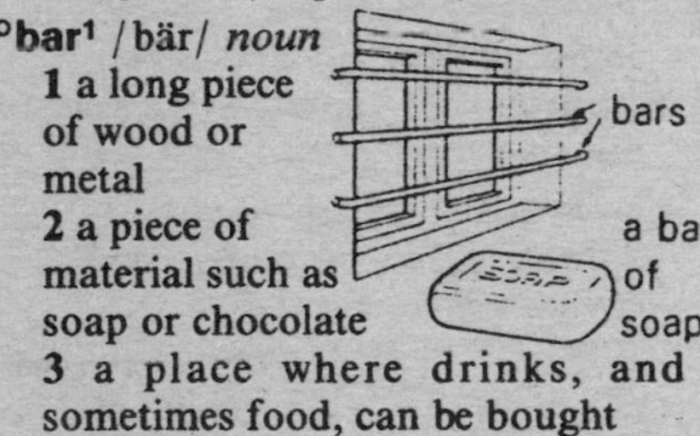

3 a place where drinks, and sometimes food, can be bought

°**bar**[2] *verb* (*present participle* **barring,** *past* **barred**)
1 to close firmly with a bar: *She* **barred** *the door.*
2 to block: *The soldiers* **barred** *the way to the airport.*

barbed wire /bärbd' wīr'/ *noun (no plural)*
wire with short sharp points in it: *a* **barbed wire** *fence*

barber /bär' bər/ *noun*
a person who cuts hair

°**bare** /bâr/ *adjective*
1 uncovered: *Don't walk on that broken glass with* **bare** *feet.*
2 empty: *a* **bare** *room* (= with no furniture)
barely *adverb* almost not: *He had* **barely** *enough money to buy food.*

bargain[1] /bär' gən/ *verb*
to talk about the price of something with the buyer or seller: *She* **bargained** *with the trader until he sold her the fruit cheaply.*

bargain[2] *noun*
something bought for a little money, but worth more

barge /bärj/ *noun*
a large boat with a flat bottom, used for carrying things on rivers

bark[1] /bärk/ *verb*
to make the sound made by a dog
bark *noun*

bark[2] *noun (no plural)*
the strong outer covering of a tree

barn /bärn/ *noun*
a building in which farm animals and harvested crops are kept

barometer /bə räm' ə tər/ *noun*
an instrument which helps us to know what the weather will be

barracks /bar' iks/ *plural noun*
buildings in which soldiers live

°**barrel** /bar' əl/ *noun*
1 a large round container with flat ends
2 the long metal tube of a gun

oil barrel
gun barrel

barren /bar' ən/ *adjective*
1 not able to have children or young ones, or having no fruit
2 so poor that crops cannot grow: *The desert is* **barren** *land.*

barrier /bar' ē ar/ *noun*
a fence or wall: *The police put a* **barrier** *across the road.*

°**base** /bās/ *noun*
1 the bottom of something; the part something stands on: *A bottle has a flat* **base.**
2 the place where something starts: *That company has offices all over the world, but their* **base** *is in New York.*

baseball /bās′ bôl″/ *noun (no plural)*
a ball game played by two teams of nine players

°**basin** /bā′ sən/ *noun*
1 a round, wide, open dish
2 a **washbasin**

basis /bā′ səs/ *noun* (*plural* **bases**) /bā′ sēz/
the starting point or central idea of something: *What is the* **basis** *of your opinion?*

°**basket** /bas′ kət/ *noun*
a container made of thin bent wood used for carrying or holding things

baskets

°**basketball** /bas′ kət bôl″/ *noun*
a game in which two teams try to throw a ball through a basket (= net)

°**bat**[1] /bat/ *noun*
a piece of wood used for hitting the ball in some games

bat[2] *verb* (*present participle* **batting,** *past* **batted**)
to use or hit something with a bat

bat[3] *noun*
a small animal that flies at night

batch /bach/ *noun*
a number of things together: *a* **batch** *of cookies*

bath[1] /bath/ *noun* (*plural* **baths** /baths/)
a large water container in which the whole body can be washed: *I* **have a bath** (= wash in a bath) *every day.*

°**bathe** /bāTH/ *verb* (*present participle* **bathing** /bā′ THing/, *past* **bathed** /bāTHd/)
1 to put something in water; wash in water: *to* **bathe** *a wound*
2 to swim in a river or the sea
bathing suit *noun* what we wear for bathing

bathroom /bath′ ro͞om″/ *noun*
a room where people wash or have a bath or use the toilet.

batter /bat′ ər/ *verb*
to hit hard, again and again

battery /bat′ ə rē/ *noun* (*plural* **batteries**)
a box that produces or stores electricity: *Our car won't start because the* **battery** *is dead* (= worn out).

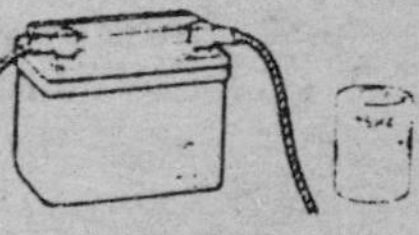
batteries

°**battle**[1] /bat′ əl/ *noun*
a fight between people or things

battle[2] *verb* (*present participle* **battling,** *past* **battled**)
to fight

bay /bā/ *noun*
a part of the shore that curves inward

bay

bazaar /bə zär′/ *noun* a market

B.C. /bē sē/
Before Christ (used in dates)

°**be** /bē/ *verb*
present tense

singular	*plural*
I **am**	*We* **are**
You **are**	*You* **are**
He/She/It **is**	*They* **are**

past tense

singular	*plural*
I **was**	*We* **were**
You **were**	*You* **were**
He/She/It **was**	*They* **were**

present participle **being**
past participle **been**
1 (used to describe or give information about people or things and to join words for people or things to the qualities or position they have): *The sunflower* **is** *a beautiful flower.* **Were** *you in the garden? My grandmother* **was** *a cook. Please* **be** *quick!*
2 (used to make some parts of other verbs): *What* **are** *you* **doing?** *I* **am painting** *a picture of a plane.*

beach /bēch/ *noun* (*plural* **beaches**)
a shore covered in sand or stones, where people go to swim

bead /bēd/ *noun*
a small ball of glass or other material, with a small hole for string or wire to pass through: *She wore a string of* **beads** *around her neck.*

beak /bēk/ *noun*
the hard pointed mouth of a bird (picture at **bird**)

beam¹ /bēm/ *noun*
1 a large, long, heavy piece of wood etc., used in building
2 a line of light shining from some bright object

beam² *verb*
to smile brightly and happily

°**bean** /bēn/ *noun*
the large seed, often used for food, of any **bean** plant: *We cook and eat* **green beans.** *We make coffee from* **coffee beans.**

bear¹ /bâr/ *noun*
a large, and sometimes fierce, animal with a thick coat

°**bear²** *verb* (*past tense* **bore** /bôr/, *past participle* **borne** /bôrn/)
1 to carry; support: *That won't* **bear** *your weight.*
2 to allow something to go on without complaining: *I can't* **bear** *that loud music!*
3 to have a child or young ones

beard /bērd/ *noun*
hair on a face below the mouth

beast /bēst/ *noun*
1 an animal
2 an unkind or cruel person

°**beat¹** /bēt/ *verb* (*past tense* **beat,** *past participle* **beaten**)
1 to hit many times
2 to move regularly in time: *His heart* **beat** *fast after the race.*
3 to defeat; do better than: *We played football but we couldn't* **beat** *them.*

beat² *noun*
a single stroke or movement as part of a regular group: *a* **drumbeat**/*a* **heartbeat**

°**beautiful** /bū′ tə fəl/ *adjective*
very good-looking; very pleasing: *What a* **beautiful** *day!*
beautifully /bū′ tə fəl lē/ *adverb: The children danced* **beautifully.**

°**beauty** /bū′ tē/ *noun*
1 *(no plural)* being beautiful: *a flower of great* **beauty**
2(*plural* **beauties**) something or someone beautiful

°**because** /bi kuz′/
for the reason that: *The roof is wet* **because** *it is raining.*

beckon /bek′ ən/ *verb*
to silently signal someone to come to you

°**become** /bi kum′/ *verb* (*present participle* **becoming** /bi kum′ ing/, *past tense* **became** /bi kām′/, *past participle* **become**)
1 to change or grow to be: *The prince* **became** *king when his father died.*
2 to happen to: *I haven't seen Simon for days; what's* **become of** *him?*

°**bed** /bed/ *noun*
1 the thing we sleep on: *What time did you* **go to bed** *last night? You should* **make your bed** *before you go to school.*
2 the base or bottom of something: *There has been no rain for months, so the* **river bed** *is dry.*
bedclothes *plural noun* all the covers put on a bed
bedroom *noun* a room for sleeping in

°**bee** /bē/ *noun*
a stinging, flying insect that makes honey

bee

beehive *or* **hive** *noun* a house, often a wooden box, made for bees to live in

beef /bēf/ *noun (no plural)*
the meat we get from cattle

been /bin/ see **be**

°**beer** /bēr/ *noun*
1 *(no plural)* an alcoholic drink made from grain
2 a glass or bottle of this drink

beetle /bēt′ əl/ *noun*
an insect whose outside wings make a hard cover for its body

°**before** /bi fôr′/ *adverb, preposition*
1 earlier than: *She was there* **before** *8 o'clock. I have seen you* **before** (= before this time), *but I can't remember where.*
2 in front of
beforehand *adverb* before something happens: *She knew I was coming because I telephoned her* **beforehand.**

°**beg** /beg/ *verb* (*present participle* **begging,** *past* **begged**)
1 to ask for money or food
2 to ask seriously: *I* **begged** *her not to go.*
beggar *noun* someone who lives by begging

begin /bi gin′/ *verb* (*present participle* **beginning,** *past tense* **began** /bi gan′/, *past participle* **begun** /bi gun′/)
to start: *The film* **begins** *at 2 o'clock. After running half a mile, I* **began** *to feel tired.*
beginning *noun* the start

behalf /bi haf′/ *noun*
instead of; for: *I have come* **on behalf of** *my brother; he's ill. I paid the money* **on your behalf** (= for you).

°**behave** /bi hāv′/ *noun*
to act in a good or bad way: *The baby* **behaved** *very well last night; he didn't cry at all. Please* **behave** *yourself* (= behave properly)!

behavior *noun (no plural): Everyone praises the children's good* **behavior.**

°**behind** /bi hīnd'/ *preposition, adverb*
at the back (of): *He hangs his coat on a nail* **behind** *the door. My brother went in front and I walked* **behind** *(him).*

being[1] /bē' ing/ see **be**

being[2] *noun*
a person: *Men, women, and children are* **human beings.**

°**believe** /bi lēv'/ *verb (present participle* **believing,** *past* **believed)**
1 to think someone is honest, right or true: *Simon says he gave you the money, and I* **believe** *him. The soldiers all* **believe in** *their leader.*
2 to think something is true: *I* **believe** *that he'll do what he said.*
belief /bi lef'/ *noun* believing; things we believe are right: *That man has a strong* **belief** *in God.*

°**bell** /bel/ *noun*
a round, hollow metal object that sounds when it is struck

bellow /bel' ō/ *verb*
to make a loud, deep sound: *"Go away!" he* **bellowed** *angrily.*

belly /bel' ē/ *noun (plural* **bellies)**
the stomach, especially of an animal

°**belong** /bi lông'/ *verb*
1 to be one's own: *That book* **belongs** *to me.*
2 to be a member of: *Do you* **belong** *to the Scouts?*
belongings *plural noun* one's own property

°**below** /bi lō'/ *adverb, preposition*
at a lower place; lower than; under: *The children threw sticks from the bridge into the river* **below.** *My brother is in the class* **below** *mine.*

°**belt** /belt/ *noun*
a piece of cloth or leather, worn round the middle of the body: *I need a* **belt** *to keep up my trousers.*

bench /bench/ *noun (plural* **benches)**
1 a long wooden seat
2 a table at which someone works, in a factory or for woodwork

°**bend**[1] /bend/ *verb (past* **bent** /bent/)
1 to make into a curve: *He* **bent** *the wire.*
2 to bend one's body: *She* **bent** *(over) to pick up a book from the floor.*

°**bend**[2] *noun*
a curve: *a* **bend** *in the road*

°**beneath** /bi nēth'/ *preposition*
below; under: *Shall we rest in the shade* **beneath** *these trees?*

benefit[1] /ben' ə fit/ *noun*
help; advantage: *I did it for his* **benefit** (= to help him).

benefit[2] *verb*
to be useful or helpful to: *The plants* **benefited from** (= were helped by) *the rain.*

bent[1] /bent/ *adjective*
curved: *I can't draw a straight line; my ruler is* **bent.**

bent[2] see **bend**

°**berry** /ber' ē/ *noun (plural* **berries)**
a small soft fruit

beside /bi sīd'/ *preposition*
at the side of: *"Come and sit* **beside**

me," he said.

besides /bi sīdz′/ *adverb*
too; also: *I don't want to come out now, and* **besides,** *I must work.*

°**best** /best/ *adjective, adverb, noun*
most good; most well; the most good thing: *This picture is* **the best** *(picture) you have painted.*

bet[1] /bet/ *verb* (*present participle* **betting,** *past* **bet** *or* **betted)**
to risk (money) on the result of a future event: *He* **bet** *me one dollar that the school team would win.*

bet[2] *noun*
an agreement to bet, or the money betted: *a* **bet** *of one dollar*

betray /bi trā′/ *verb*
to be unfaithful; give away a secret or break a promise: *I asked you not to tell anyone, but you* **betrayed** *me. The expression on his face* **betrayed** *his feelings.*

°**better** /bet′ ər/ *adjective, adverb*
more good; in a way that is more good: *That song is* **better** *than the other one; I like it* **better.** *My father was ill, but he is* **better** (= not so ill) *now. You* **had better** (= ought to) *lock the door when you go out.*

°**between** /bi twēn′/ *preposition*
1 (showing where): *There is a fence* **between** *his garden and our garden.*
2 (showing when): *Come* **between** *five and six o'clock.*
3 (showing how things are joined): *There is a railroad* **between** *the two cities.*
4 (showing how things are divided): *She shared the oranges* **between** *the two children.*

beware /bi wâr′/ *verb*
(used to tell someone to be careful of something): **Beware of** *the dog!*

beyond /bi yond′/ *adverb, preposition*
past; on the other side of; farther away: *My house is two miles* **beyond** *the school. From the top of that hill you can see the country* **beyond.**

bib /bib/ *noun*
a piece of material that is tied under a child's chin to protect the child's clothes while the child is eating

Bible /bī′ bəl/ *noun*
the religious book of the Christian and Jewish faiths
biblical /bib′ lə kəl/ *adjective: Joseph and Mary are* **biblical** *names.*

°**bicycle** /bī′ sik əl/ *or* **cycle** *or* **bike** /bīk/ *noun*
a machine with two wheels for riding on

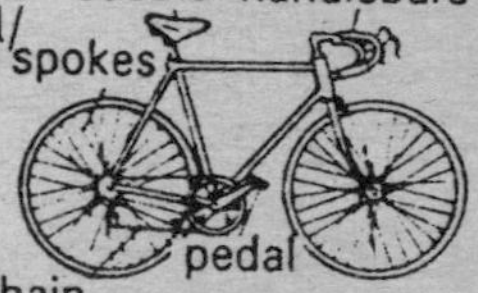

bicycle

bid[1] /bid/ *noun*
an offer of an amount of money in order to buy something: *My uncle wants to sell his farm, and he has already had two large* **bids** *for it.*

bid[2] *verb* (*present participle* **bidding,** *past* **bid)**
to make an offer of money in order to buy something: *He* **bid** *ten dollars for the bicycle.*

°**big** /big/ *adjective* **(bigger, biggest)**
large in size, weight, number, importance, etc.: *How* **big** *is the school you go to? A cow is* **bigger** *than a goat.*

bill /bil/ *noun*
1 a piece of paper showing the amount you must pay for

something: *How much was the* **bill** *for the electricity?*
2 a plan for a new law: *The government is considering the new education* **bill.**

billion /bil′ yən/ *noun, adjective*
the number 1,000,000,000 (= a thousand million)

billy goat /bil′ ē gōt″/ *noun*
a male goat

bin /bin/ *noun*
a large container often with a lid, for bread, flour, coal, etc., or for waste: *They filled the* **bin** *with grain.*

bind /bīnd/ *verb* (*past* **bound**)
to tie with rope or string

binoculars /bə nok′ yə lərz/ *plural noun*
a pair of special glasses to make things in the distance look bigger

binoculars

biography /bī og′ rə fē/ *noun* (*plural* **biographies**)
the story of a person's life

biology /bī ol′ ə jē/ *noun (no plural)*
the scientific study of living things: *In* **biology** *we study plants and animals.*
biological /bī ə loj′ ik əl/ *adjective*
biologist /bī ol′ ə jist/ *noun*
someone who studies biology

°**bird** /burd/ *noun*
an animal with wings and feathers (see)

°**birth** /burth/ *noun*
being born; being brought into the world: *My sister* **gave birth** *to a daughter yesterday.*

birthday /burth′ dā″/ *noun*
the day of the year on which a person was born

biscuit /bis′ kit/ *noun*
a dry, thin cake, often sweet

bishop /bish′ əp/ *noun*
a Christian priest who looks after churches in a large area

°**bit** /bit/ *noun*
a small piece or amount: *He ate every* **bit** *of food. He dug the garden* **bit by bit** (= slowly, a little at a time).

°**bite**[1] /bīt/ *verb* (*present participle* **biting** /bīt′ ing/, *past tense* **bit** /bit/, *past participle* **bitten** /bit n/)
to cut or wound with the teeth: *Jane's dog* **bit** *me. She was* **bitten** *by mosquitoes.*

°**bite**[2] *noun*
1 an act of biting: *This apple's good; do you want a* **bite?**
2 a wound made by biting: *She was covered with insect* **bites.**

°**bitter** /bit′ ər/ *adjective*
1 having a sharp sour taste: **bitter** *fruit*
2 angry: *a* **bitter** *quarrel*
3 very cold: *a* **bitter** *wind*

°**black**[1] /blak/ *adjective*
1 (of) the darkest color; of the color of the words in this book: *At night the sky looks* **black.**
2 with dark-colored skin: *Some of the children were* **black,** *others were white.*

black[2] *noun*
1 *(no plural)* black color: *He was dressed* **in black.**
2 a person with dark-colored skin

blackboard /blak′ bôrd″/ *noun*
the board on which the teacher writes

blacksmith /blak′ smith′/ *noun*
a man who works with iron and makes shoes for horses

°**blade** /blād/ *noun*
1 the flat cutting part of anything sharp
2 a long flat leaf of grass, or anything with such a shape

blades

°**blame**[1] /blām/ *verb* (*present participle* **blaming,** *past* **blamed)**
to say that someone is the cause of something bad: *The policeman* **blamed** *the car driver for causing the accident.*

°**blame**[2] *noun (no plural)*
the cause of something bad: *The car driver took the* **blame** *for the accident.*

blank /blangk/ *adjective*
1 without writing or other marks: *a* **blank** *piece of paper*
2 not showing any expression: *She looked at him with a* **blank** *face.*

blanket /blang′ kit/ *noun*
a thick woolen cloth, used as a cover on a bed

blare /blâr/ *verb* (*present participle* **blaring,** *past* **blared)**
to sound loudly and unpleasantly: *The radio was* **blaring.**

blast[1] /blast/ *noun*
1 a sudden strong movement of wind or air: *There was a* **blast** *of wind as she opened the door.*
2 a sound made by instruments like a horn: *The driver gave a* **blast** *on his horn.*

blast[2] *verb*
1 to break something up by explosions: *They've* **blasted** *away the rock to build the new road.*
2 to begin a space flight: *The spaceship* **blasted off.**

blaze[1] /blāz/ *noun*
1 a very strong fire: *The fire burned slowly at first, but soon became a* **blaze.**
2 brightly shining light or color: *The flowers were a* **blaze** *of color.*

blaze[2] *verb* (*present participle* **blazing,** *past participle* **blazed)**
to burn strongly

bleach[1] /blēch/ *verb*
to make white: *Did you* **bleach** *this tablecloth? It looks very clean. Her hair was* **bleached** (= made lighter) *by the sun.*

bleach[2] *noun (no plural)*
something used for bleaching things, usually clothes

bleak /blēk/ *adjective*
cold and unpleasant: *a* **bleak** *wind*

bleat /blēt/ *verb*
to make the sound of a sheep, goat, etc. **bleat** *noun*

°**bleed** /blēd/ *verb* (*past* **bled** /bled/)
to lose blood: *The cut on my arm* **bled** *for a long time.*

blend[1] /blend/ *verb*
1 to mix together: **Blend** *the sugar and eggs.*
2 to go well together: *When they sing, their voices* **blend** *nicely.*

blend[2] *noun*
a mixture produced by blending

bless /bless/ *verb* (*past tense* **blessed** /blest/)
to ask God's favor for something: *The holy man* **blessed** *the ship.*
blessing *noun* 1 asking or receiving God's help 2 something one is glad of: *His son is a great* **blessing** *to him.*

blew /blo͞o/ see **blow**

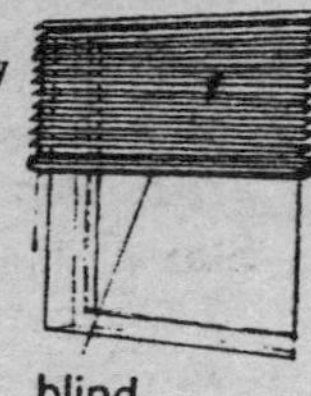
blind

blind¹ /blīnd/ *adjective*
not able to see: **blind** *in one eye*
blindness *noun*

blind² *noun*
a piece of material which can be pulled down to cover a window

blindfold /blīnd′ fōld/ *verb*
to cover someone's eyes with material so that he or she cannot see

blink /blink/ *verb*
to shut and open the eyes quickly

blister /blis′ tər/ *noun*
a swelling under the skin, filled with liquid, usually caused by rubbing or burning

°**block¹** /blok/ *noun*
1 a solid mass or piece of wood, stone, etc.
2 a large building divided into separate parts: *an* **office block**
3 a building or group of buildings between two streets: *Turn left after two* **blocks.**
4 something that prevents movement: *The police put up a* **roadblock** *outside the city.*

°**block²** *verb*
to prevent movement: *The police have* **blocked** *the road.*
blockage *noun: There's no water in the tap; perhaps there's a* **blockage** *in the pipe.*

blond *or* **blonde** /bländ/ *noun, adjective*
(a person) with light-colored hair and skin

°**blood** /blud/ *noun (no plural)*
the red liquid that flows through the body
blood vessel *noun* any of the tubes in the body that carry blood
bloody *adjective* **(bloodier, bloodiest)** covered with blood

bloom¹ /blo͞om/ *noun*
a flower: *What beautiful* **blooms!**

bloom² *verb*
to have flowers: *These flowers* **bloom** *in the spring.*

blossom¹ /blos′ əm/ *noun*
the flower of a flowering tree

blossom² *verb*
to have flowers: *Those trees are* **blossoming.**

blot¹ /blot/ *noun*
a dirty mark, such as that of ink on paper

blot² *verb* (*present participle* **blotting,** *past* **blotted)**
1 to make a blot on something: *He dropped his pen and* **blotted** *his book.*
2 to dry ink with special paper: *He* **blotted** *the page carefully with* **blotting paper.**

blouse /blous *or* blouz/ *noun*
a loose garment for women, reaching from the neck to about the waist

blouse

°**blow¹** /blō/ *verb* (*past tense* **blew** /blo͞o/, *past participle* **blown** /blōn/)
1 to move air; send air out quickly: *I* **blew** *the dust off the table.*
2 (of wind, air, etc.) to move: *The wind* **blew** *hard all night.*
3 to make air go into something: *He* **blew** *a whistle. She* **blew up** *the flat tire of her bicycle with a pump.*
4 to break by exploding: *The soldiers* **blew up** *the bridge.*

°**blow²** *noun*
1 a hard stroke with the hand or a weapon, etc.: *a* **blow** *on the head*
2 a shock: *It was a great* **blow** *to her when her mother died.*

°**blue** /blo͞o/ *adjective, noun*
(of) the color of the sky when there are no clouds: *The sea is* **blue.**

blunt /blunt/ *adjective*
not sharp: *a* **blunt** *knife*

blush /blush/ *verb*
to become red in the face, from shame or another cause

°**board¹** /bôrd/ *noun*
1 a long, thin, flat piece of wood: *wooden* **floorboards**
2 a flat surface used for a special purpose: *Our teacher wrote on the* **blackboard.** *Read the notices on the school* **bulletin board.**
3 a group of people who have a special job, like running a company
on board *or* **aboard** *adverb* on or onto a ship or public vehicle: *We went* **on board** *the ship.*

board² *verb*
1 to cover with wooden boards: *He* **boarded up** *the broken window.*
2 to go on board: *He* **boarded** *the bus/plane/ship/train/taxi.*
boarder *noun* a person who pays to live and eat in someone else's home

boast /bōst/ *verb*
to praise oneself: *He* **boasted** *that he could run very fast.*

°**boat** /bōt/ *noun*
1 a small open ship: *a fishing* **boat**
2 any ship: *Are you going to Europe by* **boat** *or plane?*

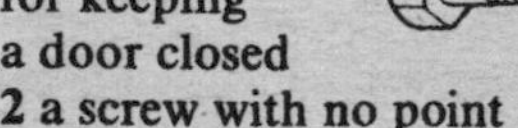
boats

bob /bob/ *verb* (*present participle* **bobbing,** *past* **bobbed)**
to move quickly up and down: *The small boat* **bobbed** *up and down on the lake.*

°**body** /bod′ ē/ *noun* (*plural* **bodies)**
1 the whole of a person or animal, but not the mind
2 the central part, not the head, arms, or legs: *He had a cut on his leg and two more on his* **body.**
3 a dead person or animal
4 a group of people who do something together: *The town is controlled by a* **body** *called the Town Council.*

°**boil¹** /boil/ *verb*
1 to become so hot, or make liquid so hot that it gives off steam
2 to cook food in boiling water: **Boil** *the eggs for five minutes.*

boil² *noun*
a painful swelling under the skin

bold /bōld/ *adjective*
brave; without fear: *By his* **bold** *actions, he saved the children from the fire.*
boldly *adverb*

bolt¹ /bōlt/ *noun*
1 a piece of metal or wood used for keeping a door closed
2 a screw with no point

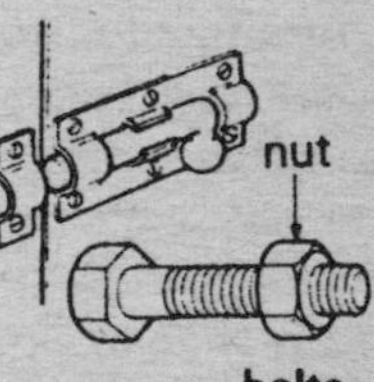

bolts

bolt² *verb*
1 to fasten with a bolt: **Bolt** *the door, please.*
2 to run away suddenly: *The horse* **bolted** *and threw its rider to the ground.*

bomb[1] /bomb/ *noun*
a container full of material that will explode

bomb[2] *verb*
to drop bombs on: *The air force* **bombed** *two towns.*
bomber /bomb′ ər/ *noun* a plane built to carry and drop bombs

bond /bond/ *noun*
1 a feeling, likeness, etc. that joins people together: *a* **bond** *of friendship*
2 a written promise, usually to pay money

°**bone** /bōn/ *noun*
one of the hard white parts in a person's or animal's body

bonfire /bon′ fīr/ *noun*
a big fire made in the open air

bonnet /bon′ it/ *noun*
1 a hat tied under the chin
2 the part of a car's body that covers the engine

°**book**[1] /bŏŏk/ *noun*
sheets of paper fastened together, for reading or writing: *You are reading a* **book** *now.*
bookcase *noun* a piece of furniture for storing books

book[2] *verb*
to arrange something you want to do later: *We've* **booked** *seats for tomorrow's football game*

boom /bōōm/ *noun*
a loud, hollow sound, like a big gun

boot /bōōt/ *noun*
1 a shoe that covers the foot and ankle

boot

border /bôr′ dər/ *noun*
1 an edge: *a blue dress with a white* **border**
2 the dividing line between two countries

bore[1] /bôr/ *verb* (*present participle* **boring,** *past* **bored**)
to make someone tired or uninterested, by something dull: *I'm* **bored** *with this job.*
boredom *noun (no plural)* being bored
boring *adjective: a* **boring** *job*

bore[2] *noun*
an uninteresting or dull person or thing

bore[3] see **bear**

bore[4] *verb* (*present participle* **boring,** *past* **bored**)
to make a round hole in something: *This machine can* **bore** *through solid rock.*

°**born** /bôrn/ *adjective*
given life: *The baby was* **born** *yesterday.*

borne /bôrn/
see **bear**

°**borrow** /bor′ ō/ *verb*
to get the use of something which you are going to give back later: *I've left my pen at home; may I* **borrow** *yours?*

boss /bôs/ *noun* (*plural* **bosses**)
someone who employs or controls people
bossy /bôs ē/ *adjective* (**bossier, bossiest**) liking to give orders: *a* **bossy** *little girl*

botany /bot′ ə nē/ *noun (no plural)*
the scientific study of plants
botanical /bə tan′ ik əl/ *adjective*
botanist *noun* a person who studies botany

°**both** /bōth/
this one and that one; the two: *Hold the dish with* **both** *hands. My brother and my sister* **both** *ran to help me.*

bother¹ /boTH′ ər/ *verb*
to cause trouble to oneself or someone else: *He didn't* **bother** *to answer my letter. I'm sorry to* **bother** *you, but could you help me?*

bother² *noun (no plural)*
trouble or difficulty: It was a **bother** *to relight the fire.*

°**bottle¹** /bot′ əl/ *noun*
a tall round glass or plastic container, with a narrow neck: *a* **milk bottle**

bottle jar

bottle² *verb*
to put into a bottle: *This is where they* **bottle** *the milk.*

°**bottom** /bot′ əm/ *noun*
1 the lowest part or base of something: *The price is on the* **bottom** *of the box.*
2 the ground below the sea, etc.: *It sank to the* **bottom** *of the sea.*
3 the last part: *Go to the* **bottom** *of the street. My friend is at the* **bottom** *of* (= in the lowest position in) *the class.*

bought /bôt/ see **buy**

boulder /bōl′ dər/ *noun*
a large rock

bounce /bouns/ *verb (present participle* **bouncing,** *past* **bounced)**
1 to spring or jump back: *The baby was* **bouncing** *on the bed.*

bounce

2 to make something do this: *The children were* **bouncing** *a ball.*

bound¹ /bound/ *adjective*
1 going toward: *This train is* **bound for** *the city.*
2 sure to: *If you work hard, you are* **bound to** *pass the exams.*

bound² see **bind**

bound³ *verb*
to jump about: *The young animals were* **bounding** *about the field.*

bound⁴ *noun*
a big jump

boundary /boun′ drē/ *noun (plural* **boundaries)**
the dividing line between two places: *Where is the* **boundary** *of the football field?*

bow¹ /bou/ *verb*
to bend the top part of the body forward to show respect: *Everyone* **bowed** *to the President.*

bow² *noun*
an act of bowing: *a* **bow** *of respect*

bow³ /bō/ *noun*
1 a piece of wood held in a curve by a string, used with an **arrow** as a weapon
2 a long thin piece of wood with tight strings fastened along it, used for playing musical instruments that have strings (picture at **violin**)
3 a knot used for ornament in the hair, for tying shoes, etc.: *She tied the ribbon* **in a bow.**

bowl /bōl/ *noun*
a deep round dish or container: *She dropped the* **bowl** *of water. Fill the* **sugar bowl,** *please.*

bowl

°**box**[1] /box/ *noun* (*plural* **boxes**)
a container with stiff, straight sides, made from wood, cardboard, plastic or metal: *a* **box** *of fruit*

box[2] *verb* (*past tense* **boxed**)
to fight with tightly closed hands: *Richard* **boxes** *well; he's the best* **boxer** *in our school.*
boxing *noun (no plural)*

°**boy** /boi/ *noun*
a malc child: *They have five children: three* **boys** *and two girls.*

bracelet /brās' lit/ *noun*
a band or chain worn around the wrist or arm

bracelets

bracket[1] /brak' it/ *noun*
a piece of wood or metal put on a wall to support something: *We use* **brackets** *to hold up a shelf.*

bracket[2] *noun*
one of the signs [ ]: *In the sentence "Do you want any [more] fruit?", [more] is* **in brackets.**

brag /brag/ *verb* (*present participle* **bragging,** *past* **bragged**)
to praise oneself: *He* **bragged** *that he had passed the exam easily.*

°**brain** /brān/ *noun*
the part inside the head with which we think

brake[1] /brāk/ *noun*
something for slowing down or stopping a bicycle, car, train, etc.

brake[2] *verb* (*present participle* **braking,** *past* **braked**)
to use brakes: *The driver* **braked** *quickly to avoid an accident.*

°**branch**[1] /branch/ *noun* (*plural* **branches**)
1 a part of a tree that grows from the main stem (picture at **tree**)
2 part of a business: *The company's head office is in the city, but it has* **branches** *all over the country.*

°**branch**[2] *verb*
to divide into two parts: *Follow the road until it* **branches.**

brand[1] /brand/ *noun*
1 the name of a particular kind of goods made by one company: *What* **brand** *of soap do you like?*
2 a mark, often made by burning, to show ownership: *These cattle have our* **brand** *on them.*
brand-new *adjective* unused: *His bike is* **brand-new.**

brand[2] *verb*
to put a brand on: *We've* **branded** *our cattle.*

°**brass**[1] /bras/ *noun (no plural)*
a very hard, bright yellow metal, made by mixing copper (see) and zinc (see)

°**brass**[2] *adjective*
made of brass: **brass** *ornaments*

°**brave** /brāv/ *adjective*
without fear, or not showing it: *a* **brave** *fireman* **bravely** *adverb*
bravery /brāv' re/ *noun (no plural): The firemen showed great* **bravery.**

°**bread** /bred/ *noun (no plural)*
a food made from flour, and baked: *a* **loaf of bread** (= a large baked piece of bread)

°**breadth** /bredth/ *noun (no plural)*
the distance from one side of something to the other; how broad something is: *What's the* **breadth** *of this river?*

°**break**[1] /brāk/ *verb* (*past tense* **broke** /brōk/, *past participle* **broken** /brok' ən/)

1 to cause to fall to pieces: *The stone* **broke** *the window.*
2 to fall to pieces: *The cup* **broke** *on the floor. Our truck* **broke down** (= would not go further) *outside town. The thieves* **broke into** *the office* (= they broke something to get in) *and stole some money. Fire* **broke out** (=suddenly started) *in the kitchen. The police* **broke up** *the fighting crowd* (= they separated them and told them to go away).

break[2] *noun*
1 an opening made by breaking or being broken: *The sun shone through a* **break** *in the clouds.*
2 a short rest: *Let's have a* **break.**

°**breakfast** /brek' fəst/ *noun*
the first meal of the day

breast /brest/ *noun*
1 one of the two parts on the front of a woman's body that can give milk
2 the top part of the front of the body

°**breath** /breth/ *noun*
air taken into and let out from the body: *He took a deep* **breath** *and jumped into the water. How long can you* **hold your breath** (= stop breathing)?
breathless *adjective* breathing quickly, because of excitement or exercise

°**breathe** /brēth/ *verb* (*present participle* **breathing,** *past* **breathed)**
to take air into the body and let it out

°**breed**[1] /brēd/ *verb* (*past* **bred** /bred/)
1 to produce young: *Some animals will not* **breed** *in cages.*
2 to keep animals so that they will produce young ones: *He* **breeds** *cattle.*

breed[2] *noun*
a type of animal: *a* **breed** *of cattle*

breeze /brēz/ *noun*
a light wind

brew /broo͞/ *verb*
1 to make drinks such as tea, coffee, or beer
2 to be going to happen: *I think a storm is* **brewing.**
brewery /broo͞' ə ē/ *noun* (*plural* **breweries)** a place where beer is made

bribe[1] /brīb/ *verb* (*present participle* **bribing,** *past* **bribed)**
to offer to give someone money or a present, so that he or she will do wrong to help you: *He tried to* **bribe** *the policeman to let him go.*

bribe[2] *noun*
something given in bribing: *A policeman should never* **take bribes.**
bribery /brīb ər ē/ *noun (no plural)*

brick /brik/ *noun*
1 a block of baked clay, used in building
2 *(no plural)* bricks as material: *a house built of* **brick**

bricks

bride /brīd/ *noun*
a woman who is going to be married, or who has just been married
bridal /brīd' əl/ *adjective* of a bride or wedding
bridesmaid /brīdz' mad″/ *noun* a girl or woman who helps a bride at her wedding

bridegroom /brīd′ gro͞om/ *or* **groom** /gro͞om/ *noun*
a man who is going to be married, or who has just been married

bridge /bridj/ *noun*
a thing that carries a road, railway, path etc. over something: *a* **bridge** *across the river*

bridges

bridle /brīd′ əl/ *noun*
leather bands put on a horse's head in order to control it

brief /brēf/ *adjective*
lasting a short time: *The meeting was very* **brief.**
briefly *adverb: to explain* **briefly**

briefcase /brēf′ kās/ *noun*
a thin flat case for papers or books

°**bright** /brīt/ *adjective*
1 sending out light: *The sun was very* **bright.**
2 having a clear color; not dull: *a* **bright** *yellow dress*
3 clever: *a* **bright** *pupil*

brilliant /bril′ yənt/ *adjective*
1 very bright; shining brightly: *a* **brilliant** *color*
2 very clever: *a* **brilliant** *student*

brim /brim/ *noun*
1 the edge of a cup, glass, or bowl
2 the part of a hat that stands out sideways

°**bring** /bring/ *verb* (*past* **brought** /brôt/)
to carry something, or go with someone, to the speaker: *Has anyone* **brought** *a ball to school today? If you take that book home,* **bring** *it* **back** *tomorrow.*

bring up *verb* to care for and educate children until they are grown-up

brisk /brisk/ *adjective*
quick and active: *a* **brisk** *walk*

brittle /brit′ əl/ *adjective*
hard, but easily broken: *Glass is a* **brittle** *material.*

°**broad** /brôd/ *adjective*
wide: **broad** *shoulders*

broadcast[1] /brôd′ kast″/ *verb* (*past* **broadcast**)
to send out by radio or television to the public
broadcaster *noun* someone who speaks on radio or television

broadcast[2] *noun, adjective*
something that is broadcast: *The news* **broadcast** *will be at 9 o'clock.*

broke /brōk/ see **break**

broken /brō kən/ *adjective*
1 in pieces: *a* **broken** *window*
2 not working: *a* **broken** *clock*

bronze /bronz/ *noun (no plural)*
a hard metal; made by mixing copper (see) and tin (see)

brooch /brōch/ *noun* (*plural* **brooches**)
an ornament that is pinned on clothes

brood[1] /bro͞od/ *noun*
a family of young birds

brood[2] *verb*
to think deeply and sadly about something

brook /bro͝ok/ *noun* a small stream

broom /bro͞om/ *noun*
a brush with a long handle

broom

°brother /bruTH′ ər/ *noun*
a boy or man with the same parents as another person: *Peter is Mary's* **brother.**
brother-in-law *noun* (*plural* **brothers-in-law**) the brother of your wife or husband, or the husband of your sister

brought /brôt/ see **bring**

brow /brou/ *noun*
the part of the face between the eyes and the hair

°brown /broun/ *adjective, noun*
(of) a dark color like coffee or earth: **brown** *eyes*

bruise[1] /bro͞oz/ *noun*
a mark left on the skin when the skin has been injured

bruise[2] *verb* (*present participle* **bruising,** *past* **bruised**)
to mark with a bruise: *She fell and* **bruised** *her knee.*

°brush[1] /brush/ *noun* (*plural* **brushes**)
an instrument with a handle made of sticks, stiff hair, etc. for cleaning or painting or tidying

brushes

°brush[2] *verb*
to clean or tidy with a brush: *Have you* **brushed** *your hair?*

brute /bro͞ot/ *noun*
an animal; a cruel person who acts like an animal
brutal /bro͞ot′ əl/ *adjective: a* **brutal** *criminal*
brutally *adverb*

bubble[1] /bub′ əl/ *noun*
a hollow ball of liquid containing air or gas: *You can see* **bubbles** *in soapy water.*

bubble[2] *verb* (*present participle* **bubbling** /bub′ ling/, *past* **bubbled** /bub′ əld/)
to make bubbles: *The water was* **bubbling** *gently in the pan.*

buck /buck/ *noun*
a male deer (see) or rabbit (see)

°bucket /buck′ ət/ *or* **pail** /pāl/ *noun*
a container made of metal or plastic, with a handle, for holding or carrying water, etc.

buckle /buck′ əl/ *noun*
a fastener, used for joining the ends of a belt

bud /bud/ *noun*
a young leaf or flower before it opens (picture at **flower**)

budge /buj/ *verb* (*present participle* **budging,** *past* **budged**)
to make something heavy move a little: *I can't* **budge** *this rock.*

budget /buj′ it/ *noun*
a plan of how to spend money: *a government's* **budget**

bug /bug/ *noun*
an insect that drinks juices from plants or animals

bugle /bū′ gəl/ *noun*
a musical instrument like a horn

°build /bild/ *verb* (*past* **built** /bilt/)
to make something by putting pieces together: *That house is* **built** *of brick.*
building *noun* something with a roof and walls that has been built to stay in one place: *The new hospital is a big* **building.**

bulb /bulb/ *noun*
1 a round part of some plants, from which the rest of the

bulbs

plant grows
2 any object of this shape, especially the part of an electric lamp that gives out light

bulge[1] /bulj/ *verb* (*present participle* **bulging,** *past* **bulged)**
to swell outwards: *His pocket was* **bulging** *with candy.*

bulge[2] *noun*
a swelling shape

bull /bu̇l/ *noun*
the male form of cattle and some other animals
bullock *noun: A* **bullock** *is a young bull which is unable to be the father of young ones.*

bulldozer /bu̇l′ dō″ zər/ *noun*
a powerful machine that moves earth to make land flat

bullet /bu̇l′ it/ *noun*
a piece of metal that is fired from a gun

bully[1] /bu̇l′ ē/ *noun* (*plural* **bullies)**
a person who likes to hurt weaker people or make them afraid

bully[2] *verb* (*present participle* **bullying,** *past* **bullied)**
to act like a bully to someone: *He's always* **bullying** *smaller boys.*

bump[1] /bump/ *verb*
to knock (against): *I* **bumped** *my head on a low branch.*

bump[2] *noun*
1 a sudden blow: *a* **bump** *on the head*
2 a raised round swelling on the body where it has been hit
bumper *noun*
a metal bar at the front or back of a car, etc. to protect the body if it bumps something

bumper

bun /bun/ *noun*
a small round sweet roll

bunch /bunch/ *noun* (*plural* **bunches)**
several things of the same kind fastened together: *a* **bunch** *of flowers*

bundle /bun′ dəl/ *noun*
a number of things tied or held together: *a* **bundle** *of clothes*

bungalow /bung′ gə lō/ *noun*
a house that has only a ground floor

bunk /bungk/ *noun*
a narrow bed which is sometimes fixed to the wall, often put one on top of another, to save space

buoy /bo͞o′ e *or* boi/ *noun*
a floating object used to show ships where there are rocks

buoy

burden /bur′ dən/ *noun*
something heavy that is carried: *He could not carry the* **burden** *alone.*

burglar /bur′ glər/ *noun*
a person who breaks into buildings to steal things
burglary *noun* (*plural* **burglaries)**: *The police were asking questions about the* **burglaries** *in our village.*

°**burn**[1] /burn/ *verb* (*past* **burned** /burnd/ *or* **burnt** /burnt/)
1 to be on fire: *The house is* **burning** *— help!*
2 to set on fire: *We* **burnt** *the old furniture.*
3 to harm or destroy by fire: *How did you* **burn** *your fingers? The building* **burned down** (= nothing was left).

°burn² *noun*
a wound or mark caused by burning: *a* **burn** *on his arm*

burrow /bur′ ō/ *noun*
a hole in the ground made as a home by some small animals

°burst¹ /burst/ *verb* (*past* **burst**)
1 to break because of force inside: *You'll* **burst** *that bag if you put any more things in it.*
2 to do something suddenly: *He* **burst** *into the room. She* **burst into tears** (= began to cry suddenly).

°burst² *noun*
something which happens suddenly: *a* **burst** *of laughter*

bury /ber′ ē/ *verb* (*present participle* **burying,** *past* **buried** /ber′ ēd/)
1 to put a dead person into the ground
2 to put or hide something in the ground: *The dog* **buried** *the bone.*
burial /ber′ e əl/ *noun* the ceremony of burying a dead person

°bus /bus/ *noun* (*plural* **buses**)
a large vehicle that carries people for a small payment

bus

bus stop *noun*
a place where buses stop for people to get on and off

°bush /bůsh/ *noun*
1 (*plural* **bushes**) a small tree
2*(no plural)* wild country that has not been cleared

°business /biz′ nis/ *noun*
1 *(no plural)* trading: **Business** *has been bad this year.*
2 (*plural* **businesses**) an activity that earns money; a place for trade: *He has a* **business** *in the town.*
3 *(no plural)* what is important to you: *Please leave me alone and* **mind your own business** (= look after your own things). *It's* **none of your business** (= nothing to do with you).
businessman *noun* (*plural* **businessmen**) someone whose work is trading

°busy /biz′ ē/ *adjective* **(busier, busiest)**
working; not free; having a lot to do: *He is* **busy** *now. He's* **busy** *writing letters.*
busily *adverb*

°but /but/
and yet; although it is true, it is also true that: *On the mountain it was sunny* **but** *it was cold.*

butcher /bůch′ ər/ *noun*
a person who kills animals for food and sells meat

butter /but′ ər/ *noun (no plural)*
yellow fat made from milk: *Do you want some* **butter** *on your bread?*

butterfly /but′ ər flī″/ *noun* (*plural* **butterflies**)
an insect that has four wings with bright colors and patterns on them

butterfly

°button /but′ ən/ *noun*
1 a small round object which is pushed through a hole to fasten clothes
2 a round object which is pushed to start or stop something
buttonhole *noun* the hole that a button goes through

°buzzer *noun* an electric instrument that makes a buzzing noise

°by /bī/ *preposition, adverb*
1 near; beside: *a table* **by** *the bed*

2 through; by way of: *Did you come* **by** *train?*
3 before: *Please do it* **by** *tomorrow.*
4 past: *He walked* **by** *me without seeing me.*
5 (to show who or what does something): *We were awakened* **by** *a loud noise. This story is* **by** *a famous writer.*
6 (to show how or with what): *I repaired the door* **by** *putting a nail in it. He took me* **by** *the hand.*

Cc

c /sē/

cab /kab/ *noun*
1 a taxi
2 the part of a truck where the driver sits

cabbage /kab′ ij/ *noun*
a vegetable with many large green leaves

cabin /kab′ in/ *noun*
1 a room on a ship or airplane
2 a small wooden house

cabinet /kab′ nit/ *noun*
1 *a medicine* **cabinet**
2 the people in a government who advise the President, Prime Minister, etc.

cable /kā′ bəl/ *noun*
1 a thick rope
2 wires that carry electricity or telephone calls
3 a message sent by cable

cackle /kak′ əl/ *verb* (*present participle* **cackling,** *past* **cackled**)
to make a noise like a hen

cactus /kak′ təs/ *noun* (*plural* **cacti** *or* **cactuses**) a prickly plant with thick stems that grows in hot, dry places

cacti

cafe /ka fā′/ *noun*
a place where you can buy drinks and simple meals

°**cage** /kāj/ *noun*
a box with metal bars where birds or animals are kept

°**cake** /kāk/ *noun*
a sweet, cooked food made of flour, fat, and eggs: *to bake a* **cake**

calculate /kal′ kyə lāt″/ *verb* (*present participle* **calculating,** *past* **calculated**)
to use numbers to find the answer to a problem: *Have you* **calculated** *the cost of the journey?*
calculation *noun*

calendar /kal′ ən der/ *noun*
a list of days, weeks, and months of the year

calf[1] /kaf/ *noun* (*plural* **calves** /kavz/)
the young form of cattle and some other animals

calf[2] *noun*
the part of the leg between the knee and the ankle

°**call**[1] /kôl/ *verb*
1 to name: *They* **called** *him John.*
2 to shout: *to* **call** *for help*
3 to visit: *He* **called on** *me last Tuesday.*
4 to telephone: *I* **called** *my sister today.*
5 to ask to come: *Mother* **called** *the doctor.*

°**call**[2] *noun*
1 a shout: *a* **call** *for help*
2 a visit: *a* **call** *from the doctor*
3 the act of talking to someone on the telephone: *There's a* **call** *for you, Mr. Brown.*

°**calm** /käm/ *adjective*
quiet; peaceful: *The sea was* **calm** *after the storm. He was* **calm** *when I told him the bad news.*
calmly *adverb*

came /kām/ see **come**

camel /kam′ əl/ *noun*
a large animal with one or two humps (see) on its back used to

carry things and people in deserts

°**camera** /kam′ rə/ *noun* an instrument for taking photographs

cameras

camouflage[1] /kam′ ə fläj″/ *noun* special clothes or colors which make a person or animal seem to be part of the surroundings: *The soldier fixed leaves to his green clothes as* **camouflage** *in the forest.*

camouflage[2] *verb* (*present participle* **camouflaging,** *past* **camouflaged)** to hide by using camouflage

camp[1] /kamp/ *noun* a place with tents or huts where people live for a time

camp[2] *verb* to live in a camp

camping *noun: The children liked* **camping.**

campaign /kam pān′/ *noun*
1 battles and movements of soldiers in a war
2 a plan to get a result: *a* **campaign** *to stop people smoking*

°**can**[1] /kan/ *verb* to know how to; be able to: **Can** *she swim? No, she* **can't** (= can not). *She* **cannot** (= can not) *swim.*

can[2] *noun* a container made of metal: *Food in* **cans** *is called* **canned** *food.*

canal /kə nal′/ *noun* a man-made river: *The* **canals** *take water to the rice fields.*

canary /kə nâr′ ē/ *noun* (*plural* **canaries)** a small yellow bird with a sweet song

cancel /kan′ səl/ *verb* (*present participle* **cancelling,** *past* **cancelled)** to stop some planned event: *We had to* **cancel** *the match, because so many people were ill.*

cancer /kan′ sər/ *noun* a serious illness in which a growth (see) spreads in the body

candidate /kan′ də dāt″/ *noun*
1 a person who hopes to be chosen for something
2 a person who takes an examination

candle /kan′ dəl/ *noun* a long piece of wax (see) with a string in the middle which burns to give light

cane[1] /kān/ *noun* a hollow stick from some plants like sugar

cannon /kan′ ən/ *noun* a large gun

cannot /kan′ ot *or* kə not′/ see **can**

canoe /kə no͞o′/ *noun* a narrow, light boat

can't /kant/ see **can**

canteen /kan tēn′/ *noun* a place where people in a factory, school, or office can eat meals

canvas /kan′ vəs/ *noun* strong cloth used to make tents, bags, etc.

cap /kap/ *noun*
1 a soft hat
2 the covering for the end of a bottle or tube

capable /kā′ pə bəl/ *adjective* able to do something: *Are you* **capable of** *climbing that tree? She* *is my most* **capable** (= cleverest) *student.*

capacity /kə pas′ ə tē/ *noun*
1 the amount something can contain: *That bowl has a* **capacity** *of two pints.*
2 ability: *Paul has a great* **capacity** *for working hard.*

cape /kāp/ *noun*
1 a high piece of land which goes out into the sea
2 a covering for the shoulders and arms

°**capital** /kap′ ə təl/ *noun*
1 the chief city of a country, where the government is
2 a large letter: A, D, H *are* **capital letters;** *a, d, h are small letters. Write your name in* **capitals.**

°**captain** /kap′ tən/ *noun*
1 the person who controls a ship or aircraft
2 an officer in the army or the navy (see)
3 the leader of a team or group

captive /kap′ tiv/ *noun*
a prisoner
captivity *noun (no plural): They were* **in captivity** (= prisoners) *for a week.*

capture /kap′ chər/ *verb* (*present participle* **capturing,** *past* **captured**)
to take as a prisoner

°**car** /kär/ *noun*
a vehicle on wheels, driven by an engine, that you can travel in

car

parking lot *noun* a place where cars can be left

caravan /kar′ ə van″/ *noun*
a group of animals or vehicles that travel together

carbon /kär′ bən/ *noun (no plural)*
a chemical found in coal, and in all living things

carcass /kär′ kəs/ *noun* (*plural* **carcasses**)
the dead body of an animal or bird

°**card** /kärd/ *noun*
a piece of stiff thick paper: *A* **playing card** *has signs and numbers on it, and is used with others in games. A* **Christmas card** *has a picture and a message on it, and is sent at Christmas.*

°**cardboard** /kärd′ bôrd″/ *noun (no plural)*
stiff, thick paper used for making boxes, book covers, etc.

cardigan /kär′ di gən/ *noun*
a short woolen coat usually worn over a shirt

cardigan

cardinal /kärd′ nəl/ *noun*
1 an important priest of the Roman Catholic (see) church
2 a bright red bird common in North America

°**care[1]** /kâr/ *verb* (*present participle* **caring,** *past* **cared**)
1 to feel interest or worry: *Does she* **care about** *her work?*
2 to look after: *His son* **cared for** *him when he was ill.*
3 to like or love: *She* **cares for** *him very much.*

°**care[2]** *noun*
1 the act of looking after a person or thing: **Take care of** *your brother while I am away.*
2 thought: *When you are crossing the road,* **take care!**
3 something that makes you sad:

He was worried by all the **cares** *of the family.*

careful *adjective: Be* **careful** *when you cross the road.*

careless *adjective:* **Careless** *driving causes accidents.*

cargo /kär′ gō/ *noun (plural* **cargoes)**
something carried on a ship or in an airplane: *a* **cargo** *of cotton/of oil*

carpentry /kär′ pən trē/ *noun*
the art of making things out of wood

carpenter *noun* a person who does carpentry as a job

carpet /kär′ pit/ *noun*
a large mat used to cover the floor

carriage /kar′ ij/ *noun*
1 a small vehicle for transporting babies (a buggy)
2 a vehicle pulled by horses instead of a motor

carrot /kar′ ət/ *noun*
a vegetable with a long orange or red root

°**carry** /kar′ e/ *verb (present participle* **carrying,** *past* **carried)**
1 to take something somewhere: *He* **carried** *the food to the table.*
2 (used in sentences like these): **Carry on** (= go on) *reading! I have* **carried out** (= done) *my work.*

°**cart** /kärt/ *noun*
a wooden vehicle, pulled by horses or oxen, and used for carrying goods

carton /kärt′ ən/ *noun*
a cardboard box for holding goods: *a* **carton** *of eggs*

carve /kärv/ *verb (present participle* **carving,** *past* **carved)**
1 to cut wood or stone into shapes: *He* **carved** *the figure of a woman from a piece of wood.*
2 to cut meat into pieces: *She* **carved** *the chicken.*

°**case**[1] /kās/ *noun*
1 something that is true or has happened: *It's raining!* **In that case,** *put on your coat before you go. Take a hat with you* **in case** (= because it might happen that) *the sun is very hot.*
2 (the facts about) a question that is decided in a court (see) of law: *a difficult* **case** *to prove*
3 one example of an illness: *There are three* **cases** *of fever in school.*

case[2] *noun*
a box or bag for carrying or covering things: *He took a* **case** *full of clothes with him.*

cash[1] /kash/ *noun*
coins and paper money: *Have you any* **cash?**

cash[2] *verb*
to get cash in return for a check (see): *I* **cashed** *a check at the bank.*

cashier /ka shēr′/ *noun: A* **cashier** *takes and gives out money in a bank or shop.*

cassette /kə set′/ *noun*
a small plastic container holding tape (see) that plays music when fitted into a **cassette recorder** or tape recorder (see)

cast /kast/ *noun*
the people acting in a play: *He was in the* **cast** *of the school play.*

castle /kas′ əl/ *noun*
a large strong building made so that no one can attack the people inside

casual /kazh' wəl *or* kazh' o͞o əl/ *adjective*
1 not planned or arranged: *a* **casual** *meeting*
2 not used for a special time or place: *He was wearing* **casual** *clothes, not his school ones.*
casually *adverb*

°**cat** /kat/ *noun*
1 a small animal often kept in houses to catch mice (see)
2 any of the larger wild animals that are like the house cat: **Lions** *and* **leopards** *are some of the big* **cats.**

cat

catalogue /kat' ə lôg"/ *noun*
a list of something in a special order: *a* **catalogue** *of all the books in the library*

°**catch**[1] /kach/ *verb* (*past* **caught** /kôt/)
1 to get in the hand and hold: *She threw the ball and I* **caught** *it.*
2 to run after and take hold of: *We ran after the dog and* **caught** *it.*
3 to get: *I* **caught** *the train. She* **caught** *a cold. I walked fast but I couldn't* **catch up** *with you* (= couldn't get to where you were).

catch[2] *noun* (*plural* **catches**)
1 a metal fastener for a window or door
2 something that is caught

category /kat' ə gôr" ē/ *noun* (*plural* **categories**)
a sort: *There are different* **categories** *of books in a library.*

caterpillar /kat' ər pil" ər/ *noun*
the young form of a butterfly (see) or moth (see), which is like a worm with short legs

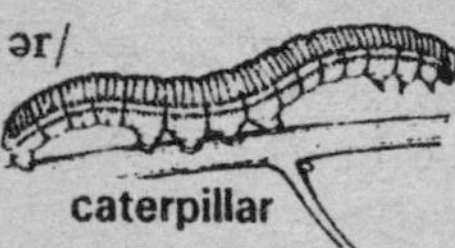
caterpillar

cathedral /kə thē drəl/ *noun*
the chief church in a city

Catholic *or* **Roman Catholic** /kath' lik/ *noun, adjective*
(a Christian) belonging to the church whose head is the Pope

°**cattle** /kat' əl/ *plural noun*
large animals kept for meat, milk, and skins

cauliflower /kô' li flou" ər/ *noun*
a vegetable with a hard white flower

°**cause**[1] /kôz/ *verb* (*present participle* **causing,** *past* **caused**)
to make something happen; be the reason: *The heavy rain* **caused** *the flood.*

°**cause**[2] *noun*
1 a person or thing that makes something happen; a reason: *The heavy rain was the* **cause** *of the flood.*
2 something you believe in or care about: *They were all fighting for the same* **cause.**

caution /kô' shən/ *noun*
great care: *Drive with* **caution.**
cautious *adjective: He was* **cautious** *when he was riding the bicycle.*
cautiously *adverb*

cave /kāv/ *noun*
a hollow place under the ground or in the side of a mountain or rock

cease /sēs/ *verb* (*present participle* **ceasing,** *past* **ceased**)
to stop: *Her mother never* **ceases** *telling you about her troubles.*
ceaseless *adjective: The* **ceaseless** *rain was bad for the crops.*
ceaselessly *adverb*

ceiling /sē′ ling/ *noun*
the inside of the roof of a room

celebrate /sel′ ə brāt″/ *verb* (*present participle* **celebrating,** *past* **celebrated**)
to show you are happy about a special event, especially by having a party or feast

celebration *noun: There was a great* **celebration** *when the baby was born.*

cell /sel/ *noun*
1 a small room in which a prisoner lives
2 a very small piece of living substance: *We lose a few skin* **cells** *every time we wash our hands.*

cellar /sel′ ər/ *noun*
a room under the ground in a house

cement /sə ment′/ *noun*
a powder which becomes hard like stone when mixed with water; it is used in building

cemetery /sem′ ə ter″ ē/ *noun* (*plural* **cemeteries**)
an area of ground where dead bodies are put under the earth

census /sen′ səs/ *noun* (*plural* **censuses**)
a count of the people in a country

cent /sent/ *noun*
a small coin used in some countries

°**center** /sen′ ter/ *noun*
1 the middle: *We went into the* **center** *of town.*
2 a place where a lot of people come with a special purpose: *The doctors worked at the Health* **Center.** *Have you seen the new shopping* **center?**

central /sen′ trəl/ *adjective* in the middle

centigrade /sen′ tə grād″/ *noun (no plural)*
a way of measuring temperature (= how hot something is): *In the summer, the temperature is sometimes forty* **degrees centigrade (40° C).**

°**centimeter** /sen′ tə mē″ tər/ *noun*
a measure of length: *There are a hundred* **centimeters** *in a meter.* **cm** *is a short way of writing* **centimeter.**

century /sen′ chə rē/ *noun* (*plural* **centuries**)
(a period of) one hundred years: *It was built in the 19th* **century.**

cereal /sēr′ ē əl/ *noun*
a crop such as wheat, rice, and maize, used as a food

°**ceremony** /ser′ ə mo″ nē/ *noun* (*plural* **ceremonies**)
a number of things done at a special happening: *The marriage* **ceremony** *took place in the church.*

certain[1] /sur′ tən/ *adjective*
sure: *I am* **certain** *he told me to come at two o'clock.*

certainly *adverb: Will you help me please?* **Certainly!** (= Of course!)

certain[2] *adjective*
some: *People who smoke cannot travel in* **certain** *parts of the train.*

certificate /sər tif′ ə kit/ *noun*
a written paper saying something important: *Your* **birth certificate** *tells people when you were born.*

chain[1] /chān/ *noun*
a number of metal rings joined together: *She wore a gold* **chain** *around her neck.*

chain[2] *verb*
to tie with a chain: *The*

chain

dog was **chained (up)** *to the wall.*

°**chair** /châr/ *noun*
a piece of furniture you sit on, with four legs and a back

chairman /châr′ mən/ (*plural* **chairmen**) /men/ *or* **chairwoman** (*plural* **chairwomen**) *or* **chairperson** (*plural* **chairpersons**) *noun*
a person who controls a meeting

°**chalk** /chôk/ *noun*
1 a soft white substance
2 a piece of this substance used for writing on a blackboard

challenge[1] /chal′ ənj/ *verb* (*present participle* **challenging,** *past* **challenged**)
1 to offer to fight or play a game against: *Their school* **challenged** *ours to a football game.*
2 to test or question: *I did not think he was right, so I* **challenged** *him.*

challenge[2] *noun*
1 an offer to fight or play against someone
2 a test of ability: *This examination is a real* **challenge.**

champion /cham′ pē ən/ *noun*
someone who is the best at something
championship *noun* a competition to find who is the best at something: *Our team won the swimming* **championships.**

°**chance** /chans/ *noun*
1 something unexpected: *I met him* **by chance.**
2 something which may happen: *There is a* **chance** *that I will be chosen for the team.*
3 a time when something may be done: *I haven't had a* **chance** *to read my letter.*
4 a risk: *He is* **taking a chance** *by driving his car so fast.*

°**change**[1] /chānj/ *verb* (*present participle* **changing,** *past* **changed**)
1 to become or make different: *This town has* **changed** *since I was a child. You said you were going to the supermarket; won't you* **change your mind** *and stay here?*
2 to take or put something in the place of something else: *She took the dress back to the shop and* **changed** *it (for another).*
3 to put on different clothes: *He* **changed** *when he arrived home from school.*

°**change**[2] *noun*
1 something that has become different: *You will see many* **changes** *in the village since last year.*
2 money you get back when you give too much for something: *I gave him a dollar and he gave me 20 cents* **change.**

channel[1] /chan′ əl/ *noun*
a narrow piece of flowing water: *The English* **Channel** *is between France and England. They cut a* **channel** *from the river to bring water to the field.*

channel[2] *verb* (*present participle* **channelling,** *past* **channelled**)
to make flow in one direction: *They* **channelled** *the water toward the field.*

chant[1] /chant/ *verb*
to say in a singing way: *He* **chanted** *a prayer. The crowd* **chanted** "*We want jobs!*"

chant[2] *noun*
words said in this way

chapel /chap′ əl/ *noun*
a small church or part of a church

chapter /chap′ tər/ *noun*
part of a book: *Open your books at* **Chapter 3.**

°**character** /kar′ ik tər/ *noun*
1 what a person or thing is like: *He has a strong but gentle* **character.** *The new buildings have changed the* **character** *of the village.*
2 a person in a book, film, or play
characteristic *noun* something that is typical of someone or something: *Kindness is one of his* **characteristics.**

charcoal /chär′ kol″/ *noun (no plural)*
wood made black by slow heating under earth and used for burning

charge¹ /chärj/ *verb (present participle* **charging,** *past* **charged)**
1 to ask money for: *The fruit seller* **charged** *me too much money.*
2 to say that a person has done something wrong: *He was* **charged with** *stealing a car.*
3 to run or hurry: *The little boy* **charged** *into the room.*

charge² *noun*
1 a price asked for something: *a* **charge** *for the use of the telephone*
2 a statement that a person has done wrong: *a* **charge** *of stealing*
3 a hurried attack
4 care: *I was* **in charge of** *my sister* (= I looked after her).

charity /char′ ə tē/ *noun*
1 goodness and kindness: *She helped him out of* **charity.**
2 (*plural* **charities**) a group of people who give money, food, etc. to those who need it

charm¹ /chärm/ *verb*
to please greatly
charming *adjective* beautiful; pleasing

charm² *noun*
1 pleasing behavior: *He had great* **charm:** *everyone liked him.*
2 a thing or words that are said to be magic (see): *He has a stone which he says is a lucky* **charm.**

chart /chärt/ *noun*
1 a map, especially of an area of sea
2 a large piece of paper with information on it in pictures and writing

°**chase¹** /chās/ *verb (present participle* **chasing,** *past* **chased)**
to run after: *The boy* **chased** *the dog.*

chase² *noun*
an act of chasing: *He caught it after a long* **chase.**

chat¹ /chat/ *verb (present participle* **chatting,** *past* **chatted)**
to talk in a friendly way

chat² *noun*
a friendly talk: *to have a* **chat**

chatter /chat′ ər/ *verb*
to talk quickly, especially about unimportant things: *They just sat and* **chattered.**

°**cheap** /chēp/ *adjective*
costing only a little money: *A bicycle is much* **cheaper** *than a car.*

°**cheat¹** /chēt/ *verb*
to deceive; do something which is not honest: *He didn't play the game fairly — he* **cheated.**

°**cheat²** *noun*
a person who is not fair or honest

check¹ /chek/ *verb*
to make sure that something has been done well or is in good order: *You should* **check** *your bicycle before you ride it.*

check²
noun 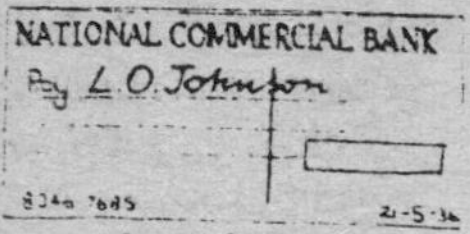
1 a printed piece of paper which you write on, and which can be exchanged for money at the bank
2 an act of checking: *a police* **check** *on cars and trucks*
3 a pattern of squares: *The material had* **checks** *on it. It was* **checked** *material.*

°**cheek** /chēk/ *noun*
one of the two parts on each side of the face under the eyes

cheeky /chēk′ ē/ *adjective* **(cheekier, cheekiest)**
not polite or respectful: *He is* **cheeky** *to his teacher.*

°**cheer¹** /chēr/ *verb*
1 to make happy: *The children's laughter* **cheered (up)** *the old woman.*
2 to shout because you are pleased

°**cheer²** *noun*
a shout of happiness or to support someone or something: *Let's give three* **cheers** *for our team — they've won!*
cheerful *adjective* smiling and happy
cheerfully *adverb*

cheese /chēz/ *noun*
a food made from thickened milk

°**chemical¹** /kem′ i kəl/ *noun*
a substance, especially one made by or used in chemistry (see)

°**chemical²** *adjective*
of or made by chemistry (see)

chemist /kem′ ist/ *noun*
a person who studies chemistry
°**chemistry** *noun* the science which studies substances like gas, metals, liquids, etc., what they are made of, and what they do

°**chest** /chest/ *noun*
1 the front of the body between the shoulders and the stomach
2 a large box: *a tool* **chest**

chew /cho͞o/ *verb*
to break up food with the teeth

°**chick** /chik/ *noun*
a young bird, especially a young chicken

°**chicken** /chik′ ən/ *noun*
a bird kept by people for its eggs and meat

°**chief¹** /chēf/ *adjective*
the most important
chiefly *adverb* mostly: *He kept animals —* **chiefly** *cattle, with some pigs.*

°**chief²** *noun*
a leader; ruler; head of a group or tribe: *the* **chief** *of police*

chieftain /chēf′ tən/ *noun*
a chief, especially of a tribe or large family group

°**child** /chīld/ *noun* (*plural* **children** /child′ rən/)
1 a young person older than a baby
2 a **son or daughter:** *They have three* **children.**
childhood *noun* the time when you are a child
childish *adjective* like or for a child: *a* **childish** *game*
childishly *adverb*

chime /chīm/ *verb* (*present participle* **chiming,** *past* **chimed)**
to make a sound like a bell: *The clock* **chimed** *three o'clock.*
chime *noun*

chimney /chim′ nē/ *noun*
a pipe which takes smoke away from a fire

chimpanzee /chim′ pan zē″/ *noun*
an African animal like a monkey but without a tail: **Chimpanzees** *are apes* (see).

°**chin** /chin/ *noun*
the part of the face below the mouth

china /chī′ nə/ *noun (no plural)*
things like cups and plates, or the special kind of white earth from which they are made

chip[1] /chip/ *noun*
1 a small piece of something broken off: *a cup with a* **chip** *out of it*
2 a thin slice of fried potato
3 a very small piece of metal or plastic used in computers to store information or make the computer work. Sometimes called a **microchip.**

chip[2] *verb* (*present participle* **chipping,** *past* **chipped)**
to break a small piece off something hard: *He* **chipped** *the cup when he dropped it.*

chirp /churp/ *noun*
a short high sound made by some birds and insects

°**chocolate** /chäk′ lət/ *noun, adjective*
(a candy or food) made from cocoa (see): **chocolate** *cake*

°**choice** /chois/ *noun*
the act of choosing or something chosen: *She had to* **make a choice** *between the two dresses. Her* **choice** *was the blue one.*

choir /kwīr/ *noun*
a number of people who sing together: *the school* **choir**

choke /chōk/ *verb* (*present participle* **choking,** *past* **choked)**
to be unable to breathe because of something in the throat: *to* **choke on** *a fish bone*

°**choose** /cho͞oz/ *verb* (*present participle* **choosing,** *past tense* **chose** /chōz/, *past participle* **chosen** /chōz′ ən/)
to pick out from a number of things or people the one you want: *She* **chose** *to study chemistry.*

chop[1] /chop/ *verb* (*present participle* **chopping,** *past* **chopped)**
to cut with an ax or sharp knife

chop[2] *noun*
a piece of meat with a bone cut from the side of an animal's body

chorus /kôr′ əs/ *noun* (*plural* **choruses)**
1 a group of singers
2 a part of a song which is repeated

christen /kris′ ən/ *verb*
to give a Christian name to: *They* **christened** *the baby John.*
christening *noun* the ceremony in which a baby is given its Christian name

°**Christian** /kris′ chən/ *noun, adjective*
(a person) following the teachings of Jesus Christ

°**Christmas** /kris′ məs/ *noun*
the day of the year on which the birth of Jesus Christ is celebrated

chuckle /chuk′ əl/ *verb* (*present participle* **chuckling,** *past* **chuckled)**
to laugh quietly: *He* **chuckled** *at the funny story.*
chuckle *noun*

°**church** /church/ *noun* (*plural* **churches)**
a building that Christians meet and pray in

cigar /si gär′/ *noun*
tobacco (see) leaves rolled together for smoking

°cigarette /sig′ ə ret″/ *noun*
tobacco (see) cut into small pieces and rolled in paper for smoking

cinema /sin′ ə mə/ *noun*
a building where you see films; a theater

°circle /sur′ kəl/ *noun*
1 something round; a ring: *They sat in a* **circle** *around the fire.*
2 a group of people
circular *adjective*

circulate /sur′ kyə lāt″/ *verb* (*present participle* **circulating,** *past* **circulated**)
to go around: *Blood* **circulates** *around your body.*
circulation *noun*

circumference /sər kum′ frəns/ *noun*
distance around

circumstances /sur′ kəm stans″ əs/ *plural noun*
the facts about what happens: **In/under the circumstances** (= considering what has happened), *I won't come.*

circus /sur′ kəs/ *noun*
a show given by people and trained animals, often in a large tent (see)

citizen /sit′ ə zən/ *noun*
a person who lives and has special rights in a country or town

city /sit′ ē/ *noun* (*plural* **cities**)
a large town

civil /siv′ əl/ *adjective*
1 polite: *Be* **civil** *to the principal.*
2 not part of the armed forces (see)
civil service *noun: The* **civil service** *is all the people who work for a government except the armed forces.*

civilian /sə vil′ yən/ *noun*
a person who is not in the armed forces (see)

civilize /siv′ ə līz″/ *verb* (*present participle* **civilizing,** *past* **civilized**)
to change the way that people live together, by making laws and having government and education
civilization *noun* people sharing their way of life and living in one place at a time

claim[1] /klām/ *verb*
1 to ask for something that you say is yours: *I* **claimed** *the coat that the teacher found.*
2 to say that something is true: *He* **claimed** *that he hadn't done it, but I didn't believe him.*

claim[2] *noun*
something that is claimed: *They made* **a claim** *for insurance money.*

clang /klang/ *noun*
the sound of one piece of metal hitting another: *There was a* **clang** *as he dropped the tools.*
clang *verb*

clap[1] /klap/ *verb* (*present participle* **clapping,** *past* **clapped**)
to make a sound by hitting your hands together, often to show that we like something: *When the singer finished, we* **clapped.**

clap[2] *noun*
1 the sound of clapping
2 the sudden sound of thunder: *a* **clap** *of thunder.*

clash[1] /klash/ *verb*
1 to hit or fight: *The police* **clashed** *with the angry crowd.*
2 (of colors) to look wrong together: *His shirt* **clashed** *with his coat.*

clash[2] *noun*
1 an act of clashing: *a* **clash** *with the police*
2 a loud noise of metal on metal: *the* **clash** *of weapons*

clasp[1] /klasp/ *verb*
to hold tightly: *He* **clasped** *my arm with fear.*

clasp[2] *noun*
something that fastens two things together: *He had a gold* **clasp** *on his belt.*

°**class** /klas/ *noun* (*plural* **classes**)
1 a group of people who learn together: *She was in a* **class** *of thirty students.*
2 a group of people or things of the same kind: *Cats belong to one* **class** *of animals, fish to another.*
classroom *noun: There are fourteen pupils in the* **classroom.**

clatter /klat′ ər/ *noun*
the loud noise of things being knocked together: *The pans fell with a* **clatter.**
clatter *verb*

clause /klôz/ *noun*
a group of words in a sentence that contains a verb: *The sentence "As I was walking home, I met my friend" contains two* **clauses.** *"As I was walking home" is one* **clause,** *and "I met my friend" is another.* Look at **phrase.**

claw[1] /klô/ *noun*
one of the sharp, hard points on the foot of a bird or animal

claw[2] *verb*
to tear with the claws: *The cat* **clawed** *the chair.*

°**clay** /klā/ *noun*
soft, sticky earth from which pots and bricks are made

°**clean**[1] /klēn/ *adjective*
not dirty: *That shirt is dirty; here is a* **clean** *one.*

°**clean**[2] *verb*
to make something clean; take dirt from something: *Have you* **cleaned** *the kitchen?*
cleaner *noun* a person who cleans

°**clear**[1] /klēr/ *adjective*
1 easy to understand: *It was* **clear** *that he wanted to be alone.*
2 easy to see or hear: *a* **clear** *voice*
3 easy to see through: **clear** *water*
clearly *adverb* **1** in a clear way: *Please speak more* **clearly,** *we can't hear you.* **2** without any doubt: **Clearly,** *he's very clever!*

°**clear**[2] *verb*
1 to take away: *to* **clear** *plates from a table*
2 to clean; tidy; put away: *They* **cleared up** *the kitchen.*

clergyman /klur′ jē man″/ *noun* (*plural* **clergymen** /men/)
religious minister

clerk /klurk/ *noun*
a person who works in an office and writes letters

°**clever** /klev′ ər/ *adjective*
quick at learning and understanding things
cleverly *adverb*

click /klick/ *noun*
a single light sound like a door shutting
click *verb*

cliff /klif/ *noun*
an area of high, steep rock, often close to the sea

climate /klī mət/ *noun*
the weather that a place has

°**climb**[1] /klīm/ *verb*
to go up: *The two boys* **climbed (up)** *the tree.*

climb² *noun*
an act of climbing; the distance climbed: *a long* **climb** *up the hill*

cling /kling/ *verb* (*past* **clung** /klung/)
to hold on tightly: *The baby monkey* **clung to** *its mother.*

clinic /klin′ ik/ *noun*
a place where people go to see a doctor

clip¹ /klip/ *noun*
a small metal object used for fastening something: *The letters were held together with a* **paper clip.**

clip² *verb* (*present participle* **clipping,** *past* **clipped)**
1 to hold with a clip: *The letters were* **clipped** *together.*
2 to cut with a sharp instrument: *He* **clipped** *his fingernails.*

cloak /klōk/ *noun*
a loose piece of clothing, worn on top of everything else

cloak

°**clock** /klok/ *noun*
a machine that tells you what time it is
clockwise /klok′ wīz″/ *adverb* in the same direction as the hands of a clock. **Counter clockwise** is the opposite way.

°**close¹** /klōz/ *verb* (*present participle* **closing,** *past* **closed)**
to shut: *The shop is* **closed** *today.* (= not open for business)

°**close²** /klōs/ *adjective*
1 near: *I live* **close** *to the shops. They were standing* **close together** (= very near each other).
2 liking or loving: *Peter and John are* **close** *friends.*

°**cloth** /klôth/ *noun*
1 a soft substance made of wool, cotton, etc.; material: *She bought some* **cloth** *to make some new dresses.*
2 a piece of cloth: *A red* **tablecloth** *covered the table.*

°**clothes** /klōz/ *plural noun*
things we wear
clothing /klōTH′ ing/ *noun (no plural)* things that are used as clothes

clothes

°**cloud** /kloud/ *noun*
a mass of very small drops of water floating in the sky
cloudy *adjective* **(cloudier, cloudiest)** having lots of cloud

clown /kloun/ *noun*
a person whose job is to make people laugh

°**club¹** /klub/ *noun*
a group of people who meet for some purpose: *a bridge* **club**

club² *noun*
a large heavy stick

clue /klo͞o/ *noun*
something which helps you find the answer to a difficult question: *The police found a* **clue** *which will help them catch the robber.*

clumsy /klum′ zē/ *adjective* **(clumsier, clumsiest)**
likely to drop things or move in an awkward way: *You are* **clumsy!** *You've knocked over my cup of coffee!*
clumsily *adverb*

clung /klung/ see **cling**

clutch /kluch/ *verb*
to take hold of something tightly: *The falling man* **clutched** *the rope.*

coach[1] /kōch/ *noun* (*plural* **coaches**)
1 a bus, or part of a train, that can carry many people
2 a four-wheeled covered vehicle drawn by horses

coach[2] *verb*
to give special lessons: *He* **coached** *her for the English examination.*

coach[3] *noun* (*plural* **coaches**)
a person who gives special lessons: *Our football* **coach** *trains the team.*

coal /kōl/ *noun (no plural)*
black hard material dug out of the ground and burned to give heat

coarse /kôrs/ *adjective*
rough; not smooth or fine

°**coast** /kōst/ *noun*
the land next to the sea: *a town on the* **coast**
coastline *noun: From the ship, they saw the rocky* **coastline.**

°**coat** /kōt/ *noun*
a piece of clothing with coverings for the arms worn over everything else

coax /kōks/ *verb*
to persuade by kindness: *She* **coaxed** *him to take the medicine.*

cobweb /kob' web"/ *noun*
the thin net spun by a spider (see), in which flies and insects are caught

cobweb

cock /kok/ *noun*
a male bird, especially a male chicken

cocoa /kō' kō/ *noun*
1 a brown powder made from the seeds of a tree, from which chocolate is made
2 a hot drink made from this powder

°**coconut** /kō' kə nut"/ *noun*
a large brown nut with a hard shell, and a hollow center filled with juice

coconut

cod /kod/ *noun* (*plural* **cod**)
a sea fish used for food

code /kōd/ *noun*
a way of using words, letters, numbers, etc. to keep messages a secret: *The letter was written* **in code** *and I could not understand it.*

°**coffee** /kôf' ē/ *noun*
1 *(no plural)* (a drink made from) a brown powder from the seeds of the coffee tree
2 a cup of this drink: *Two* **coffees,** *please!*

coffin /kôf' in/ *noun*
a box in which a dead body is put

coil[1] /koil/ *verb*
1 to gather a rope, wire, or pipe in rings one above the other
2 to go around in a ring: *The snake* **coiled** *around the tree.*

coil[2] *noun*
a set of rings joined to each other; a continuous circling shape: *a* **coil** *of rope*

°**coin** /koin/ *noun*
a piece of money made of metal

°**cold**[1] /kōld/ *adjective*
having very little heat; not hot: *a* **cold** *drink*

°**cold**² *noun*
1 an illness of the nose and throat: *I've got a* **cold.**
2 *(no plural)* cold weather; absence of heat: *I don't like the* **cold.**

collapse /kə laps'/ *verb* (*present participle* **collapsing,** *past* **collapsed)**
to break into pieces; fall down: *The roof of the old house* **collapsed.** *The old man* **collapsed** *in the street.*

collar /kol' ər/ *noun*

1 the part of your clothes worn around the neck: *The* **collar** *of his shirt was dirty.*
2 a leather or metal band put around the neck of an animal

°**collect** /kə lekt'/ *verb*
to gather together in the same place: *A crowd had* **collected** *to watch the ceremony. I* **collect** *stamps from all over the world.*
collection *noun: a large* **collection** *of stamps*

°**college** /kol' ij/ *noun*
a place where people study after they have left high school

collide /kə līd'/ *verb* (*present participle* **colliding,** *past* **collided)**
to come together with great force: *The two trains* **collided.**
collision /kə lizh' ən/ *noun: a* **collision** *between two trains*

colon /kō' lən/ *noun*
the sign : which in this book comes before an example

colonel /kur' nəl/ *noun*
an officer in the army

colony /kol' ə nē/ *noun* (*plural* **colonies)**
a country that is under the control of another country
colonial /kə lō' nē əl/ *adjective* of or about a colony

°**color**¹ /kul' ər/ *noun*
the quality that makes things look green, red, yellow, etc.: *The* **color** *of leaves is green in summer.*
colorful *adjective* bright; having a lot of colors: **colorful** *clothes*

°**color**² *verb*
to put color onto something: *Sarah is* **coloring** *the picture in her book.*

column /kol' əm/ *noun*
1 a large post used to support a part of a building
2 a long narrow piece of printing in a newspaper or book
3 a row: *Can you add up this* **column** *of figures?*

°**comb**¹ /kom/ *noun*
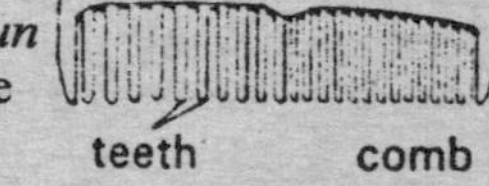

a thin piece of plastic, metal, etc. with teeth, used to make hair tidy

°**comb**² *verb*
to arrange with a comb: *Have you* **combed** *your hair?*

combine /kəm bīn'/ *verb* (*present participle* **combining,** *past* **combined)**
to join or mix together: *The two small shops* **combined** *to make one large one.*
combination /kom" bə nā' shən/ *noun: His character is a* **combination** *of strength and kindness.*

°**come** /kum/ (*present participle* **coming** /kum' ing/, *past tense* **came,** *past participle* **come)**
to move toward the person

speaking: "**Come** *here Mary, I want to speak to you!*" "*I'm going out. Are you* **coming** *with me?*" *My shoe has* **come off** (= it is not on my foot any more). *We were walking to town when we* **came across** (= found) *a cat in the road. I* **come from** *London* (= I was born there, my home is there).

comedy /kom′ ə dē/ *noun* (*plural* **comedies**)
a funny play, film, etc.; something that makes us laugh

°**comfort¹** /kum′ fərt/ *noun*
being free from pain, trouble, etc.: *He lived* **in comfort** (= he had enough money to live well).

°**comfort²** *verb*
to give help or show kindness to someone in pain or trouble: *She* **comforted** *the ill child.*
comfortable *adjective: This is a very* **comfortable** *chair* (= it is nice to sit in).
comfortably *adverb*

comic¹ /kom′ ic/ *adjective*
that makes us laugh; funny

comic² *noun*
a picture or strip of pictures in a newspaper or magazine that tells a joke

comma /kom′ ə/ *noun*
the sign , used in writing to divide up a sentence

command¹ /kə mand′/ *verb*
1 to order: *I* **command** *you to go!*
2 to be in charge of: *A general is a man who* **commands** *a large number of soldiers.*

command² *noun*
1 an order
2 power: *The officer is* **in command** *of his men.*

comment¹ /kom′ ent/ *verb*
to say something about a special thing: *He* **commented** *on the bad road.*

comment² *noun*
something said: *He made a* **comment** *about the bad road.*
commentary /kom′ ən ter″ ē/ *noun* a description spoken during a special event, match, etc.
commentator /kom′ ən tāt″ ər/ *noun: A* **commentator** *is a person who gives a commentary on the radio or television.*

commerce /kom′ ərs/ *noun*
business; buying and selling
commercial *adjective: A* **commercial** *course includes subjects that would be useful in business.*

commit /kə mit′/ *verb* (*present participle* **committing,** *past* **committed**)
to do something wrong: *A robbery was* **committed** *last night.*

committee /kə mit′ ē/ *noun*
a group of people chosen to do a job: *The tennis* **committee** *arranges all the matches.*

°**common** /kom′ ən/ *adjective*
1 found everywhere; usual: *Palms are* **common** *trees in Africa. If you have* **common sense,** *you don't do silly or careless things.*
2 shared by several people; belonging to or used by several people: *The park is* **common** *property: everyone can use it.*

Commonwealth /kom′ ən welth″/ *noun*
a group of independent countries which used to be a part of the British empire (= under the control of Britain)

communicate /kə mū′ nə kāt″/ *verb* (*present participle* **communicating**, *past* **communicated**)
to speak or write to; be understood by: *If you know English, you can* **communicate** *with people everywhere. We* **communicate** *by letter.*
communication *noun:* **Communication** *between people who speak different languages is difficult.*
communications *plural noun* roads, railroads, radio, telephones, and all other ways of moving or sending information between places

community /kə mū′ nə tē/ *noun* (*plural* **communities**)
the people living in one place, who share some things: *All the children in our* **community** *go to the same school.*

°**companion** /kəm pan′ yən/ *noun*
a person you are with, often a friend: *He was my travelling* **companion** *for many months.*

°**company** /kum′ pə nē/ *noun*
1 people to be with: *I had no* **company** *on the journey.*
2 (*plural* **companies**) a group of people doing business; a firm: *I work for a mining* **company**.

comparative /kəm par′ ə tiv/ *noun, adjective*
a word or a form of a word that shows that something is bigger, smaller, better, worse, etc. than something else: *This pen is quite good, but that one is* **better**. "Better" is a **comparative**. Look at **superlative**.

°**compare** /kəm pâr′/ *verb* (*present participle* **comparing**, *past* **compared**)
to decide in what way things are alike or different: *I* **compared** *my shoes* **with** *my sister's.*
comparison /kəm par′ ə sən/ *noun: My shoes are small* **in comparison with** *my sister's.*

compass /kum′ pəs *or* kom′ pəs/ *noun*
an instrument with a metal needle that always points north and south

compel /kəm pəl′/ *verb* (*present participle* **compelling**, *past* **compelled**)
to force: *The floods* **compelled** *us to turn back.*

°**compete** /kəm pēt′/ *verb* (*present participle* **competing**, *past* **competed**)
to try to win a race, prize, etc.: *Five children* **competed in** *the race.*
competition /kom′ pə tish′ ən/ *noun* a test of who is best at something: *She came first in a drawing* **competition**.
competitor /kəm pet′ ə tər/ *noun* a person who competes

°**complain** /kəm plān/ *verb*
to say that something is not good, or that you are unhappy or angry with something: *We* **complained about** *the bad food.*
complaint *noun: We made a* **complaint** *about the food.*

°**complete**[1] /kəm plēt/ *adjective*
1 whole; with nothing left out: *a* **complete** *set of stamps*
2 total: *a* **complete** *waste of time*

completely *adverb: Have you* **completely** *finished your work?*

complete[2] *verb (present participle* **completing,** *past* **completed)**
to finish: *to* **complete** *a piece of work*

complicated /kom′ plə kā″ tid/ *adjective*
difficult to understand; not simple: *A car engine is a* **complicated** *machine.*

compliment[1] /kom′ plə mənt *or* kom′ plə ment″/ *noun*
something nice said about someone

compliment[2] *verb*
to say something nice to someone: *He* **complimented** *my mother* **on** *her driving.*

compose /kəm pōz′/ *verb (present participle* **composing,** *past* **composed)**
1 to form out of parts: *Cakes are* **composed** *of flour, shortening, eggs, and sugar.*
2 to write or make up: *to* **compose** *songs and music*
composer *noun* a person who composes music.
composition /kom″ pə zish′ ən/ *noun* something composed, often a story: *to write a* **composition**

°**compound** /kom′ pound″/ *noun*
a building or group of buildings and the land around: *The army* **compound** *covers a square mile.*

compulsory /kəm pul′ sər ē/ *adjective*
that must be done: *Learning science is* **compulsory** *at our school — we have no choice.*

computer /kəm pū′ tər/ *noun*
a machine that can store information and work out answers quickly: *A small computer is called a* **microcomputer.**

conceal /kən sēl′/ *verb*
to hide: *He* **concealed** *the candy in his pocket.*

concentrate /kon′ sən trāt″/ *verb*
to keep your thoughts or attention on one thing: *Are you* **concentrating on** *your work?*

concern[1] /kən surn′/ *noun*
worry: *He shows no* **concern** *for his children.*
concerned *adjective* worried

concern[2] *verb*
to be about: *This letter* **concerns** *you.*
concerning *preposition* about: *I spoke to him* **concerning** *his behavior*

concert /kon′ sərt/ *noun*
music played for a lot of people

conclude /kon klo͞od′/ *verb (present participle* **concluding,** *past* **concluded)**
1 to finish: *The principal* **concluded** *her speech quickly.*
2 to decide: *When I had heard his story, I* **concluded** *that he had told me the truth.*
conclusion /kən klo͞o′ shən/ *noun: My* **conclusion** *was that the boy had told me the truth.*

concrete /kon′ krēt *or* kon krēt′/ *noun (no plural)*
a gray powder **(cement),** mixed with sand and water, which becomes very hard and is used for building

condemn /kən dem′/ *verb*
to send someone to prison for a crime

°**condition** /kən dish′ ən/ *noun*
1 the state of someone or something: *The car is in very good* **condition.** *Weather* **conditions** *are*

bad today.
2 something that must happen before something else happens: *One of the* **conditions** *of having the job was that I had to learn German. I was given the job on the* **condition** *that I learned German.*

conduct[1] /kon′ dəkt/ *verb*
to lead or guide: *The principal* **conducted** *us around the school.*
conductor *noun* **1** a person who controls a group of people playing music **2** a person who sells tickets on a bus or train

conduct[2] *noun (no plural)*
behavior

cone /kōn/ *noun*
a round shape that is pointed at one end, like the end of a sharp pencil

conference /kon′ frəns/ *noun*
a meeting of people to find out what they think about a special thing: *a doctor's* **conference**

confess /kən fes′/ *verb*
to tell about the things you have done wrong: *When the police questioned the man, he* **confessed.**
confession /kən fesh′ ən/ *noun: He* **made a confession.**

confident /kon′ fə dent/ *adjective*
feeling sure or safe: *I was* **confident that** *I had passed the examination.*
confidence *noun (no plural): She has a lot of* **confidence;** *she doesn't mind giving a speech to the whole school.*

confirm /kən furm′/ *verb*
to give proof (of): *Please* **confirm** *your telephone message by writing to me.*
confirmation /kon″ fər mā′ shən/ *noun (no plural)* proof

conflict[1] /kon′ flikt/ *noun*
a fight or argument: *a* **conflict** *between two groups of children*

conflict[2] /kən flikt′/ *verb*
to disagree: *The two stories* **conflicted,** *so I did not know what to believe.*

confuse /kən fūz′/ *verb (present participle* **confusing,** *past* **confused)**
to mix up in your mind: *I* **confused** *the two boys, because they looked so alike.*
confusion *noun* mixing up; disorder: *The room was* **in** *complete* **confusion.**

congratulate /kən grach′ ə lāt″/ *verb*
to say you are pleased about a happy event: *I* **congratulated** *them* **on** *the birth of their baby.*
congratulations /kən grach″ ə lā′ shənz/ *plural noun:* **Congratulations** *on the birth of your baby!*

conjunction /kən jungk′ shən/ *noun*
a word that joins two parts of a sentence: *I walked to the shop* **and** *I bought some fruit.* **"And"** *is a conjunction.*

°**connect** /kə nekt′/ *verb*
to join: *Will you* **connect** *this wire to the television?*
connection *noun: The television isn't working; is there a loose* **connection?**

conquer /kong′ kər/ *verb*
to defeat in war: *to* **conquer** *the enemy*
conquest /kon′ kwest″/ *noun: the* **conquest** *of the enemy*

conscience /kon′ shəns/ *noun*
the feeling inside you which tells you whether something is right or

wrong: *His* **conscience** *troubled him after he took the money.*

conscious /kon′ shəs/ *adjective*
awake and knowing what is happening around you: *He became* **conscious** *a few minutes after the accident.*
consciously *adverb*

consent[1] /kən sent′/ *verb*
to agree: *I asked my mother if I could go out, and she* **consented.**

consent[2] *noun*
agreement: *I had to get my mother's* **consent** *before I went.*

consequence /kon′ sə kwens″/ *noun*
something that happens as a result: *As a* **consequence** *of being in the hospital, Jane decided that she wanted to become a nurse.*
consequently *adverb*

conservation /kən sur vā′ shən″/ *noun*
saving and protecting: *There is a need for the* **conservation** *of trees, or there will soon be no forests.*

°**consider** /kən sid′ ər/ *verb*
to think about: *I'm* **considering** *changing my job.*
consideration *noun: They gave the plan careful* **consideration** (= thought). *She shows great* **consideration** *to* (= cares about the wishes of) *her parents.*

consist /kən sist′/ *verb*
to be made (of): *A knife* **consists of** *a blade and a handle.*

consonant /kon′ sə nənt/ *noun*
a written letter, or the sound of a letter, which is not *a, e, i, o,* or *u.* Look at **vowel.**

constant /kon′ stənt/ *adjective*
happening all the time: **constant** *rain*
constantly *adverb*

constituency /kən stich′ ə wən sē/ *noun* (*plural* **constituencies**)
a group of people that choose one member of government (see)

constitution /kon″ stə tōō′ shən/ *noun*
a set of laws governing a country, club, etc.
constitutional *adjective*

construct /kən strukt′/ *verb*
to build or make: *to* **construct** *a bridge*
construction *noun* **1** building: *a* **construction** *company* **2** something that is built

consul /kon′ səl/ *noun*
a person who represents his country in a foreign town: *The* **consul** *gave us information about colleges in his country.*

consult /kən sult′/ *verb*
to ask or look at for information: *I* **consulted** *George about buying a car.*

consume /kən sōōm′/ *verb* (*present participle* **consuming,** *past* **consumed)**
to eat or use up: *The big car* **consumed** *a lot of gasoline.*
consumption *noun (no plural): The gasoline* **consumption** *of the big car was very high.*

contact[1] /kon′ takt/ *verb*
to talk or write to: *She* **contacted** *me as soon as she arrived.*

°**contact**[2] *noun*
touching or coming together: *The two wires were* **in contact.** *She* **comes into contact with** (= meets) *many people.*

°**contain** /kən tān′/ *verb*
to have inside; hold: *The speech*

contained *some interesting ideas.*

container *noun: A* **container** *is a box, pot, or anything you can put something into.*

content /kən tent′ *or* kon′ tent/ *adjective*
happy; pleased: *Is he* **content** *with his work?*

contented *adjective*

contents /kon′ tents/ *plural noun*
what is in something: *The* **contents** *of the box fell onto the floor.*

contest /kon′ test/ *noun*
a fight or competition

continent /kon′ tə nənt/ *noun*
one of the seven large masses of land on the earth: *Europe is a* **continent.**

continental /kon″ tə nen′ təl/ *adjective*

°**continue** /kən tin′ ū/ *verb* (*present participle* **continuing,** *past* **continued**)
to go on: *Please* **continue** *reading.*

continual *adjective* happening often: **continual** *arguments*

continuous *adjective* never stopping: *a* **continuous** *noise*

contract /kon′ trakt *or* kən trakt′/ *noun*
a written agreement to do work or sell goods at an agreed price

contrary[1] /kon′ trer ē/ *noun*
the opposite: "*You must be tired.*" "**On the contrary,** *I feel wide awake.*"

contrary[2] *adjective*
opposite: *He passed the examination,* **contrary** *to what I expected.*

contrast[1] /kən trast′/ *verb*
to compare two things and find the differences between them: *The hot, sunny day* **contrasted** *greatly with the cold, rainy night.*

contrast[2] /kon′ trast″/ *noun*
difference: *There is a great* **contrast** *between good and evil.*

contribute /kən trib′ ūt/ *verb* (*present participle* **contributing,** *past* **contributed**)
to give with other people: *We all* **contributed** *money to buy Richard's present.*

contribution /kon″ trə bū′ shən/ *noun: Peter collected all the* **contributions.**

control[1] /kən trōl/ *verb* (*present participle* **controlling,** *past* **controlled**)
to have power over someone or something; decide or guide the way something or someone works: *That woman* **controls** *the newspaper. This handle* **controls** *the flow of electricity* (= makes it more or less strong).

control[2] *noun*
power; guidance: *He was* **in control** *of the car. The horse got* **out of control,** *and the rider fell to the ground.*

convenient /kən vēn′ yənt/ *adjective*
useful or suitable: *The school is in a* **convenient** *place, near my home.*

convenience *noun: My mother likes the* **convenience** *of living close to the shops.*

convent /kon′ vent/ *noun*
a place where nuns (= women who lead a religious life) live

°**conversation** /kon″ vər sā′ shən/ *noun*
a talk: *I had a long* **conversation** *with your teacher.*

convert /kən vurt′/ *verb*
to change into something else: *That building has been* **converted into** *a school.*
conversion /kən vur′shən/ *noun*

convey /kən vā′/ *verb*
to take or carry (usually over a long distance): *The truck* **conveyed** *machinery across the country.*

convict[1] /kən vikt′/ *verb*
to decide in a law court (see) that somebody is guilty of a crime: *He was* **convicted** *of stealing.*

convict[2] /kən′ vikt *or* kon′ vikt/ *noun*
a person who has been convicted of a crime

convince /kən vins′/ *verb* (*present participle* **convincing,** *past* **convinced)**
to make a person believe something: *He* **convinced** *me that I should study law.*

°**cook**[1] /ko͝ok/ *verb*
to make food ready to eat by heating it: *I haven't* **cooked** *the dinner. Does he* **cook** *well?*

°**cook**[2] *noun*
a person who cooks: *Sarah is a very good* **cook** (= she cooks well).

°**cool**[1] /ko͞ol/ *adjective*
1 not warm, but not very cold: *The room was* **cool** *after the sun had gone down.*
2 calm: *Don't get excited about the examination; keep* **cool.**

cool[2] *verb*
to make or become cool: *We* **cooled down** *by swimming in the river.*

cooperate /kō op′ ə rāt/ *verb* (*present participle* **cooperating,** *past* **cooperated)**
to work with (one another): *If we all* **cooperate,** *we'll soon finish.*
cooperation *noun: Thank you for your* **cooperation.**
cooperative *adjective* willing to help other people

copper /kop′ ər/ *noun*
a red-gold metal

°**copy**[1] /kop′ ē/ *verb* (*present participle* **copying,** *past* **copied)**
to make or do something exactly the same as something else: *I* **copied** *the letters into my book.*

°**copy**[2] *noun* (*plural* **copies)**
something that is the same as something else: *Please send a* **copy** *of this letter to Mr. Brown.*

cord /kôrd/ *noun*
thin rope

cork /kôrk/ *noun*
1 a light substance that comes from the bark (= outside part of the stem) of a tree
2 a piece of this, used to fill the holes in the tops of bottles

°**corn** /kôrn/ *noun*
large green plant with a tube-shaped vegetable that is covered with kernels

°**corner** /kôr′ nər/ *noun*
an angle; the place where two lines, streets, etc. meet each other: *The table stood in the* **corner** *of the room. His house is on the* **corner** *of School Road and Green Street.*

corporation /kôr″ pə rā′ shən/ *noun*
business group which operates as a person under the law

corpse /kôrps/ *noun*
a dead body, usually of a person

°**correct**[1] /kə rekt′/ *adjective*
right; not wrong: *a* **correct** *answer*

correct[2] *verb*
to make right: *Please* **correct** *this mistake.*

correctly *adverb*
correction *noun: He made several* **corrections** *to the letter.*

correspond /kôr″ ə spond′/ *verb*
to write and receive letters from: *to* **correspond** *with a friend*
correspondence *noun (no plural)* letters

corridor /kôr′ ə dər/ *noun*
a long narrow part of a building, with rooms on each side of it: *Go down the* **corridor,** *to the third room on the left.*

cosmetics /kos met′ iks/ *plural noun*
substances put on the skin, especially of the face, and on the hair to make them look prettier

°**cost**[1] /kôst/ *noun*
the price you pay when you buy something: *The* **cost** *of the house was too high for me.*

°**cost**[2] *verb (past* **cost)**
to have as a price: *How much did that tie* **cost?** *It* **cost** *five dollars!*
costly *adjective* costing a lot of money: *The ring was very* **costly.**

costume /kos′ to͞om/ *noun*
clothes worn for a special reason, or to represent a country or time in history: *Her* **national costume** *showed which country she came from.*

cot /kot/ *noun*
a lightweight bed that usually folds up to a smaller size

cottage /kot′ ij/ *noun*
a small house in the country: *a thatched* (see) **cottage**

°**cotton** /kot′ ən/ *noun (no plural)*
a plant grown in hot countries for the fine white threads **(cotton)** which cover its seeds, and which are made into thread or material: *She sewed the* **cotton** *dress with* **cotton** *(thread).*

couch /kouch/ *noun (plural* **couches)**
a long seat on which you can sit or lie down

couch

°**cough**[1] /kôf/ *noun*
a sharp noise made by sending air out of the lungs (see) suddenly: *The child had a bad* **cough,** *so his mother took him to the doctor.*

°**cough**[2] /kôf/ *verb*
to make the noise of a cough: *The child was* **coughing** *all night.*

°**could** /ku̇d/ *verb*
1 (the word for can in the past): *Before I had a bicycle, I* **couldn't** (= could not) *visit my friend.*
2 (used in sentences like these): *She would help us if she* **could,** *but she can't.*
3 (used as a polite way of asking someone something): **Could** *you help me, please?*

council /koun′ səl/ *noun*
a group of people who are chosen to make laws or decisions or to advise people: *The town* **council** *will decide where to plant the trees.*
councillor or councilor *noun* a member of a council

°**count**[1] /kount/ *verb*
1 to say numbers in the right order: *to* **count** *from 1 to 100*
2 to name one by one to find out how many there are; add up: *She* **counted** *the books — there were fourteen of them.*

count[2] *noun*
an act of counting: *There were so many cars that I* **lost count** (= could not remember how many).

counter /koun′ tər/ *noun*
1 a long table between buyers and sellers in a shop

2 a small round piece of plastic or wood used in playing games

°**country** /kun′ trē/ *noun*
1 (*plural* **countries**) an area ruled by one government: *France and Germany are European* **countries.**
2 the land that is not a town: *He lives in the* **country.**
countryside *noun (no plural)* land outside towns and cities

couple /kup′ əl/ *noun*
two people or things usually thought of together: *I waited a* **couple** *of hours. My brother and his wife are a happy* **couple.**

coupon /ko͞o′ pon *or* kū′ pon/ *noun*
a piece of paper that can be exchanged for goods or money: *I've kept the special* **coupon** *from the box of detergent, so that I can get my next box cheaper.*

°**courage** /kur′ ij/ *noun*
not being afraid; bravery: *The soldier had shown great* **courage** *in the battle.*
courageous /kə rā′ jəs/ *adjective*

course /kôrs/ *noun*
1 the way that something happens or the time when something is happening: *During the* **course** *of the journey, we saw a lot of new places.* **Of course** (= you can be sure) *I'll write to you when I am away.*
2 the path or direction of something: *The* **course** *of the river was marked on the map. The plane had to* **change course** *and go another way.*
3 part of a meal: *We had three* **courses:** *soup, meat and vegetables, and fruit.*
4 a set of lessons: *What* **course** *are you taking at college?*

court /kôrt/ *noun*
1 a place where someone is questioned about a crime, and where people decide whether he is guilty or not
2 an open space where games are played: *a* **tennis court**
3 a king or queen (see) and all the people who live with them

cousin /kuz′ ən/ *noun*
the child of an aunt or uncle

°**cover**[1] /kuv′ ər/ *verb*
to put something over something else: *She* **covered** *the table with a cloth.*

°**cover**[2] *noun*
something that is put over something else: *The book had a blue* **cover.**

°**cow** /kou/ *noun*
the full grown female form of cattle: *I have ten* **cows** *and one bull* (see).

coward /kou′ ərd/ *noun*
a person who avoids pain or danger because he has no courage: *I never go to the dentist; I'm really a* **coward.**
cowardly *adjective:* **cowardly** *behavior*

cowboy /kou′ boi″/ *noun*
a man who rides a horse and looks after cattle

crab /krab/ *noun*
a sea animal with ten legs and a hard shell

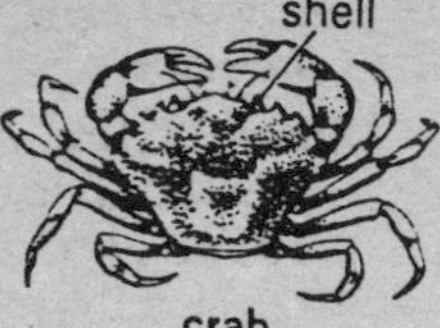

°**crack¹** /krak/ *verb*
1 to break, but not into separate parts: *One of these cups is* **cracked.**
2 to make a sharp noise, like the noise of thunder or a gun

°**crack²** *noun*
1 a thin line where something is broken: *There's a* **crack** *in this cup!*
2 a sharp noise: *a* **crack** *of thunder*

cradle /krā′ dəl/ *noun*
a bed for a baby which can be swung from side to side

craft /kraft/ *noun*
1 a job or trade needing skill, especially with your hands: *He knew the* **craft** *of making furniture. He was a* **craftsman.**
2 *(no plural)* a boat or plane

cram /kram/ *verb* (*present participle* **cramming,** *past* **crammed**)
to fill or force in: *Lots of people were* **crammed** *into the bus.*

crane /krāne/ *noun*
a tall machine for lifting heavy things from one place to another

°**crash¹** /krash/ *noun* (*plural* **crashes**)
1 a loud noise, like something large falling over: *The car hit the tree with a* **crash.**
2 an accident when vehicles hit each other: *a car* **crash**

°**crash²** *verb*
to make the noise of a crash: *The cars* **crashed** *into each other.*

crate /krāt/ *noun*
a big wooden box: *a* **crate** *of fruit*

crawl /krôl/ *verb*
to go along slowly, often on hands and knees: *The baby* **crawled** *toward his father. The insects were* **crawling** *across the wall.*

crayon /krā′ on/ *noun*
a soft colored pencil

crazy /krā′ zē/ *adjective*
mad; foolish: *He's* **crazy** *to drive his car so fast.*

creak /krēk/ *verb*
to make the sound of a door which has not been oiled: *The door* **creaked** *as she opened it.*
creak *noun*

cream¹ /krēm/ *noun (no plural)*
the fatty part of the milk that rises to the top

cream² *adjective, noun*
(of) the color of this milk, yellowish-white

create /krē āt′/ *verb* (*present participle* **creating,** *past* **created**)
to make something new: *He* **created** *his house from stone and his own ideas.*
creation *noun*

creature /krē′ chər/ *noun*
an animal or insect

credit /kred′ it/ *noun*
1 attention and approval: *We both made the machine, but James was given the* **credit** *for it.*
2 buying things and paying for them later: *We bought the furniture* **on credit.**

°**creep** /krēp/ *verb* (*past* **crept**)
to move quietly, often with the body close to the ground

crest /krest/ *noun*
1 feathers that stick up on top of a bird's head
2 the top of something: *the* **crest** *of a hill*

crew /kro͞o/ *noun*
the people who work on a ship

cricket[1] /krik′ ət/ *noun*
a ball game played by two teams of eleven players each

cricket[2] *noun*
a small brown insect that makes a noise which seems to go on all the time

cried /krīd/ see **cry[1]**

cries /krīz/ see **cry[2]**

°**crime** /krīm/ *noun*
something that is wrong and can be punished by the law: *Killing people is a* **crime.**
criminal /krim′ ə nəl/ *noun: The person who carries out a crime is a* **criminal.**
criminal *adjective*

crimson /krim′ zən/ *adjective, noun*
(of) a deep red color, like blood

cripple[1] /krip′ əl/ *noun*
a person who has an arm or leg that he cannot use, or who cannot walk

cripple[2] *verb* (*present participle* **crippling,** *past* **crippled**)
to hurt someone so that he cannot use his arms and legs: *She was* **crippled** *in the car accident.*

crisis /krī′ səs/ *noun* (*plural* **crises**)
a time when something serious or dangerous happens: *We had a* **crisis** *at work today — Jane fell down the stairs.*

crisp[1] /krisp/ *adjective*
1 firm and dry; easily broken: *The outside of fresh bread is* **crisp.**
2 firm and fresh: **crisp** *apples*

criticize /krit′ i sīz/ *verb* (*present participle* **criticizing,** *past* **criticized**)
to say what is wrong with something; find faults in something: *The teacher* **criticized** *my work — he said it was very badly written.*
critic /krit′ ik/ *noun* a person who criticizes
critical /krit′ ə kəl/ *adjective: She was very* **critical** *of my work.*
criticism /krit′ i siz″ əm/ *noun: I listened to all her* **criticisms.**

croak /krōk/ *verb*
to make a low, hard sound in the throat, like a frog (see)

crockery /krok′ ə rē/ *noun*
plates, cups, and other things which we use for eating

crocodile /krok′ ə dīl″/ *noun*
a large animal **(reptile)** of hot places, which can swim

crocodile

crooked /krook′ id/ *adjective*
bent or curved: *a* **crooked** *road*

°**crop** /krop/ *noun*
1 food that is grown: *Which* **crops** *does he grow?*
2 vegetables, grain, etc. that are cut or gathered at one time: *a* **crop** *of apples*

°**cross[1]** /krôs/ *noun* (*plural* **crosses**)
a shape with four arms (X)

°**cross[2]** *verb*
to go over: *They* **crossed** *the road.*

crossing *noun* a special place where you may cross a road

cross[3] *adjective*
feeling angry: *Why are you* **cross** *with me?*

crossroads /krôs′ rōdz/ *plural noun*
a place where several roads meet each other

crossword /krôs′ wurd″/ *noun*
a game in which words have to be guessed so that the letters will fit empty places in a picture

crouch /krouch/ *verb*
to make the body come close to the ground by bending the knees: *She* **crouched** *by the fire to get warm.*

crow /krō/ *noun*
a large black bird with a hard, low cry

crowd[1] /kroud/ *noun*
a large mass of people: *a* **crowd** *(of people) at the football game*

crowd[2] *verb*
to come together in a large group: *They all* **crowded** *around the teacher.*

crowded *adjective* full of people: *I don't like the market; it is too* **crowded.**

crown[1] /kroun/ *noun*
a special hat made of metal, beautiful stones, etc., worn by a king or queen for ceremonies

crown[2] *verb*
to make someone king or queen

crude /kro͞od/ *adjective* **(cruder, crudest)**
1 raw; in a natural state: **Crude** *oil has to be made pure before it can be used by man.*
2 rude: *a* **crude** *joke*

°**cruel** /kro͞o′ əl/ *adjective*
liking to hurt other people or animals: *He is* **cruel** *to animals.*

cruelly *adverb*
cruelty *noun:* **cruelty** *to animals*

crumb /krumb/ *noun*
a little piece of something you can eat, like bread: *He dropped* **crumbs** *of cake all over the table.*

crumble /krum′ bəl/ *verb (present participle* **crumbling,** *past* **crumbled)**
to break up into little pieces: *The walls of that old house are* **crumbling.**

°**crush** /krush/ *verb*
to hurt or damage by pressing heavily: *Her hand was* **crushed** *under the bricks.*

crust /krust/ *noun*
the hard part on the outside of bread or some other things: *He ate a* **crust** *(of bread).*

crutch /kruch/ *noun* (*plural* **crutches)**
a piece of wood or metal that supports a person who cannot walk well: *to walk* **on crutches**

crutches

°**cry**[1] /krī/ *verb (past* **cried** /krīd/)
1 to call out loudly: *The boy* **cried** *for help.*
2 to have water running from the eyes: *She started to* **cry** *when she heard the sad news.*

°**cry**[2] *noun (plural* **cries)**
a shout; a call: *They heard a* **cry** *for help.*

cub /kub/ *noun*
a young one of any of the big cats or of a fox (see)

cube /kūb/ *noun*
a solid shape that has a square on every side
cubic /kū' bik/ *adjective*

cucumber /kū' kəm bər/ *noun*
a long, thin green vegetable which can be eaten without cooking

cuddle /kud' əl/ *verb* (*present participle* **cuddling,** *past* **cuddled**)
to hold someone close to your body, in a loving way: *She* **cuddled** *her little boy.*

cuff /kuf/ *noun*
the end of a sleeve (= arm of a shirt, dress, etc.)

°**cultivate** /kul' tə vāt"/ *verb* (*present participle* **cultivating,** *past* **cultivated**)
to grow plants on land that has been specially prepared: *The land by the river was* **cultivated.**
cultivation *noun (no plural)*

culture /kul' chər/ *noun*
the way of life of a group of people: *These two countries have different* **cultures.**

cunning /kun' ing/ *adjective*
clever at deceiving people: *For a long time nobody knew he told lies, because he is so* **cunning.**

°**cup** /kup/ *noun*
1 a container that you can drink from, usually having a handle: *a* **cup** *of tea*
2 a prize, shaped like a bowl, usually made of metal

°**cure¹** /kūr/ *verb* (*present participle* **curing,** *past* **cured**)
to make someone better when they have been ill: *I hope the doctor can* **cure** *the pain in my shoulder.*

°**cure²** *noun*
a way of making better: *a* **cure** *for an illness*

curious /kūr' ē əs/ *adjective*
wanting to know about things or people: *It is good to be* **curious** *about the world around you.*
curiously *adverb*
curiosity /kūr" ē os' it te/ *noun (no plural): He is full of* **curiosity.**

curl¹ /kurl/ *verb*
to roll or bend in a round or curved shape: *The snake* **curled** *around the branch. She* **curled** *her hair.*

curl² *noun*
a roll or round shape: *Her hair was in* **curls.**
curly *adjective* **(curlier, curliest): curly** *hair*

currency /kur' ən sē/ *noun* (*plural* **currencies**)
the money used in a country: *"Have you any Canadian* **currency?***" Yes, I have $10.*

current /kur' ənt/ *noun*
a flow of water, electricity, etc.: *Don't swim in the river, the* **current** *is very fast.*

curry /kur ē/ *noun* (*plural* **curries**)
food cooked with special plants that make it taste hot: *chicken* **curry** *and rice*
curried *adjective:* **curried** *chicken*

curse¹ /kurs/ *verb* (*present participle* **cursing,** *past* **cursed**)
1 to wish harm to come to someone: *He* **cursed** *the person who had stolen his money.*
2 to speak angry words: *He* **cursed** *when he hit his head on the shelf.*

curse² *noun*
1 something you say asking for harm to come to someone
2 angry words

curtain /kur′ tən/ *noun*
a piece of cloth hung up to cover a window, door, or part of a room

°**curve¹** /kurv/ *noun*
a smooth round shape; a bend: *a* **curve** *in the road*

°**curve²** *verb* (*present participle* **curving,** *past* **curved**)
to make a curve; bend: *The river* **curved** *around the hill.*

cushion /kush′ ən/ *noun*
a bag filled with soft material to sit on or rest against

°**custom** /kus′ təm/ *noun*
a special way of doing something that a person or group of people has: *It is the* **custom** *to say "How do you do?" when you meet someone.*

customary /kus′ tə mer″ ē/ *adjective* usual: *He talked to us with his* **customary** *kindness.*

°**customer** /kus′ tə mər/ *noun*
a person who buys from a shop or market

customs /kus′ təmz/ *plural noun*
a department of the government that controls what is brought into a country: *At the airport, the* **customs** *officers searched his case.*

°**cut¹** /kut/ *verb* (*present participle* **cutting,** *past* **cut**)
to break with a knife or blade: *He* **cut** *the apple in half. He has* **cut** *his leg, and it is bleeding. She* **cut** *her hair* (= made it shorter). **Cut down** *the tree* (= cut it so that it falls down). *He was* **cutting up** *the chicken* (= cutting it into pieces). *The girl* **cut out** *a picture from the newspaper* (= took it out by cutting the paper around the edge).

°**cut²** *noun*
1 an opening or wound made by cutting: *a* **cut** *on the leg*
2 something made shorter or stopped: *I need a* **haircut.**

cutlery /kut′ lər ē/ *noun (no plural)*
metal things used in eating: *Knives and forks are* **cutlery.**

cycle¹ /sī′ kəl/ *noun*
a bicycle

cyclist /sī′ klist/ *noun* a person who rides a bicycle

°**cycle²** *verb* (*present participle* **cycling,** *past* **cycled**)
to ride a bicycle: *He* **cycles** *to school every day.*

cylinder /sil′ ən dər/ *noun*
a long round shape like a tube or a pencil

cylindrical /sil″ in′ drə kəl/ *adjective*

Dd

daddy /dad′ dē/ (*plural* **daddies**) *or* **dad** *noun*
father

dagger /dag′ ər/ *noun*
a short knife used as a weapon

daily /dā′ lē/ *adjective, adverb*
every day: *I catch the bus* **daily.**

dairy /dâr′ ē/ *noun* (*plural* **dairies**)
a place where milk is kept and foods from milk are made; a shop where these things are sold

dam¹ /dam/ *noun*
a wall built to keep water at a high level

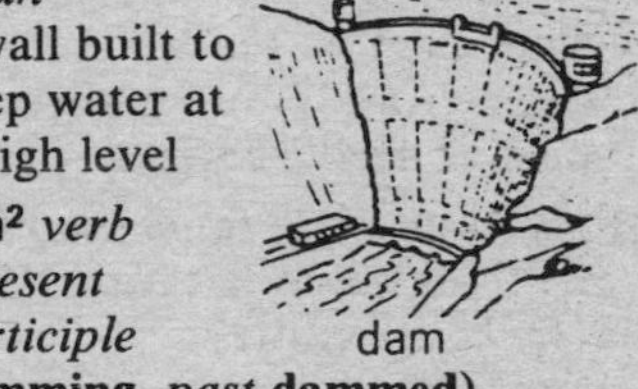

dam

dam² *verb* (*present participle* **damming,** *past* **dammed**)
to put a dam across something: *The river was* **dammed (up)** *to make a lake.*

°**damage¹** /dam′ ij/ *noun*
harm, especially to things

°**damage²** *verb* (*present participle* **damaging,** *past* **damaged**)
to hurt; cause damage to: *The cars are badly* **damaged** *in the accident.*

damp /damp/ *adjective*
rather wet: *These clothes aren't dry yet; they're still* **damp.**

°**dance¹** /dans/ *verb* (*present participle* **dancing,** *past* **danced**)
to move to music, or as if to music
dancer *noun*

°**dance²** *noun*
1 a set of movements you do to music: *to learn a new* **dance**
2 a party where there is dancing: *Are you going to the* **dance?**

°**danger** /dān′ jər/ *noun*
1 the possibility of loss or harm: *There is always* **danger** *(of floods) in a storm. He put his life* **in danger** *when he ran across the busy street.*
2 something that causes danger: *the* **dangers** *of smoking*
dangerous *adjective: a* **dangerous** *bend in the road*

°**dare** /dâr/ *verb* (*present participle* **daring,** *past* **dared**)
to be brave enough to: *David* **dared (to)** *climb the tree. She* **dare not** *tell her sister that she has lost her money.*

°**dark¹** /därk/ *adjective*
1 like night; not light or bright: *It was getting* **dark,** *so we hurried home.*
2 of a deep color, nearer black than white: *He wore a* **dark** *suit.*
darkness *noun (no plural): We couldn't see the houses in the* **darkness.**

dark² *noun*
the lack of light: *We could not see in the* **dark.**

darling /där′ ling/ *noun, adjective*
a name for someone who is loved: **Darling,** *go now, or you will be late.*

dart¹ /därt/ *noun*
a sharp-pointed metal weapon thrown by the hand, also used in the game of darts

dart² *verb*
to go quickly: *The bird* **darted** *across the river.*

dash[1] /dash/ *verb*
to go quickly: *She* **dashed** *home from school.*

dash[2] *noun* (*plural* **dashes**)
the sign — used in writing to show a short space, or to separate two parts of a sentence

°**date**[1] /dāt/ *noun*
the day, month and year: *What is the* **date** *today? The* **date** *of this battle was 1857.*

date[2] *noun*
a small, sweet, brown fruit

°**daughter** /dôt′ ər/ *noun*
a female child: *They have three* **daughters** *and one son.*

dawn /dôn/ *noun*
the time when the sun rises: *I woke up at* **dawn.**

°**day** /dā/ *noun*
1 the time when it is light; the opposite of night: *In the* **day,** *we work and go out, but at night we sleep.*
2 twenty-four hours: *It hasn't stopped raining for* **days.**
daylight *noun: How many hours of* **daylight** *do we have in a day?*
daytime *noun: In the* **daytime,** *we go to school, but in the evenings we play.*

°**dead**[1] /ded/ *adjective*
not living: *My grandfather has been* **dead** *for ten years.*
deadly *adjective* (**deadlier, deadliest**) causing death: *This seed is* **deadly** *if you eat it.*

dead[2] *noun*
dead people: *After the battle, they counted* **the dead.**

deaf /def/ *adjective*
not able to hear: *I've called you three times, are you* **deaf?**

deal[1] /dēl/ *noun*
1 a business arrangement: *Let's* **make a deal** — *I'll clean your bicycle if you let me ride it today.*
2 a lot: *He has* **a great deal** *of work to do.*

deal[2] *verb* (*past* **dealt** /delt/)
1 to do business with; buy and sell: *I have* **dealt with** *this farmer for years.*
2 to do what is necessary: *I can't* **deal with** *all this work, I need someone to help me.*
3 to give: **I dealt (out)** *the pieces of cake, one to each child.*
dealer *noun* a person who buys and sells something

dear[1] /dēr/ *adjective*
loved: *He is my* **dearest** *friend. She began the letter with* **"Dear** *James".*
dearly *adverb*

°**death** /deth/ *noun*
being dead, or dying: *The* **death** *of his father was sudden.*

debate[1] /di bāt′/ *noun*
a public talk about something important: *a* **debate** *about the punishment for criminals*

debate[2] *verb* (*present participle* **debating,** *past* **debated**)
to talk about something important: *The government is* **debating** *the education laws.*

debt /det/ *noun*
money owed: *His* **debt** *is $30 which he must pay me. He is* **in debt** *to me* (= he owes me money).

decay[1] /di kā′/ *verb*
to go bad: *His teeth had* **decayed,** *because he never cleaned them.*

decay[2] *noun*
the state of being bad: *tooth* **decay**

°**deceive** /di sēv′/ *verb (present participle* **deceiving,** *past* **deceived)**
to make someone believe what is not true: *He* **deceived** *her into thinking he could drive a car.*
deceit *noun (no plural): He got the money* **by deceit.**

°**December** /di sem′ bər/ *noun*
the 12th month of the year

decent /dē′ sənt/ *adjective*
good enough: *a* **decent** *house*

°**decide** /di sīd′/ *verb (present participle* **deciding,** *past* **decided)**
to think that you will do one thing; choose what to do: *I* **decided to** *go home, although they asked me to stay at the party. She could not* **decide** *which dress to buy.*
decision /di sizh′ ən/ *noun: She could not* **make a decision** *about the dresses.*

deck /dek/ *noun*
a part of a ship, bus, etc. where passengers sit or stand

declare /di klâr′/ *verb (present participle* **declaring,** *past* **declared)**
to say in public what we think or decide: *I* **declared** *at the meeting that I did not support the leader. One country* **declared war** *on another.*
declaration /dek′ lə ra″ shən/ *noun*

decorate /dek′ ə rāt″/ *verb*
to make prettier with ornaments, color, etc.: *She* **decorated** *the room with flowers.*
decoration *noun:* **decorations** *in the room*

decrease[1] /di krēs′/ *verb (present participle* **decreasing,** *past* **decreased)**
to get less or fewer: *The number of children in the school has* **decreased** *this year.*

decrease[2] /dē′ krēs *or* di krēs′/ *noun (no plural)*
getting less or fewer: *There was a* **decrease** *in the number of children in school.*

deed /dēd/ *noun*
something that you do: *He was punished for his bad* **deeds.**

°**deep** /dēp/ *adjective*
1 going down a long way: *This is a* **deep** *river; it is 50 feet* **deep.** *He has a* **deep** *voice.*
2 strong or dark in color: *He has* **deep** *brown eyes.*
3 felt strongly: *Her love for the child was very* **deep.**
depth /depth/ *noun: What is the* **depth** *of the river? Nobody knew the* **depth** *of her love for the child.*

deer /dēr/ *noun (plural* **deer)**
an animal which has horns and which runs fast

°**defeat**[1] /di fēt′/ *verb*
to beat; win over: *They were* **defeated** *in the football game.*

°**defeat**[2] *noun*
loss; being beaten: *The football team suffered a* **defeat.**

defend /di fend′/ *verb*
to fight for in order to protect: *She had to* **defend** *herself against the guard dog.*
defense *noun*

definite /def′ ə nit/ *adjective*
clear; sure: *Let's fix a* **definite** *date for the next meeting.*
definitely *adverb: I can't tell you* **definitely** *when I will come.*

defy /di fī'/ *verb* (*present participle* **defying,** *past* **defied** /di fīd'/)
to be ready to fight against; show no respect for: *The child* **defied** *his mother and didn't go to school.*
defiant /di fī' ənt/ *adjective: The* **defiant** *child was punished.*

degree /di grē'/ *noun*
1 a measurement of heat or angle (°): *The temperature* (= heat) *today is two* **degrees** *hotter than yesterday.*
2 a piece of paper saying that you have completed training at a university (see): *He passed his examinations and now has a* **degree** *in English.*

°**delay**[1] /di lāy'/ *noun*
a time of waiting: *There was a* **delay** *while father went back to the house to get his money.*

°**delay**[2] *verb*
to make something take a longer time; wait: *The letter was* **delayed** *three days by the train accident.*

deliberate /di lib' ər it/ *adjective*
planned or done on purpose: *She knew she had written the wrong word; it was a* **deliberate** *mistake.*
deliberately *adverb: I didn't knock it over* **deliberately,** *it was an accident.*

delicate /del' ə kit/ *adjective*
fine; easily harmed or broken: *a* **delicate** *glass/a* **delicate** *child who is often ill*

delicious /di lish' əs/ *adjective*
good to eat: *The soup is* **delicious.**

delight[1] /di līt'/ *noun (no plural)*
joy: *to laugh with* **delight**

delight[2] *verb*
to give joy to: *I was* **delighted** *to be invited to her party.*

deliver /di liv' ər/ *verb*
1 to bring goods to a special place: *Some new books have been* **delivered** *to the school.*
2 to help a mother have a baby: *Which doctor* **delivered** *the baby?*
delivery *noun* (*plural* **deliveries**): *a* **delivery** *of books*

demand[1] /di mand'/ *verb*
to ask strongly for: "*Give me my book at once!*" she **demanded** *rudely.*

demand[2] *noun*
something asked for: *He listened to the workers'* **demand** *for more money. Teachers are* **in demand** (= needed) *in this area.*

democracy /di mok' rə sē/ *noun*
a government or country where everyone has an equal right to choose the leaders, by voting (see)

demolish /di mol' ish/ *verb*
to knock down; destroy: *All these old houses are going to be* **demolished.**
demolition *noun*

demonstrate /dem' ən strāt"/ *verb* (*present participle* **demonstrating,** *past* **demonstrated**)
to show clearly: *He* **demonstrated** *how to use the new machine.*
demonstration *noun: to give a* **demonstration**

den /den/ *noun*
a place in which a wild animal lives

dense /dens/ *adjective*
thick: **dense** *forest*

dentist /den' tist/ *noun*
a doctor who looks after your teeth

deny /di nī'/ *verb* (*present participle* **denying,** *past* **denied** /di nīd'/)
to say something is not true: *He*

said that I had stolen his bicycle, but I **denied** *it.*

depart /di pärt/ *verb*
to leave; go away: *When does the next train* **depart?**
departure /di pär′ chər/ *noun: The* **departure** *of the train was delayed.*

°**department** /di pärt′ mənt/ *noun*
a part of a business, company, government, etc.: *He teaches in the History* **department** *of the college. A* **department store** *is a big shop which sells many kinds of goods.*

°**depend** /di pend′/ *adverb*
1 to be a result of: *"Are you going for a walk?" "That* **depends on** *the weather." "Are you coming with us?" "It* **depends** (= I have some doubts about it)."
2 to need; trust: *She* **depends on** *him to take her to school every day. Can I* **depend** *on your help?*
dependent *adjective: She is completely* **dependent on** *her daughter for money.*

deposit[1] /di poz′ it/ *verb*
1 to put down: *He* **deposited** *his books on the kitchen table.*
2 to put into a bank: *She* **deposited** *her money in the bank.*

deposit[2] *noun*
money you pay to show that you want something and will pay the rest later: *He put a* **deposit** *on a house.*

depot /dē′ pō/ *noun*
a place where goods or vehicles are stored

depress /di pres′/ *verb*
to make someone feel sad: *He was* **depressed** *because he had not passed his examinations.*
depression /di presh′ ən/ *noun*
feeling sad: *A vacation will help his* **depression.**

depth /depth/ *noun* see **deep**

deputy /dep′ yə te/ *noun* (*plural* **deputies**)
someone who is second in importance to the head of something: *When the police chief was away, the* **deputy** *head did his job.*

descend /di send′/ *verb*
to go down: *to* **descend** *the steps*
descendant *noun* a person in your family who lives after you

°**describe** /di skrīb′/ *verb* (*present participle* **describing,** *past* **described**)
to tell about; say what something is like: *I will* **describe** *you: you are 5 feet tall, quite strong, you laugh a lot, and you like reading.*
description *noun: That is a* **description** *of you.*

°**desert**[1] /dez′ ərt/ *noun*
a large empty, usually very dry, place where almost nothing grows: *the Sahara* Desert

desert[2] /di zurt′/ *verb*
to leave completely: *He* **deserted** *his family and went to the city.*

°**deserve** /di zurv′/ *verb* (*present participle* **deserving,** *past* **deserved**)
to be worth: *He has worked very hard; he* **deserves** *more money.*

design[1] /di zīn′/ *noun*
1 a pattern: *a* **design** *on material*
2 a plan: **designs** *for a new house*

design[2] *verb*
to make a plan for something: *Who* **designed** *the new house?*

desire[1] /di zīr′/ *noun*
a strong wish: *I had a* **desire** *to go swimming.*

desire² *verb* (*present participle* **desiring,** *past* **desired**)
to want very much: *She* **desires** *money, and she will do everything she can to get it.*

°**desk** /desk/ *noun*
a worktable, often with space inside it for keeping books, pens, etc.

despair¹ /di spâr′/ *noun*
a feeling of not being able to hope: *I was* **in despair** *when my daughter went to live in New York — I knew she would never come back.*

despair² *verb*
to have no hope: *I* **despair of** *ever seeing my daughter again.*

desperate /des′ prit *or* des′ pər it/ *adjective*
ready to do anything to get what you want: *The man lost in the desert was* **desperate** *for water.*
desperately *adverb*

despise /di spīz′/ *verb* (*present participle* **despising,** *past* **despised**)
to hate a person or thing because you think it is not worth anything: *She* **despises** *cheap clothes and will only wear the best.*

despite /di spīt′/ *preposition*
in spite of: **Despite** *the bad weather we enjoyed our vacation.*

dessert /di zurt′/ *noun*
a sweet food that you eat at the end of a meal

destination /des″ tə nā′ shən/ *noun*
the place you are going to: *It took us all day to reach our* **destination.**

°**destroy** /di stroi′/ *verb*
to break up or get rid of completely: *The fire* **destroyed** *all my books.*
destruction /di struk′ shən/ *noun (no plural): The fire caused the* **destruction** *of my books.*

detail /di tāl′ *or* dē′ tāl/ *noun*
one of the small points which make up the whole of something: *Give me all the* **details** *of the accident —tell me what happened* **in detail.**

detect /di tekt′/ *verb*
to discover: *I* **detected** *a smell of gas. A policeman* **detects** *criminals.*
detective *noun* a special policeman who finds out who has done a crime

detergent /di tur′ jənt/ *noun*
a sort of soap for washing clothes, dishes, etc.

deteriorate /di ter′ ē ə rāt″/ *verb* (*present participle* **deteriorating,** *past* **deteriorated**)
to get worse: *Your work has* **deteriorated** *in the last month.*

determine /di tur′ min/ *verb* (*present participle* **determining,** *past* **determined**)
to make up your mind firmly; decide: *I am* **determined to** *do better than Anne.*
determination *noun: That girl has great* **determination;** *I am sure she will do well.*

detest /di test′/ *verb*
to hate: *I* **detest** *cheese; I can't eat it.*

°**develop** /di vel′ əp/ *verb*
to grow: *Several industries are* **developing** *in this area. Some children* **develop** *more slowly than others. When a photograph is*

developed, *the film is treated with special liquids so that the picture can be seen.*

development *noun* **1** something new in the growth of something: *an exciting* **development** *in the story of the robbery* **2** *(no plural)* growing: *The* **development** *of this industry will take several years.*

device /di vīs′/ *noun*
a useful thing or trick: *a* **device** *for opening bottles*

devil /dev′ əl/ *noun*
a bad being, thought to cause all the bad things in people's lives

devote /di vōt′/ *verb* (*present participle* **devoting,** *past* **devoted)**
to give your time, thoughts, etc. completely to: *She* **devoted** *all her time to her job.*

dew /do͞o/ *noun (no plural)*
water which forms on the ground, on plants, etc. when the sun has set

diagonal /dī ag′ ə nəl/ *noun*

diagram /dī′ ə gram/ *noun*
a plan drawn to explain an idea, or how something works

dial[1] /dī′ əl/ *noun*
a round part of a machine or instrument, often with numbers on it

dials

dial[2] *verb* (*present participle* **dialing,** *past* **dialed)**
to make a telephone call by moving the dial to get the right numbers

diameter /dī am′ ə tər/ *noun*
distance across a circle, measured through the center

diamond /dī′ mənd/ *noun*
a very hard, clear stone that is worth a lot of money: *a ring with a* **diamond** *in the center*

diary /dī′ rē *or* dī′ ə rē/ *noun* (*plural* **diaries)**
a book in which you can write down things that have happened or things to remember each day

dice /dīs/ *noun (plural of* **die)**
small square blocks with a different number of spots on each side (from 1 to 6), used in games

dictate /dik′ tāt/ *verb* (*present participle* **dictating,** *past* **dictated)**
to say something for someone else to write: *I* **dictated** *a letter to my secretary.*

dictation *noun*

°**dictionary** /dik′ shən er″ ē/ *noun* (*plural* **dictionaries)**
a book which tells you what words mean and how to spell them

did /did/ *verb*
(past tense of the verb **do**): *I* **did** *all my homework, but my sister* **didn't** (= did not) *do hers.*

°**die** /dī/ *verb* (*present participle* **dying,** *past* **died** /dīd/)
to stop living: *to* **die of** *an illness*

diesel /dē′ zəl/ *noun (no plural)*
engine that burns heavy oil instead of gasoline

diet /dī′ ət/ *noun*
1 what you eat
2 special food eaten by people who want to get thinner, or people who are ill: *She is* **on a diet.**

differ /dif′ ər/ *verb*
to be different: *My sister and I* **differ** *in many ways. She* **differs from** *me in many ways.*

°**different** /dif′ rənt/ *adjective*
not the same: *I don't like that dress, I want a* **different** *one.*

difference *noun*

°**difficult** /dif′ ə kəlt *or* dif′ ə kult″/ *adjective*
hard to do or understand; not easy: *a* **difficult** *question*
difficulty *noun (plural* **difficulties**): *This question is full of* **difficulties.** *Do you have any* **difficulty** *with English?*

°**dig** /dig/ *verb* (*present participle* **digging,** *past* **dug** /dug/)
to cut downwards into something; make a hole by cutting and taking material from: *He is* **digging** *in his garden. He has* **dug up** *some vegetables. She* **dug** *a fork into the vegetable. The old miner was* **digging** *for gold.*

digest /dī jest′/ *verb*
to take food into the body from the stomach: *Some foods are easier to* **digest** *than others.*
digestion /dī jes′ chən *or* di jes′ chən/ *noun*

dignity /dig′ nə tē/ *noun*
1 a person's feeling of her own worth: *Although she is very poor, she has not lost her* **dignity.**
2 serious and calm behavior: *It is difficult to act with* **dignity** *when you are angry about something.*

dim /dim/ *adjective*
not very bright: *a* **dim** *light*
dimly *adverb*

din /din/ *noun*
loud noise: *What a* **din** *the children are making!*

°**dinner** /din′ ər/ *noun*
usually the largest meal of the day

°**dip** /dip/ *verb* (*present participle* **dipping,** *past* **dipped**)
to put something into a liquid and then take it out again: *She* **dipped** *her hand in the sea to find out how cold it was.*

°**direct**[1] /di rekt′/ *adjective*
straight: *Which is the most* **direct** *way to the station?*
directly *adverb* straight: *We live* **directly** *opposite the school. You must go to bed* **directly** *after dinner.*

direct[2] *verb*
to tell someone the way to go or what to do: *I* **directed** *the traveler to the hotel.*
°**direction** *noun* where someone or something is going or pointing; the way: *In which* **direction** *are you going, north or south?*
director *noun* a person who controls a business: *He is one of the* **directors** *of the company.*
directory *noun (plural* **directories**) a book to tell you where people live or what their telephone numbers are

°**dirt** /durt/ *noun*
anything which stops something being clean; something that has to be washed off: *There is some* **dirt** *on your coat.*
dirty *adjective* **(dirtier, dirtiest)** having dirt on it; not clean: *My shoes were* **dirty.**

disabled /dis ā′ bəld/ *adjective*
not being able to move your body easily because of some illness or wound: *The* **disabled** *man could not use the stairs. Blind people and deaf people are* **disabled,** *too.*

disadvantage /dis″ əd van′ tij/ *noun*
something that makes things more

difficult for you: *This child is* **at a disadvantage** *in school because she cannot hear well. One of the* **disadvantages** *of this house is that it is very far from the city.*

disagree /dis″ ə grē′/ *verb* (*past* **disagreed**)
not to agree: *He said it would rain, but I* **disagreed with** *him — I was sure it wouldn't rain.*
disagreement *noun: a small* **disagreement** *about the weather*

disappear /dis″ ə pēr′/ *verb*
to go away; be no longer seen: *The boy* **disappeared** *around the corner.*

°**disappoint** /dis″ ə point′/ *verb*
to be less interesting, nice, etc. than you expected, and so make you sad: *Don't be* **disappointed** *if you lose; next time you might win!*
disappointment *noun: He could not hide his* **disappointment** *when his team lost the game.*

disaster /di zas′ tər/ *noun*
something very bad, especially something that happens to a lot of people: *The floods were a* **disaster:** *hundreds of people were killed and crops destroyed.*

discs

disc /disc/ *noun*
any round flat thing: *The dog had a* **disc** *on a band round its neck, with the name of its owner on it. A* record (see) *can also be called a* **disc.**

discipline /dis′ ə plin/ *noun (no plural)*
teaching you to obey and control yourself: *Soldiers have to learn* **discipline** *in the army.*

discount /dis′ kount/ *noun*
some money taken off the price of something: *We will give you a* **discount** *if you pay now.*

discourage /dis kur′ ij/ *verb* (*present participle* **discouraging,** *past* **discouraged**)
to take away or try to take away the wish to do something from someone: *The schoolteachers* **discourage** *smoking.*

°**discover** /dis kuv′ ər/ *verb*
to find or find out: *Scientists* **discovered** *that there was no water on the moon.*
discovery *noun* (*plural* **discoveries**) something discovered: *a new* **discovery** *in medical science*

discriminate /dis krim′ ə nāt/ *verb* (*present participle* **discriminating,** *past* **discriminated**)
to treat a person or people in a different way from others, because of race or religion or another reason: *In the United States, employers are not allowed to* **discriminate against** *women.*
discrimination *noun (no plural):* **Discrimination** *against women is not allowed.*

discuss /dis kus′/ *verb*
to talk about: *I want to* **discuss** *your work with you.*
discussion *noun: a* **discussion** *about his work*

disease /di zēz′/ *noun*
illness: *a* **disease** *of the eyes*

disgrace /dis grās′/ *noun (no plural)*
the loss of other people's good opinion of you: *He was in* **disgrace** *because he had lied.*

disguise[1] /dis gīz′/ *verb* (*present participle* **disguising,** *past* **disguised**) to try to look like someone else, as a trick: *The policeman* **disguised** *himself as a farmer, so that the criminals would not notice him.*

disguise[2] *noun*
something that you wear to make you look like someone else

disgust[1] /dis gust′/ *verb*
to give someone a strong feeling of not liking to see, taste, or smell something unpleasant
disgusting *adjective: The bad fish had a* **disgusting** *smell.*

disgust[2] *noun*
a strong feeling of dislike: *The smell filled me with* **disgust.**

°**dish** /dish/ *noun* (*plural* **dishes**)
1 a container for food: *a* **dish** *of rice*
2 part of a meal: *We had a fish* **dish** *and a meat* **dish.**

dishonest /dis on′ ist/ *adjective*
not honest

disinfect /dis″ in fekt′/ *verb*
to clean thoroughly with special chemicals: *The ill man's room was* **disinfected** *when he got better.*
disinfectant *noun* a chemical used to disinfect

dislike[1] /dis līk′/ *verb* (*present participle* **disliking,** *past* **disliked**)
not to like: *He likes cats, but* **dislikes** *dogs. He* **dislikes** *reading.*

dislike[2] *noun*
not liking; something that is not liked: *I felt a strong* **dislike** *of the new teacher.*

disloyal /dis loi′ əl/ *adjective*
not faithful or true to someone: *She is* **disloyal** *to her family; she says bad things about them.*

dismal /diz′ məl/ *adjective*
dull or sad; not bright or happy: *a* **dismal,** *rainy day*

dismay /dis mā′/ *noun (no plural)*
a feeling of loss and fear: *"Someone's robbed my house!" she said* **in dismay.**

dismiss /dis mis′/ *verb*
to send away: *The children were* **dismissed** *and sent home. He was* **dismissed** *from his job.*

disobey /dis″ ə bā′/ *verb*
not to do what you are told; not to obey: *Jane's mother told her to stay inside, but she* **disobeyed** *(her) and went out.*
disobedience /dis″ ə bē′ dē əns/ *noun (no plural): She was punished for her* **disobedience.**
disobedient *adjective*

disorganized /dis ôr′ gə nīzd/ *adjective*
untidy; not in order: *Her desk is very* **disorganized.**

display[1] /dis plā′/ *verb*
to show something so that many people can see it: *The children's work was* **displayed** *on the wall.*

display[2] *noun*
a show: *All the parents were looking at the* **display** *of children's work. The work was* **on display.**

dispose /dis pōz′/ *verb* (*present participle* **disposing,** *past* **disposed**)
to get rid of: *I have* **disposed of** *my old clothes.*

dispute /dis pūt′/ *noun*
a quarrel: *We had a* **dispute** *about how much money he owes me.*

dissatisfied /dis sat′ is fīd″/ *adjective*
not pleased enough: *I have tried to write this story four times, but I am still* **dissatisfied** *with it.*

dissolve /di solv′/ *verb* (*present participle* **dissolving,** *past* **dissolved)**
to mix completely with a liquid: *Sugar* **dissolves** *in hot tea.*

distant /dis′ tənt/ *adjective*
far: *The foreign visitors came from a* **distant** *country.*
° **distance** *noun: What* **distance** *do you have to walk to school? I could see the bus coming* **in the distance** (= far away).

distinct /dis′ tinkt′/ *adjective*
1 clear; easily seen or heard: *The hills were* **distinct** *against the sky.*
2 separate; different: *There are several* **distinct** *languages in every African country.*
distinctly *adverb: I told you* **distinctly** *not to go to the park, so why did you go?*

distinguish /dis ting′ gwish/ *verb*
to see or hear clearly; notice: *Can you* **distinguish** *the different musical instruments playing now?*
distinguished *adjective* famous

distress[1] /dis tres′/ *noun (no plural)*
a feeling of sadness or difficulty: *The mother was* **in distress** *when her baby became ill.*

distress[2] *verb*
to make someone sad: *The mother was* **distressed** *by her baby's illness.*

distribute /dis trib′ ūt/ *verb* (*present participle* **distributing,** *past* **distributed)**
to give or send to different people or places: *We* **distributed** *the books to the schoolchildren.*
distribution *noun (no plural): the* **distribution** *of the books*

district /dis′ trikt/ *noun*
a part of a country, city, etc.: *He doesn't live in this* **district.**

disturb /dis turb′/ *verb* (*present participle* **disturbing,** *past* **disturbed)**
1 to break the calm state of a person; make someone feel worried: *Please don't* **disturb** *me while I'm working. I have heard some bad news which has* **disturbed** *me very much.*
2 to move something out of order: *Please don't* **disturb** *the papers on my desk.*
disturbance *noun* a breaking of the calm state; trouble: *There has been a* **disturbance** *in the street: someone has been hurt.*

ditch /dich/ *noun* (*plural* **ditches)**
a deep narrow place for water to run, especially by a road or field

dive /dīv/ *verb* (*present participle* **diving,** *past* **dived)**
to go head first into water: *He* **dived** *into the swimming pool. She* **dived** *to the bottom of the river.*
diver *noun* a person who works under water and wears special instruments to help him breathe

°**divide** /di vīd′/ *verb* (*present participle* **dividing,** *past* **divided)**
1 to split into pieces: *The road* **divided** *into three, and I took the middle road.*
2 to share: *We* **divided** *the apple between us.*
3 to find out how many times a number will go into another: *I* **divided** *39 by 3. The answer was 13.*
division /di vizh′ ən/ *noun* **1** dividing sums: *I haven't learned*

how to do **division** *yet.* **2** part of something: *Which* **division** *of the company do you work in?*

divine /di vīn′/ *adjective*
of or like a god or God

divorce[1] /di vors′/ *verb* (*present participle* **divorcing,** *past* **divorced)**
to arrange by law for a husband and wife to separate, so that either may marry again: *"When did she* **divorce** *her husband?" "They got* **divorced** *last year."*

divorce[2] *noun*
an act of divorcing: *She got a* **divorce** *from him last year.*

dizzy /diz′ ē/ *adjective* **(dizzier, dizziest)**
feeling as if things are turning around you, and you are going to fall: *I feel* **dizzy** *when I look out of a high window.*

°**do[1]** /do͞o/ *verb*
present tense

singular	*plural*
I **do**	*We* **do**
You **do**	*You* **do**
He/She/It **does**	*They* **do**

past tense **did**
past participle **done**
present participle **doing**
to act; carry out: *When you have* **done** *your school work, you can* **do** *something else. What have you* **done with** *your bicycle? I put it in the yard. I can't* **do without** (= live comfortably without) *my books.*

°**do[2]** *verb*
1 (used with **not** before another verb, to say that something is not so): *I* **do not** *like apples — I* **don't** (= do not) *like oranges, either.*
2 (used with another verb, to ask a question): **Don't** *you want to come to see the film?*
3 (used with **not,** to tell someone not to do something): **Do not** *leave your bag in the bus.*
4 (used to make another verb stronger): *You're wrong if you think I don't like school; I* **do** *like it!*

dock[1] /dok/ *noun*
a place where ships are loaded and unloaded

dock[2] *verb*
(of a ship) to come into a dock

°**doctor** /dok′ tər/ *noun*
a person who looks after people's health

dodge /dodj/ *verb* (*present participle* **dodging,** *past* **dodged)**
to move quickly to one side to avoid something: *He* **dodged** *the book I threw at him.*

does /duz/ *verb*
(the part of the verb **do** that we use with **he, she,** and **it**): *Anna* **does** *a lot of jobs in the house, but her sister* **doesn't** (= does not).

°**dog** /dôg/ *noun*
an animal with four legs and a tail, that eats meat: *Some people keep* **dogs** *in their houses.*

doll /dol/ *noun*
a toy made to look like a person

dollar /dol′ ər/ *noun*
the money used in the United States and some other countries

dome /dōm/ *noun*
a high, rounded roof

dome

domestic /də mes′ tik/ *adjective*
1 found in or to do with the home: **domestic** *jobs like cleaning and cooking*

2 not wild: *Cattle are* **domestic** *animals.*

dominate /dom′ ə nāt″/ *verb* (*present participle* **dominating,** *past* **dominated)**
to have power over: *That child* **dominates** *all the smaller children.*

donate /dō nāt′/ *verb* (*present participle* **donating,** *past* **donated)**
to give: *The businessman* **donated** *a lot of money to the hospital.*

donation /dō nā′ shən/ *noun: a* **donation** *of money to the hospital*

donor /dō′ nər/ *noun* someone who gives: *She is a* **blood donor** (= she gives her blood to be used in the hospital).

done /dun/ see **do**

donkey /don′ kē/ *noun*
an animal like a small horse with long ears

donkey

don't /dōnt/ see **do**

°**door** /dôr/ *noun*
the entrance to a building or room; the flat piece of wood, metal, etc. which shuts the entrance: *Will you wait at the* **door?** *Please open the* **door** *for me.*

doorway *noun* the opening for an entrance to a room or a building: *He stood in the* **doorway** *and watched me.*

dormitory /dôr′ mə tôr″ ē/ *noun* (*plural* **dormitories)**
a room for several people to sleep in: *Students sleep in* **dormitories** *when they live at college.*

dose /dōs/ *noun*
an amount of medicine that you should take at one time: *Here is your medicine — the* **dose** *is two spoonfuls every four hours.*

°**dot** /dot/ *noun*
a small round mark: *On the map towns were marked by a red* **dot.** *A small "i" has a* **dot** *over it.*

double[1] /dub′ əl/ *adjective, adverb, noun*
1 twice as much: *He took a* **double** *share of the candy, two bags instead of one.*
2 with two parts: *a* **double** *door*
3 made for two: *a* **double** *bed*

double[2] *verb* (*present participle* **doubling,** *past* **doubled)**
to become or make twice as big or twice as much: *He worked so well that I* **doubled** *his wages.*

°**doubt**[1] /dout/ *verb*
to be unsure of something: *I* **doubt if** *he will pass the examinations.*

°**doubt**[2] *noun*
reason for being unsure about: *I have (my)* **doubts** *about whether he is the best man for the job. There is no* **doubt** *that he is guilty.*

doubtful *adjective* unsure: *It is* **doubtful** *that he will come.*

doubtless *adverb* surely: *He will* **doubtless** *arrive by the next train.*

dough /dō/ *noun (no plural)*
a soft mixture of flour and water: *We use* **dough** *to make bread.*

°**down** /doun/ *adverb, preposition, adjective*
in or to a lower place: *Sit* **down,** *please, and put your bags* **down** *on the floor. The children ran* **down** (= along) *the road. The men are* **down** *by the river.*

downward (*also* **downwards)** *adverb* from a higher to a lower place; toward the ground or floor: *She climbed* **downward** *to a lower branch of the tree. He fell face* **downward** *in the sand.*

upside down *or* **upside-down** *adverb*
with the top part **downward:** *If you hold the bottle* **upside down,** *all the liquid will run out.*

upside-down

downhill /doun′ hil′/ see **hill**

downstairs /doun′ stârz′/ see **stairs**

doze[1] /dōz/ *verb* (*present participle* **dozing,** *past* **dozed**)
to sleep lightly for a short time: *I* **dozed (off)** *for about an hour.*

doze[2] *noun*
a short sleep: *to have a* **doze**

dozen /duz′ ən/ *noun*
twelve: *I want a* **dozen** *eggs, please. There were* **dozens of** (= a lot of) *people there.*

Dr. /dok′ tər/
the short way of writing **doctor** in a name: **Dr.** *Brown*

drag /drag/ *verb* (*present participle* **dragging,** *past* **dragged**)
to pull along behind you: *The bag was too heavy to carry, so he had to* **drag** *it into the house.*

dragon /drag′ ən/ *noun*
an imaginary animal in stories that is said to breathe fire

drain[1] /drān/ *noun*
a pipe or hollow which takes dirty water away: *Your kitchen* **drain** *has become blocked by tea leaves.*

drain[2] *verb*
1 to flow away; make water flow away: *Some farmers have to* **drain** *water off their fields. The water* **drained away** *slowly.*
2 to become drier as water flows away: *After I washed the plates, I left them to* **drain.**

drama /drä′ mə/ *noun*
1 stories that can be acted; plays
2 excitement: *I like the* **drama** *of a big storm.*

dramatic /drə mat′ ik/ *adjective*
exciting: *a* **dramatic** *scene*

drank /drangk/ see **drink**

°**draw** /drô/ *verb* (*past tense* **drew** /dro͞o/, *past participle* **drawn** /drôn/)
1 to make a picture, especially with a pencil or pen: *I* **drew** *(a picture of) my cat. I like* **drawing** *cats.*
2 to pull or pull up: *The cart was* **drawn** *by oxen.*
3 to come: *The day of the party* **drew** *nearer.*

drawing *noun* **1** *(no plural)* making pictures: **Drawing** *is my favorite lesson.* **2** a picture done by pen or pencil: *She had done a* **drawing** *of her mother.*

°**drawer** /drôr/ *noun*
a box that fits into a piece of furniture, with handles so that it can be pulled out and pushed in

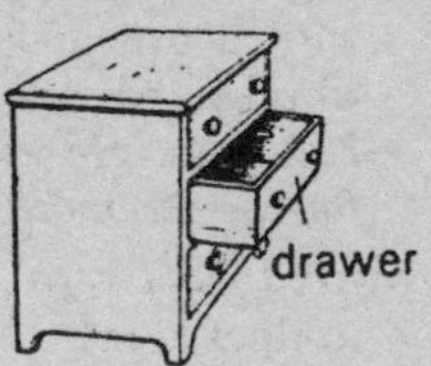

chest of drawers

chest of drawers *noun* a piece of furniture with several drawers

dreadful /dred′ fəl/ *adjective*
very bad or unpleasant: *There's been a* **dreadful** *accident — two people have died. I've had a* **dreadful** *day — everything seems to have gone wrong.*

°dream¹ /drēm/ *verb* (*present participle* **dreaming,** *past* **dreamt** /dremt/ or **dreamed** /drēmd/)
1 to imagine things while you are asleep: *I* **dreamt about** *my teacher last night.*
2 to imagine something nice: *I* **dream of** *being the best skier in the town.*

°dream² *noun*
1 something that you imagine while you are asleep: *a frightening* **dream**
2 something nice that you imagine, or that you want to do: *It is my* **dream** *to come first in the race.*

drench /drench/ *verb*
to make completely wet: *I was* **drenched** *in the storm.*

°dress¹ /dres/ *verb*
1 to put on and wear clothes: *He is* **dressed** *very well. She likes to* **dress up** (= put on nice, special clothes) *for a party.* **Dress yourself** *quickly.*
2 to clean and put a bandage on a wound: *I* **dressed** *his cut hand.*

°dress² *noun*
1 (*plural* **dresses**) a piece of clothing with a top and a skirt, worn by women and girls
2 clothes: *He was in special* **dress** *for the ceremony.*

drift /drift/ *verb*
to float along: *The piece of wood was* **drifting** *down the river.*

drills

drill¹ /dril/ *verb*
to make a hole in something with a special machine: *to* **drill** *a hole in the wall*

drill² *noun*
a machine for making holes

°drink¹ /dringk/ *verb* (*present participle* **drinking,** *past tense* **drank** /drangk/, *past participle* **drunk** /drungk/)
to take liquid into the mouth and swallow it: *He* **drank** *some milk. Would you like something to* **drink?**

°drink² *noun*
some liquid taken and swallowed: *Can I have a* **drink?** *Would you like a* **drink** *of water?*

drip¹ /drip/ *verb* (*present participle* **dripping,** *past* **dripped**)
to fall or let fall in drops: *The rain* **dripped** *through the trees. The trees* **dripped.**

drip² *noun*
a small drop: **Drips** *of water fell down her neck.*

°drive¹ /drīv/ *verb* (*present participle* **driving,** *past tense* **drove** /drōv/, *past participle* **driven** /driven/)
to make a vehicle move in the direction you want: *Can you* **drive** *(a car)? I* **drove** *to town yesterday.*
driver *noun: a bus* **driver**

drive² *noun*
1 a journey by road vehicle: *It is a short* **drive** *to the village.*
2 a road going to a house only: *He left his car in the* **drive.**

droop /dro͞op/ *verb*
to hang down: *The flowers* **drooped** *soon after we picked them.*

°drop¹ /drop/ *verb* (*present participle* **dropping,** *past* **dropped**)
to fall or let fall: *The plate* **dropped** *from her hands. She* **dropped** *the plate. Why don't you* **drop in** (= visit us) *tomorrow?*

°drop² *noun*
a small amount of liquid: *A few* **drops** *of rain landed on the roof.*

drought /drout/ *noun*
a time when no rain falls and the land becomes very dry

drove /drōv/ see **drive**

drown /droun/ *verb*
to die by not being able to breathe under water: *Don't play by the river in case you fall in and* **drown!**

drug /drug/ *noun*
medicine: *This drug will get rid of the pain in your back.*

°**drum**[1] /drum/ *noun*
1 a musical instrument made of a round hollow box with skin stretched tightly over it, which is beaten
2 a metal container for oil, water, etc.

drums

°**drum**[2] *verb* (*present participle* **drumming,** *past* **drummed)**
to beat or make music on a drum
drummer *noun*

drunk[1] /drungk/ *adjective*
having had too much alcohol: *The man who started singing outside our house was* **drunk.**
Drunken means the same as drunk, but can only be used with a noun: *a* **drunken** *man*

drunk[2] see **drink**

°**dry**[1] /drī/ *adjective* (**drier** /drī′ ər/, **driest** /drī′ est/)
not containing water; not wet: *This coat will keep you* **dry** *in the rain.*

°**dry**[2] *verb* (*present participle* **drying,** *past* **dried** /drīd/)
to make or become dry: *The clothes* **dried** *quickly outside. She* **dried** *her hair in the sun.*

duchess /duch′ is/ *noun*
the wife of a duke (see)

duck /duk/ *noun*
a bird that swims on water and can be kept by people for its eggs and meat

duckling /duk′ ling/ *noun*
a young duck

due /do͞o/ *adjective*
1 owed; that should be paid or given: *Our thanks are* **due** *to him.*
2 expected: *The train is* **due** *at five. I am* **due for** (= it is time for me to have) *a raise in pay.*
due to *preposition* because of; caused by: *His illness was* **due to** *bad food.*

duet /do͞o et′/ *noun*
a song or piece of music for two people

dug /dug/ see **dig**

duke /do͞ok/ *noun*
the title of a man from a very important family, especially in Britain

°**dull** /dul/ *adjective*
1 not bright or light: *a* **dull,** *cloudy day/a* **dull** *brown color*
2 not interesting or clever; *a* **dull** *speech*

dumb /dum/ *adjective*
not able to speak

°**dump**[1] /dump/ *verb*
to leave, drop, or throw away: *We* **dumped** *our bags on the floor. There are special places where you can* **dump** *things you don't want.*

dump[2] *noun*
a place where things can be thrown away: *They dumped their old car in the town* **dump.**

°**during** /dūr′ ing/ *preposition*
1 all the time that something is going on: *They swim every day* **during** *the summer.*
2 at some time while something else

is happening: *He fell asleep* **during** *the lesson.*

dusk /dusk/ *noun (no plural)*
the time when the sun has just set: *It is difficult to see clearly at* **dusk.**

°**dust**[1] /dust/ *noun (no plural)*
fine powder carried in the air or lying on dry ground: *There is a lot of* **dust** *on this table.*

dust[2] *verb*
to clean dust from: *She* **dusted** *the table.*

dusty *adjective* **(dustier, dustiest):** *a* **dusty** *road*

°**duty** /do͞o′ tē/ *noun* (*plural* **duties**)
1 what you ought to do: *It is your* **duty** *to look after your children.*
2 a time when you are looking after things: *Only one doctor is* **on duty** *today — the other doctor is* **off duty.**

dwarf /dwôrf/ *noun*
a person, plant, or animal that is much smaller than usual

dye[1] /dī/ *verb* (*present participle* **dyeing,** *past* **dyed** /dīd/)
to give a color to: *She* **dyed** *her hair black.*

dye[2] *noun*
something that gives a lasting color: **Dyes** *come from plants or from chemicals.*

Ee

° **each** /ēch/
every one separately: **Each** *child has an exercise book for his own work. The two brothers help* **each other** (=each brother helps the other).

°**eager** /ē′ gər/ *adjective*
very anxious to do something: *The boy was* **eager** *to show me his stamps.*
eagerly *adverb*

eagle /ē′ gəl/ *noun*
a large bird that kills other creatures for food

eagle

°**ear** /ēr/ *noun*
1 one of the parts on each side of the head with which you hear
2 the part of a plant where the seed is: *an* **ear** of corn
earring /ēr′ ring *or* ēr′ ing/ *noun: Ornaments worn in or on the ears are called* **earrings.**

°**early** /ur′ lē/ *adjective, adverb* **(earlier, earliest)**
1 before the usual or agreed time: *We agreed to meet at seven o'clock but I was* **early;** *I arrived at half past six. The bus arrived* **early.**
2 near the beginning (of a day, year, etc.): *It often rains in the* **early** *morning. Do you get up* **early?**

°**earn** /urn/ *adjective*
to get money in return for work you do: *He has* **earned** *a lot of money by working in the evenings.*

°**earth** /urth/ *noun*
1 the world on which we live: *The* **earth** *goes around the sun once a year. We live on* **Earth.**
2 *(no plural)* the substance on the ground in which plants can grow: *She put the seeds in the* **earth.**
earthquake *noun* a strong and sudden shaking of the ground

°**ease¹** /ēz/ *noun (no plural)*
the ability to do something without difficulty: *He passed the examination* **with ease.**

ease² *verb* (*present participle* **easing,** *past* **eased**)
to make better: *The medicine* **eased** *the pain.*

°**east** /ēst/ *noun, adjective, adverb*
the direction from which the sun comes up in the morning: *Our house faces* **east.** *There is a strong* **east** *wind* (=from the east).
eastern /ēs′ tərn/ *adjective* in or of the east
eastward *adverb* toward the east: *to travel* **eastward**

°**easy** /ē′ zē/ *adjective* **(easier, easiest)**
not difficult; done with no trouble: *It was an* **easy** *job, and we did it quickly.*
easily *adverb: He did the job* **easily.**

°**eat** /ēt/ *verb* (*present participle* **eating,** *past tense* **ate** /āt/ *past participle* **eaten** /ēt′ ən/)
to put food into the mouth and swallow it: *Have you* **eaten** *your breakfast yet?*

echo¹ /ek′ ō/ *verb*
(of a sound) to come back again: *Our voices* **echoed** *in the empty room.*

echo² *noun* (*plural* **echoes**)
a sound that comes back to you: *the* **echoes** *of our voices*

eclipse /i klips'/ *noun*
a time when the light from the sun (or moon) is blocked by the moon (or Earth)

economy /i kon' ə mē/ *noun*
the management of money: *The country's* **economy** *depends on the amount of goods it sells abroad. It is good* **economy** *to buy well made shoes, as they will last longer.*
economic /ek"ə näm' ik *or* ē"kə näm' ik/ *adjective: What is the* **economic** *state of the country?*
economical *adjective* cheap: *Going by train is more* **economical** *than going by plane.*

°**edge** /ej/ *noun*
1 the outside end of something: the part which is farthest from the middle: *The* **edge** *of the plate was blue.*
2 the cutting part of a knife, ax, etc.: *That knife has a sharp* **edge.**

editor /ed'i tər/ *noun*
a person who prepares books or newspapers before they are printed
edition /i dish' ən/ *noun* a book or newspaper brought out at a special time

°**educate** /ej' ə kāt/ *verb*
(*present participle* **educating,** *past* **educated)**
to teach people: *Schoolteachers* **educate** *children.*
education *noun (no plural)* teaching and learning: **Education** *is given to children by the government in many countries.*
educational *adjective* helping you to learn: *an* **educational** *toy*

eel /ēl/ *noun*
a long fish shaped like a snake

effect /i fekt'/ *noun*
a result: *Alcoholic drink can have a bad* **effect** *on your body.*
effective *adjective* getting the result you want: *The medicine is an* **effective** *cure for a headache.*

efficient /i fish' ənt/ *adjective*
working well and getting a lot of things done: *an* **efficient** *secretary*
efficiently *adverb*

effort /ef' ərt/ *noun*
the use of strength in trying to do something: *With a great* **effort** *he pushed open the door. Please put more* **effort** *into your school work.*

e.g. /ē' gē/
for example: *They keep animals,* **e.g.** *goats and cattle.*

°**egg** /eg/ *noun*
a rounded thing from which baby birds, snakes, fish, or insects come: *We eat hens'* **eggs.**

eight /āt/ *noun, adjective*
the number 8
eighth /āth/ *noun, adjective*
number 8 in order; 8th

eighteen /ā' teen"/ *noun, adjective*
the number 18
eighteenth *noun, adjective*
number 18 in order; 18th

eighty /ā' tē/ *noun, adjective*
the number 80
eightieth /ā' tē əth/ *noun, adjective*
number 80 in order; 80th

either /ē' THər *or* ī' THər/
1 one or the other of two: *Both skirts are too small, so I can't wear* **either** *(of them).* **Either** *the father* **or** *his sons drive the truck.*
2 (used in sentences with **not**): *I haven't been to England, or to Germany,* **either.**

elaborate /i lab′ ər it/ *adjective*
having many different parts or needing a lot of different sorts of work done on it

elastic[1] /i las′ tic/ *adjective*
which goes back to its first shape after being stretched or pulled: *Rubber is an* **elastic** *substance.*

elastic[2] *noun*
a material which is elastic: *a belt made of* **elastic**

°**elbow** /el′ bō/ *noun*
the part of your arm which bends it in the middle

°**elder** /el′ dər/ *adjective*
the older of two: *Which brother did you see, the* **elder** *or the younger?*

°**eldest** /el′ dest/ *adjective*
the oldest of three or more: *My* **eldest** *brother lives abroad.*

elect /i lekt′/ *verb*
to choose, usually by vote (see): *The government is made up of men and women* **elected** *by the people of the country.*

election *noun* a time when we choose people for special positions: *The primary* **elections** *will be next month. Who won the* **election?**

°**electricity** /i lek″ tris′ ə tē/ *noun*
power for lighting, heating, machinery, etc. that is sent through wires: *Do you use* **electricity** *for cooking?*

electric /i lek′ trik/ *adjective*
working by electricity: *an* **electric** *cooker*

electrical *adjective* about electricity: *The furnace isn't working because of an* **electrical** *fault.*

electrician /i lek″ trish′ ən/ *noun: An* **electrician** *repaired the furnace.*

elegant /el′ ə gənt/ *adjective*
graceful and beautiful: **elegant** *clothes*

elegantly *adverb*

element /el′ ə mənt/ *noun*
one of the very simple substances from which everything is made: *Gold and iron are* **elements** *but brass is not, because it is made by mixing two other metals.*

elementary /el′ ə men′ trē/ *adjective*
having to do with the beginning of something: *an* **elementary** *reading book for a child who is learning to read*

elephant /el′ ə fənt/ *noun*
a very large animal which has two long curved teeth **(tusks)** and a long nose **(trunk)**, and lives in hot places

eleven /i lev′ ən/ *noun, adjective*
the number 11: **Eleven** *minus one is ten* (11–1 = 10).

eleventh *noun, adjective* number 11 in order; 11th

eliminate /i lim′ ə nāt″/ *verb* (*present participle* **eliminating,** *past* **eliminated)**
to take out; get rid of: *She has been* **eliminated** *from the swimming race because she did not win any of the early heats.*

°**else** /els/ *adverb*
1 other; different; instead: *If you don't like eggs I can cook something* **else.**
2 more; as well: *Would you like something* **else** *to eat?*
3 (used in some questions and phrases): *It's not here; where* **else**

can we look? If the train has gone, how **else** *can we get home. Hold the bottle in both hands* **or else** (=if not) *you may drop it.*

elsewhere *adverb* in or to some other place: *They left the village and went* **elsewhere.**

embarrass /im bar′ əs/ *verb*
to make someone feel nervous or silly in front of other people: *When I began to sing, he laughed and made me* **embarrassed.**

embarrassment *noun (no plural)*

embassy /em′ ba sē/ *noun* (*plural* **embassies)**
a place where people work to represent their own country in another country

embrace[1] /im brās′/ *verb* (*present participle* **embracing,** *past* **embraced)**
to hold in the arms to show love: *The child* **embraced** *his parents.*

embrace[2] *noun*
holding in the arms: *a loving* **embrace**

embroider /im broi′ dər/ *verb*
to sew with ornamental patterns: *to* **embroider** a dress

embroidery *noun (no plural): The dress was covered with beautiful* **embroidery.**

emerge /i murj′/ *verb* (*present participle* **emerging,** *past* **emerged)**
to come out: *The baby birds* **emerged from** *their eggs.*

emergency /i mur′ jən se/ *noun* (*plural* **emergencies)**
a sudden happening that needs something done about it all at once: *The hospital has to treat* **emergencies** *such as car accidents. In an* **emergency,** *telephone the police.*

emotion /i mō′ shən/ *noun*
a feeling: *Anger and love are strong* **emotions.**

emperor /em′ pər ər/ *noun*
a ruler of a country or several countries

empire /em′ pīr/ *noun* a group of countries ruled by an emperor

empress /em′ pres/ *noun* a female ruler of a country or several countries; the wife of an emperor

emphasize /em′ fa sīz″/ *verb* (*present participle* **emphasizing,** *past* **emphasized)**
to show that something is important: *He* **emphasized** *the need for hard work.*

°**employ** /im ploi′/ *verb*
to give work to: *I am* **employed** *by the National Bank, which* **employs** *hundreds of people.*

employee /im ploi′ ē/ *noun* a person who is employed by someone else: *There are ten* **employees** *in his firm.*

employer *noun* a person who employs others

employment *noun (no plural): He left his home to look for* **employment.**

°**empty**[1] /em′ te/ *adjective* **(emptier, emptiest)**
having nothing inside: *The house is* **empty,** *no one is living there.*

°**empty**[2] *verb* (*present participle* **emptying,** *past* **emptied)**
to take everything out of: *He* **emptied** *the box of books (onto the floor).*

enable /in ā bəl/ *verb* (*present participle* **enabling,** *past* **enabled**) to make possible: *The new machine* **enables** *us to cut and tie up our wheat quickly.*

enamel /i nam′ əl/ *noun* a kind of paint for metal: *The iron pan was covered with white* **enamel.**

enclose /in klōz/ *verb* (*present participle* **enclosing,** *past* **enclosed**) to shut something in: *The football field is* **enclosed** *by a wall. When I wrote to my parents, I* **enclosed** *a photograph of the baby (in the letter).*

enclosure /in klō′ zho͝or/ *noun: They put the cattle into an* **enclosure.**

°**encourage** /in kur′ ij/ *verb* (*present participle* **encouraging,** *past encouraged*) to give praise or hope to someone so that he will do something: I **encouraged** *her to work hard and to try for the examinations.*

encyclopedia /in sī″ klə pē′ dē ə/ *noun* a book that gives you knowledge about a lot of things; it is usually arranged in alphabetical order

°**end**[1] /end/ *noun* the farthest point or edge of anything: *When you get to the* **end** *of this road, turn right. At the* **end** *of the lesson, we went home.* **In the end** (=at last), *we found the house.*

°**end**[2] *verb* to finish: *When the lesson* **ended,** *we went home.*

ending *noun* the end of a story, film, play, or word: *The story had a happy* **ending.**

endless *adjective: There is* **endless** *work to do when you have children in the house.*

endure /in dūr/ *verb* (*present participle* **enduring,** *past* **endured**) to bear: *I can't* **endure** *loud music.*

endurance *noun (no plural)* the power to bear something or to keep doing something for a long time: *Long distance races are a test of a runner's* **endurance.**

enemy /en′ ə mē/ *noun* (*plural* **enemies**) a person or country that is not friendly to you or that wants to harm you: *The two countries are* **enemies.**

energy /en′ ər jē/ *noun (no plural)* power to do things or to make things work: *I have no* **energy** *left after playing football. Coal and oil give us* **energy** *for heating, lighting, moving things, etc.*

energetic /en″ ər jet′ ik/ *adjective: He is an* **energetic** *boy; he enjoys sports.*

energetically *adverb*

engaged /in gājd′/ *adjective*
1 busy or being used: *The principal is* **engaged** *— can you come back later? The telephone number you want is* **engaged;** *try again in a few minutes.*
2 having promised to marry someone: My brother is **engaged** *to Anne; they will be married next year.*

engagement *noun: My brother has just told me about his* **engagement** *to Anne. I have three* **engagements** (=things to do which will make me busy) *today — so can I see you tomorrow?*

°**engine** /en′ jin/ *noun* a machine which uses gasoline, oil, gas, electricity, or steam and which makes things work or move: *a car* **engine**

engineer /en″ jə nēr′/ *noun*
a person who plans and makes machines, roads, bridges, etc.
engineering *noun (no plural)* the science or job of an engineer: *He is studying* **engineering** *at college.*

°**enjoy** /in joi′/ *verb*
to get pleasure from: *I* **enjoy** *my job.* **enjoyable** *adjective*
enjoyment *noun (no plural): I get a lot of* **enjoyment** *from my job.*

enlarge /in lärj′/ *verb (present participle* **enlarging,** *past* **enlarged)**
to make bigger: *to* **enlarge** *a photograph*

enormous /i nôr′ məs/ *adjective*
very large: *an* **enormous** *plate of food*

°**enough** /i nuf′/ *adjective, adverb, noun*
as much as is needed: *There is* **enough** *paper here. Are you sure there is* **enough** *(of it)? That seat is not big* **enough** *for five people.*

°**enter** /en′ tər/ *verb*
to go or come in: *He* **entered** *the room quietly.*

entertain /en″ tər tān′/ *verb*
to do something to amuse or interest people: *He* **entertained** *us with stories about life abroad.*
entertainment *noun: If you want* **entertainment** *in the city, you can go to a film or play.*

enthusiasm /in thōō′ zē az″ əm/ *noun (no plural)*
an eager feeling of wanting to do something: *He plays football with* **enthusiasm.**
enthusiastic /in thōō″ zē as′ tik/ *adjective*

entire /in tīr′/ *adjective*
whole; complete: *The* **entire** *class will be there.*
entirely *adverb: I agree with you* **entirely.**

°**entrance** /en′ trəns/ *noun*
1 a place where you go in: *He stood in the* **entrance** *of the hospital.*
2 going or coming in: *The music played for the* **entrance** *of the dancers.*

entry /en′ trē/ *noun (plural* **entries)**
entrance: *That road sign says "No* **entry**", *which means that cars cannot go into the road.*

envelope /en′ vel ōp/ *noun*
a folded paper cover for a letter

envelope

environment /in vī′ rə mənt/ *noun*
the conditions surrounding something: *The children have a happy* **environment** *at school.*

envy¹ /en′ vē/ *noun (no plural)*
the feeling of anger or bitterness because someone has more of something or a better life than you have: *He was filled with* **envy** *because Richard passed the examination and he did not.*
envious /en′ vē us/ *adjective: He was* **envious** *of my new car.*

envy² *verb (present participle* **envying,** *past* **envied)**
to feel envy: He **envied** *his friend.*

epidemic /ep″ ə dem′ ik/ *noun*
an illness that spreads quickly to a lot of people

°**equal¹** /ē′ kwəl/ *adjective*
the same as: *I gave the three children* **equal** *sums of money.*
equality /i kwal′ ə tē/ *noun (no plural)* being equal: *All three children have* **equality** *in our family — they are all treated in*

the same way.

equally *adverb: They are both* **equally** *good at reading.*

equal² *noun*
someone who is as good as someone else: *All people should be treated as* **equals** *by the law.*

equal³ *verb (present participle* **equaling,** *past* **equaled)**
1 to be the same as: *Three and five* **equals** *eight* (3 + 5 = 8).
2 to be as good, clever, etc. as: *None of us can* **equal** *Sarah — she's always first in her class.*

equator /i kwā′ tər/ *noun*
an imaginary line that runs around the middle of the Earth

equip /i kwip′/ *verb (present participle* **equipping,** *past* **equipped)**
to give things that are useful for doing something: *Our school is* **equipped with** *a radio and a television.*

equipment *noun (no plural): Our school has been given some new* **equipment** *— a radio and a television.*

erect¹ /i rekt′/ *adjective*
standing straight: *to stand* **erect**

erect² *verb*
to put up: *They* **erected** *the hut in two hours.*

errand /er′ ənd/ *noun*
a short journey made to do something useful or necessary: *My mother asked me to go* **on an errand** *— she wanted me to buy some food.*

error /er′ ər/ *noun*
a mistake: *This work is full of* **errors!**

erupt /i rupt′/ *verb*
to burst out: *Volcanoes are mountains from which melted rock* **erupts.**

escalator /es′ kə lā″ tər/ *noun*
moving stairs which can take you up or down without your walking

escalator

°**escape¹** /es kāp/ *verb (present participle* **escaping,** *past* **escaped)**
to get free from: *to* **escape** *from prison*

°**escape²** *noun*
the act of escaping: *The prisoner* **made his escape** *at night.*

escort /es kôrt′/ *verb*
to go with someone: *A group of soldiers* **escorted** *the President.*

escort /es′ kôrt/ *noun: an* **escort** *of soldiers*

°**especially** /es pesh′ əl ē/ *adverb*
1 very; more than usual: *She is* **especially** *good at science.*
2 most of all: *I would like a bicycle,* **especially** *a blue one.*

essay /es′ ā/ *noun*
a piece of writing on a special thing: *She wrote an* **essay** *on "My Family".*

essential /ə sen′ shəl / *adjective*
necessary; very important: *If you travel abroad, it is* **essential** *that you have the right papers.*

estate /ə stāt′/ *noun*
a large piece of land, usually with a house on it: *A* **housing estate** *is a piece of land on which a group of houses has been built. A* **real estate agent** *is a person who arranges the buying and selling of houses.*

estimate¹ /es′ tə māt/ *verb (present participle* **estimating,** *past*

estimated)
to make a reasonable guess: *I* **estimate** *that the journey will take three hours.*

estimate² /es′ tə mit/ *noun*
a guess

etc. /et set′ rə/
and so on: *There are lots of things to buy — tea, sugar, bread,* **etc.**

°**even¹** /ē′ vən/ *adjective*
1 flat and smooth: *an* **even** *surface*
2 equal: *He won the first game and I won the second, so we're* **even.**
3 (of a number) that can be divided exactly by two: *2 and 4 are* **even** *numbers, but 3 and 5 are odd numbers.*
evenly *adverb: Divide the candy* **evenly** *among the three boys* (= give the same number to each boy).

°**even²** *adverb*
1 more than we usually expect: *He let me use his bicycle and he* **even** *said I could keep it all day.*
2 still; yet: *Yesterday it rained hard, and today it's raining* **even** *harder.*

°**evening** /ēv′ ning/ *noun*
the time between the end of the afternoon and when you go to bed

°**event** /i vent′/ *noun*
a happening, often an important one: *What* **events** *do you remember from your school days?*

eventually /i ven′ cho͞o əl ē/ *adverb*
at last; in the end: *I looked everywhere for my glass and* **eventually** *found it under my chair.*

°**ever** /ev′ ər/ *adverb*
1 at any time: *Have you* **ever** *been abroad? She used to sing well, but now she sings better* **than ever.**
2 always: *I have lived here* **ever since** *I was a child. I would like to stay here* **for ever.**

°**every** /ev′ rē/
each one; not missing out one: *I have read* **every** *book in the bookcase.*

everybody /ev′ rē bud″ ē/ *or* **everyone**
every person: **Everybody** *wanted to watch the game.*

everyday /ev′ rē dā″/ *adjective*
usual; not special: *This is an* **everyday** *dress; I shall wear something better to the party.*

everything /ev′ rē thing″/
every thing; all things: *I got* **everything** *I needed in the market.*

everywhere /ev′ rē hwâr/ *adverb*
in or to every place: *I looked* **everywhere** *for my watch, but I couldn't find it.*

evidence /ev ə dəns/ *noun* *(no plural)*
words or things which prove something: *You say that John took your book, but have you any* **evidence** *of that?*
evident *adjective* clear: *It is* **evident** *that you have done the job well.*
evidently *adverb*

evil /ē vəl/ *adjective*
very bad: *It was* **evil** *to kill the old woman and steal all her money.*

ex- /eks/
used of someone who used to be what is said, but no longer is: *She is his* **ex-wife.**

°**exact** /ig zakt′/ *adjective*
completely correct: *Can you tell me the* **exact** *time?*
exactly *adverb: It is* **exactly** *four*

o'clock, not one minute more or one minute less.

exaggerate /ig zaj′ ə rāt″/ *verb* (*present participle* **exaggerating,** *past* **exaggerated**)
to make something seem bigger, better, worse, etc. than it really is: *When he had been ill, he* **exaggerated** *and said he had nearly died.*

exaggeration *noun*

°**examination** /ig zam″ ə nā′ shən/ *noun*
a test of knowledge: *Have you* **passed the examination** *you took last month? No, I* **failed that examination** *but I'm taking it again next year.*

exam *noun:* **Exam** *is short for examination and is nearly always used in spoken English.*

examine /ig zam′ in/ *verb* (*present participle* **examining,** *past* **examined**)
1 to look at closely: *The doctor* **examined** *my throat.*
2 to give someone an examination

°**example** /ig zam′ pəl/ *noun*
one thing taken from a number of things of the same kind to show what the other things are like: *I showed my new employer some* **examples** *of my work. You can use any two colors —* **for example,** *red and yellow.*

exceed /ik sēd′/ *verb*
to be more than: *If your truck* **exceeds** *this weight, you cannot cross the bridge.*

excellent /ek′ sə lənt/ *adjective*
very good: *This is* **excellent** *work, Paul.*

excellently *adverb*

°**except** /ik sept′/
apart from; not including: *I have washed all the clothes* **except** *your shirt.*

exception /ik sep′ shən/ *noun*
something which is different from what is usually expected: *Most children like candy, but she is the* **exception** *— she will not eat it!*

exceptional *adjective* unusual, especially unusually good: *an* **exceptional** *pupil*

exceptionally *adverb*

excess /ik ses′ *or* ek′ ses/ *noun, adjective*
more than is usual or allowed: *You have to pay for* **excess** *luggage* (see) *on a plane.*

°**exchange**[1] /iks chānj′/ *verb* (*present participle* **exchanging,** *past* **exchanged**)
to change something for something else

°**exchange**[2] *noun*
an act of exchanging: *We made an* **exchange** *— she had my dress and I had hers.*

°**excite** /iks sīt′/ *verb* (*present participle* **exciting,** *past* **excited**)
to give strong and pleasant feelings; cause to lose calmness: *The game excited the children and they all started to shout.*

excited *adjective* having strong and pleasant feelings; not calm

excitement *noun: The* **excitement** *of the games has made them tired.*

exciting *adjective* able to make someone excited: **exciting** *news*

exclaim /iks klām′/ *verb*
to shout out or say loudly in surprise: *"Look, there's James on*

television!" **exclaimed** *Peter.*

exclamation /eks″ klə mā′ shən/ *noun*

exclamation mark /eks″ klə mā′ shən märk/ *noun*
the sign ! used in writing to show surprise, shock, etc., or when calling someone: *Come here!*

exclude /iks kloōd′/ *verb* (*present participle* **excluding,** *past* **excluded**)
to keep someone or something out: *We had to* **exclude** *John from the team because he hurt his leg.*

excursion /ik skur′ zhən/ *noun*
a short journey, for pleasure: *We went on an* **excursion** *to the city.*

°**excuse**[1] /ik skūz′/ *verb* (*present participle* **excusing,** *past* **excused**)
to forgive: *I* **excused** *James's bad work, as I knew he had been ill.* **Excuse me** *(troubling you), could you tell me the way to the station?*

°**excuse**[2] /ik skūs′/ *noun*
a reason given when you ask someone to forgive you: *I haven't done the work well; my* **excuse** *is that I have been ill.*

execute /ek′ sə kūt″/ *verb* (*present participle* **executing,** *past* **executed**)
to kill as a punishment decided by law

execution *noun*

°**exercise**[1] /ek′ sər sīz/ *noun*
using your body to make it stronger or more healthy: *Running is good* **exercise.**

°**exercise**[2] *verb* (*present participle* **exercising,** *past* **exercised**)
to use part of the body: *He was* **exercising** *his arms by swinging from a rope.*

exhaust[1] /ig zôst′/ *verb*
to make very tired: *We are all* **exhausted** *after the journey.*

exhaust[2] *noun (no plural)*
burnt gas which comes out from the back of a car

exhibit /ig zib′ it/ *verb*
to show in public: *She* **exhibited** *her paintings at our school.*

exhibition /ek′ sə bish′ ən/ *noun: an* **exhibition** *of paintings*

exile /eg′ zīl/ *noun*
someone who is not allowed to live in his own country as a punishment: *He had been five years* **in exile** (= made to live abroad).

exist /ig zist′/ *verb*
to be: *The elephant* (see) *is the largest land animal that* **exists.**

existence *noun (no plural): The elephant is the largest land animal in* **existence.**

exit /eg′ zit *or* ek′ sit/ *noun*
the way out of a place: *Where is the* **exit?**

expand /ik spand′/ *verb*
to grow or make larger: *The business has* **expanded** *from having one office to having twelve.*

expansion /ik span′ shən/ *noun*

°**expect** /ik spekt′/ *verb*
to think that something will happen: *Do you* **expect** *to win the race? Yes, I* **expect** *I will win.*

expedition /ek″ spə dish′ ən/ *noun*
a journey, usually a long onc to find out something: *an* **expedition** *to find the beginning of the Nile River*

expel /ik spel′/ *verb* (*present participle* **expelling,** *past* **expelled**)
to send away, especially from a school: *The pupils were* **expelled** *for stealing.*

expulsion /ik spul′ shən/ *noun*

expensive /ik spen′ siv/ *adjective*
costing a lot of money: *It is*

expensive *to travel by plane.*

expense *noun* cost; money spent: *What are the* **expenses** *of moving house?*

experience[1] /ik spēr′ ē əns/ *noun*
1 something that happens to you: *The accident was an* **experience** *she will never forget.*
2 *(no plural)* work you have done before of the same sort: *Have you any* **experience** *at teaching?*

experience[2] *verb* (*present participle* **experiencing,** *past* **experienced)**
to have something happen to you: *to* **experience** *fear*

experienced *adjective* having done something before: *an* **experienced** *teacher*

experiment[1] /ik sper′ ə mənt/ *noun*
a careful test done to see whether something is true: *We can learn by* **experiment** *that oil and water will not mix.*

experiment[2] *verb*
to make a careful test to see if something is true: *We* **experimented** *by putting oil and water together, and we saw that they did not mix.*

expert /ek′ spərt/ *noun*
a person who is very good at something special: an **expert** *in cooking/a cooking* **expert**

°**explain** /ik splān′/ *verb*
to make clear: *Can you* **explain** *why you were late?*

explanation /ek″ splə nā′ shən/ *noun: What is your* **explanation** *for being late?*

°**explode** /ik splōd′/ *verb* (*present participle* **exploding,** *past* **exploded)**
to burst with a loud noise: *When you blow air into a paper bag, and then hit the bag, it* **explodes.**

explosion *noun: The* **explosion** *was caused by a burst gas pipe.*

explosive /-siv/ *noun*
something that makes things explode: *The miners put some* **explosives** *in the mine, to loosen the coal.*

explore /ik splôr′/ *verb*
(*present participle* **exploring,** *past* **explored)**
to find out about a place by going and looking: *Have you really* **explored** *your nearest town?*

exploration /eks″ plə rā′ shən/ *noun*

explorer *noun* a person who travels into an unknown area to find out about it

export[1] /ik spôrt′ *or* eks′ pôrt/ *verb*
to send something out of the country to be sold abroad: *South Africa* **exports** *fruit.*

export[2] /eks′ pôrt/ *noun*
something that is exported: *Fruit is one of South Africa's* **exports.**

expose /ik spōz′/ *verb* (*present participle* **exposing,** *past* **exposed)**
to uncover: *He* **exposed** *the wound on his arm.*

°**express**[1] /ik spres′/ *verb*
to say clearly: *He wanted to* **express** *his thanks but he could not think of the best words.*

expression *noun* **1** something that is said: *You should not use that* **expression** *— it's not polite.*
2 the look on someone's face: *a sad* **expression**

express[2] *noun*
a fast train which makes only a few stops on its journey

extend /ik stend′/ *verb*
to stretch out; make larger or longer: *The boss* **extended** *our*

vacation by a day.

extension *noun* something that extends: *We built an* **extension** *onto the school, so now we have two more classrooms.*

extensive /-siv/ *adjective* spreading over a large area: *The school has* **extensive** *playing fields.*

extent /ik stent′/ *noun* the area that something spreads over: *What is the* **extent** *of your garden?*

external /ik stur′ nəl/ *adjective* of or on the outside: *the* **external** *walls of a house*

extinguish /ik sting′ gwish/ *verb* to put out: *to* **extinguish** *a fire*

extinguisher *noun* a container of chemicals which will put out a fire quickly

extra /eks′ trə/ *adjective, adverb, noun* more than usual; more than is expected: *Can I have* **extra** *time to finish my work? This hotel charges* **extra** *for a room with a bath.*

extract /ik strakt′/ *verb* to take out: *The dentist* (see) **extracted** *my tooth.*

extraordinary /ik strôr′ də nar″ ē/ *adjective* very unusual or strange: *I heard an* **extraordinary** *story the other day.*

extravagant /ik strav′ ə gənt/ *adjective* spending too much money: *She's very* **extravagant** *— she spends all her money on clothes.*

extravagance *noun*

extreme /ik strēm′/ *adjective* the farthest possible: *She lives at the* **extreme** *edge of the forest.*

extremely *adverb* very: *I am* **extremely** *hot.*

°**eye** /ī/ *noun* **1** the part of the head with which you see **2** a small hole at one end of a needle

eyebrow *noun* the hairy line above the eye

eyelash *noun* one of the hairs growing on the part of the eye which shuts

eyelid *noun* either of the pieces of skin which shut over the eye

eyesight *noun (no plural): Her* **eyesight** *is very good; she can see a ship far out in the sea.*

Ff

fable /fā′ bəl/ *noun*
a story which teaches something about good behavior

fabric /fa′ brik/ *noun*
woven material; cloth: *She bought some* **fabric** *to make shirts from.*

°**face**[1] /fās/ *noun*
1 the front part of the head, with the eyes, nose, and mouth
2 the front of other things, such as a **clock face**

°**face**[2] *verb* (*present participle* **facing,** *past* **faced**)
to have the front forward; look at: *Our house* **faces** *the school. I knew he was angry and I could not* **face** *him* (= I wasn't brave enough to meet him).

facilities /fə sil′ ə tēz/ *plural noun*
something for you to use, especially in a public place: *Are there washing* **facilities** *in the school?* (= is there somewhere you can wash, with soap, running water etc.?)

°**fact** /fakt/ *noun*
something that is true; something that has happened: *It is a* **fact** *that you are reading this sentence. I said it was Tuesday, but* **in fact** (= really) *it was Monday.*

°**factory** /fak′ trē *or* fak′ tə rē/ *noun* (*plural* **factories**)
a place where things are made, often by machines

fade /fād/ *verb* (*present participle* **fading,** *past* **faded**)
to lose color or brightness: *If you leave that blue dress in the sun, it will* **fade.**

Fahrenheit /fâr′ ən hīt″/ *noun (no plural)*
a way of measuring temperature (= how hot something is): *Water freezes at* **32 degrees Fahrenheit (32° F).**

°**fail** /fāl/ *verb*
1 not to do well, or not to do what you intend: *He tried to jump the wall, but he* **failed.** *Our crops* **failed** *because there was no rain.*
2 not to pass (an examination): *He* **failed** *his English examination.*
failure /fāl′ yər/ *noun: The* **failure** *of the crops meant that there was no food.*

faint[1] /fānt/ *verb*
to lose the feeling of being awake suddenly and fall down: *She* **fainted** *because of the heat.*

°**faint**[2] *adjective*
not strong; not clear: *a* **faint** *sound of music/a* **faint** *light*

°**fair**[1] /fâr/ *adjective*
1 equally good to everyone; just: *It is not* **fair** *that my brother has a bicycle and I haven't.*
2 good, but not very good: *His writing is good, but his reading is only* **fair.**
3 pale: *English people usually have* **fair** *skin.*
fairly *adjective* a bit but not very: *This bed is* **fairly** *soft.*

fair[2] *noun*
a gathering of people to buy and sell things and to amuse themselves

fairy /fār′ ē/ *noun* (plural **fairies**)
a small imaginary person who can do things that ordinary people cannot do

faith /fāth/ *noun*
belief in something: *I have* **faith** *in you; I am sure you will do well.*
faithfully *adverb: He delivered the newspapers* **faithfully** *even in bad weather.*

°**fall¹** fôl/ verb
(*present tense* **fell** /fel/, *past participle* **fallen** /fôl′ ən/)
to drop to a lower place: *The price of food has* **fallen.** *Rain was* **falling** *steadily. The apples* **fell off** *the tree. The pile of books* **fell over** (= fell to the ground).

°**fall²** *noun*
an act of falling: *The child had a bad* **fall** *and hurt himself. There has been a* **fall** *in the price of food.*

false /fôls/ *adjective*
1 not true: *Is this statement true or* **false?**
2 not real: **false** *teeth*
falsely *adverb*

fame /fām/ *noun (no plural)*
being well known
°**famous** /fām′ əs/ *adjective*
well known: *This town is* **famous** *for its beautiful buildings.*

familiar /fə mil′ yər/ *adjective*
known; often seen or heard; usual: *This song sounds* **familiar.** *Are you* **familiar with** (= do you know) *this type of car?*

°**family** /fam′ lē/ *noun*
(*plural* **families**)
a group of relatives

famine /fam′ in/ *noun*
a time when there is no food

fan¹ /fan/ *noun*
an instrument for moving the air to make us cooler: *The electric* **fan** *made his office cool.*

fan² *verb* (*present participle* **fanning,** *past* **fanned)**
to make the air move: *She* **fanned** *herself with the newspaper to cool her face.*

fancy¹ /fan′ sē/ *adjective* **(fancier, fanciest)**
not usual or plain: **fancy** *clothes*

°**far** /fär/ *adverb, adjective*
(farther /fär′ THər/, **farthest** *or* **further** /fur′ THər/, **furthest)**
1 not near; a long distance away: *How* **far** *is it to town? It isn't* **far away. As far as** *I know* (= what I know), *he has gone to town.*
2 very much: *She is* **far** *better than I at writing.*

fare /fār/ *noun*
an amount of money that you pay for traveling somewhere: *a bus* **fare**/*a taxi* **fare**

°**farm** /färm/ *noun*
buildings and land where people grow food or keep animals
farmer *noun* a person who owns or works on a farm
farming *noun (no plural)* the job of farmers: **Farming** *is difficult when the weather is bad.*
farmyard *noun: Outside the farmhouse is the* **farmyard,** *where the chickens and dogs live.*

fascinate /fas′ ə nāt″/ *verb* (*present participle* **fascinating,** *past* **fascinated)**
to make someone feel very strong interest: *The city* **fascinates** *him.*
fascination *noun* very strong interest: *The city has a* **fascination** *for him.*

fashion /fash′ ən/ *noun*
the way of dressing or doing something that is considered best

at one time: *Is it the* **fashion** *to wear short skirts? Yes, short skirts are* **in fashion.**

fashionable /fash′ ən ə bəl/ *adjective: Short skirts are* **fashionable** *now.*

fashionably *adverb*

°**fast**[1] /fast/ *adjective*

1 quick; not slow: *He is a* **fast** *runner. The clock is (a minute)* **fast** (= it shows a time which is later than the real time).

2 firmly fixed

°**fast**[2] *adverb*

1 quickly: *to run* **fast**

2 firmly; tightly: *The boat stuck* **fast** *in the mud.*

fast[3] *verb*

to eat no food, usually for religious reasons

°**fasten** /fas′ ən/ *verb*

to fix firmly; join or tie together: *She* **fastened** *her coat.*

fastener /fas′ ən ər/ *noun: The* **fastener** *on her skirt broke.*

°**fat**[1] /fat/ *adjective* **(fatter, fattest)**

having a wide, rounded body; not thin: *I think he's too* **fat.**

fatten /fat′ ən/ *verb* to make a person or animal fat

°**fat**[2] *noun (no plural)*

an oily substance, especially the oil that comes from meat when it is cooked: *She skimmed the* **fat** *from the stew.*

fatal /fāt′ əl/ *adjective*

causing death: *a* **fatal** *car accident*

fatally *adverb*

fate /fāt/ *noun (no plural)*

the power which seems to cause everything to happen: *When they met again after ten years, they felt that* **fate** *brought them together.*

°**father** /fä′ THər/ *noun*

a male parent

father-in-law *noun (plural* **fathers-in-law**) the father of your wife or husband

°**fault** /fôlt/ *noun*

something that is wrong; a mistake or weak point: *His greatest* **fault** *is that he talks too much. Who broke the cup? It's my* **fault,** *I dropped it.*

faultless *adjective* having no faults; perfect: **faultless** *work*

°**favor** /fā′ vər/ *noun*

something kind done for somebody: *May I* **ask you a favor?** *Will you* **do me a favor** *and lend me some money? I am* **in favor of** (= I like the idea of) *stopping work now.*

favorable /fāv′ rə bəl/ *adjective* good and suitable: **favorable** *weather for working outside.*

favorite /fāv′ rit/ *adjective* that is liked best of all: *Oranges are my* **favorite** *fruit.*

°**fear**[1] /fēr/ *verb*

to be afraid of: *He did not* **fear** *the snake. I* **fear** (= I am worried) *that you'll be late if you don't go now.*

°**fear**[2] *noun*

the feeling of being afraid: *He was shaking with* **fear.**

fearful *adjective* causing fear; very bad: *a* **fearful** *sound*

fearless *adjective* without fear; never afraid: a **fearless** *soldier*

°**feast**[1] /fēst/ *noun*

a large meal of good food for a special reason

°**feast**[2] *verb*

to eat a feast

°**feather** /feth′ ər/ *noun*
one of the things which cover birds, like a thin stick with soft hairs

feather

feature /fē′ chər/ *noun*
1 any part of the face, especially eyes, nose, and mouth: *Her eyes were her best* **feature.**
2 a part of something that you notice specially: *The unusual chair was a* **feature** *of the room.*

February /feb′ ū er″ ē *or* feb′ roo͞ er″ ē/ *noun*
the second month of the year

federal /fed′ rəl/ *adjective*
having several states or countries joined under one government, but able to look after certain things themselves: *Nigeria is a* **federal** *country.*

federation /fed″ ə rā shən/ *noun: The small countries joined together into a* **federation.**

fee /fē/ *noun*
money charged by a doctor, school, etc.

feeble /fē′ bəl/ *adjective*
weak: *I felt* **feeble** *when I was ill.*

feed /fēd/ *verb* (*present participle* **feeding,** *past* **fed** /fed/)
to give food to: *Have you* **fed** *the animals?*

feel /fēl/ *verb* (*present participle* **feeling,** *past* **felt** /felt/)
1 to touch; know through your senses: *I* **feel** *cold. I* **felt** *the branch touch my face. I* **feel** *afraid.*
2 to think: *I* **feel** *that he doesn't like me.*

feeling *noun* something that is felt: *Her words gave me a* **feeling** *of pleasure, I* **have a feeling** (= I think) *he'll come.*

feet /fēt/ see **foot**

fell /fel/ see **fall**

fellow /fel′ ō/ *noun*
a man: *Who's that old* **fellow?**

female[1] /fē′ māl/ *adjective*
belonging to the sex of women: **Female** *animals give birth to young ones.*

female[2] *noun*
a female person or animal: *We've got three cats — two* **females** *and a male.*

feminine /fem′ ə nin/ *adjective*
like or of a woman

°**fence**[1] /fens/ *noun*
a wooden or wire wall round something: *The* **fence** *kept the dog in the yard.*

fence[2] /fens/ *verb* (*present participle* **fencing,** *past* **fenced)**
to put a fence around something

fern /furn/ *noun*
a green plant that has no flowers and grows in wet or shady places

fern

ferry /fer′ ē/ *noun* (*plural* **ferries)**
a boat that takes people or things across water: *A* **ferry** *crosses the river every hour.*

fertile /fur′ təl/ *adjective*
having good earth for things to grow: *His farm is on* **fertile** *land.*

fertilize /fur′ təl īz/ *verb* (*present participle* **fertilizing,** *past* **fertilized)**
to make fertile: **Fertilizer** *is a substance put on land to* **fertilize** *it.*

festival /fes′ tə vəl/ *noun*
a time when people get together to amuse themselves, dance, sing, etc.

fetch /fech/ *verb*
to go somewhere and bring

something back: *Will you* **fetch** *some water?*

°**fever** /fē′ vər/ *noun*
an illness when you feel hot, have a headache, etc.
feverish *adjective: I felt* **feverish** *all night.*

°**few** /fū/
not many: **Few** *people like snakes. Are your friends here? Yes,* **a few** (= some, but not many) *are here.*

fiber /fī′ bər/ *noun*
a thin thread of plant or animal substance, especially when used to make something: *Coconut* **fiber** *can be made into mats.*

°**field** /fēld/ *noun*
a piece of ground, usually with a fence or wall around it, usually used for farming: *a* **field** *of corn*

°**fierce** /fērs/ *adjective*
wild; angry; cruel: *a* **fierce** *dog/a* **fierce** *storm*
fiercely *adverb*

fifteen /fif tēn′/ *adjective, noun*
the number 15
fifteenth *adjective, noun*
number 15 in order; 15th

fifty /fif′ tē/ *adjective, noun*
the number 50
fiftieth /fif′ tē ith″/ *adjective, noun* number 50 in order; 50th

fig /fig/ *noun*
a fruit which is full of small seeds

°**fight**[1] /fīt/ (*present participle* **fighting,** *past* **fought** /fôt/)
to use your body or weapons against someone or something: *What are the boys* **fighting** *about?*

°**fight**[2] *noun*
an act of fighting: *The two boys had a* **fight.**

°**figure** /fig′ yər/ *noun*
1 a written number like 3 or 8
2 a shape, especially the shape of a human body: *I could see a tall* **figure** *near the door.*

file[1] /fīl/ *noun*
1 a cardboard cover for papers
2 a metal instrument with a rough edge for making things smooth
3 a line of people: *They went into the school* **in single file.**

files

file[2] *verb* (*present participle* **filing,** *past* **filed**)
1 to put papers into a file: *to* **file** *letters*
2 to make something smooth with a file
3 to walk in a line one behind the other: *The children* **filed** *into the classroom.*

°**fill** /fil/ *verb*
to put as much as possible or needed into something: *He* **filled (up)** *the bucket with water. Will you* **fill in** (= put answers in the spaces in) *this printed paper?*
filling *noun: I have a* **filling** (= something put into a hollow part) *in my tooth.*

°**film**[1] /film/ *noun*
1 a story shown in a theater or on television
2 a band put into a camera on which photographs are made
3 a thin covering: *a* **film** *of oil on water*

°**film**[2] *verb*
to photograph something on film; make a film: *The television company is* **filming** *in our town.*

filthy /fil′ thē/ *adjective* **(filthier, filthiest)**
very dirty

fin /fin/ *noun*
a part of a fish which helps it to swim (picture at **fish)**

final /fīn′ əl/ *adjective*
coming at the end; last: *The* **final** *thing she did before she left the house was to lock the door.*
finally *adverb: She* **finally** *agreed with me.*

finance[1] /fi nans′ *or* fī′ nans/ *noun (no plural)*
controlling large sums of money: *People who work in banks know about* **finance.**
financial /fi nan′ shəl/ *adjective: The bank gave him* **financial** *advice.*
financially *adverb*

finance[2] *verb* (*present participle* **financing,** *past* **financed)**
to give the money for something: *The government will* **finance** *the building of the new roads with the taxes it collects.*

°**find** /fīnd/ *verb*
(*present participle* **finding,** *past* **found** /found/)
to see or get something after you have been looking for it: *After looking in every room for my glasses, I* **found** *them in the kitchen, but I* **found** *that* (= I saw that it was true that) *they were broken. I* **found out** (= discovered) *later who had broken them.*

°**fine[1]** /fīn/ *adjective*
1 nice; pleasant; very good: *a* **fine** *piece of work*/**fine** *weather*
2 very thin: **fine** *lines*

fine[2] *noun*
money paid as a punishment: *to pay a* **fine** *of one hundred dollars*

fine[3] *verb* (*present participle* **fining,** *past* **fined)**
to make someone pay a fine: *The man was* **fined** *one hundred dollars.*

°**finger** /fing′ gər/ *noun*
one of the five long parts of your hand

°**finish** /fin′ ish/ *verb*
to end: *The game* **finished** *at four o'clock. Have you* **finished (doing)** *your work? You can use the scissors when I've* **finished with** *them* (= finished using them).

°**fire** /fīr/ *noun*
things that are burning: *He* **set fire to** (= made burn) *the dry grass. The grass* **caught fire.** *The grass was* **on fire** *for a short time. A* **fireplace** *is an area in a house where you can light fires.*
fire-brigade *noun: The men who fight fires are called* **firemen,** *and a group of them who work together is called a* **fire company.**
firework *noun* a cardboard tube filled with powder, which burns with bright lights or a loud noise

°**firm[1]** /furm/ *adjective*
fixed and steady: *You must always build on* **firm** *ground. The teacher was* **firm** *and did not change her mind.*
firmly *adverb: She told him* **firmly** *that he must sit down and wait his turn* (= in a way he could not argue with).

°**firm[2]** *noun*
a group of people running a business; company

°**first** /furst/
1 coming before all others; earliest: *The* **first** *boy who came in was James.* **First** *we'll have breakfast,*

then we'll walk to school.
2 (used in some phrases): **At first** *it was very hot, but then it got cooler.* **First of all** (= before everything else) *tell us your name.*

first aid /furst' ād'/ *noun* *(no plural)*
simple help that anyone can learn to give an ill or wounded person

°**fish¹** /fish/ *noun* (*plural* **fish** *or* **fishes**)
a cold-blooded animal that lives in water: *A person who catches* **fish** *is a fisherman* /fish' ər mən/.

fish² *verb*
to try to catch fish: *They are* **fishing** *in the river.*
fishing *noun (no plural)* catching fish: *They went* **fishing** *yesterday.*

fist /fist/ *noun*
the hand with fingers closed tightly together: *He hit me with his* **fist.**

°**fit¹** /fit/ *adjective*
1 not ill; well; *Do you feel* **fit?**
2 good enough: *This food is not* **fit for** *your visitors.*

°**fit²** *verb* (*present participle* **fitting,** *past* **fitted**)
to be the right size for: *The trousers don't* **fit** *him, they are too small.*

five /fīv/ *adjective, noun*
the number 5
fifth /fifth/ *adjective, noun* number 5 in order: 5th

°**fix** /fiks/ *verb*
1 to put in place firmly: *He* **fixed** *a picture to the wall.*
2 to mend: *I asked the boy to* **fix** *the bicycle.*
3 to arrange: *We have* **fixed** *a date for the school dance.*

fizzy /fiz' ē/ *adjective* **(fizzier, fizziest)**
(of a drink) having carbonation in it

°**flag** /flag/ *noun*
a piece of cloth with a special pattern on it, used as the sign of a country, club, etc.

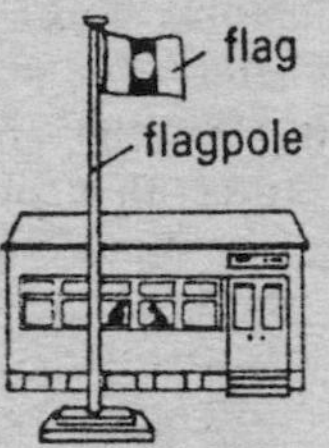

flagpole *noun* a tall pole at the top of which a flag is hung

flake /flāk/ *noun*
a small thin piece: *We watched the* **flakes** *of snow fall.*

°**flame** /flām/ *noun*
a bright piece of burning gas that you see in a fire: *The house was in* **flames** (= burning).

flap¹ /flap/ *verb* (*present participle* **flapping,** *past* **flapped**)
to wave up and down: *The bird* **flapped** *its wings.*

flap² *noun*
a piece of something which hangs down over an opening: *a* **flap** *on a pocket*

°**flash¹** /flash/ *noun*
a sharp sudden light: *a* **flash** *of lightning*

°**flash²** *verb*
to shine for a moment; move quickly: *He* **flashed** *the light in my eyes. The cars* **flashed past** (= went past quickly).

flask /flask/ *noun*
a sort of bottle: *A* **vacuum flask** *(thermos) keeps cool drinks cool and hot drinks hot.*

°**flat¹** /flat/ *adjective*
not hilly or sloping; with no pieces sticking out: *That building has a*

flat roof. The car tires were **flat** (= had no air in them).

flatten /flat′ ən/ *verb* to make something flat: *The rain* **flattened** *the corn.*

flatter /flat′ ər/ *verb*
to say that someone is better, nicer, etc. than she really is: *She only* **flatters** *you so you will help her.*

flattery /flat′ ar ē/ *noun (no plural)*

flavor /flā′ vər/ *noun*
a taste: *This cake has an unusual* **flavor.**

flea /flē/ *noun*
a very small jumping insect that drinks blood from animals and people

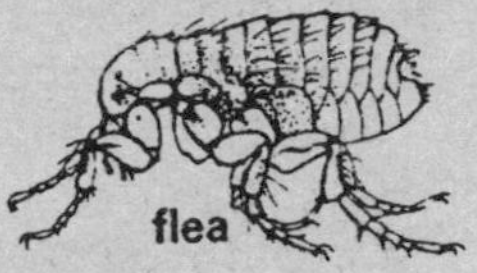

flea

flee /flē/ *verb* (*present participle* **fleeing,** *past* **fled**)
to run away: *The cat* **fled** *from the dog.*

fleece /flēs/ *noun*
the wool of a sheep or goat

fleet /flēt/ *noun*
a lot of ships together, especially warships: *a* **fleet** *of fishing boats*

flesh /flesh/ *noun (no plural)*
the soft part of the body; meat: *The knife cut the* **flesh** *of his arm.*

flew /flo͞o/ see **fly**[1]

flight /flīt/ *noun*
flying: *The airplane* **flight** *took three hours. They saw the birds* **in flight.**

°**float** /flōt/ *verb*
to stay on the surface of a liquid; not to sink: *A boat* **floats** *on water.*

flock /flok/ *noun*
a number of sheep, goats, birds, etc. together: *a* **flock** *of sheep*

°**flood**[1] /flud/ *noun*
a great quantity of water staying in places that are usually dry: *The* **floods** *swept away many homes.*

°**flood**[2] *verb*
to cover with water: *The river rose and* **flooded** *the fields.*

°**floor** /flôr/ *noun*
1 the part of a room you walk on: *a wooden* **floor**
2 all the rooms on one level: *We live on the third* **floor.**

°**flour** /flou′ ər/ *noun (no plural)*
fine powder made from wheat, or sometimes from other grain: *Bread is made from* **flour.**

flourish /flur′ ish/ *verb*
1 to grow well: *Plants* **flourish** *in this earth.*
2 to wave about

°**flow**[1] /flō/ *verb*
(of liquids or gases) to move: *The water* **flowed** *down the hill.*

°**flow**[2] *noun (no plural)*
a flowing movement: *The* **flow** *of air was stopped when she closed the window.*

°**flower**[1] /flou′ ər/ *noun*
the part of a plant which holds the seeds and which is usually brightly colored

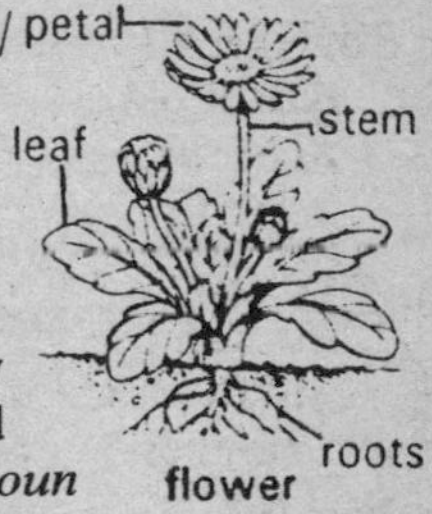

petal
stem
leaf
roots
flower

flower bed *noun* an area of earth with flowers planted in it

flown /flōn/ see **fly**[1]

flu /flo͞o/ see **influenza**

fluent /flo͞o′ ent/ *adjective*
speaking a language smoothly and

easily: *He speaks* **fluent** *German.*
fluently *adverb*

fluff /fluf/ *noun (no plural)*
soft fine bits that come off animals, wool, etc.

fluid¹ /flo͞o′ id/ *noun*
something that flows: a liquid

fluid² *adjective*
liquid; not solid; able to flow

flute /flo͞ot/ *noun*
a musical instrument which you blow

flute

°**fly¹** /flī/ *verb (present participle* **flying,** *past tense* **flew** /flo͞o/, *past participle* **flown** /flōn/)
1 to move through the air: *Birds were* **flying** *above the houses. The plane* **flew** *from Paris to Rome.*
2 to go quickly: *She* **flew** (= ran) *out of the house.*

fly² *noun (plural* **flies**)
a small flying insect

foal /fōl/ *noun*
a baby horse

foam /fōm/ *noun (no plural)*
the white substance which we sometimes see on top of water: *We see* **foam** *on water with a lot of soap in it.*

fog /fog/ *noun (no plural)*
thick cloud that forms close to the ground: *The* **fog** *was so thick that I could not see my way.*
foggy *adjective* **(foggier, foggiest):** *a* **foggy** *night*

°**fold¹** /fōld/ *verb*
to turn part of something over the other part: *She* **folded** *the letter so that it would fit into her bag.*
folder *noun* a cardboard cover for papers, etc.

°**fold²** *noun*
a part of something which has been folded over another part

folk /fok/ *noun (no plural)*
people: *The old* **folk** *sat and talked.*

°**follow** /fol′ ō/ *verb*
to go after: *The children* **followed** *their mother into the room. We* **followed** (= went along) *the road to the top of the hill. He didn't* **follow** (= understand) *what the teacher was saying.*

fond /fond/ *adjective*
loving: *She has* **fond** *parents. I am not* **fond of** (= I do not like) *eating meat.*

°**food** /fo͞od/ *noun (no plural)*
what you eat: *Is there enough* **food** *for everyone?*

fool¹ /fo͞ol/ *noun*
someone silly: *I'm a* **fool;** *I left my coat on the train.*
foolish *adjective* not reasonable; silly
foolishly *adverb*

fool² *verb*
to trick or deceive: *He* **fooled** *me into giving him money. Don't* **fool around** (= behave like a fool).

foot /fo͝ot/ *noun (plural* **feet** /fēt/)
1 the part of your leg that you stand on: *We decided to go* **on foot** (= walking).
2 the bottom of something: *the* **foot** *of a hill*
3 a measure of length equal to twelve inches: *The man was six* **foot/feet** *two (inches).*
football *noun* a game in which two teams try to score points against each other in a period of time.
footpath *noun: This is a*

footpath; *cars are not allowed.*
footprint *noun* the mark of a foot: *He left* **footprints** *behind him on the sand.*
footstep *noun* the sound of someone walking: *I heard* **footsteps** *in the room behind me.*

°**for** /fôr/ *preposition*
1 meant to be used in this way: *This knife is* **for** *cutting bread.*
2 meant to be given to or used by: *This book is* **for** *you — you can keep it.*
3 (showing how far or how long): *She has lived in this town* **for** *many years. I waited* **for** *three hours.*
4 going to: *The train* **for** *New York*
5 at a price of: *She bought the dress* **for** *one hundred dollars.*
6 as a sign of; with the meaning of: *What is the word* **for** *"tree" in your language?*
7 (used in sentences like these): *He worked* **for** *peace when he was in the government. It is hard* **for** *me to understand this work.*
for example, for instance showing an example of what is meant: *You can buy fruit here — oranges and bananas,* **for example.**

forbid /fər bid'/ *verb* (*present participle* **forbidding,** *past tense* **forbade** /fər bād'/, *past participle* **forbidden)**
to say no to something that someone wants to do: *I* **forbid** *you to go swimming.*

°**force**[1] /fôrs/ *verb* (*present participle* **forcing,** *past* **forced)**
to make happen, using strength: *She* **forced** *her daughter to go to school. Don't* **force** *the door* (= make it open using strength).

°**force**[2] *noun*
1 *(no plural)* strength: *You must use* **force** *to open that bottle.*
2 a group of specially trained people like the army, etc.: *He joined the* **police force.**

ford /fôrd/ *noun*
a place where you can walk across a river

forecast /fôr' kast"/ *noun*
saying what you think will happen: *a weather* **forecast**

°**forehead** /fôr' əd *or* fôr' hed"/ *noun*
the front of the head above the eyes, where no hair grows

°**foreign** /fôr ən/ *adjective*
of or from another country: *a* **foreign** *language*
foreigner *noun: He is not from this country, he is a* **foreigner.**

foreman /fôr' mən/ *noun*
a man who controls a group of workmen

°**forest** /fôr' ist/ *noun*
an area where a lot of trees grow thickly together

forever /fôr ev' ər/ *adverb*
always; for all time; continually: *I shall remember that happy day* **forever.**

forge /fôrj/ *verb* (*present participle* **forging,** *past* **forged)**
to make a copy of something in order to deceive: *He was sent to prison for* **forging** *money.*
forgery /fôr' jər ē/ *noun* (*plural* **forgeries)** making copies in order to deceive; a copy made like this: *This letter is a* **forgery!**

°**forget** /fər get'/ *verb* (*present participle* **forgetting,** *past tense* **forgot** /fər got'/, *past participle* **forgotton** /fər got' ən/)

not to have a memory of; not to remember: *She* **forgot** *to mail the letter.*

°**forgive** /fər giv′/ *verb* (*present participle* **forgiving,** *past tense* **forgave** /fər gāv/, *past participle* **forgiven)**
to stop being angry with someone: *Please* **forgive** *me — I didn't mean to be rude.*

°**fork¹** /fôrk/ *noun*
1 an instrument with a handle and two or more points at the end: *We use a* **fork** *to eat food. A big* **fork** *is used to dig the earth.*
2 the place where something divides into two: *When you get to the* **fork** *in the road, go right.*

forks

fork² *verb*
to divide into two: *The road* **forks** *soon after the bridge.*

°**form¹** /fôrm/ *noun*
1 a shape: *a candy in the* **form** *of an egg*
2 a piece of printed paper on which you have to write things: *If you fill in this* **form,** *you can take books out of the library.*

°**form²** *verb*
to make: *We* **formed** *a club for people who liked cars.*
formation *noun* making: *the* **formation** *of a club*

formal /fôr′ məl/ *adjective*
obeying the firm laws and customs of your people in every way: *a* **formal** *meeting with the leader of the government* **formally** *adverb*

former /fôr′ mər/ *adjective*
1 the first of two: *There are Jane and Anne; the* **former** (Jane) *is wearing a green dress.*
2 earlier in time: *The owner of that shop is Mr. Johnson — the* **former** *owner was Mrs. Brown.*
formerly *adverb: The shop was* **formerly** *owned by a woman.*

formula /fôr′ myə lə/ *noun* (*plural* **formulas)**
a list of substances used to make something: *This plastic is made from a new* **formula.**

fort /fôrt/ *noun*
a strong place which can protect the people inside from attack
fortress /fôr′ tris/ *noun* a large fort

fortune /fôr′ chən/ *noun*
1 *(no plural)* luck or chance: *It was his good* **fortune** *to be chosen to play for the school.*
2 a very large amount of money: *He made a* **fortune** *by selling houses.*
fortunate /fôr′ chə nit/ *adjective* lucky: *You are very* **fortunate** *to have so many kind relatives.*
fortunately *adverb: You have a headache? Well,* **fortunately** *I have some medicine with me.*

forty /fôr′ tē/ *adjective, noun*
the number 40
fortieth /fôr′ tē ith/ *adjective, noun* number 40 in order; 40th

°**forward** /fôr′ wərd/ *adverb*
toward the front; away from the back: *When the lights were green, the cars moved* **forward.** *She is* **looking forward to** (= thinking about with pleasure) *seeing you.*

fought /fôt/ see **fight**

foul /foul/ *adjective*
unpleasant or dirty: *a* **foul** *smell/* **foul** *weather*

found¹ /found/ see **find**

found² *verb*
to start: *He* **founded** *the school in 1954.*
foundation *noun*
foundations *plural noun* the parts of a building under the ground

fountain
fount' ən/
noun
water thrown high into the air from a pipe

fountain

four /fôr/ *adjective, noun*
the number 4: *I have* **four** *brothers.*
fourth *adjective, noun* number 4 in order; 4th

fourteen /fôr' tēn/ *adjective, noun*
the number 14
fourteenth *adjective, noun* number 14 in order; 14th

fowl /foul/ *noun*
a bird, usually one that is kept for food: *Chickens and ducks are two types of* **fowl.**

fox /foks/ *noun* (*plural* **foxes**)
a wild animal like a dog, with a thick tail

fraction /frak' shən/ *noun*
a part, especially a small part: *A half* (½) *is a* **fraction** *of one* (1).

fracture¹ /frak' chər/ *verb* (*present participle* **fracturing,** *past* **fractured**)
to break: *His leg was* **fractured** *in an accident.*

fracture² *noun*
a break

fragment /frag' mənt/ *noun*
a piece broken off from something: *a* **fragment** *of glass*

frail /frāl/ *adjective*
weak: *He is* **frail** *after his illness.*

°**frame¹** /frām/
noun
1 the bars around which a building, car, etc. is made: *a building with a steel* **frame**
2 a piece of wood or metal around a picture

picture frame

door frame

frame² *verb* (*present participle* **framing,** *past* **framed**)
to put a frame around

°**free¹** /frē/ *adjective*
1 able to do what you like; not shut up or in prison: *You are* **free** *to go where you want.*
2 not working: *Are you* **free** *this evening?*
3 not costing any money
freedom *noun (no plural): The children enjoyed the* **freedom** *of the school holidays.*
freely *adverb: You can speak* **freely** (= say what you want to say) *here.*

°**free²** *verb* (*past* **freed**)
to make someone or something free: *They* **freed** *the birds from the cages.*

freeze /frēz/ *verb* (*present participle* **freezing,** *past tense* **froze** /frōz/, *past participle* **frozen**)
to change from a liquid into a solid: *When water* **freezes** *it becomes ice.*
freezer *noun* a machine that keeps food very cold, so that it keeps fresh for a long time: *We keep* **frozen** *food in a* **freezer.**

°**frequent** /frē' kwent/ *adjective*
happening often: *I enjoyed his*

frequent *visits.*
frequently *adverb*

°**fresh** /fresh/ *adjective*
1 picked, killed, etc. a short time ago: *These vegetables are* **fresh;** *I picked them this morning.*
2 new: *Use a* **fresh** *page.*
3 pleasantly cool: *The air smelled* **fresh** *after the rain.*

°**Friday** /frī′ dā/ *noun*
the sixth day of the week

°**friend** /frend/ *noun*
a person you like and feel you can trust: *He is my* **friend.** We are **friends.** *Peter is Jane's* **boyfriend** (= special male friend) — *Jane is Peter's* **girlfriend.**
friendly *adjective: He is* **friendly** (= kind and helpful) *to us all.*
friendship *noun* being friends: *The boys have had a long* **friendship.**

fright /frīt/ *noun*
being frightened: *His face showed* **fright** *when he saw the accident.*

frighten /frīt′ ən/ *verb*
to make someone afraid: *He was* **frightened** *by the fierce dog.*

fringe /frinj/ *noun*
1 threads, hair, etc. hanging down in a straight line: *a* **fringe** *around the edge of a bed cover*
2 edge: *on the* **fringe** *of the*

frog /frog/ *noun*
a small jumping animal that can live in water or on land

°**from** /frəm *or* from/ *preposition*
1 starting at: *The train goes* **from** *Paris to Rome.*
2 given or sent by: *This letter is* **from** *my uncle.*
3 out of; away: *books* **from** *the library*
4 using: *Bread is made* **from** *flour.*
5 because of: *She was nearly crying* **from** *the pain of her cut leg.*

°**front** /frunt/ *noun, adjective*
the side opposite the back; the forward part: *My sister is waiting* **in front of** *the school. I went out by the* **front** *door.*

frontier /fron′ tēr′/ *noun*
the dividing line between two countries

frost /frôst/ *noun (no plural)*
frozen water that stays on every outdoor surface in cold weather: *The trees were white with* **frost.**

frown[1] /froun/ *verb*
to draw the eyebrows (= hairy lines above the eyes) down over the nose, as you do when you are angry or thinking: *He* **frowned** *as he tried to work out the math problem.*

frown[2] *noun*
a frowning expression

froze /frōz/ see **freeze**

°**fruit** /fro͞ot/ *noun* (*plural* **fruit**)
the part of a plant which carries the seeds; it is often sweet and good to eat: *Would you like some* **fruit** *— an apple or an orange?*

fry /frī/ *verb* (*present participle* **frying,** *past* **fried**)
to cook in hot oil over a fire: *She* **fried** *the eggs in a* **frying pan.**

fuel /fūl/ *noun*
a substance that burns to give heat, light, etc.: *Gas and coal are* **fuels.**

fulfil /fəl fil′/ *verb* (*present participle* **fulfilling,** *past* **fulfilled**)
to do what you have promised or

are expected to do: *He has* **fulfilled** *the orders that I gave him.*

°**full** /fůl/ *adjective*
having as much as it will hold: *The cup is* **full** — *it is* **full of** *milk.*
fully *adverb*

full stop /fůl′ stop′/

°**fun** /fun/ *noun (no plural)*
amusement: *The children had great* **fun** *playing by the river.*

function[1] /fungk′ shən/ *noun*
how something works; what something does: *The* **function** *of a clock is to show you the time.*

function[2] *verb*
to work: *This machine isn't* **functioning** *well.*

fund /fund/ *noun*
an amount of money collected for something special: *a* **fund** *to help poor children*

funeral /fūn′ rəl *or* fū′ nər əl/ *noun*
the ceremony held when someone dies

fungus /fung′ gəs/ *noun*
(*plural* **fungi** /fun′ gī *or* fun′ jī/ *or* **funguses**)
a plant which has no leaves or flowers

funnel /fun′ əl/ *noun*
1 a tube wide at the top and narrow at the bottom, used for pouring things into a narrow opening: *He poured the gasoline into the car through a* **funnel.**
2 a pipe to take smoke from a ship or engine.

°**funny** /fun′ ē/ *adjective* **(funnier, funniest)**
1 making you laugh; amusing: *a* **funny** *joke*
2 strange; unusual: *I had a* **funny** *feeling that you would come. What's that* **funny** *smell?*

fur /fur/ *noun (no plural)*
the soft hair on some animals: *Cats have* **fur.**

furious /fūr′ ē əs/ *adjective*
very angry: *I was* **furious** *when he crashed my car.*

furnace /fur′ nəs/ *noun*
a large covered fire in which metals are melted, or which makes heat for a home.

furnish /fur′ nish/ *verb*
to put furniture in: *She rents a* **furnished** *apartment* (= with furniture in it). *to* **furnish** *a house*

°**furniture** /fur′ ni chər/ *noun (no plural)*
things used in a house, like beds, tables, and chairs

°**further** /fur′ THər/, **furthest** see **far**

fuss[1] /fus/ *noun*
a worried and excited state: *My parents always* **make a fuss** *if I stay out late.*

fuss[2] *verb*
to behave in an unnecessary, worried or excited way: *Don't* **fuss** *over the children, they can take care of themselves.*
fussy *adjective* **(fussier, fussiest):** *I am not* **fussy** *about what I eat* (= I don't mind what I eat).

°**future**[1] /fū′ chər/ *noun (no plural)*
time that will come; things that have not happened yet: *He has a good* **future** *with that company; it is doing well.* **In the future,** *please write your name clearly.*

°**future**[2] *noun, adjective*
talking about an action that will happen later: *The sentence "We will see them tomorrow" has the verb in the* **future.** Look at **tense.**

Gg

°**gain** /gān/ *verb*
to win or get: *The team* **gained** *100 yards in the first half.*

gale /gāl/ *noun*
a very strong wind

gallery /gal′ rē *or* gal′ ə rē/ *noun* (*plural* **galleries**)
a building or a large long room where you can see pictures on the walls, or other artistic things: *Let's visit the art* **gallery.**

gallon /gal′ ən/ *noun*
a measure of liquid equal to 8 pints

gallop[1] /gal′ əp/ *verb*
to run very fast: *The horse* **galloped** *across the plains.*

gallop[2] *noun*
galloping: *He set off at a* **gallop.**

gamble /gam′ bəl/ *verb (present participle* **gambling,** *past* **gambled)**
to try and win money on games, races, etc.: *He is a* **gambler.** *He spends all his money on* **gambling.**

°**game**[1] /gām/ *noun*
something you play, with rules that tell you what to do: *Football is a team* **game.** *a* **game** *of cards*

game[2] *noun (no plural)*
wild animals or birds which people hunt: *Animals like lions are called* **big game.**

gang[1] /gang/ *noun*
a group of people: *a* **gang** *of young men (*= a group of friends)/*a* **gang** *of criminals*

gang[2] *verb*
to form a gang: *The older children* **ganged up** *against the younger ones.*

garage /gə räzh′/ *noun*
a place where cars, buses, etc. are kept or repaired

garden[1] /gärd′ ən/ *noun*
a place where trees, flowers, or vegetables are grown, near a house or in a public place

garden[2] *verb*
to work in a garden: *He enjoys* **gardening.**
gardener *noun*

°**garment** /gär′ mənt/ *noun*
a piece of clothing: *Why did you leave these* **garments** *on the floor?*

°**gas** /gas/ *noun*
1 any substance like air; not liquid or solid: *The air we breathe is made chiefly of two* **gases.**
2 *(no plural)* a short word for gasoline

gasp[1] /gasp/ *verb*
to take in a breath quickly: *I* **gasped** *as I jumped into the cold river.*

gasp[2] *noun*
the sound of gasping: *a* **gasp** *of surprise*

°**gate** /gāt/ *noun*
a sort of door which closes an opening in a wall or fence: *The school has iron* **gates** *between the yard and the road.*

gates

°**gather** /gaTH′ ər/ *verb*
1 to bring together: *She* **gathered up** *her books and left.*
2 to know from something that has been said: *I* **gather** *that you like football.*

gathering *noun* a lot of people together in one place: *There was a large* **gathering** *(of people) at the ceremony.*

gauge[1] /gāj/ *verb (present participle* **gauging,** *past* **gauged)**
to measure: *I tried to* **gauge** *how many people were there.*

gauge[2] *noun*
something that measures: *A* **gas gauge** *shows the amount of gas left in a car.*

gave /gāv/ *see* **give**

gay /gā/ *adjective*
happy and cheerful: *It was a* **gay** *picture, with lots of color in it.*

gaze /gāz/ *verb (present participle* **gazing,** *past* **gazed)**
to look steadily: *The child* **gazed** *at the toys in the shop window.*

gear /gēr/ *noun*
a set of wheels with teeth in an engine. They work together to make the wheels of a car go faster or more slowly: *The truck driver* **changed gears** *to go up the hill.*

geese /gēs/ *see* **goose**

gem /jem/ *noun*
any sort of stone which is worth a lot of money and is used as an ornament

°**general**[1] /jen′ ral *or* jen′ ər əl/ *adjective*
about, for, or by everyone or everything: *Today is a* **general** *holiday. I like games* **in general** (= most or all games), *and especially football.*

generally *adverb: It is* **generally** *(= usually) hot in summer.*

general[2] *noun*
a very important officer in the army

generate /jen′ ə rāt″/ *verb (present participle* **generating,** *past* **generated)**
to make: *When coal burns, it* **generates** *heat.*

generator *noun* a machine that makes electricity

generation /jen″ ə rā′ shən/ *noun*
the people born at a certain time: *My parents and I belong to different* **generations.**

°**generous** /jen′ rəs *or* jen′ ər əs/ *adjective*
giving what you can: *He is very* **generous** *— he often buys things for other people.*

generosity /jen″ ə ros′ ə tē/ *noun (no plural): He was famous for his* **generosity.**

genius /jēn′ yəs/ *noun*
someone who is much cleverer than anyone else

°**gentle** /jent′ əl/ *adjective*
not rough; quiet and kind: *a* **gentle** *kiss/a* **gentle** *wind*

gently *adverb: You must hold the baby* **gently.**

gentleman /jent′ əl man/ *noun* (*plural* **gentlemen** /-mən/ *)*
1 a kind, polite man
2 a polite word for a man: *When he made a speech, he began by saying "Ladies and* **gentlemen"**.

genuine /jen′ ū in/ *adjective*
real and true: *This ring is* **genuine** *gold.*

genuinely *adverb* truly: *She was* **genuinely** *frightened by the storm.*

geography /jē og′ rə fē/ *noun (no plural)*
the study of the earth and the people who live on it: *In our* **geography** *class, we are learning*

about rivers.

geology /jē ol′ ə je/ *noun (no plural)*
the study of rocks, and how they were made

geometry /jē om′ ə trē/ *noun (no plural)*
the study of measuring shapes, lines, etc.

germ /jurm/ *noun*
a very small piece of living substance that can grow in animals or people, often giving them an illness

germinate /jur′ mə nāt″/ *verb (present participle* **germinating,** *past* **germinated)**
(of plants) to start to grow: *Seeds will not* **germinate** without water.

germination

germination *noun (no plural)*

gesture¹ /jes′ chər/ *noun*
a movement of the hands, head, etc. made to express something

gesture² *verb (present participle* **gesturing,** *past* **gestured)**
to make a gesture: *He* **gestured** *angrily at me.*

°**get** /get/ *verb (present participle* **getting,** *past* **got** /got/ *)*
1 to take, have, or buy: *I* **got** *a letter from Maria this morning. I must* **get** *some fruit in the market. I* **have got** *a dog.*
2 to become: *I* **got** *angry with him.*
3 to make be or happen: *He* **got** *the shirt clean in hot water. He is still asleep, he hasn't* **gotten up** (= got out of bed) *yet.*
4 to arrive: *When we* **got to** *the station, the train was waiting.*
5 must: *I* **have got to** *see him today.*

ghost /gōst/ *noun*
the form of a dead person which a living person thinks he sees
ghostly *adjective* frightening, as if there were ghosts

giant¹ /jī′ ənt/ *noun*
a very, very large person, usually only talked about in stories

giant² *adjective*
very large: *a* **giant** *snake*

giddy /gid′ ē/ *adjective* **(giddier, giddiest)**
having a turning feeling in the head: *She felt* **giddy** *when she looked down from the high bridge.*

gift /gift/ *noun*
something given; a present

gigantic /jī gan′ tik/ *adjective*
very, very big: *The new airplane looked like a* **gigantic** *bird.*

giggle /gig′ əl/ *verb (present participle* **giggling,** *past* **giggled)**
to laugh in a silly way: *The girls were* **giggling** *in class.*

gills /gilz/ *plural noun*
part of a fish, near its head, through which it breathes (picture at **fish)**

ginger /jin′ jər/ *noun*
1 a plant with stems under the ground
2 a powder made from these stems which gives food a hot taste

giraffe /jə raf′/ *noun (plural* **giraffe** *or* **giraffes)**
a tall African animal with a very long neck and very long legs and large brown spots on its coat

°**girl** /gurl/ *noun*
a female child: *She has two children, a* **girl** *and a boy.*

°**give** /giv/ *verb (present participle* **giving,** *past tense* **gave** /gāv/ *past participle* **given** /giv′ ən/)
1 to let someone have: *Have you* **given** *him your telephone number? The supermarket is* **giving away** (= letting people have for no money) *a box of sugar to everyone who comes today.*
2 to bring a feeling to: *The child* **gave** *his parents much worry.*
3 to stop: *I have* **given up** *smoking cigarettes. I can't guess the answer to your question, I* **give in** (= I have stopped trying to guess). *The criminal* **gave himself up** (= stopped trying to run away from the police).

°**glad** /glad/ *adjective*
happy: *I am* **glad** *to see you.*
gladly *adverb* willingly: *He* **gladly** *lent me the money.*

glance¹ /glans/ *verb (present participle* **glancing,** *past* **glanced)**
to look quickly: *She* **glanced** *along the road to see if he was coming.*

glance² *noun*
looking quickly: *She saw* **at a glance** *that he was coming.*

glare¹ /glâr/ *verb (present participle* **glaring,** *past* **glared)**
1 to shine with an unpleasantly bright light: *The sun* **glared** *down.*
2 to look hard and unpleasantly: *She* **glared** *at me.*

glare² *noun*
unpleasant brightness: *The* **glare** *of the sun made her eyes hurt.*

°**glass** /glas/ *noun*
1 *(no plural)* a clear hard substance used for windows
2 (*plural* **glasses**) a cup made of **glass,** without a handle

glasses /glas′ əs/ *plural noun* specially shaped pieces of glass or plastic which help people to see better, held on the nose by a frame

glasses

gleam /glēm/ *verb*
to shine faintly: *The moonlight* **gleamed** *on the river.*
gleam *noun*

glide /glīd/ *verb (present participle* **gliding,** *past* **glided)**
to move very smoothly
glider *noun* an airplane without an engine (picture at **aircraft**)

glimpse¹ /glimps/ *noun*
a very quick sight: *I just* **caught a glimpse** *of the plane as it flew over.*

glimpse² *verb (present participle* **glimpsing,** *past* **glimpsed)**
to see very quickly: *He* **glimpsed** *his friend in the crowd.*

glitter /glit′ ər/ *verb*
to shine with a light that flashes: *The sea* **glittered** *in the sun.*
glitter *noun*

globe /glōb/ *noun*
1 a ball representing the earth, with all the countries, seas, etc. marked on it
2 anything round like a ball

gloom /glo͞om/ *noun*
1 darkness: *In the* **gloom** *of the thick forest, he nearly lost his way.*
2 a feeling of sadness: *He was deep in* **gloom** *because his girlfriend had gone away.*
gloomy *adjective* **(gloomier, gloomiest):** *a* **gloomy** *day/a* **gloomy** *expression on his face*

glory /glôr′ ē/ *noun (no plural)*
fame and respect that is given to someone who has done something great

glorious /glôr′ ē əs/ *adjective: Isn't it a* **glorious** (= very beautiful) *day?*

glove /gluv/ *noun* one of a pair of coverings for the hands

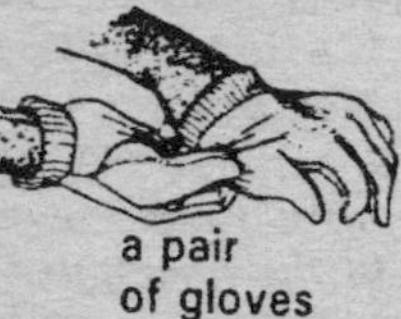
a pair of gloves

glow¹ /glō/ *verb* to shine with a warm-looking light: *The dying fire* **glowed** *in the dark.*

glow² *noun* a warm shine: *the* **glow** *of a sunset*

glue¹ /glo͞o/ *noun (no plural)* a substance used for sticking things together: *She stuck the handle onto the cup with* **glue.**

glue² *verb (present participle* **glueing** or **gluing,** *past* **glued)** to stick with glue: *She* **glued** *the handle onto the cup.*

gnaw /nô/ *verb* to bite something until it is worn away: *The rat* **gnawed** *a hole in the wooden box.*

°**go¹** /gō/ *verb (present participle* **going** /gō′ ing/, *past tense* **went** /went/, *past participle* **gone** /gôn/*)* to move: *Are you* **going** *to school today? The food* **goes** (= has a special place) *in the pantry. Please* **go on** (= continue) *reading. They* **went out** *to a party. When a light or a fire* **goes out,** *it stops shining or burning. I* **am going to** *wear* (= will wear) *the blue dress tomorrow. Will you* **go through** *this work* (= look at it) *and make sure there are no mistakes?*

go² *noun* a try: Can I **have a go** *at fixing the bicycle?*

goal /gōl/ *noun*
1 a place to which you try to hit or kick the ball in games like soccer: *The* **goalkeeper** *is the player who guards the* **goal.**
2 a point won when the ball goes to that place: *to score a* **goal**

°**goat** /gōt/ *noun* an animal like a sheep that is kept for milk and for its hairy coat

goat

god /god/ *noun* a being to whom people pray, and who is believed to control the world
goddess *noun* a female god

°**gold** /gōld/ *noun (no plural)*
1 a yellow metal that costs a lot of money: *She wore a* **gold** *ring.*
2 the color of this metal
golden *adjective* like or made of gold: *a* **golden** *sky*

golf /golf/ *noun (no plural)* a game in which a small ball is hit into a number of holes arranged on a large piece of land called a **golf course**

gong /gong/ *noun* a flat piece of metal that is hung up and hit with a stick to make a noise

°**good¹** /go͝od/ *adjective* **(better** /bet′ ər/, **best** /best/ *)*
1 not wrong or bad; right: *He is a* **good** *man — he always tries to do what is right.*
2 suitable; useful: *This material is quite* **good,** *but that one is* **better.** *Fruit is* **good for** *you.*
3 well behaved: *Children, be* **good!**
4 nice; pleasant: *We had a* **good** *time at the party.*
5 (used in greeting people): **Good morning,** *doctor!* **Good night,**

children, sleep well! I must go now — **goodbye!**

°**good**[2] *noun (no plural)*
what is right or useful: *We should try to do* **good** *to other people* (= help them).
goodness *noun (no plural)* **1** being good, especially for the health: *There is a lot of* **goodness** *in milk.* **2** (to show surprise): **Goodness!** *It's late. I must go!*
goods *plural noun* things which are bought, sold, or owned: *What* **goods** *does your shop sell?*

goose /gōōs/
(plural **geese** /gēs/*)*
a large strong bird that can swim on water

gorgeous /gôr' jəs/ *adjective*
very nice or beautiful: *a* **gorgeous** *dress*

gorilla /gə ril' ə/ *noun*
a very large, strong animal, like a monkey, that is the largest ape

gossip[1] /gos' ip/ *noun*
1 *(no plural)* talk about people, often unkind: *You shouldn't listen to* **gossip.**
2 a person who talks like this

gossip[1] *verb*
to talk gossip: *They sat and* **gossiped** *all evening.*

got /got/ *see* **get**

gourd /gôrd/ *noun*
a large fruit, or its hard shell which is used as a container

°**govern** /guv' ərn/ *verb*
to be in control of: *A lot of people help to* **govern** *a country.*
government /guv' ər mənt *or* guv' ərn mənt/ *noun*
the people who control what happens in a country
governor *noun* a person who controls a country or state

gown /goun/ *noun*
1 a long dress for a woman: *a beautiful silk* **gown**
2 a loose, long piece of clothing worn by special people: *The doctor in the hospital wore a* **gown** *over his ordinary clothes.*

grab /grab/ *verb (present participle* **grabbing,** *past* **grabbed)** to take hold of quickly and roughly: *He* **grabbed** *the book and ran away.*

grace /grās/ *noun (no plural)*
1 a nice way of moving: *She walks with* **grace.**
2 a short prayer before or after a meal: *Who is going to say* **grace?**
graceful *adjective* with grace
gracefully *adverb*
gracious /grā' shəs/ *adjective*
showing kindness: *a* **gracious** *smile*

grade[1] /grād/ *noun*
a level, size, or quality: *We sell three* **grades** *of eggs.*

grade[2] *verb (present participle* **grading,** *past* **graded)**
to put into groups according to size, quality, etc.: *We have* **graded** *the eggs into several sizes.*
gradual /graj' ōō əl/ *adjective*
happening slowly: *a* **gradual** *improvement in his work*
°**gradually** /graj' ōō ə lē/ *adverb*

graduate[1] /graj' ōō āt"/ *verb (present participle* **graduating,** *past* **graduated)**
to take and pass the last examination at a college: *She* **graduated** *from an American college. She* **graduated** *in history.*

graduate[2] /graj' ōō it/ *noun*
a person who

has graduated; *a* **graduate** *of a college*

°**grain** /grān/ *noun*
1 *(no plural)*
a crop like wheat, corn, or rice that has seeds which we eat: **Grain** *is used for making flour.*
2 a seed or small piece of something: *a few* **grains** *of salt*

gram /gram/ *noun*
a measure of weight: *There are 1,000* **grams** *in a kilogram.*
g. is a short way of writing **gram(s)**

grammar /gram′ ər/ *noun (no plural)*
the laws of a language: *English* **grammar** *is quite difficult to learn.*

grand /grand/ *adjective*
very large and fine: *He lives in a* **grand** *house.*
grandchild *noun* the child of your child
granddaughter *noun* the daughter of your child
grandfather *noun* the father of one of your parents
grandmother *noun* the mother of one of your parents
grandson *noun* the son of your child

grant[1] /grant/ *verb*
to give; allow: *The children were* **granted** *a holiday from school.*

grant[2] *noun*
an allowed sum of money: *The government gave us a* **grant** *to build another classroom.*

grape /grāp/ *noun*
a small round juicy fruit that grows in bunches (see) on a grape vine in warm places

a bunch of grapes

grapefruit /grāp′ fro͞ot/ *noun*
a large yellow or green fruit that is like an orange, but not as sweet

graph /graf/ *noun*
a picture or line that shows how something changes: *They made a* **graph** *of how hot the weather was every day for a month.*
graph paper *noun: Paper with squares on it for making graphs is called* **graph paper.**

grasp /grasp/ *verb*
1 to take hold of firmly: *I* **grasped** *the cat by the back of its neck.*
2 to understand or learn: *I could not* **grasp** *what the teacher said.*

°**grass** /gras/ *noun (no plural)*
a low plant with thin leaves that cattle eat: *We sat on the* **grass** *to have our picnic* (see).
grassy *adjective* **(grassier, grassiest):** *a* **grassy** *river bank*

grasshopper /gras′ hop″ ər/ *noun*
an insect with strong back legs for jumping

grate[1] /grāt/ *noun*
a metal frame where a fire is lit

grate[2] *verb (present participle* **grating,** *past* **grated)**
to cut into small thin pieces with a special instrument (a **grater**): *to* **grate** *cheese*

°**grateful** /grāt′ fəl/ *adjective*
feeling that you want to thank someone: *I am* **grateful** *to you for helping me.*
gratefully *adverb*
gratitude /grat′ ə to͞od/ *noun (no plural): I am full of* **gratitude** *to you for helping me.*

grave[1] /grāv/ *noun*
a hole in the ground where a dead

body is placed, and then covered with earth

grave[2] *adjective*
serious: *a* **grave** *accident*
gravely *adverb:* **gravely** *ill*

gravel /grav′ əl/ *noun (no plural)*
a mixture of small stones and sand used for roads

gravity /grav′ ə tē/ *noun (no plural)*
the force which brings things down to Earth: *When you let go of something,* **gravity** *makes it fall to the floor.*

°**gray** /grā/ *adjective, noun*
(of) the color of rain clouds: *She wore a* **gray** *dress.*

graze[1] /grāz/ *verb (present participle* **grazing,** *past* **grazed)**
1 to eat grass: *Cattle were* **grazing** *in the field.*
2 to hurt the skin by rubbing it against something: *He* **grazed** *his knee when he fell.*

graze[2] *noun*
a small wound on the surface of the skin

grease[1] /grēs/ *noun (no plural)*
oil or fat: *You put* **grease** *on a wheel to make it turn more easily.*

grease[2] *(present participle* **greasing,** *past* **greased)**
to put grease on something
greasy *adjective* **(greasier, greasiest)** covered with grease

°**great** /grāt/ *adjective*
very large, important, etc.: *We learn about* **great** *people in history. He is my greatest* (= best) *friend. It gives me* **great** (= a lot of) *pleasure to see you all tonight. The party was* **great** (= very enjoyable)!
great grandchild *noun* the son **(great grandson)** or daughter **(great granddaughter)** of a grandchild
great grandparent *noun* the father **(great grandfather)** or mother **(great grandmother)** of a grandparent

greed /grēd/ *noun (no plural)*
the feeling that you want more than enough: *He can't stop eating candy — it's just* **greed!**
greedy *adjective* **(greedier, greediest):** *He's so* **greedy** *he ate all our candy.*

°**green** /grēn/ *adjective, noun*
(of) the color of growing leaves and grass: *She wore a* **green** *dress. She was dressed in* **green.**
greenhouse *noun* a little house, made of glass, for growing plants

°**greet** /grēt/ *verb*
to welcome with words or actions: *He* **greeted** *her by saying "Good morning".*
greeting *noun: She sent* **greetings** (= good wishes) *to my mother on her birthday.*

grew /gro͞o/ *see* **grow**

°**grey** see **gray**

grief /grēf/ *noun (no plural)* great sadness: *She did not show her* **grief** *when her son died.*

grin[1] /grin/ *verb (present participle* **grinning,** *past* **grinned)**
to smile widely, showing the teeth: *He* **grinned** *with pleasure when he was given the money.*

grin[2] *noun*
a wide smile: *"I've been given some money!" he said with a* **grin.**

grind /grīnd/ *verb*
(present participle **grinding,** *past* **ground** /ground/*)*
to crush something so that it

becomes powder: *We* **grind** *grain to make flour.*

grip[1] /grip/ *verb (present participle* **gripping,** *past* **gripped)**
to hold onto: *She* **gripped** *her mother's hand.*

grip[2] *noun*
a hold: *She took a firm* **grip** *on the heavy case.*

groan /grōn/ *verb*
to make a low, sad noise: *He* **groaned** *with pain.*
groan *noun*

grocer /grōs′ ər/ *noun*
a person who sells dry foods like sugar, tea, and rice: *Have you been to the* **grocer's?**
groceries *plural noun* the goods you can buy in a grocery
grocery *noun* a grocer's shop

groove /gro͞ov/ *noun*
a narrow line cut into something: *When we play a record* (see), *the needle moves along very small* **grooves** *to make the sound.*

°**ground**[1] /ground/ *noun (no plural)*
the surface of the earth: *Trees grow in the* **ground.** *The* **ground floor** *of a building is on the same level as the* **ground.**
grounds *plural noun* garden or land around a building

ground[2] see **grind**

°**group** /gro͞op/ *noun*
a number of people or things together; quantity: A **group** *of girls was waiting by the school.*

°**grow** /grō/ *verb (present participle* **growing,** *past tense* **grew** /gro͞o/, *past participle* **grown** /grōn/*)*
1 to get bigger: *Children* **grow (up)** *fast. I am* **growing** *an orange tree* (= I have planted the seed and I am waiting for it to get bigger).
2 to become: *The weather* **grew** *colder.*
grown-up *adjective, noun* a full-grown person: *The* **grown-ups** *talked while the children played.*
growth /grōth/ *noun (no plural)* an act or amount of growing; something which grows: *The child's* **growth** *was fast.*

growl /groul/ *verb*
to make a low angry noise in the throat: *The dog* **growled** *at the visitors.*
growl *noun*

grubby /grub′ ē/ *adjective* **(grubbier, grubbiest)**
dirty: **grubby** *hands*

grumble /grum′ bəl/ *verb (present participle* **grumbling,** *past* **grumbled)**
to complain: *She was* **grumbling** *about the cost of food.*

grumpy /grump′ ē/ *adjective* **(grumpier, grumpiest)**
bad-tempered: *a tired and* **grumpy** *child*
grumpily *adverb*

grunt /grunt/ *verb*
to make a short, low noise like a pig
grunt *noun*

guarantee[1] /gar″ ən tē/ *noun*
a promise: *He gave me a* **guarantee** *that he would repair the car today. The new radio had a* **guarantee** *with it* (= a document saying that if anything was wrong with it, it would be fixed free).

guarantee[2] *verb* (*past* **guaranteed)**
to promise: *He* **guaranted** *that he would do it today.*

°**guard**[1] /gärd/ *noun*
1 a person who guards
2 *(no plural)* guarding: *The soldiers*

were **on guard** *all night.*

guardian /gärd′ ē ən/ *noun*
a person who looks after a child if his parents are dead or away

guerilla /gə ril′ ə/ *noun*
a person who fights secretly against the government or against an army

°**guess**[1] /ges/ *verb*
to give an answer that you feel may be right: *I'm not sure how old David is — I* **guess** *he's five.*

°**guess**[2] *noun*
something you think is right, but do not know: *If you don't know the answer, make a* **guess.**

guest /gest/ *noun*
a visitor to someone's house: *We have three* **guests** *to dinner. This hotel has ninety* **guests.**

°**guide**[1] /gīd/ *verb (present participle* **guiding,** *past* **guided)**
to lead or show the way to: *He* **guided** *the old woman across the busy street.*

°**guide**[2] *noun*
a person or thing that guides: *He is a* **guide** *and shows visitors around the town. We have bought a* **guide (book)** *to the town, with maps in it.*
guidance *noun (no plural)* help: *I did the work with my teacher's* **guidance.**

°**guilt** /gilt/ *noun (no plural)*
knowing you have done wrong: *The* **guilt** *of the criminal* (= the fact that he had done wrong) *was proved.*
guilty *adjective* **(guiltier, guiltiest):** *I felt* **guilty** *when I spent all his money.*

guitar /gi tär′/ *noun* 
a musical instrument with strings that you pluck (= pull and let go quickly)

guitar

gulf /gulf/ *noun*
a narrow piece of sea with land on three sides of it: *the Persian* **Gulf**

gulp[1] /gulp/ *verb*
to swallow quickly: *He* **gulped (down)** *the water.*

gulp[2] *noun*
a swallow: *He drank it* **in one gulp.**

gum /gum/ *noun*
1 *(no plural)* a sticky substance used for joining things together: *There is* **gum** *on the back of a stamp.*
2 the pink part of your mouth where the teeth grow

°**gun** /gun/ *noun*
an instrument which sends out bullets (= small pieces of metal) very fast, used for hurting or killing animals or people: *Soldiers carry* **guns.**

gust /gust/ *noun*
a sudden strong wind: *A* **gust** *of wind blew the leaves along.*

gutter /gut′ ər/ *noun* 
an open pipe for water along the edge of a roof or the side of a road: *The* **gutter** *took away the rainwater from the roof.*

gutter
gutter

gymnastics /jim nas′ tiks/ *plural noun*
exercises for the body: *We do* **gymnastics** *in a* **gymnasium** /jim nāz′ ē əm/.
gym /jim/ *noun:* **Gym** *is short for* **gymnastics** *and for* **gymnasium.**

Hh

°**habit** /hab′ it/ *noun*
something you always do: *I have a* **habit** *of getting up late every day.*

had /had/ *verb*
past tense of the verb **have:** *He* **had** *lots of cloth last week, but he* **hadn't** *any today.*

hail[1] /hāl/ *noun (no plural)*
drops of rain that are so cold they have frozen and become hard: *There was a* **hail storm** *yesterday.*
hailstone *noun* a hard, cold drop of rain

hail[2] *verb*
to rain in hard drops: *It's* **hailing.**

°**hair** /hâr/ *noun*
1 *(no plural)* fine threads which grow on the skin of men and animals: *His* **hair** (= the hair on his head) *is black.*
2 one of these threads: *This hair brush is full of* **hairs!**
hairdresser *noun: A person who cuts and shapes your hair as a job is a* **hairdresser.**

°**half** /haf/ *noun*
(*plural* **halves** /havz/)
one of the two equal parts of anything: *I had* **half** *the apple and my brother had the other* **half.** *We had* **half each.** *It's* **half past** *ten* (= 30 minutes after ten o'clock). **Halfway** (= when I had gone half the distance) *to school, I met my teacher.*

hall /hôl/ *noun*
1 a large room or building: *The children were in the school* **hall.**
2 the room just inside the front door of a house: *Hang your coat in the* **hall.**

halt[1] /hôlt/ *verb*
to stop: *The policeman* **halted** *us. The car* **halted** *by the house.*

halt[2] *noun (no plural)*
a stop: *The car came to a* **halt.**

halve /hav/ *verb*
(present participle) **halving,** *past* **halved)**
to divide in half: James and I **halved** *the apple* (= we each had half of it).

ham /ham/ *noun (no plural)*
meat from a pig's leg that is kept from going bad by salt or by smoke

°**hammer[1]**
/ham′ ər/
noun
a tool with a metal head and a wooden handle, used for knocking nails into things or for breaking things

hammer

°**hammer[2]** *verb*
to hit with a hammer: *She* **hammered** *the nail in the wood.*

°**hand[1]** /hand/ *noun*
1 the end part of your arm, with which you hold things: *This toy was made* **by hand** (= not by machine). *I* **shook hands** (= took hold of the right hand firmly with my right hand) *with the teacher.*
2 the part of a clock which moves to show the time: *When the* **minute hand** *points to twelve and the* **hour hand** *points to three, it's three o'clock.*
handbag *noun* a woman's bag for small things, held in the hand
handful *noun* the amount that can be held in the hand: *a* **handful** *of rice*

handwriting *noun* writing done by hand: *Your* **handwriting** *is very good.*

handy *adjective* **(handier, handiest)** suitable or near: *This house is* **handy** *for the market.*

°**hand²** *verb*
to give with the hands: **Hand** *me that plate, please.* **Hand in** *your books to the teacher at the end of the lesson. The teacher* **handed out** *the books* (= gave one to each person).

handicap¹ /han′ dē kap″/ *noun*
something that makes it difficult to do well: *His sore leg will be a* **handicap** *in the race.*

handicap² *verb*
(*present participle* **handicapping,** *past* **handicapped)**
to make it difficult for someone to do well: *I expected her to do well in the examination, but she has been* **handicapped** *by her illness.*

°**handkerchief** /hang′ kər chif/ *noun*
a square piece of cloth for cleaning the nose

°**handle¹** /hand′ əl/ *noun*
part of a tool or instrument that you hold in the hand

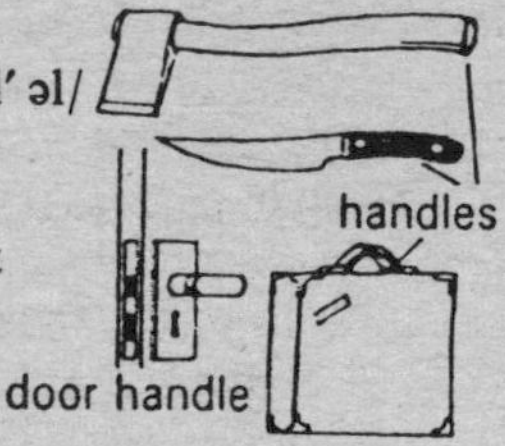

handles

door handle

°**handle²** verb
(*present participle* **handling,** *past* **handled)**
1 to use: *He learned how to* **handle** *an ax.*
2 to control: *I can't* **handle** *children.*

handlebars /hand′ əl bärz″/ *plural noun*
the part of a bicycle that you hold when you ride it (picture at **bicycle**)

handsome /han′ səm/ *adjective*
nice to look at (usually used of men)

°**hang** /hang/ *verb*
1 (*past* **hung** /hung/) to fasten something at the top so that the lower part is free: *I* **hung** *my coat* **(up)** *on a hook.*
2 (*past* **hanged)** to kill, usually as a punishment, by holding someone above the ground with a rope around his neck
3 (*past* **hung)** to wait: *He* **hung about** *outside my house.*

hanger *noun* a specially shaped piece of wire or wood for hanging clothes on: *a* **coat hanger**

°**happen** /hap′ ən/ *verb*
1 to take place; be: *The accident* **happened** *outside my house.*
2 to do by chance: *I* **happened** *to be in the market yesterday when a fire started.*

happening *noun* an event: *There were some unusual* **happenings** *at school last week.*

°**happy** /hap′ ē/ *adjective* **(happier, happiest)**
feeling very pleased: *I am* **happy** *to see you again.*

happily *adverb: They were laughing* **happily.**

happiness *noun (no plural)* pleasure; being happy: *After they got married, they had many years of* **happiness.**

°**harbor** /här′ bər/ *noun*
a place where ships may shelter safely: *The boats in the* **harbor** *were safe during the storm.*

°**hard¹** /härd/ *adjective*
1 not moving or soft when touched; firm like rock or metal: *This*

ground is too **hard** *to dig.*
2 difficult to do or understand: *Is science* **harder** *than English?*

°**hard²** *adverb*
a lot; very much: *It's raining* **hard.** *Are you working* **hard?**

harden /härd′ ən/ *verb*
to become hard: *The earth* **hardens** *under the hot sun.*

hardly /härd′ lē/ *adverb*
almost not at all; only just: *It was so dark that I could* **hardly** *see. He* **hardly ever** (= almost never) *eats meat.*

hare /hâr/ *noun*
an animal like a rabbit (see), that has long ears and long back legs

hare

°**harm¹** /härm/ *noun (no plural)*
hurt: *The child fell over but* **came to no harm** (= was not hurt). **There is no harm in** *asking him for a job* (= Nothing bad will happen if you ask).
harmful *adjective* bad; hurtful: *Smoking* **is harmful** *to your health.*
harmless *adjective* which cannot do harm: *a* **harmless** *snake*

°**harm²** *verb*
to do harm; hurt: *Our dog won't* **harm** *you.*

harsh /härsh/ *adjective*
hard to bear; cruel: **harsh** *weather/a* **harsh** *punishment*
harshly *adverb: He spoke to the child* **harshly.**

harvest¹ /här′ vist/ *noun*
1 the time when the crops are gathered: *We all helped with the* **harvest.**
2 the amount gathered: *a good fruit* **harvest**

harvest² *verb*
to gather a crop: *Have you* **harvested** *your crops?*

has /haz/ *verb*
the part of the verb **have** that we use with **he, she** and **it:** *She* **has** *three children, but she* **hasn't** *any sons.*

haste /hāst/ *noun*
hurry; quick movement or action: *In my* **haste** *I forgot my coat.*
hasty *adjective* **(hastier, hastiest)** done in a hurry: *He ate a* **hasty** *lunch.*
hastily *adverb*

°**hat** /hat/ *noun*
something worn on the head

hats

hatch¹ /hach/ *verb*
to come out of an egg: *The chickens* **hatched** *this morning.*

hatch² *noun (plural* **hatches***)*
an opening in a wall or in the floor: *She passed food through the* **hatch** *from the kitchen.*

°**hate** /hāt/ *verb (present participle hating, past* **hated***)*
not to like: *I* **hate** *snakes.*
hatred /hā′ trid/ *or* **hate** *noun (no plural): She looked at me with an expression of* **hatred.**

haul /hôl/ *verb*
to pull (something heavy): *They* **hauled** *the boat up onto the shore.*

haunt /hônt/ *verb*
(of ghosts (see) or spirits) to visit or be in a place: *People say that old house is* **haunted.**

°**have**[1] /hav/
present tense

singular	*plural*
I **have**	*We* **have**
You **have**	*You* **have**
He/She/It **has**	*They* **have**

past **had**
present participle **having**
a word that helps another word to say that something happened in the past: *We* **have given** *some food to the goat. When I arrived, she* **had** *already* **gone** *away. The teacher* **hasn't** (= has not) **locked** *the door.* **I've** (= I have) *told you this story before.*
have to *or* **have got to** *verb* must: *We* **have to** *leave now, so that we can catch the bus.* **We've got to** *go now.*

°**have**[2] *verb*
1 to own; hold; keep: *Do you* **have** *any fruit? I* **haven't** *any today.*
2 (used with some other things): *I* **have** *an idea! My father* **has** *no time to play with us.*
Have got is often used instead of **have: Have** *you* **got** *any fruit? No, I* **haven't got** *any fruit.*

hawk /hôk/ *noun*
a large bird that kills small animals and birds for food

hay /hā/ *noun (no plural)*
dry grass fed to cattle

hazard /haz′ ərd/ *noun*
a danger: *There are many* **hazards** *in a journey across Africa.*
hazardous *adjective*

haze /hāz/ *noun (no plural)*
fine cloud which stops you seeing clearly: *mountains covered in* **haze**
hazy *adjective* **(hazier, haziest)** not clear: *Since it was* **hazy,** *we couldn't see the mountains.*

°**he** /hē/ *pronoun*
(plural **they** /THā/)
the male person or animal that the sentence is about: **He** *is my brother:* **he's** (= he is) *twelve and* **he's** (= he has) *got brown eyes. Be careful of that dog,* **he** *bites.*

°**head**[1] /hed/ *noun*
1 the top part of your body, where eyes, ears, and mouth are
2 what we think with: **Use your head!** (= Think!) *Don't* **lose your head** (= get excited), *just* **keep your head** (= stay calm).
3 the top of something: *The* **head** *of the hammer fell off the handle.*
4 a chief person: *the* **head** *of the government*
5 the front: **At the head of** *the line of cars was a bus.*
headache *noun: My head hurts inside; I've got a* **headache.**
heading *noun* something written at the top of a piece of writing
headlight *noun* one of the big lights at the front of a car

headline *noun* words printed in large letters at the top of a newspaper story

head[2] *verb*
1 to be at the front or the top of something: *The bus* **headed** *the line of cars.*
2 to go toward something: *The thirsty animals* **headed for** *the water.*
3 to hit a ball with the head

headquarters /hed′ kwôr″ tərz/ *plural noun*
the chief office of a business or other group

heal /hēl/ *verb*
to make or get better: *The wound on my arm has* **healed.**

°**health** /helth/ *noun (no plural)*
the state of your body; how you are: *His* **health** *is not good* (= he is often ill).
healthy *adjective* **(healthier, healthiest):** *You look very* **healthy** (= well in body). *It is* **healthy** (= good for the health) *to eat fruit.*

°**heap**[1] /hēp/ *noun*
a number of things put untidily on top of each other: *A* **heap** *of old clothes was lying in the corner.*

heap[2] *verb*
to put into a large heap: *He* **heaped** *his plate with food.*

°**hear** /hēr/ *verb (present participle* **hearing,** *past* **heard** /hurd/*)*
1 to get sounds through the ears: *I* **heard** *the rain on the roof.*
2 to get news of: *Have you* **heard from** *John since he has been abroad? I have* **never heard of** *her* (= I don't know her).
hearing *noun (no plural): My* **hearing** *is very good; I can hear the bell two miles away.*

°**heart** /härt/ *noun*
1 the part of your body in your chest that pumps the blood around the body
2 what we feel with: *He has a kind* **heart** (= he is kind by nature).
3 the middle: *in the* **heart** *of the forest*
heartbeat *noun* the movement or sound the heart makes as it pumps the blood around the body
heartless *adjective* without kind feelings; cruel

°**heat**[1] /hēt/ *noun*
1 *(no plural)* the feeling of something hot: *The* **heat** *of the sun made her feel ill.*
2 a race run earlier than the chief race, to decide who will run in it: *The winners of the* **heats** *run in the chief race.*

°**heat**[2] *verb*
to make something hot: *We* **heated** *the soup on the cooker.*
heater *noun* a machine that heats: *She used an electric* **heater** *to warm the room.*

heave /hēv/ *verb (present participle* **heaving,** *past* **heaved***)*
to lift or pull with difficulty: I **heaved** *the heavy box up the steps.*

heaven /hev′ ən/ *noun*
a place where God or the gods are said to live, and where good people are believed to go after they die: *Will you go to* **heaven** *or hell?*
heavenly *adjective* **1** of or from heaven: *God is our* **heavenly** *father.* **2** very pleasant: *What a* **heavenly** *day!*

°**heavy** /hev′ ē/ *adjective*
(heavier, heaviest)
weighing a lot: *How* **heavy** *was the baby when he was born? We had* **heavy** (= a large amount of) *rain today.* **Heavy** *trucks can damage roads and buildings.*

hedge /hej/ *noun*
small trees planted between fields or along roads to make a wall

°**heel** /hēl/ *noun*
1 the back part of the foot below the ankle
2 the back part of the bottom of a shoe: *shoes with high* **heels**

°**height** /hīt/ *noun*
how tall or far from the ground something is: *He measured the* **height** *of the bridge.*

heir /âr/ *noun*
a person who gets money or goods when someone dies: *Richard was his father's only* **heir**, *as he had no brothers or sisters.*

held /held/ see **hold**

helicopter /hel′ i kop′ tər/ *noun*
a sort of airplane with blades which go around on its top, which can go straight up from the ground and stay still in the air

helicopter

hell /hel/ *noun*
a place where the devil (see) is said to live, and where bad people are believed to go after they die

hello /he′lō *or* hə lō′/
a greeting said when you meet someone you know: **Hello,** *Jane!*

helmet /hel′ mit/ *noun*
a covering which protects the head from being hit: *The man on the motorcycle wore a* **helmet.**

°**help**[1] /help/ *verb*
to do something or part of something for someone: *I can't lift this box — will you* **help** *me please?* **Help yourself** *to the food* (= take what you want). *I* **can't help** (= I can't stop) *crying. I'm so sad.*

helpful *adjective: The* **helpful** *boy carried my bags for me.*

helping *noun* the amount of food on a plate: *Would you like a second* **helping** *of soup?*

helpless *adjective: The rain is coming into my house and I am* **helpless** (= I can do nothing about it).

°**help**[2] *noun*
someone or something that helps: *It will be a* **help** *if you carry the basket.*

hem[1] /hem/ *noun*
the sewn bottom edge of a skirt, shirt, etc.: *Are you going to* **let down** *or* **take up the hem** *of that dress* (= make the dress longer or shorter)?

hem[2] *verb (present participle* **hemming,** *past* **hemmed)**
to sew the hem of something

hemisphere /hem′ is fēr″/ *noun*
1 one half of a sphere (see): *If you cut a round fruit into two, each half is a* **hemisphere.**
2 one of two parts of the world: *The* **Northern Hemisphere** *is the part of the world north of the equator* (see), *and the* **Southern Hemisphere** *is south of the equator.*

°**hen** /hen/ *noun*
a female chicken

°**her** /hur/ *pronoun*
1 a woman or girl, (used in sentences like this): *Give* **her** *the book. I had a letter from* **her.**
2 belonging to a woman or girl: **Her** *baby is sleeping in* **her** *arms.*

herb /urb *or* hurb/ *noun*
any plant used for medicine or for giving a special taste to food

herd[1] /hurd/ *noun*
a group of animals of the same kind: *a* **herd** *of cattle*

herd[2] *verb*
to drive animals as a herd: *He* **herded** *his cattle into the yard.*

°**here** /hēr/ *adverb*
at or to this place: *Come* **here** *and sit by me.*

hero /hēr′ o/ *noun*
(*plural* **heroes)**
a man who does something great

or brave: *The football player was Paul's* **hero** *when he was at school.*

heroic /hi rō′ ik/ *adjective*

heroine /her′ ō in/ *noun* a woman who does something great or brave

hers /hurz/ *pronoun*
something belonging to a woman or girl: *Is the pen* **hers?** *Yes, it's* **her** *pen.*

herself /hur ″self′/ *pronoun (plural* **themselves***)*
1 the same female person as the one the sentence is about: *The woman dressed* **herself** *in her best clothes. She went for a walk* **by herself** (= alone). *She lifted that heavy box* **by herself** (= without help).
2 (used to give **she** a stronger meaning): *She gave me some money, although she* **herself** *didn't have much money.*

hesitate /hez′ ə tāt″/ *verb (present participle* **hesitating,** *past* **hesitated***)*
to stop what you are doing for a short time: *He* **hesitated** *before he answered because he didn't know what to say.*

hesitation *noun*

°**hide**[1] /hīd/ *verb (present participle* **hiding,** *past tense* **hid** /hid/, *past participle* **hidden***)*
to put in a place not known to other people: *Where did you* **hide** *the money? I* **hid** *behind the door, so that no one would see me. She* **hid** *her feelings* (= no one knew what she felt).

hide[2] *noun*
the skin of an animal

°**high** /hī/ *adjective*
1 tall, or far from the ground: *The* **highest** *mountain in Africa is Mount Kilimanjaro. It is nearly 20,000 feet* **high.**
2 great: **high** *prices/a* **high** *wind*
3 not low in sound: *a* **high** *voice*

highlands /hī′ landz/ *plural noun* land which has a lot of hills, or is high up in the hills

highness *noun* a title of a prince (see) or princess (see)

highway *noun* a chief road

hijack /hī′ jak″/ *verb*
to force the driver of a plane, train, etc. to take you somewhere or give you something

hijacker *noun*

°**hill** /hil/ *noun*
a piece of ground higher than usual: small mountain: *I climbed up the* **hill** *and ran down the other side; I had to go slowly* **uphill,** *but I could run* **downhill.**

°**him** /him/ *pronoun*
a man or boy (used in sentences like this): *Give* **him** *the book. I had a letter from* **him.**

himself /him self′/ *pronoun (plural* **themselves** /THem selvz′ *or* THəm selvz′/)
1 the same male person as the one the sentence is about: *The man dressed* **himself** *in his best clothes. He stayed at home* **by himself** (= alone). *He lifted that heavy box* **by himself** (= without help).
2 (used to give **he** a stronger meaning): *He gave me some money, although he* **himself** *didn't have much money.*

hinder /hin′ dər/ *verb*
to prevent or make it more difficult for someone to do something: *I haven't cooked the dinner because the children* **hindered** *me.*

Hindu /hin′ dōō/ *noun*

a person who follows the main religion of India **(Hinduism)**

hinge /hinj/ *noun*
an instrument which joins two pieces of metal, wood, etc. and allows one piece to swing away from the other: *The lid of the suitcase had a broken* **hinge,** *so it wouldn't open easily.*

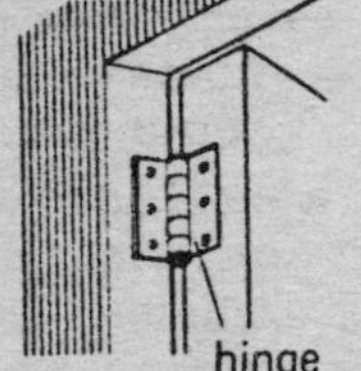

hint¹ /hint/ *verb*
to say something in a way that is not direct: *He* **hinted** *that he was looking for another job.*

hint² *noun*
something said in a way that is not direct: *When she said she was tired, it was a* **hint** *that she wanted us to go.*

hip /hip/ *noun*
the part of your body where it joins your legs

hippopotamus /hip″ ə pot′ ə məs/ *noun (plural* **hippopotamuses***)*
a large African animal that lives in rivers

hire /hīr/ *verb (present participle* **hiring,** *past* **hired***)*
to pay for the use of something or for someone's help: *He* **hired** *a car for two days.*

his /hiz/ *pronoun*
1 belonging to a man or boy: *My uncle took* **his** *children to school.*
2 something belonging to a man or boy: *That pen is my brother's; I know it is* **his.** *It is* **his,** *not hers.*

hiss /his/ *verb*
to make a sound by forcing air out through the teeth: *Snakes* **hiss.**

°**history** /his′ trē *or* his′ tə rē/ *noun (no plural)*
learning about the past: *a* **history** *lesson at school*

historic /his tôr′ ik/ *adjective*
causing important changes: *a* **historic** *meeting between the two leaders*

historical /his tôr′ i kəl/ *adjective* of history; in or about the past: *a* **historical** *play*

°**hit¹** /hit/ *verb (present participle* **hitting,** *past* **hit***)*
to bring down (something) hard on something else: *He* **hit** *me with his hand. The falling tree* **hit** *a car.*

°**hit²** *noun*
1 a blow or stroke, especially a good one: *He aimed at the mark on the wall and hit it exactly — it was a good* **hit.**
2 a song or film which everybody likes: *That song was a* **hit** *last year.*

hoard¹ /hôrd/ *verb*
to collect and store, but not use: *She* **hoards** *her money — she never spends it.*

hoard² *noun*
a lot of something which has been stored: *a* **hoard** *of money*

hoarse /hôrs/ *adjective*
(of the voice) rough, as when your throat is sore or dry: *His voice was* **hoarse** *after talking for an hour.*

hobby /hob′ ē/ *noun (plural* **hobbies***)*
something you do to amuse yourself: *He works in a bank, but his* **hobby** *is building model boats.*

hockey /hok′ ē/ *noun (no plural)*
a game played by two teams who use curved sticks to hit an object into a net

hoe /hō/
noun
a tool used to loosen the ground

hoes

hoist /hoist/ *verb*
to pull up: *You* **hoist** *a flag when you pull it to the top of its pole.*

°**hold**[1] /hōld/ *verb*
(present participle **holding,** *past* **held** /held/*)*
1 to have in the hand: *She was* **holding** *a book (in her hand).*
2 to have inside: *This bottle* **holds** *one quart.*
3 to arrange **and** *give (an event): We're* **holding** *a party next week.*
4 to have: *He* **holds** *an important position at the bank. The policemen* **held up** (= stopped) *all the traffic.*

°**hold**[2] *noun*
1 holding in the hand: *Can you get* **hold of** *that rope?*
2 the place on a ship where goods are stored

°**hole** /hōl/ *noun*
an empty space or opening in something: *I fell into a* **hole** *in the road.*

°**holiday** /hol′ ə dā″/ *noun*
a time when you do not work or go to school: *When I was* **on holiday,** *I visited my uncle.*

°**hollow** /hol′ ō/ *adjective*
having an empty space inside: *A water pipe is* **hollow.**

°**holy** /hō′ lē/ *adjective*
(holier, holiest)
of God or of the gods: *The Bible is a* **holy** *book.*

°**home** /hōm/
noun, adjective, adverb
the place where someone lives: *Her* **home** *is far away, so we don't often see her. We ran* **home** *to have our dinner. I stayed* **at home** *to read.*
homework *noun* work given to you at school to be done at home

°**honest** /on′ ist/ *adjective*
not lying or deceiving people; truthful: *I gave James too much money by mistake, but he was* **honest** *— he gave me some back.*
honestly *adverb*
honesty *noun (no plural): He was praised for his* **honesty** *when he returned the money.*

honey /hun′ ē/ *noun (no plural)*
sweet, sticky liquid that bees collect from flowers, and that people can eat
honeymoon /hun′ ē mo͞on″/ *noun* a vacation taken by people who have just gotten married

honor /on′ ər/ *noun (no plural)*
great respect: *The things that he has done have brought* **honor** *to our country. I have cooked a special meal* **in honor of** (= to show our respect for) *our visitors.*

honor[2] *verb*
to respect: *He was* **honored** *for his courage in battle.*

hood /hood/ *noun*
1 a piece of clothing that covers the head and neck
2 the covering of a convertible: *It's raining. Put the* **hood** *up.*

hoof /hu̇f *or* ho͞of/
noun
(plural
hooves
/hu̇fs *or* ho͞ovs/)
the foot of a horse, cow, sheep, or goat

°**hook**[1] /ho͝ok/ *noun*
a bent piece of metal or hard

plastic: *He hung his coat on the* **hook** *behind the door. She caught a fish on her* **hook.**

°**hook**[2] *verb*
to fasten with hooks or onto a hook: *My dress* **hooks** *at the back.*

hoop /ho͞op/ *noun*
a round band; a ring: *The barrel had two metal* **hoops** *around it.*

hoot /ho͞ot/ *verb*
to make or cause to make a low whistle on one note: *The bus driver* **hooted** *at the man who stepped onto the road.*
hoot *noun*

hop /hop/ *verb (present participle* **hopping,** *past* **hopped***)*
1 to move on one foot: *She* **hopped** *across the room because she had hurt her foot.*
2 to jump with both legs together, like some birds and animals.

°**hope**[1] /hōp/ *verb*
to wish for and expect: *I* **hope** *to go to college.*

°**hope**[2] *noun*
wishing and expecting: *I* **gave up hope** *of going to college when I failed my examinations.*
hopeful *adjective: I am* **hopeful** *that she will come tomorrow.*
hopefully *adverb: The dog waited* **hopefully** *beside the table for some food.*
hopeless *adjective: It is* **hopeless** *to go on learning science — I shall never understand it! I am* **hopeless** (= very bad) *at science.*
hopelessly *adverb:* **hopelessly** *lost*

horizon /hə rī′ zən/ *noun*
the line between the land or sea and the sky: *I could see a ship on the* **horizon.**
horizontal /hôr″ ə zont′ əl/ *adjective* going from side to side: *On a map there are* **horizontal** *lines and* **vertical** (= going up and down) *lines.*

°**horn** /hôrn/
1 one of the two hard pieces sticking out from the heads of some animals
2 the instrument on a car, bus, etc. which makes a noise to warn people
3 a musical instrument that you blow into

horrify /hôr′ ə fī″/ *verb*
(present participle **horrifying,** *past* **horrified)**
to shock or make someone feel fear: *I was* **horrified** *by the news.*

horror /hôr′ ər/ *noun*
great fear and shock: *The man saw with* **horror** *that there had been a bad accident.*
horrible /hôr ə bəl/ *adjective* very unpleasant: *There was a* **horrible** *accident here yesterday.*
horrid /hôr′ id/ *adjective* unpleasant: **horrid** *food*

°**horse** /hôrs/ *noun*
an animal with long legs that eats grass and can pull a cart or carry people

horseback *noun: There were two soldiers* **on horseback** (= riding horses).
horseshoe *noun* a piece of iron shaped like a half circle which is nailed to a horse's foot to protect it

hose[1] /hōs/ *noun*
a long piece of tube which bends easily, used for getting water from one place to another

hose[2] *verb (present participle* **hosing,** *past* **hosed)**
to put water onto something from a hose: *Will you* **hose down** *my car — it's very dirty.*

°**hospital** /hos′ pit əl/ *noun*
a building where ill people are taken to be looked after and given medicine

hospitality /hos″ pə tal′ ə tē/ *noun (no plural)*
welcome and kindness to visitors: *The people of your village showed me great* **hospitality.**

host /hōst/ *noun*
the person whose house a visitor is in, or who is paying for a meal for someone: *Mr. Brown was our* **host** *at the party.*
hostess /hōs′ tis/ *noun: They thanked their* **hostess,** *Mrs. Brown.*

hostage /hos′ tij/ *noun*
a person taken and kept by someone so that someone else will do what he wants

hostel /hos′ təl/ *noun*
a building where students, people away from their families, etc. can live

hostile /hos′ təl/ *adjective*
not friendly: *Ever since I got better marks than Richard, he has been* **hostile** *to me.*

°**hot** /hot/ *adjective* **(hotter, hottest)**
1 having a lot of heat; not cold: *The sun is very* **hot.** *Here is some* **hot** *tea for you.*
2 having a strong, burning taste: *Pepper makes food taste* **hot.**

°**hotel** /hō tel′/ *noun*
a building where visitors can sleep and eat meals if they pay

hound /hound/ *noun*
a dog used for hunting or racing

°**hour** /our/ *noun*
a measure of time; sixty minutes: *He went away for* **half an hour.** *Our business* **hours** (= the time when we are open for business) *are 9:30 to 5:30.*

°**house** /hous/ *noun*
a building that people live in
household /hous′ hōld/ *noun* all the people who live in a house together
housewife *noun (plural* **housewives)** a woman who works in the house for her family

hover /huv′ ər/ *verb*
to stay in the air without moving: *Some birds* **hover** *when they look for animals to kill on the ground.*
hovercraft *noun* a sort of boat that travels over land or water by floating on air pushed out by its engines

hovercraft

°**how** /how/ *adverb*
1 (used in questions to ask in what way): **How** *do you open this box?*
2 (used in questions about time, amount, or size): **How much** *money did you pay?* **How many** *children are there in the school?*
3 (used to ask about health): **How** *are you? I'm very well, thank you.* **How do you do?** *is a greeting we use when we first meet people.*
4 (used to show surprise or pleasure): **How** *beautiful those flowers are!*

however /how ev′ ər/ *adverb*
1 in whatever way; it does not matter how: *He can answer the question* **however** *hard it is.*
2 but: *I don't think we can do it* —**however,** *we'll try.*

howl /houl/ *verb*
to cry loudly and with a long breath: *The dog* **howled** *when it was locked in the house. Wind* **howled** *round the house.*
howl *noun*

hug[1] /hug/ *verb (present participle* **hugging,** *past* **hugged)**
to put the arms round someone and hold them: *He* **hugged** *his daughter.*

hug[2] *noun*
hugging: *He gave her a* **hug.**

huge /hūj/ *adjective*
very large: *a* **huge** *amount of food*

°**hum** /hum/ *verb (present participle* **humming,** *past* **hummed)**
1 to make a low, steady noise like a bee
2 to sing with the lips closed: *She* **hummed** *(a song).*

°**human** /hū′ mən/ *adjective*
of or like a person: *We are all* **human beings.**

humble /hum′ bəl/ *adjective*
1 having a simple opinion of yourself; not proud: *The doctor was* **humble** *about his work, although he cured many people.*
2 simple or poor: **humble** *people*

humor /hū′ mər/ *noun (no plural)*
being able to laugh at things or to make others laugh: *He has no* **sense of humor** — *he never laughs at anything.*
humorous *adjective* funny

hump /hump/ *noun*
a round lump: *A camel* (see) *has a* **hump** *on its back.*

hundred /hun′ drid/ *noun, adjective*
the number 100: *That farmer has* **a hundred** *cows, and this one has* **two hundred.**
hundredth *noun, adjective* number 100 in order; 100th

hung /hung/ see **hang**

°**hunger** /hung′ gər/ *noun (no plural)*
the feeling of wanting to eat: *If you have nothing to eat for a day, you feel great* **hunger.**
hungry /hung′ grē/ *adjective* **(hungrier, hungriest):** *Can I have an apple? I'm* **hungry.**

°**hunt** /hunt/ *verb*
1 to chase and kill animals or birds for food or sport
2 to look for: *I* **hunted for** *my book everywhere.*
hunter *noun* a person who hunts animals or birds

hurl /hurl/ *verb*
to throw hard: *He* **hurled** *the brick through the window.*

hurray /hə rā′/
a word you shout when you are pleased about something: *Our team has won!* **Hurray!**

hurricane /hur′ ə kān″/ *noun*
a great storm with a strong wind

°**hurry**[1] /hur′ ē/ *verb (present participle* **hurrying,** *past* **hurried)**
to move or do something quickly: *I'm late — I must* **hurry (up)!**

hurry[2] *noun*
hurrying: *You always seem to be* **in a hurry.**

°**hurt** /hurt/ *verb (past* **hurt)**
to give pain or cause damage: *My leg* **hurts.** *I* **hurt** *it playing football.*

It won't **hurt** *your bicycle if you leave it outside. She's* **hurt** (= sad) *because you haven't visited her.*

°**husband** /huz' bənd/ *noun*
the man to whom a woman is married

°**hut** /hut/ *noun*
a small, usually wooden, building

hydrogen /hī' drə jən/ *noun (no Plural)*
a very light, colorless gas

hyena /hī ēn' ə/ *noun*
a wild animal like a large dog

hygiene /hī' jēn"/ *noun (no plural)*
keeping yourself and your home clean

hygienic *adjective* clean

hymn /him/ *noun*
a religious song

hyphen /hī' fən/ *noun*
the sign - used between two parts of a word or two words joined together, as in *half-mast*

Ii

°**I** /ī/ (*plural* **we** /wē/) *pronoun*
the person who is speaking: *He wants bananas, but* **I** *want oranges.* **I'm** (= I am) *very glad to see you.* **I've** (= I have) *been waiting a long time.* **I'll** (= I will *or* I shall) *wait a little longer. When* **I'd** (= I had) *written the story, I read it to my friend. I thought that* **I'd** (= I would *or* I should) *miss the bus, but I didn't.*

°**ice** /īs/ *noun (no plural)*
water which is so cold that it has become hard: *He put some* **ice** *in his drink to make it cold.*

ice cream *noun* a sweet food made from very cold milk fat with different tastes added

icy /ī' sē/ *adjective* very cold **(icier, iciest)**

iceberg /īs' burg"/ *noun*
a very large mass of ice floating in the sea

icing /ī' sing/ *noun (no plural)*
a mixture of sugar and other ingredients, put on top of cakes

°**idea** /ī dē' ə/ *noun*
a thought; something formed in the mind: *I've had an* **idea.** *We could play football! What time is it? I* **have no idea** (= I do not know).

ideal /ī dē əl *or* ī dēl'/ *adjective*
the best possible: *This book is* **ideal** *— it's exactly what I needed.*

identical /ī den'ti kəl/ *adjective*
exactly the same: *The two bowls are* **identical,** *they are the same size, shape, and color.*

identify /ī den'tə fī"/ *verb*
(*present participle* **identifying,** *past* **identified)**
to say who someone is or what something is: *Can you* **identify** *the three plants in the picture?*

identification *noun (no plural)* saying or showing who someone is or what something is: *Have you any* **identification** (= something that shows who you are)?

identity *noun* (*plural* **identities)** who someone is or what something is: *Can you prove your* **identity?**

idiom /id' ē əm/ *noun*
a group of words which when used together have a special meaning: *"I've got cold feet" is an* **idiom** *— it doesn't only mean that my feet feel cold, it can also mean that I am afraid.*

idle /īd' əl/ *adjective*
1 doing no work: **idle** *machines in a factory*
2 lazy: *He never does any work — he's* **idle.**

idol /īd' əl/ *noun*
a figure that people respect and honor. *They prayed to an* **idol.**

i.e. /ī ē/
this is what is meant: *The best pupil in the class,* **i.e.** *Peter, won the prize.*

°**if** /if/
1 on condition that: *You can catch the bus* **if** *you go now.*
2 whether: *I don't know* **if** *he will play or not.*
3 (used in phrases like this): *Do you like coffee?* **If so** (= if you do

like it), *have a cup of coffee.* **If not** (= if you do not like it), *I'll make you a cup of tea.*

ignorant /ig′ nər ənt/ *adjective*
not knowing much: *She is very* **ignorant** *about her own country.*
ignorance *noun (no plural): Her* **ignorance** *is surprising.*

ignore /ig nôr′/ *verb (present participle* **ignoring,** *past* **ignored)**
to take no notice of; pretend someone or something is not there: *I tried to tell her, but she* **ignored** *me.*

°**ill**[1] /il/ *adjective* (**worse** /wurs/, **worst** /wurst/)
not feeling healthy; unwell: *She can't go to school because she is* **ill.**
illness *noun* (*plural* **illnesses**): *He has had a bad* **illness,** *but he is better now.*

ill[2] *adverb*
(often joined to other words) badly: *The cruel man* **ill treated** *his children.*

illegal /i lē′ gəl/ *adjective*
not allowed by law: *It is* **illegal** *to steal things.*

illegible /i lej′ ə bəl/ *adjective*
not able to be read: **illegible** *writing*

illuminate /i lo͞o′ mə nāt″/ *verb (present participle* **illuminating,** *past* **illuminated)**
to light up: *The river was* **illuminated** *by the setting sun.*

illustrate /il′ əs trāt″/ *verb (present participle* **illustrating,** *past* **illustrated)**
to add pictures to: *The book was* **illustrated** *with color photographs.*

illustration *noun: Who drew these* **illustrations?**

illustration

image /im′ ij/ *noun*
1 a picture in the mind, or in a mirror: *He saw the* **image** *of his face in the mirror.*
2 a figure made of stone, wood, etc.

°**imagine** /i maj′ in/ *verb (present participle* **imagining,** *past* **imagined)**
1 to have a picture in the mind of: *When he talked about the city, I tried to* **imagine** *it.*
2 to think: *John* **imagines** *that we don't like him.*
imaginary *adjective: He told a story about an* **imaginary** (= not real) *land.*
imagination *noun: You didn't really see it — it was just your* **imagination.**

imitate /im′ ə tāt/ *verb (present participle* **imitating,** *past* **imitated)**
to copy: *She* **imitated** *the way her teacher talked.*
imitation *noun: This isn't a real gun — it's only an* **imitation.**

immediate /i mē′ dē it/ *adjective*
happening at once: *I need an* **immediate** *answer.*
immediately *adverb: She came* **immediately.**

immense /i mense′/ *adjective*
very large: *He made an* **immense** *amount of money in business.*
immensely *adverb: I am* **immensely** *pleased to have this job.*

immunize /im′ ū nīz″/ *verb (present participle* **immunizing,** *past* **immunized)**

to put a special substance into the body, usually by an injection, to prevent an illness (see **inject**)

immunization *noun (no plural)*

impatient /im pā′ shənt/ *adjective*
not able to wait for something to happen: *It is no use getting* **impatient** *when you are waiting for a train.*

impatience *noun (no plural)*
impatiently *adverb*

imperative /im per′ ə tiv/ *noun, adjective*
the form of a verb we use when we are telling someone to do something: *In the sentence "Come over here!", "come" is in the* **imperative.**

impertinent /im pur′ tə nənt/ *adjective*
rude, especially to older people: *She scolded her son for being* **impertinent.**

impertinence *noun (no plural)*

impolite /im″ pə līt/ *adjective*
not polite; rather rude: *I think I was* **impolite** *when I asked the woman how old she was.*

import¹ /im pôrt′/ *verb*
to bring into a country for use there: *We* **import** *many automobiles in our country.*

import² /im′ pôrt″/ *noun*
something that is imported: *Cocoa is one of our* **imports.**

°**important** /im pôrt′ ənt/ *adjective*
having power; of great value: *The principal is the most* **important** *person in the school. It is* **important** *that we tell the truth.*

°**importance** *noun (no plural): The* **importance** *of telling the truth cannot be doubted.*

impossible /im pos′ ə bəl/ *adjective*
not possible; not able to happen: *I can't come today; it's* **impossible.**

impossibly *adverb: That piece of work looks* **impossibly** *difficult.*

impress /im pres′/ *verb*
to cause strong good feelings or thought: *His teacher was so* **impressed** *by his work, that she showed it to the principal.*

impression *noun: His work made a great* **impression** *on his teacher.*

impressive *adjective: His work was very* **impressive.**

imprison /im priz′ ən/ *verb*
to put in prison: *He was* **imprisoned** *for two years.*

imprisonment *noun: He was given two years'* **imprisonment.**

°**improve** /im prōōv′/ *verb (present participle* **improving,** *past* **improved)**
to make or get better: *Your reading has* **improved** *this year, but you must try to* **improve** *your writing.*

improvement *noun: There have been great* **improvements** *in your reading, but your writing still needs* **improvement.**

impulse /im′ puls″/ *noun*
a sudden wish to do something: *She had an* **impulse** *to buy a new dress. She bought the dress* **on impulse.**

impulsive *adjective: An* **impulsive** *person does things without thinking carefully about them first.*

°**in** /in/ *preposition, adverb*
1 (showing where): *Don't stand* **in** *the sun, sit* **in** *the shade.*
2 at or to the inside of a place: *We ran to the water and jumped* **in.**

3 during; before the end of: *The house was built* **in** *1978. He woke up* **in** *the middle of the night.*
4 at home or in an office: *My brother is out now but he will be* **in** *this evening.*
5 using: *She spoke* **in** *a quiet voice. The words were written* **in** *pencil.*
6 wearing: *The guard was* **in uniform.**
7 (used in phrases like this): *Emily was* **in tears** (= crying). *Are all your family* **in good health** (= well)? *That kind of shirt is* **in** (= liked and worn by a lot of people) *this year.*

°**inadequate** /in ad′ ə kwit/ *adjective*
not enough: *The food was* **inadequate** *for ten people — there was only enough for five.*

incapable /in kā′ pə bəl/ *adjective*
not able to do something: *Since her accident, she has been* **incapable of** *walking.*

°**inch** /inch/ *noun* (*plural* **inches**)
a measure of length, equal to 2.5 centimeters. *There are twelve* **inches** *in a foot.* **in.** is a short way of writing **inches.**

incident /in′ sə dənt/ *noun*
an event; something that happens: *Were there any exciting* **incidents** *during your journey?*

incline /in′ klīn/ *verb* (*present participle* **inclining,** *past* **inclined**)
to be inclined to to want to or be likely to: *I am* **inclined to** *be ill after eating fish.*

°**include** /in kloo͞d′/ *verb* (*present participle* **including,** *past* **included**)
1 to have as part of: *His class* **includes** *the two cleverest students in the school.*
2 to count or think of someone or something as part of: *I* **included** *my uncle in my list of people to thank.*

income /in′ kum″/ *noun*
all the money you receive: *What is your* **income** *from your job?* **Income tax** *is taken by the government from what you earn, to be spent on schools, roads, hospitals, etc.*

incomplete /in kəm plēt′/ *adjective*
not finished: *This list of names is* **incomplete:** *you have left out Paul.*

inconvenient /in kən vēn′ yənt/ *adjective*
not suitable; causing difficulty: *This shelf is at an* **inconvenient** *height. It's too high for me to reach.*
inconvenience *noun (no plural)*

incorrect /in kə rekt′/ *adjective*
not right; wrong: *The answer to the sum is* **incorrect.**
incorrectly *adverb*

°**increase**[1] /in krēs′/ *verb* (*present participle* **increasing,** *past* **increased**)
to make or grow larger: *My wages have* **increased** *this year. My employer has* **increased** *my wages.*

°**increase**[2] /in′ krēs/ *noun*
getting larger: *an* **increase** *in wages*

indeed /in dēd/ *adverb*
1 really: *Did he say that? He did* **indeed.**
2 (used to make **very** even stronger): *He runs very fast* **indeed.**

indefinite /in def′ ə nit/ *adjective*
not clear or fixed: *He gave an* **indefinite** *answer. I am staying for an* **indefinite** *time.*
indefinitely *adverb: I am staying here* **indefinitely.**

independent /in di pen′ dənt/ *adjective*

able to look after yourself; not governed by anyone or anything else: *Although she is young, she is very* **independent.**

independence *noun (no plural): The United States gained its* **independence** *in 1776.*

index /in′ deks/ *noun* (*plural* **indexes**)
a list in a book of what can be found in it, and on what page

indicate /in′ də kāt″/ *verb* (*present participle* **indicating,** *past* **indicated)**
to show: *On this map, the towns are* **indicated** *by a red dot.*

indication *noun: There is no* **indication** (= nothing to show) *that you have worked hard.*

indignant /in dig′ nənt/ *adjective*
angry because of something that appears wrong: *I was* **indignant** *because I felt that I had been punished unfairly.*

indignantly *adverb: "It isn't fair!" she said* **indignantly.**

indirect /in″ də rekt′/ *adjective*
not direct; not straight: *We went to the house by an* **indirect** *road.*

indirectly *adverb*

individual[1] /in də vij′ o͞o əl/ *noun*
a person: *All* **individuals** *seen leaving school early will be punished.*

individual[2] *adjective*
single; for one person only: *The children had* **individual** *desks.*

individually *adverb: The children were taught* **individually,** *not in a group.*

indoor /in′ dôr″/ *adjective*
inside a building: *If it rains, we play* **indoor** *games.*

indoors /in′ dôrz″/ *adverb*
inside a building: *Let's stay* **indoors** *today.*

°**industry** /in′ dəs trē/ *noun* (*plural* **industries)**
making things in factories: *Our town has a lot of* **industry.** *What are the important* **industries** *in the town?*

industrial /in dus′ trē əl/ *adjective: an* **industrial** *town* (= with a lot of industry)

infant /in′ fənt/ *noun*
a baby or young child

infect /in fekt′/ *verb*
to give an illness to: *One of the boys in the class had a fever and he soon* **infected** *other children.*

infection *noun: My brother has a throat* **infection.**

infectious *adjective: An* **infectious** *illness is one that you can give to other people.*

infinite /in′ fə nit/ *adjective*
endless; so large that it cannot be imagined: **Infinite** *space surrounds the earth.*

infinitely *adverb: It is* **infinitely** (= very much) *easier to drive a car than to repair it.*

inflate /in flāt/ *verb* (*present participle* **inflating,** *past* **inflated)**
to fill with air: *to* **inflate** *a tire*

influence[1] /in′ flo͞o əns/ *noun*
something that changes what happens: *My teacher's* **influence** *made me study science at college.*

influential /in″ flo͞o en′shəl/ *adjective* having great influence

influence[2] *verb* (*present participle* **influencing,** *past* **influenced)**
to change what happens: *My teacher* **influenced** *my decision to study science.*

influenza /in flōō en′ zə/ *or* **flu** /flōō/ *noun (no plural)*
an illness which causes fever, headache, and other discomfort

inform /in fôrm′/ *verb*
to tell: *The principal* **informed** *us that the school would be closed for one day next week.*

°**information** /in fər mā′ shən/ *noun (no plural)* facts; knowledge; things you want to know: *What* **information** *is on a map?*

informal /in fôr′ məl/ *adjective*
happening or done in an easy way, not according to rules: *It's not a* **formal** *party, it's an* **informal** *one, so you can wear what you like.*

informally *adverb*

ingredient /in grē′ dē ənt/ *noun*
something you put in when making something: *Flour is an* **ingredient** *of this cake.*

inhabitant /in hab′ ə tənt/ *noun*
someone who lives in a place: *the* **inhabitants** *of a village*

inherit /in her′ it/ *verb*
to get something from someone when they die: *He* **inherited** *the farm from his parents.*

inheritance *noun: The farm is his* **inheritance.**

initial[1] /i nish′ əl/ *noun*
the first letter of a name, used to stand for the name: *His name is John Smith, so his* **initials** *are J.S.*

initial[2] *adjective*
first: *Her* **initial** *plan was to walk to town, but then she decided to go by bus.*

initially *adverb*

inject /in jekt′/ *verb*
to give someone medicine through the skin, with a needle

injection

injection *noun: The doctor gave him an* **injection.**

injure /in′ jər/ *verb (present participle* **injuring,** *past* **injured)**
to harm; wound: *There were two people* **injured** *in the car accident.*

injury *noun (plural* **injuries)** a wound; damage: *The people in the accident had serious* **injuries.**

injustice /in jus′ tis/ *noun*
being unfair; something unfair: *The teacher did him an* **injustice** *when she called him a cheat.*

°**ink** /ink/ *noun (no plural)*
a colored liquid used for writing, printing, etc.

inland[1] /in′ lənd/ *adjective*
far from the sea: *an* **inland** *town*

inland[2] *adverb*
away from the sea: *We went twenty kilometers* **inland,** *up the river.*

in-law /in lô/ *noun*
used after a word to mean a person related to you through your wife or husband: *Your* **mother-in-law** *is your wife's (or husband's) mother.*

inn /in/ *noun*
a place which sells drinks and food, and is sometimes a hotel as well: *The travelers stopped to eat at a small* **inn.**

inner /in′ ər/ *adjective*
further in, or in the middle: *The* **inner** *room was reached through the kitchen.*

innocent /in′ nə sənt/ *adjective*
not guilty
innocence *noun (no plural): Her* **innocence** *has been proved.*

inquire /in kwīr′/ *verb*
(*present participle* **inquiring,** *past* **inquired)**
to ask: *If you want to know anything, just* **inquire** *at this office.*
inquiry *noun: She made an* **inquiry** *about jobs.*

insane /in sān′/ *adjective*
mad: *He must be* **insane** *to drive his car so fast.*

°**insect** /in′ sekt/ *noun*
a small animal without bones that has six legs: *Bees and ants are* **insects.**

insert /in surt′/ *verb*
to put in: **Insert** *this card in your book to mark the page.*

°**inside**[1] /in′ sīd″ *or* in sīd′/ *noun*
the part that is in the middle of something, contained by something or facing inward: *The outside of an orange is bitter, but the* **inside** *is sweet. Have you seen the* **inside** *of the house?*

°**inside**[2]
preposition, adverb, adjective
in; to or on the inside of something: *She put the money* **inside** *her bag. Don't stand out there in the sun; come* **inside.** *We eat the* **inside** *part of this fruit.*

insist /in sist′/ *verb*
to say with great firmness: *I* **insist** *that you come to school now. Mr. Brown* **insists on** *seeing you.*

inspect /in spekt′/ *verb*
to look at carefully, to see if there is anything wrong: *He* **inspected** *the building before he bought it. The government sent someone to* **inspect** *our school.*
inspection *noun: He made an* **inspection** *of the school.*
inspector *noun* **1** a person who inspects: *The Building* **Inspector** *visited our school.* **2** a police officer

install /in stôl′/ *verb*
to place machinery, etc.: *We have* **installed** *a telephone in the office.*
installation /in stə lā′ shən/ *noun*

instance /in′ stans/ *noun*
an example: *An* **instance** *of his bad behavior is that he ran away from school.*

instant /in′ stant/ *adjective*
happening or working at once: **Instant** *coffee is made as soon as you pour water on it.*
instantly *adverb* at once

°**instead** /in sted′/ *adverb*
in place of someone or something: *I didn't have a pen, so I used a pencil* **instead.**
instead of *preposition* in place of: *I came* **instead of** *my brother.*

instinct /in′ stingkt/ *noun*
a natural force which makes you do things when you haven't been taught to do them; natural feelings: *Babies drink from their mothers* **by instinct.**
instinctive *adjective: A baby's cry is* **instinctive.**

institute /in′ stə to͞ot″/ *noun*
a group, or the building it uses, of people who want to study or talk about a special thing
institution /in″ stə to͞o′ shən/ *noun: A hospital is an* **institution** *for ill people* (= a building specially for them).

instruct /in strukt′/ *verb*
to teach: *She* **instructed** *me in the use of the telephone.*
instruction *noun: Read the* **instructions** *on the packet.*
instructor *noun: He is a sports* **instructor.**

°**instrument** /in′ strə mənt/ *noun*
a tool used for doing something special: *A pen is an* **instrument** *for writing. Do you play any* **musical instrument** (= thing to make music)?

musical instruments

insult¹ /in sult′/ *verb*
to be rude to: *He* **insulted** *her by calling her a stupid fool.*

insult² /in′ sult/ *noun*
something rude said to someone: *He shouted* **insults** *at the boys.*

insurance /in shūr′ əns/ *noun (no plural)*
money paid to a company which will pay a large amount if you are in an accident, die, etc.

intelligent /in tel′ ə jənt/ *adjective*
being quick at thinking; clever
intelligence *noun (no plural)*

°**intend** /in tend′/ *verb*
to plan to do something: *Today, I* **intend** *to finish reading this book.*
intention *noun: I began reading* **with the intention of** *finishing the book, but I never did.*

°**interest¹** /in′trist *or* in′tər ist/ *noun*
wanting to know more about something; getting pleasure from studying something: *She* **takes an interest in** *everything around her. His chief* **interest** (= thing he is interested in) *is baseball.*

°**interest²** *verb*
to make someone want to know more, or get pleasure from studying: *I am very* **interested in** *stamps. I find them* **interesting.**

interfere /in′ tər fēr′/ *verb* (*present participle* **interfering,** *past* **interfered**)
to prevent someone doing what he wants to; to get in the way: *I was playing with Jane, but Anne* **interfered** *and spoiled the game.*
interference *noun*

interior /in tēr′ ē ər/ *noun (no plural)*
the inside: *The* **interior** *of the box was black.*

internal /in tur′ nəl/ *adjective*
of or on the inside: *Although the man who had fallen looked all right, he was hurt* **internally.**

international /in″ tər nash′ ən əl/ *adjective*
of, for or by many countries: *an* **international** *agreement*

interrupt /in″ tə rupt′/ *verb*
to say something when someone else is already speaking: *It is rude to* **interrupt.**

interval /in′ tər vəl/ *noun*
a time or space between things: *In between parts of a play, there is often an* **interval.** *There were trees* **at intervals** *along the road.*

interview¹ /in′ tər vū″/ *noun*
a meeting to decide if a person is suitable for a job, or to ask his opinions: *to go for an* **interview**

interview² *verb*
to talk to someone to see if he is suitable for a job, or to ask his opinions

°**into** /in′ too͞/
preposition
1 to or toward the middle of: *Come* **into** *the classroom.*
2 (used to show how people or things change): *She made the material* **into** *a dress. He cut the cake* **into** *six pieces.*

intransitive /in tran′ zə tiv/
noun, adjective
a verb whose action is not done to something or somebody; a verb that does not take an object (see): *When he had finished, he sat down. "Finish" and "sit" are* **intransitive** *verbs here.* Look at **transitive.**

introduce /in″ trə do͞os′/ *verb* (*present participle* **introducing,** *past* **introduced**)
1 to give someone's name when they first meet someone else: *He* **introduced** *his friend to me.*
2 to bring in a new thing: *to* **introduce** *a new subject in a school*
introduction /in′ trə duk″ shən/ *noun* **1** introducing someone or something **2** a piece of writing at the beginning of a book telling us about it

invade /in vād′/ *verb* (*present participle* **invading,** *past* **invaded**)
to attack and go into someone's land, house, etc.: *The army* **invaded** *the town.*
invasion *noun*

invalid /in′ və lid/ *noun*
a person made weak by illness: *He helps to look after his grandfather, who is an* **invalid.**

invent /in vent′/ *verb*
to think of and plan something completely new: *Who* **invented** *the telephone?*
invention *noun: the* **invention** *of the telephone*
inventor *noun* a person who invents

investigate /in ves′ tə gāt/ *verb* (*present participle* **investigating,** *past* **investigated**)
to find out about something by looking, asking questions, etc.: *The police are* **investigating** *the robbery.*
investigation *noun: The police* **investigation** *will take weeks.*

invisible /in viz′ ə bəl/ *adjective*
not able to be seen: *It was so cloudy that the top of the mountain was* **invisible.**

invite /in vīt′/ *verb* (*present participle* **inviting,** *past* **invited**)
to ask someone to your house, to go out with you, etc.: *She* **invited** *us to her party.*
invitation /in və tā′ shən/ *noun: We had three* **invitations** (= letters inviting us) *to parties.*

involve /in volv′/ *verb* (*present participle* **involving,** *past* **involved**)
to make be a part of: *All the children were* **involved** *in the school play. This lesson* **involves** (= needs) *a lot of work.*

°**inward** /in′ wərd/ *also* **inwards**
adverb
toward the middle or the inside: *She turns her toes* **inward** *when she walks.*

°**iron**[1] /i′ ərn/
noun
1 *(no plural)* a hard, gray metal
2 an instrument which is heated, and then used to make clothes smooth

iron

iron² *verb*
to press clothes with a hot iron to make them smooth

irregular /i reg′ yə lər/ *adjective*
not regular: *Your writing is* **irregular:** *some letters are big and some small.*
irregularly *adverb*

irrigate /ir′ ə gāt/ *verb*
(*present participle* **irrigating,** *past* **irrigated)**
to make water flow onto: *The fields are* **irrigated** *so that the crops can grow.*
irrigation *noun: We could not grow rice on this land before* **irrigation,** *because there was not enough rain.*

irritate /ir′ ə tāt″/ *verb*
(*present participle* **irritating,** *past* **irritated)**
to annoy: *The noise of the children was* **irritating** *me. Insect bites* **irritate** *your skin* (= make it sore).

is /iz/ *verb*
the part of the verb **be** that we use with **he, she** and **it:** *She* **is** *Peter's sister.* **He's** *her brother. That* **boy's** (= boy is) *in my class.* **He's not** (*or* **he isn't)** *in your class.*

Islam /iz′ läm/ *noun*
the religion of the Muslims
Islamic *adjective*

°**island** /ī′lənd/ *noun*
a piece of land surrounded by water

isolate /ī′ sə lāt″/ *verb* (*present participle* **isolating,** *past* **isolated)**
to separate; set apart from other things or people: *The farm is* **isolated;** *the nearest house is 5 kilometers away.*

issue¹ /ish′ o͞o/ *verb* (*present participle* **issuing,** *past* **issued)**
to give, send, or come out: *The teacher* **issued** *paper and pencils to all the children.*

issue² *noun*
something that comes out: *An* **issue** *of a newspaper is one day's newspaper.*

°**it** /it/ (*plural* **they** /THā/)
1 the thing or animal or baby that the sentence is about: *I've lost my book, and I can't find* **it** *anywhere.* **It's** (= it is) *not in my room.* **It'll** (= it will) *be Saturday tomorrow.*
2 (used about the weather, time, and dates, and in other phrases): **It** *is very hot today.* **It's** *nearly four o'clock.* **It** *is Thursday, September 2nd.* **It's** *a long way to the town.*

itch¹ /ich/ *verb*
to be sore and annoying, so that you want to rub it: *The insect bite* **itched** *all night.*

itch² *noun* (*plural* **itches)**
an itching feeling: *I've got an* **itch** *on my back.*

item /ī′təm/ *noun*
a thing: *There was an interesting* **item** *in the newspaper today. On the desk there were two books, a pen, and some other* **items.**

°**its** /itz/
of it; belonging to it: *She gave the baby* **its** *food. The dog hurt* **its** *foot.*

itself /it self′/ (*plural* **themselves** /THem selvz′ *or* THəm selvz′/)
the same thing, animal, or baby as the one that the sentence is about: *The baby is too young to feed* **itself.** *The house stands* **by itself** (= alone) *outside the village.*

ivory /ī′ vrē/ *noun (no plural)*
hard, yellowish-white substance taken from the tusks (= long teeth) of elephants.

Jj

jab /jab/ *verb* (*present participle* **jabbing,** *past* **jabbed**)
to push, usually with something sharp: *I* **jabbed** *the needle into my finger. He kept* **jabbing** *his finger into my back until I turned around.*

jackal /jak′ əl/ *noun*
a wild animal like a small dog that eats meat

jacket /jak′ it/ *noun*
1 a short coat with sleeves (= covering for the arms)
2 the outer covering of some things: *The paper cover of some books is called a* **dust jacket.**

jagged /jag′ id/ *adjective*
having a rough, uneven edge with sharp points: *I cut myself on the* **jagged** *edge of the can.*

jaguar /jag′ wär/ *noun*
a wild animal with a spotted coat which is one of the big cats

jail /jāl/ *noun*
prison: *The man was sent to* **jail.**

jam¹ /jam/ *verb* (*present participle* **jamming,** *past* **jammed**)
1 to press or be pressed together; pack tightly into something: *I tried to* **jam** *all my clothes into a case, but they wouldn't fit.*
2 to get stuck or stop all movement: *I can't open this window — it's* **jammed.**

jam² *noun*
so many cars, people, etc., crowded together that movement is stopped: *There are always* **traffic jams** *in the city in the morning.*

jam³ *noun (no plural)*
sweet food made of fruit boiled with sugar, usually eaten with bread

°**January** /jan′ ū er″ ē/ *noun*
the first month of the year

jar /jär/ *noun*
a container like a bottle with a short neck and a wide opening: *a* **jar** *of jam* (picture at **bottle**)

jaw /jô/ *noun*
one of the bony parts of the face in which the teeth are set

jazz /jaz/ *noun (no plural)*
a kind of music with a strong beat: *Do you like listening to* **jazz?**

jealous /jel′ əs/ *adjective*
1 unhappy because of wanting what someone else has: *I was* **jealous** *of Sarah when she got her new bicycle. I was very* **jealous** *of Sarah's new bicycle.*
2 being afraid of losing what you have: *Sarah is Jane's friend, but she is* **jealous** *if Jane plays with other girls.*
jealously *adverb*
jealousy *noun (no plural): It is silly to let* **jealousy** *spoil our friendship.*

jeans /jēns/ *plural noun*
pants made of a strong cotton cloth, usually blue: *I've got a new* **pair of jeans.**

jeep /jēp/ *noun*
a car which has a strong engine and can be used on bad roads

jeer /jēr/ *verb*
to laugh rudely at someone: *Don't* **jeer at** *the person who came last in the race — it's very unkind.*

jelly /jel' ē/ *noun*
1 (*plural* **jellies**) a sweet, soft food, often tasting of fruit
2 *(no plural)* any other thing that is between liquid and solid: *The medicine was a clear* **jelly**.

jellyfish /jel' e fish"/ *noun*
(*plural* **jellyfish** *or* **jellyfishes**)
a soft sea creature that looks like a lump of jelly (see) and can sting

jerk¹ /jurk/ *verb*
to pull or move suddenly: *She* **jerked** *the rope but it wouldn't move.*

jerk² *noun*
a short hard pull or movement: *The old bus started with a* **jerk**.

jersey /jur' zē/ *noun*
a piece of clothing, usually made of wool, that covers the top part of the body.

jet /jet/ *noun*
1 a narrow stream of gas, air, or liquid which comes out of a small hole: *The fireman sent* **jets** *of water into the burning house.*
2 an aircraft that is pushed through the air by an engine which pushes out hot air behind itself (a **jet engine**)

jetty /jet' ē/ *noun* (*plural* **jetties**)
a kind of wall built out into water, used for getting on and off boats, or for protection against the waves

Jew /jo͞o/ *noun*
member of **Jewish** religion called **Judaism**

jewel /jo͞o' əl *or* jo͞ol/ *noun*
a stone which is worth a lot of money and is used as an ornament: *She wore beautiful* **jewels** *around her neck.*

jewelry /jo͞o' əl rē/ *noun (no plural)* jewels, gold, etc. made into rings, earrings, and other ornaments.

jigsaw puzzle /jig' sô puz' əl/ *noun*
a game in which you must fit together small pieces to make one big picture

jingle /jing' gəl/ *verb* (*present participle* **jingling**, *past* **jingled**)
to make a ringing noise, like little bells: *The coins* **jingled** *in his pocket.*

°**job** /job/ *noun*
1 a piece of work that must be done: *My mother does all the* **jobs** *about the house.*
2 work that you are paid to do: *What is your* **job**? *— I'm a teacher.*

°**join¹** /join/ *verb*
1 to put or bring two or more things together: *Tie a knot to* **join** *those two pieces of rope. This road* **joins** *the two villages.*
2 to come together; meet: *Where do the two roads* **join**? *Will you* **join** *us for coffee* (= have coffee with us)?
3 to become a member of something: *He* **joined** *the army. Everyone* **joined in** (= was a part of) *the game.*

°**joint¹** /joint/ *noun*
a place where things, especially bones, are joined: *Our arms and legs bend at the* **joints** *— the elbows and knees.*

°**joint²** *adjective*
shared by two or more people: *Mr. Jones and his two sons are the* **joint** *owners of the business.*

jointly *adverb*

°**joke**[1] /jōk/ *noun*
something you say or do to make people laugh: *Our teacher told us a* **joke** *today. We all* **played a joke on** *him* (= did something to make other people laugh at him).

°**joke**[2] *verb* (*present participle* **joking,** *past* **joked**)
to tell jokes: *I didn't mean that seriously — I was only* **joking.**

jolly /jol′ ē/ *adjective* (**jollier, jolliest**)
happy; pleasant: *a* **jolly** *person*

jolt[1] /jōlt/ *noun*
a sudden shake or shock: *The truck started with a* **jolt.**

jolt[2] *verb*
to give a jolt; move with a jolt

journal /jur′ nəl/ *noun*
1 a sort of newspaper, often for special things: *The doctor reads the* **Journal** *of Medical Science.*
2 a diary (see)
journalism *noun (no plural)* the job of a journalist; the writing that a journalist does
journalist *noun* a person who works for a newspaper, and writes about the news

°**journey** /jur′ nē/ *noun*
a trip, usually a long one: *How long is the* **journey** *to the coast?*

joy /joi/ *noun*
1 *(no plural)* great happiness: *She was full of* **joy** *when her child was born.*
2 something that gives great happiness: *Her child was a* **joy** *to her.*
joyful *adjective* showing or giving joy
joyfully *adverb*

Judaism /jo͞o′ dā izm/ *noun*
religion of Jews as told in Old Testament of Bible

judge[1] /juj/ *noun*
1 a person who can decide questions of law in a court (see): *The* **judge** *decided that the man should go to prison for two years.*
2 a person who decides who wins a competition

judge[2] *verb* (*present participle* **judging,** *past* **judged**)
1 to decide if something or someone is good or bad, right or wrong, etc.; form an opinion about: Can you **judge** *which shoes are best?*
2 to act as a judge: *Who's* **judging** *the races?*
judgment *noun* **1** the decision made by a judge **2** *(no plural)* what you think or decide: *In her* **judgment,** *we shouldn't change our plans.*

judo /jo͞o′ dō/ *noun (no plural)*
a kind of fighting in which you hold and throw the other person

jug /jug/ *noun*
a container with a handle for holding and pouring liquids: *a* **jug** *of water*

juggle /jug′ əl/ *verb* (*present participle* **juggling,** *past* **juggled**)
to throw several things into the air and keep them moving by throwing and catching them, as a trick

juggler *noun*

°**juice** /jo͞os/ *noun*
the liquid that comes out of fruit and vegetables and also meat: *a*

glass of orange **juice.**

juicy *adjective* **(juicier, juiciest)** having a lot of juice: *Oranges are* **juicy.**

°**July** /jo͞o lī′/ *noun*
the seventh month of the year

jumble /jum′ bəl/ *verb*
(*present participle* **jumbling,** *past* **jumbled)**
to mix up together in an untidy way: *How can I find that letter when all your papers are* **jumbled up** *like this?*

°**jump¹** /jump/ *verb*
1 to move the body off the ground, up in the air, or over something: *She* **jumped up** *onto the chair. The dog* **jumped over** *the gate.*
2 to move quickly: *She* **jumped to her feet** (= stood up quickly).
3 to move suddenly because of fear or surprise: *That sudden noise made me* **jump.**

°**jump²** *noun*
1 moving the body off the ground: *He went over the fence in one* **jump.**
2 something that someone jumps over, in a race, etc.: *The horses raced over the* **jumps.**

jumper

jumper /jum′ pər/ *noun*
a piece of clothing, usually made of wool, that covers the top part of the body

junction /jungk′ shən/ *noun*
a place where two or more things join or meet each other: *Turn left at the* **junction** *of the two roads.*

°**June** /jo͞on/ *noun*
the sixth month of the year

jungle /jung′ gəl/ *noun*
a thick forest in hot countries

junior /jo͞on′ yər/ *adjective*
1 younger: *She teaches a* **junior** *class.*
2 lower in importance or position: *He has a* **junior** *position in the company.*

junk /junk/ *noun (no plural)*
useless things that are not wanted: *That room is full of* **junk.**

jury /jŭr′ ē/ *noun* (*plural* **juries)**
a group of people who decide if a person is guilty or not in a law court (see)

°**just¹** /just/ *adverb*
1 exactly; no more and no less: *It is his birthday; he is* **just** *ten years old.*
2 to the amount needed, but no more: *I can* **just** *reach the top shelf if I stand on my toes.*
3 a very short time ago; by a short time: *You have* **just** *missed the bus.*
4 only: *I rang up* **just** *to say hello.*
5 (used in some phrases, to make the meaning stronger): *Ada is* **just as** *clever* **as** *her brothers. I am* **just** *going to cook a meal; will you stay and eat with us? The last pupil arrived* **just as** (= at the moment when) *the lesson began.*

°**just²** *adjective*
fair and right: *a* **just** *punishment*

justice /jus′ tis/ *noun* **1** *(no plural)* being fair and just: *Everyone should be treated with* **justice. 2** *(no plural)* the power of the law: *The criminals were finally* **brought to justice.**

justly *adverb*

Kk

kangaroo /kang″ gə ro͞o′/ *noun*
an animal living in Australia that jumps along on its large back legs

kangaroo

keen /kēn/ *adjective*
having a sharp edge: *This knife is* **keener** *than that one.*

°**keep¹** /kēp/ *verb*
(*past* **kept** /kept/)
1 to have or hold something: *I don't want this book any more, so you can* **keep** *it* (= have it as your own). *Will you* **keep** *this book until next week, and give it back to me then?*
2 to store something in a place: *Always* **keep** *your money in a safe place.*
3 to give food, clothes, and things that are needed to someone: *He has to earn quite a lot of money to* **keep** *his wife and six children.*
4 to stay or make someone stay: *Her illness* **kept** *her in hospital for three weeks.* **Keep** *still while I'm cutting your hair. He* **keeps** *telling me* (= he tells me often) *but I always forget. Danger —* **keep out! Keep off** *the grass!*
keeper *noun* a person who keeps or looks after something

keep² *noun (no plural)*
the cost of someone's food, clothes, etc.: *He* **earns his keep** *by working with his uncle*

kennel /ken′ əl/ *noun*
a small house for a dog

kerosene /ker′ ə sēn/ *noun (no plural)*
colorless oil that can be burned and used for cooking and lighting

kettle /ket′ əl/ *noun*
a metal pot with a lid, and a handle, and a long curved mouth for pouring; it is used for boiling water: *Will you* **put the kettle on?**

°**key** /kē/ *noun*
1 a metal instrument used for locking and unlocking things: *We have a* **key** *for the door of the house and a* **key** *for starting the car.*

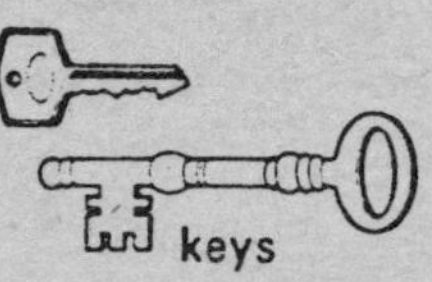
keys

2 a small part of a machine or musical instrument, that is pressed: *There are black and white* **keys** *on a piano* (see). *On a typewriter* (see), *each* **key** *has a letter on it.*
3 an answer, or something that helps you to understand: *The answers are in the* **key** *at the back of the book.*
keyhole *noun* the part of a lock that a key fits into

khaki /kak′ ē/ *adjective, noun (no plural)*
1 a yellow-brown color
2 a strong cotton cloth of this color

°**kick¹** /kik/ *verb*
to hit something with the foot; move the foot suddenly as if to hit something: *Don't* **kick** *the ball into the road. The baby was lying on its back,* **kicking** *its legs in the air.*

°**kick²** *noun*
1 an act of kicking: *If the door won't open, give it a* **kick.**

2 a feeling of pleasure or excitement: *I* **get a kick out of** *driving fast.*

kid /kid/ *noun*
1 a young goat
2 a child or young person

kidnap /kid′ nap″/ *verb* (*present participle* **kidnapping,** *past* **kidnapped)**
to take someone away and ask for money in return for bringing him or her back safely
kidnapper *noun*

kidney /kid′ nē/ *noun*
one of the two parts inside the body which remove waste liquid from the blood

°**kill** /kil/ *verb*
to make someone or something die: *Ten people were* **killed** *in the train crash.*
killer *noun* a person or thing that kills: *The* **killer** *was put in prison.*

kilogram /kil′ ə gram″/ *noun*
a measure of weight; 1,000 grams
° **kilo** /kē′ lō/ *noun* a short way of writing or saying kilogram: *a* **kilo** *of sugar*

°**kilometer** /ki lom′ ə tər *or* kil′ ə mē″ tər/ *noun*
a measure of length; 1,000 meters: *It is three* **kilometers** *to the town.*
km is a short way of writing **kilometer**

kin /kin/ *noun (no plural)*
people in your family: *The dead man's* **next of kin** (= his closest relative) *was told about his death.*

°**kind¹** /kīnd/ *noun*
a sort; type; group: *She is the* **kind** *of woman who helps people. What* **kind** *of car has he got?*

°**kind²** *adjective*
good; helpful; wanting to do things that make other people happy: *She was* **kind** *to me when I was unhappy. It's very* **kind** *of you to help me.*
kindhearted *adjective: She's very* **kindhearted** *— she always helps other people when she can.*
kindness *noun (no plural): Thank you for all your* **kindness.**

kindle /kind′ əl/ *verb* (*present participle* **kindling,** *past* **kindled)**
to begin to burn; make something burn: *This wet wood won't* **kindle.**

°**king** /king/ *noun*
a male ruler of a country, especially one who comes from a family of rulers
kingdom *noun* the land ruled by a king

°**kiss** /kis/ *verb*
to touch someone with the lips, as a sign of love or liking: *He* **kissed** *his wife when he said goodbye. He* **kissed** *her goodbye.*

°**kiss²** *noun* (*plural* **kisses)**
an act of kissing: *He gave his daughter a* **kiss.**

kit /kit/ *noun*
1 all the things needed for doing something or going somewhere: *The soldiers packed their* **kits** *for the journey.*
2 a set of small pieces from which to make something: *We made a model plane out of a* **kit.**

°**kitchen** /kich′ ən/ *noun*
a room used for cooking

kite /kīt/ *noun*
a toy with a light frame covered with plastic or cloth, which flies in the air on the end of a long string

kitten /kit′ ən/ *noun*
a young cat

knead /nēd/ *verb*
to mix and press dough (= flour and water) to make bread

°**knee** /nē/ *noun*
the joint in the middle of the leg where the leg bends

°**kneel** /nēl/ *verb*
(*past* **knelt** /nelt/)
to go down or stay on the knees: *She* **knelt down** *to pray.*

knew /no͞o/ see **know**

°**knife** /nīf/ *noun* (*plural* **knives** /nīvz/)
a blade with a handle, used for cutting

knives

knight /nīt/ *noun*
1 in Middle Ages, an armed soldier
2 in Britain, an honorary title
3 a chess piece

knit /nit/ *verb* (*present participle* **knitting,** *past* **knitted** *or* **knit**)
to join wool or other thread into a sort of cloth using long needles: *My grandmother* **knitted** *me some socks.*

knitting *noun (no plural)* making things by knitting; a piece of knitted work

knob /nob/ *noun*
a round lump, handle, or button: *Turn the door* **knob** *to open the door. This machine has lots of* **knobs** *on it — which one starts it?*

°**knock¹** /nok/ *verb*
1 to hit something, making a sharp noise: *Please* **knock** *on the door before you go in.*
2 to hit or push something: *I* **knocked over** *the glass and spilled the water. The old house was* **knocked down** (= pulled down to the ground). *The bigger man hit the other one so hard that he* **knocked** *him* **out** (= made him fall down, so that he could not know or feel anything).

°**knock²** *noun*
the sound of a blow: *a* **knock** *at the door*

°**knot¹** /not/ *noun*
a fastening made by tying two ends of something together: *to tie a* **knot** *in a piece of string*

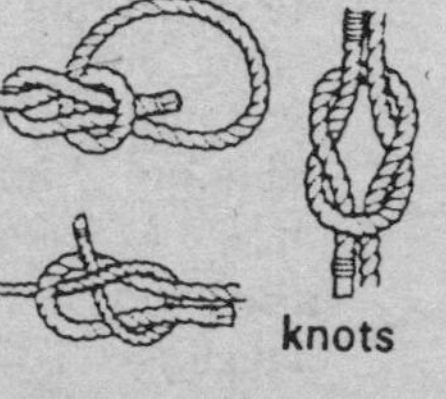
knots

°**knot** *verb* (*present participle* **knotting,** *past* **knotted**)
to tie something in a knot or with a knot: *Will you* **knot** *the rope round the post?*

°**know** /nō/ *verb*
(*past tense* **knew** /no͞o/, *past participle* **known** /nōn/)
1 to have in the mind; have learned: *Do you* **know** *what happened? I* **know** *how to swim.*
2 to have met or seen before: *I don't* **know** *that boy; who is he?*

°**knowledge** /nol′ ij/ *noun*
(no plural)
things that we know: *We go to school to get* **knowledge** *about many different things. He has a good* **knowledge** *of this area* (= he knows a lot about it).

knowledgeable *adjective* having a lot of **knowledge**

knuckle /nuk′ əl/ *noun*
one of the joints in the fingers: *Our fingers bend at the* **knuckles.**

Koran /kô′ rän/ *noun*
the holy book of the Muslims

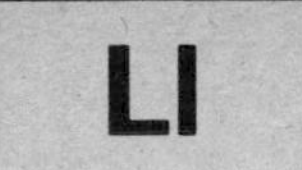

label[1] /lā′ bəl/ *noun*
a piece of paper or other material fixed to something which gives you information about it: *A* **label** *on a letter tells us where to send it.*

labels

label[2] *verb (present participle* **labeling** /lā′ bəl ing/, *past* **labeled)**
to put or fix a label on something: *The parcel was not* **labeled** *so it got lost.*

labor /lā′ bər/ *noun (no plural)*
1 hard work done with the hands: *His beautiful home was the result of many years of* **labor.**
2 the workers in a country or factory: *We don't have enough* **labor** to finish the job.

labor[2] *verb*
to work hard: *We* **labored** *all day to finish the job.*

laborer *noun* a person who works with his hands: *a farm* **laborer**

laboratory /lab′ rə tôr″ ē/ *noun* (*plural* **laboratories)**
a room or building where scientific work is done

lab /lab/ is a short way of saying **laboratory.**

lace[1] /lās/ *noun*
1 a piece of string for fastening a shoe: *I need new* **laces** *for my shoes.*
2 *(no plural)* ornamental cloth with holes in it, made from fine thread: *My dress has lots of pretty* **lace** *around the neck and sleeves.*

lace[2] *verb* (*present participle* **lacing,** *past* **laced)**
to tie with a lace: **Lace** *your shoes* **up.**

°**lack**[1] /lak/ *verb*
to have too little of something: *He* **lacked** *the strength to lift the box.*

°**lack**[2] *noun*
too little of something: *We have a great* **lack** *of water; there has been no rain.*

lad /lad/ *noun*
a boy: *He moved here when he was a young* **lad.**

°**ladder** /lad′ ər/ *noun*
two long pieces of wood or metal joined together by shorter pieces that form steps for climbing: *I need a* **ladder** *to reach the roof.*

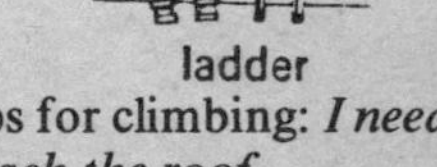
ladder

laden /lād′ ən/ *adjective*
carrying something, especially a large amount: *The truck was* **laden** *with boxes of fruit.*

ladle /lād′ əl/ *noun*
a big spoon with a long handle: *She used a* **ladle** *for serving soup.*

°**lady** /lād′ ē/ *noun* (*plural* **ladies)**
1 a polite woman
2 in Britain, the wife of a lord (see)

lag /lag/ *verb* (*present participle* **lagging,** *past* **lagged)**
to move more slowly than others: *The children were tired and* **lagged behind** *their parents.*

laid /lād/ see **lay**

lain /lān/ see **lie**

lake /lāk/ *noun*
a big pool of water with land all around it

lamb /lam/ *noun*
a young sheep

lame /lām/ *adjective*
(lamer, lamest)
not able to walk easily, usually because of a hurt leg or foot: *My horse is* **lame** *— I can't ride him.*

°**lamp** /lamp/ *noun*
an apparatus for giving light: *There are electric* **lamps** *in the streets.*
lamppost *noun* a tall post in the street with a light at the top
lampshade *noun* a cover for a lamp

°**land** /land/ *noun*
1 *(no plural)* the dry part of the earth, not covered by the sea: *The* **land** *is very dry; there has been no rain. We traveled* **by land** *until we reached the sea.*
2 a country: *After living in foreign* **lands** *for many years, the man went back home.*
landlady *noun* (*plural* **landladies**) a woman who owns a building which she lets others use or live in, in return for money
landlord *noun* a man who owns a building which he lets others use or live in, in return for money
landscape /land′ skāp/ *noun (no plural)* the way an area of land looks: *The trees and the mountains made the* **landscape** *very beautiful.*

°**land²** *verb*
1 to come to the ground or the land from the air or water: *The plane will* **land** *in five minutes.*
2 to bring a plane or ship to the ground from the air or water: *He* **landed** *the plane at the airport.*
landing *noun: The plane made a safe* **landing.**

lane /lān/ *noun*
a narrow road: *We walked down the* **lane** *to the farm.*

°**language** /lan′ gwij/ *noun*
the words people use in speaking and writing: *People in different countries speak different* **languages.**

lantern /lan′ tərn/ *noun*
a lamp in a glass case, often having a handle for carrying it

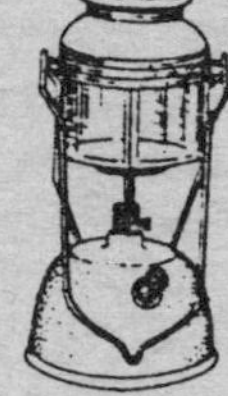
lantern

lap¹ /lap/ *noun*
1 the flat surface formed by the upper parts of the legs when you are sitting down: *Her little girl sat on her* **lap.**
2 the distance once round a track in a race: *a six-***lap** *race*

lap² *verb*
(*present participle* **lapping,** *past* **lapped**)
to drink liquid with the tongue, like a dog: *The dog* **lapped** *its water.*

°**large** /lärj/ *adjective* **(larger, largest)**
big; able to hold a lot: *They need a* **large** *house because they have nine children.*
largely *adverb* mostly: *There are few towns in this area; it is* **largely** *land for farming.*

laser /lā′ zər/ *noun*
an apparatus with a very strong, very narrow beam (see) of light used to cut metal, etc.

lash¹ /lash/ *verb*
1 to hit hard, usually with something like a whip: *The cruel man* **lashed** *the donkey, but it would*

not go any faster.
2 to fasten something tightly with a rope: *We* **lashed** *the boat to a tree.*

lash² *noun* (*plural* **lashes**)
one of the hairs that grow around the eye: *Mary has beautiful* **lashes.** **eyelash** is another word for **lash.**

lasso¹ /las′ ō *or* la sōō′/ *noun*
a long rope with a rope ring at the end, for catching animals

lasso² *verb* (*present participle* **lassoing,** *past* **lassoed)**
to catch with a lasso: *The farmer* **lassoed** *the cow.*

last¹ /last/ *adjective*
1 coming after all others: *The* **last** *boy who came in was James. Who came in* **last?**
2 happening just before this time; the time before now: *I saw my friend* **last** *week, but I haven't seen him this week. I haven't seen his brother since* **last** *July* (= July of last year). *When did you* **last** *read an exciting book?*
3 (used in some phrases): *I waited a long time, and* **at last** (= in the end) *the bus came. That is* **the last** *of the flour; there isn't any more.*
lastly *adverb* at the end: **Lastly,** *let me thank you for your help.*

last² *verb*
1 to go in time: *Our holiday* **lasted** *ten days.*
2 to stay in good condition or unchanged: *Good shoes* **last** *longer. She was very angry yesterday, but it didn't* **last;** *she was happy again today.*
3 to be enough: *Two loaves of bread will* **last** *us for two days.*

°**late** /lāt/ *adjective, adverb* **(later, latest)**
1 after the usual or agreed time: *I was* **late** *for school because I got up* **late.**
2 near the end (of a day, year, etc.): *It is very* **late** *— I should be in bed. He began the work in* **late** *May.*
lately *adverb* not long ago: *Have you been on a bus* **lately?**
latest *adjective* newest: *Have you heard the* **latest** *news? Please arrive by nine o'clock* **at the latest** (= and no later).

lather /laTH′ ər/ *noun (no plural)*
the white soapy mass on the top of water that has soap in it

latitude /lat′ ə tōōd/ *noun (no plural)*
a position on the earth shown on maps by lines (lines of latitude) that go from east to west. Look at **longitude.**

latter /lat′ ər/ *adjective*
1 the second of two: *Richard and Paul came in together; the* **latter** (= Paul) *was wearing his coat.*
2 later in time: *In the* **latter** *years of his life, my grandfather never went out of the house.*

°**laugh¹** /laf/ *verb*
to make a sound that shows you are pleased, happy, or think something is funny: *We all* **laughed** *loudly when she made a joke.*
laughter /laf′ tər/ *noun (no plural): loud* **laughter**

°**laugh²** *noun*
laughter: *We had a good* **laugh** *at his joke.*

launch¹ /lônch/ *noun*
a small boat driven by an engine

launch

launch² *verb*
to put a ship into the water, or to

send a spaceship into space

laundry /lôn′ drē/ *noun*
1 (*plural* **laundries**) a place where clothes and sheets are washed
2 *(no plural)* the clothes and sheets that are washed together at one time: *Will you carry the* **laundry** *into the kitchen?*

lava /lo′ və *or* lav′ ə/ *noun (no plural)*
very hot liquid rock that comes out of the top of a volcano (= a mountain that explodes)

lavatory /lav′ ə tôr ē/ *noun* (*plural* **lavatories**)
1 a small basin or sink
2 a room with this in it: *Where is the ladies'* **lavatory**, *please?*

°**law** /lô/ *noun*
a rule made by the government that all people must obey: *There is a* **law** *to stop people from driving too fast in towns. It is* **against the law** (= not allowed by the law) *to steal.*
lawful *adjective: It is not* **lawful** *to steal.*
lawyer /lô′ yər/ *noun* a person who has studied the laws of our country and helps us to understand them

°**lawn** /lôn/ *noun*
an area of short grass outside a house or in a park
lawnmower *noun* a machine for cutting a lawn

°**lay**[1] /lā/ *verb* (*past* **laid** /lād/)
1 to put down; put in a certain place: **Lay** *the book on the table.*
2 to make eggs and send them out of the body: *The hen* **laid** *three eggs.*

lay[2] see **lie**

layer /lā′ ər/ *noun*
a covering that is spread on top of another thing or in between two other things: *This cake has a* **layer** *of chocolate in the middle.*

°**lazy** /lā′ zē/ *adjective* **(lazier, laziest)**
not wanting to work: *a* **lazy** *pupil*
lazily *adverb*

°**lead**[1] /lēd/ *verb* (*past* **led** /led/)
1 to show someone the way, usually by going in front: *He* **led** *us to his home. The path* **led** *to his home.*
2 to be the chief person in doing a thing; be first or at the front, especially in a race or competition: *After the first half of the race, I was* **leading.**
leader *noun: Our teacher is the* **leader** *— she will show us where to go.*

°**lead**[2] /lēd/ *noun*
1 *(no plural)* guiding; going in front: *We all followed the teacher's* **lead.** *Sarah was* **in the lead** (= in front) *during the race.*

lead[3] /led/ *noun*
1 *(no plural)* a soft, gray metal
2 the part inside a pencil, that we write with

°**leaf** /lēf/ *noun* (*plural* **leaves** /lēvz/)
one of the green flat parts of a plant or tree which grow out of branches or stems: *Some plants have* **leaves** *that grow straight out of the ground.* (picture at **flower**)

leaflet /lēf′ lit/ *noun*
a piece of paper with an advertisement or a notice printed on it

league /lēg/ *noun*
1 a group of people, countries, etc. who join together to help each other: *the* **League** *of Nations*
2 a group of people or teams that

play against each other in a competition: *Our team plays in the football* **league.**

leak¹ /lēk/ *noun*
a hole or crack through which gas or liquid may pass in or out: *There's a* **leak** *in the roof — the rain's coming in.*

leaky *adjective* **(leakier, leakiest)** having a leak: *The roof is* **leaky** *and the rain comes in.*

leak² *verb*
to escape through a hole or crack; let gas or liquid escape: *The roof* **leaks;** *it lets the rain come in.*

°**lean¹** /lēn/ *verb* (*past* **leaned)**
1 to bend forward, sideways, backwards, or toward: *Do not* **lean** *out of the window too far because you might fall out.*

lean

2 to put a thing against or on another thing to support it: *She* **leaned** *her bicycle against the wall.*

lean² *adjective*
not containing fat; thin: **lean** *cattle*

leap¹ /lēp/ *verb* (*past* **leaped** *or* **leapt** /lept/)
to jump: *The dog* **leaped** *over the fence.*

leap² *noun*
a jump: *The dog made a* **leap** *over the fence.*

leap year *noun* a year, once every four years, in which February has 29 days instead of 28 days: 1992 and 1996 are **leap years.**

°**learn** /lurn/ *verb* (*past* **learned)**
1 to get knowledge of something or of how to do something: *Have you* **learned** *to swim? I am* **learning** *English.*
2 to fix in the memory: *She* **learned** *the whole lesson so that she could repeat it the next day.*

°**least** /lēst/ *adjective, adverb*
1 the smallest amount or number: *None of us had much money, but I had* (the) **least** *of all. I had the* **least** *money of us all. They arrived when I* **least** *expected them* (= when I did not expect them at all).
2 (used in some phrases): *He's going away for* **at least** (= not less than) *a week. I'm* **not in the least** (= not at all) *interested in what she says. I don't like rain or storms, and* **least of all** (= especially not) *thunder.*

°**leather** /leTH′ ər/ *noun (no plural)*
the skin of a dead animal specially prepared for use: **leather** *shoes*

°**leave¹** /lēv/ *verb* (*present participle* **leaving,** *past* **left** /left/)
1 to go away (from): *The train* **leaves** *(the station) in five minutes.*
2 to let a thing stay in a place: *When I went to school, I* **left** *my books at home.*
3 to let things stay as they are: **Leave** *the cakes alone — you can eat them later.*

leave² *noun*
a short time away from work: *The soldiers had six weeks'* **leave.**

leaves /lēvz/ see **leaf**

lecture¹ /lek′ chər/ *noun*
a talk given to teach a large number of people: *The students have* **lectures** *every day.*

lecture² *verb* (*present participle* **lecturing,** *past* **lectured)**
to give a lecture: *I am going to* **lecture** *to my students today.*

lecturer *noun*

led /led/ see **lead**

ledge /ledj/ *noun*
a narrow shelf, such as at the bottom of a window, or a narrow, flat piece of rock, on which you can stand: *a window* **ledge**

left[1] /left/ see **leave**

°**left**[2] *noun (no plural), adjective, adverb*
the opposite side to the right side: *The school is on the* **left** *of the road and his house is on the right. Turn* **left** *at the corner.*
left-handed *adjective: If you do most things with your left hand, you are* **left-handed.**

°**leg** /leg/ *noun*
1 one of the parts of the body of a man or animal used for walking: *Men have two* **legs** *and dogs have four* **legs.**
2 one of the parts on which chairs, tables, etc. stand: *a chair with a broken* **leg**

legal /lē′ gəl/ *adjective*
allowed by the law: *Stealing is not* **legal.**

legend /lej′ ənd/ *noun*
a story about people who lived in the past, which may not be true

legible /lej′ ə bəl/ *adjective*
easy to read: **legible** *writing*

leisure /lē′ zhər *or* lezh′ ər/ *noun (no plural)*
the time when you are not at work and can do what you want: *What do you do in your* **leisure** *time?*

lemon /lem′ ən/ *noun*
a yellow fruit with a sour taste, from the lemon tree, which grows in hot places

lemonade /lem″ ən ād′/ *noun (no plural)*
a drink made from lemons

°**lend** /lend/ *verb* (*past* **lent** /lent/)
to let someone use or have something for a time, after which he must give it back: *Can you* **lend** *me that book for a few days?*

°**length** /lenth/ *noun (no plural)*
the distance from one end of something to the other; how long something is: *Mary's dress is not the right* **length;** *it is too short.*
lengthy *adjective* **(lengthier, lengthiest)** long: *a* **lengthy** *speech*

lengthen /lenth′ ən/ *verb*
to make longer: *to* **lengthen** *a dress*

lens /lenz/ *noun* (*plural* **lenses**)
one of the shaped pieces of glass used to bend light in an instrument for seeing things clearly, like a pair of glasses, a camera, or microscope

leopard /lep′ ərd/ *noun* (*plural* **leopard** or **leopards**)
a wild animal with a spotted coat which is one of the big cats and lives in Africa and Asia

°**less** /les/ *noun, adverb*
1 smaller; not so much: *I don't want all that bread — please give me* **less.** *I would like* **less** *bread, please.*
2 (used in some phrases): *He does* **less and less** *work* (= a smaller amount of work) *every day — he's very lazy.*

lessen /les′ ən/ *verb*
to make or become less

°**lesson** /les′ ən/ *noun*
something you must learn; a time when you must learn things in

schools: *We had a history* **lesson** *at school this morning.*

°**let** /let/ *verb* (*present participle* **letting,** *past* **let**)
1 to allow: *My mother wouldn't* **let** *me go to the movies. Hold the ladder for me and don't* **let go** (= stop holding it). *They won't* **let** *people* **in** *without a ticket. She promised to come and help, but then she* **let** *us* **down** (= didn't do what she had promised).
2 to allow someone to use a house or some land in return for money: *They* **let** *their house to another family when they went away.*
3 (used when you ask someone to do something with you): **Let's** *go down to the river and swim.*

°**letter** /let′ ər/ *noun*
1 one of the signs we use to write words: *A, B, C, and D are the first four* **letters** *in the alphabet.*
2 a written message sent to someone by mail: *to post a* **letter**
mailbox *noun* **1** a box in the street or post office where letters are put to be sent
2 a hole or box for letters in the front of a building

lettuce /let′ əs/ *noun*
a vegetable with large, soft, green leaves which are eaten without cooking

°**level¹** /lev′ əl/ *adjective*
1 flat; without higher or lower places: *We need a* **level** *piece of ground to play football on.*
2 equal: *The water was* **level** *with the dike.*

°**level²** *noun*
a place or position of a particular height: *The house was built on two* **levels.**

level³ *verb* (*present participle* **leveling,** *past* **leveled**)
to make something flat: *We* **leveled** *the piece of ground so that we could play football on it.*

lever¹ /lev′ ər *or* lēv′ ər/ *noun*
a long bar for lifting or moving heavy things

lever

lever² *verb*
to move something with a lever: *I* **levered** *the lid off the box with a stick.*

liable /lī′ bəl/ *adjective*
likely: *Your are* **liable** *to* (= likely to) *be caught if you steal.*

liar /lī′ ər/ *noun*
someone who tells lies

liberty /lib′ ər tē/ *noun (no plural)*
being free and not forced to do what other people order: *The prisoner was given his* **liberty** *and allowed to leave the prison.*

°**library** /lī′ brer″ ē *or* lī′ brâr ē/ *noun* (*plural* **libraries**)
a collection of books that people can borrow or a room or building where they are kept: *Our town has a very good* **library.**
librarian /lī brer′ ē ən *or* lī brâr′ ē ən/ *noun* a person who works in a library

lice /līs/ see **louse**

license /lī′ sens/ *noun*
a document showing that the law allows you to do something, like drive a car: *The policeman asked to see his* **driving license.**
license *verb* (*present participle* **licensing,** *past* **licensed**) to give someone a license

lick /lik/ *verb*
to touch a thing with the tongue: *The cat cleaned itself by* **licking** *its hair.*

°**lid** /lid/ *noun*
a cover for a box, pan, or other container, which can be taken off

°**lie**[1] /lī/ *verb (present participle* **lying,** *past tense* **lay** /lā/, *past participle* **lain** /lān/)
1 to have your body flat on something: *He was* **lying** *in the shade of the tree. She* **lay** *down* (= got into a lying position) *on her bed.*
2 to stay or be: *The plates* **lay** *on the table.*

°**lie**[2] *verb (present participle* **lying,** *past* **lied)**
to say things that are not true: *I'm sorry I* **lied** *to you.*

°**lie**[3] *noun (plural* **lies)**
things said which are not true: *Why did you tell me a* **lie?**

lieutenant /lo͞o ten′ ənt/ *noun*
an officer in the army, navy (see), or police

life /līf/ *noun*
1 *(no plural)* the ability that we have to grow and feel: *Animals and plants have* **life,** *which makes them different from stones and water.*
2 (*plural* **lives** /līvz/) the time that someone is alive: *He has lived in the same village all his* **life.**
3 (*plural* **lives)** the way someone lives or spends their time: *He leads a happy* **life** *in the country.*
4 *(no plural)* activity; strength; cheerfulness: *The children were jumping about and full of* **life.**

lifetime *noun* the time for which someone is alive: *In my father's* **lifetime** *there have been many changes in the village.*

°**lift**[1] /lift/ *verb*
to pick up, often to put in a higher place: **"Lift** *me* **up** *so I can see over the fence," said the little girl.*

lift[2] *noun*
a free ride in a vehicle: *He gave me a* **lift** *to the station in his car.*

°**light**[1] /līt/ *noun*
1 *(no plural)* the thing that allows our eyes to see, that there is not enough of when it is dark: *The sun gives us* **light** *during the day.*
2 a thing that gives out light: *We use* **lights** *in the house at night so that we can see.*
lighting *noun (no plural): The* **lighting** *in this room is not bright enough for me to read.*

°**light**[2] *adjective*
1 not dark in color; brightly colored and having a lot of white: *a* **light** *blue sky*
2 easy to lift; not heavy; *The basket is very* **light:** *I can easily pick it up.*
lighten *verb* to make light or more light in weight or color

°**light**[3] *verb (past* **lit** or **lighted)**
to make a thing like a lamp, fire, or cigarette burn or give out light: *Will you* **light** *the fire for me. A* **lighter** *is an instrument for* **lighting** *a cigarette or pipe.*

°**lightning** /līt′ ning/ *noun*
(no plural)
a bright flash of light in the sky, followed by thunder, that happens during a storm

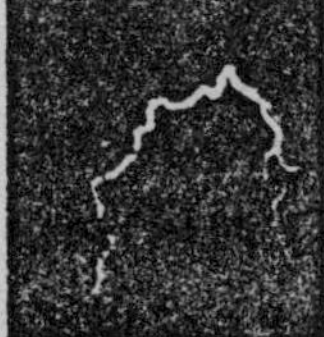
lightning

°**like**[1] /līk/ *verb* (*present participle* **liking,** *past* **liked)**
to find pleasant; enjoy: *Do you* **like** *your teacher? I* **like** *bananas.*
liking *noun: I* **have a liking for** *bananas.*

°**like**[2] *preposition*
1 in the same way as: *I wish I could sing* **like** *her.*
2 with the same qualities as: *Mary's dress is red,* **like** *mine.*

°**likely** *adjective*
1 expected: *The train is* **likely** *to be late.*
2 suitable: *She is the most* **likely** *girl to win the prize.*
likeness *noun* being or looking the same: *There is a* **likeness** *between the three brothers.*
likewise *adverb* in the same way; the same; also: *Paul always finishes his work — you should do* **likewise.**

lily /lil′ ē/ *noun* (*plural* **lilies)**
a plant with beautiful flowers and thick roots

°**limb** /lim/ *noun*
a part of the body such as an arm or leg: *Men and women have four* **limbs;** *two arms and two legs.*

lime /līm/ *noun*
a green fruit with a sour taste from a tree of the orange family which grows in hot places

°**limit**[1] /lim′ it/ *noun*
as far as you can or are allowed to go; the edge of an area of ground; a greatest amount or farthest distance: *The* **speed limit** *is the fastest speed you are allowed to drive a car at. There is a* **limit** *to the amount of money I can afford. The fence shows the* **limit** *of the field.*

°**limit**[2] *verb*
to stop a thing from going past a point or level: *My mother* **limits** *the amount of food that I eat.*

limp[1] /limp/ *adjective*
not firm or stiff: *When flowers are dying, their stems become* **limp.**

limp[2] *verb*
to walk as if one leg or foot has been hurt: *He* **limped** *off the football field.*

limp[3] *noun*
the way we walk when one leg is hurt: *to walk with a* **limp**

°**line**[1] /līn/ *noun*
1 a long very narrow mark: *Write on the* **lines** *of the paper.*
2 people or things one after the other or beside each other; a row: *How many* **lines** *of words are there on this page?*
3 a long piece of string or rope: *We have a* **washing line** *from which we hang clothes to dry.*

line[2] *verb* (*present participle* **lining,** *past* **lined)**
1 to stand in a line: *People* **lined** *the streets to see the famous man go past.* **Line up** *please, children!*
2 to cover the inside, sides, or edges of something: *The box was* **lined** *with soft paper to protect the things inside.*

linen /lin′ ən/ *noun (no plural)*
cloth made from threads from the stem of a certain plant: *Tablecloths and sheets are often made of* **linen.**

lining /lī′ ning/ *noun*
the cloth covering the inside of a piece of clothing: *The* **lining** *of my coat is torn.*

link[1] /link/ *noun*
one of several rings, usually made of metal, fitted together in a long line: *A lot of* **links** *fitted together to form a chain.*

link

link[2] *verb*
to join together or be joined with: *The two towns are* **linked** *by a railroad.*

°**lion** /lī′ ən/ *noun*
(*plural* **lions**)
a wild animal which is one of the big cats and lives in Africa
lioness /lī′ ən es/ *noun* (*plural* **lionesses**) a female lion

°**lip** /lip/ *noun*
one of the soft red edges round the mouth: *We move our* **lips** *when we speak.*
lipstick *noun* color that women put on their lips

°**liquid** /lik′ wid/ *noun*
a thing like water or milk that can be poured
liquid *adjective*

°**list**[1] /list/ *noun*
a lot of names of things written down one under another: *I must* **make a list** *of things to buy.*

list[2] *verb*
to write or say as a list: *I* **listed** *the things I wanted to buy.*

°**listen** /lis′ ən/ *verb*
to try to hear a thing; take notice of what someone is saying: **Listen** *to the noise of the wind in the trees. You should* **listen** *to the teacher if you want to learn.*

lit /lit/ see **light**[3]

°**liter** /lēt′ ər/ *noun*
a measure of liquid: *The bottle holds a* **liter** *of beer. A* **liter** *is equal to about 1¾ pints* (see).

literature /lit′ ər ə chər/ *noun*
(no plural)
good books and writing that people like to read: *Newspapers are not* **literature;** *you usually read them only once.*

litter /lit′ ər/ *noun*
1 *(no plural)* waste paper and other things left lying on the ground: **litter** *on the streets of a town*
2 a lot of animals born together: *a* **litter** *of puppies* (= young dogs)

°**little**[1] /lit′ əl/ *adjective*
(littler, littlest)
small; not big; young: *We live in a* **little** *house. The mother was carrying her* **little** *girl.*

°**little**[2] **(less** /les/, **least** /lēst/)
1 some, but not much: *There isn't much tea, but we only need* **a little** *for a cup of tea. Put* **a little** *salt on the meat. I feel* **a little** *better.*
2 a very small amount: *You eat very* **little** *— that's why you're so thin. I have too* **little** *time to finish this work. I go there very* **little** (= not often).

°**live**[1] /liv/ *verb* (*present participle* **living,** *past* **lived)**
1 to have life; not to be dead: *My grandfather is still* **living,** *but my grandmother is dead.*
2 to stay in a place or at a house; have your home somewhere: *I* **live** *in a town.*
3 to keep alive by eating something or by earning some money: *Cows* **live** *on grass. I can* **live** *on very little money.*

living *adjective* alive

live² /līv/ *adjective*
having life; not dead: *a* **live** *animal*
lively *adjective* **(livelier, liveliest):** *A* **lively** *person is full of life and is always doing things.*

liver /liv′ ər/ *noun*
a large part inside the body which cleans the blood

lizard /liz′ ərd/ *noun*
an animal with four short legs which has a skin like a snake

lizard

°**load¹** /lōd/ *noun*
things that are carried, especially by a train, truck, or ship: *The truck was carrying a* **load** *of bananas.*

°**load²** *verb*
1 to put a load on a truck, ship, or other thing for carrying loads: *We* **loaded** *the truck with bananas.*
2 to put pieces of metal (bullets) in a gun so that they can be fired out of it

°**loaf** /lōf/ *noun*
(*plural* **loaves** /lōvz/)
a piece of baked bread before it is cut up: *to bake a* **loaf** *of bread*

loan¹ /lōn/ *noun*
a thing, especially money, lent to another person: *I asked the bank for a* **loan.**

loan² *verb*
to give a loan: *The bank* **loaned** *me some money.*

loathe /lōTH/ *verb* (*present participle* **loathing,** *past* **loathed)**
to hate: *I* **loathe** *washing dishes.*

lobster /lob′ stər/ *noun*
a sea animal with a shell, a tail, and ten legs

local /lō′ kəl/ *adjective*
in the area near a place; near where you live: *My children go to the* **local** *school.*

locate /lō kāt/ *verb* (*present participle* **locating,** *past* **located)**
1 to put something in a place: *The new building will be* **located** *in the center of town.*
2 to find the place where a thing is: *I cannot* **locate** *the shop.*
location *noun: Have they decided on the* **location** *of the new building yet?*

°**lock¹** /lok/ *noun*
an instrument for fastening things like doors, gates, or drawers, that can only be opened or closed with the right key

locks

°**lock²** *verb*
to close a lock with a key: *My father accidentally* **locked** *me* **out** *of the house* (= he locked the door so that I could not get back into the house).

locker /lok′ ər/ *noun*
a small box or area, often with a lock, for keeping things: *At the station there were* **lockers** *where people could leave suitcases.*

locust /lō′ kəst/ *noun*
an insect that is a kind of grasshopper (see) and lives in large groups

lodge /loj/ *verb* (*present participle* **lodging,** *past* **lodged)**
to pay to live in a room in someone else's house: *My friend* **lodges** *in my uncle's house.*
lodger *noun: My friend is a* **lodger** *in my uncle's house.*

°**log** /log/ *noun*
a large piece of wood as it comes from a tree: *We put* **logs** *on the fire.*

°**lonely** /lōn′ lē/ *adjective* **(lonelier, loneliest)**
unhappy because you are alone: *People who have no friends can be* **lonely.**

°**long¹** /lông/ *adjective*
1 measuring a great distance or time from one end to the other: *I take a* **long** *time to walk to school because it is a* **long** *way.*
2 measuring distance or time from one end to the other: *This piece of string is 30 centimeters* **long.** *How* **long** *do you take to walk home?*

°**long²** *adverb*
1 for a long time: *He said he'd waited so* **long** *that he couldn't stay any* **longer.**
2 at a distant time: *He died* **long** *ago.* **Not long** (= a short time) *after that, he got married.*
3 (used in some phrases): *You can go out* **as long as** (= if) *you promise to be back before 9 p.m.*

long³ *verb*
to want something very much: *I* **longed for** *a bicycle.*

longitude /lon′ jə to͞od″/ *noun* *(no plural)*
a position on the earth shown on maps by lines (lines of longtitude) that go from north to south. Look at **latitude.**

°**look¹** /lo͝ok/ *verb*
1 to point the eyes towards a thing to try to see it: *The teacher told us to* **look** *at the blackboard.* **Look out** (= be careful), *there's a car coming. The children were* **looking for** (= trying to find) *a ball. My friend* **looked after** (= cared for) *my dog while I was on vacation. When you do not understand a word, you can* **look it up** (= find it) *in a dictionary. We are all* **looking forward** *to our vacation* (= waiting for it and thinking about it with pleasure).
2 to seem to be: *That dog* **looks** *dangerous. That* **looks like** *an interesting movie.*

°**look²** *noun*
1 looking; using the eyes: *Take a* **look** *at this book.*
2 the way something appears: *I don't like the* **look** *of it* (= I think it is bad).
3 the expression on a face: *an angry* **look**
looks *plural noun* the way a person appears: **Good looks** (= beauty) *are not as important as kindness.*

loom /lo͞om/ *noun*
a machine for weaving cloth

loop /lo͞op/ *noun*
a ring made by a thing like rope or string crossing itself: *She put a* **loop** *of rope around the cow's neck.*

°**loose** /lo͞os/ *adjective* **(looser, loosest)**
free or able to move easily; not tight: *The dog was tied up but the rope broke and now the dog is* **loose.**
loosen *verb: My belt is too tight; I must* **loosen** *it.*

lord /lôrd/ *noun*
in Britain a title for a man, used before his name

°**lose** /lo͞oz/ *verb* (*present participle* **losing,** *past* **lost** /lôst/)
1 not to keep; not to have something any more: *I cannot find my watch;*

I must have **lost** *it. My father has* **lost** *his job.*
2 not to do well; not to win: *Our team* **lost** *the football game.*

°**loss** /lôs/ *noun* (*plural* **losses**)
losing or a thing that is lost: *The* **loss** *of my watch meant that I had to buy a new one.*
lost /lôst/ *adjective* not knowing where you are: *The little boy went for a walk and got* **lost.**

°**lot** /lot/ *noun* or **lots** *plural noun*
a large amount or number; much: *There was* **a lot of** *mud on the ground. I picked* **lots** *of flowers.*

lotion /lō′ shən/ *noun*
a liquid for putting on the skin or wounds: *Put this* **lotion** *on the insect bites to stop them hurting.*

lotus /lō′ təs/ *noun* (*plural* **lotuses**)
a water plant of Asia with white or pink flowers and round leaves on tall stems

°**loud** /loud/ *adjective*
having or making a lot of noise; easily heard: *The teacher's voice is very* **loud;** *we can all hear it.*
loudly *adverb*
loudspeaker *noun* an electric instrument for making sounds: *There is a* **loudspeaker** *in a radio.*

lounge /lounj/ *noun*
a room in a house or hotel with comfortable chairs

louse /lous/ *noun*
(*plural* **lice** /līs/) a small insect without wings that lives on the skin of animals, birds, and people
lousy /lou′ ze/ *adjective* (**lousier, lousiest**) **1** having lice **2** bad: *What a* **lousy** *day I've had!*

°**love**[1] /luv/ *verb* (*present participle* **loving,** *past* **loved**)
1 to have a very strong warm feeling for someone: *Mothers and fathers* **love** *their children.*
2 to like very much: *Maria* **loves** *reading.*
lovable *adjective* so nice as to be loved very much: *a* **lovable** *child*
loving *adjective* showing that you love someone: *He have her a* **loving** *kiss.*
lovingly *adverb*

°**love**[2] *noun (no plural)*
strong warm feeling: *The boy* **fell in love with** *the girl* (= he started to love her).

lovely /luv′ lē/ *adjective* (**lovelier, loveliest**)
very much liked; very beautiful: *a* **lovely** *cool drink*

°**low** /lō/ *adjective*
1 near the ground; not high: *a* **low** *fence*/**low** *prices*
2 not loud; not high in sound: *a* **low** *voice*
lower /lō′ ər/ *verb* to make a thing nearer the ground or less high or loud: *They* **lowered** *the load to the ground. Please* **lower** *your voice.*
lowland *noun* land that is flat and has no mountains

loyal /loi′ əl/ *adjective*
able to be trusted by a friend or by your country: *The people stayed* **loyal** *to their country in the war.*
loyalty *noun* (*plural* **loyalties**): *The government was sure of the people's* **loyalty.**

°**luck** /luk/ *noun (no plural)*
the good and bad things that happen to you by chance: *It was good* **luck** *that I met you here; I did not expect to see you.*
lucky *adjective* (**luckier, luckiest**) having or bringing good luck: *I was* **lucky** *that I met you here.*

Some people think that black cats are **unlucky** (= bring bad luck).
luckily *adverb*

luggage /lug′ ij/ *noun* *(no plural)* the bags, suitcases, and other things you take with you when you travel

luggage

lukewarm /lo͝ok′ wôrm″/ *adjective* not very warm but not cold: *The water was* **lukewarm.**

lullaby /lul′ ə bī/ *noun* (*plural* **lullabies**) a soft song to send someone to sleep

°**lump** /lump/ *noun*
1 a hard piece of something, without a special shape: *a* **lump** *of rock*
2 a swelling on the body: *I have a* **lump** *on my head where I hit it against the door.*
lumpy *adjective* full of lumps, usually when you do not want them

lunatic /lo͞o′ nə tik/ *noun* a mad person: *He must be a* **lunatic** *to drive his car so fast.*

lunch /lunch/ *noun* (*plural* **lunches**) the meal you eat in the middle of the day

lung /lung/ *noun* one of the two parts inside the chest with which we breathe

lurk /lurk/ *verb* to wait in hiding, especially for some bad purpose: *There's someone* **lurking** *behind that bush.*

lust /lust/ *noun (no plural)* a very strong feeling of wanting something, often something bad or wrong: *a* **lust** *for money*

luxury /luk′ shar ē *or* lug′ shər ē/ *noun*
1 *(no plural)* great comfort: *They live* **in luxury** *in a very big house.*
2 (*plural* **luxuries**) something that you do not really need, but that is very pleasant: *Going to school in a car is a* **luxury.**
luxurious /luk zhoor′ ē əs *or* lug zhoor′ ē əs/ *adjective* fine and expensive; very comfortable: *a* **luxurious** *hotel*

lying /lī′ ing/ see **lie**[1] and [2]

Mm

°**machine** /mə shēn′/ *noun*
an instrument made up of many parts, used to do work: *A* **sewing-machine** *helps us to sew things more quickly.*
machine-gun *noun* a gun that fires continuously while the trigger (see) is pressed
°**machinery** *noun (no plural)* parts of a machine or a number of machines together: *The new factory contained a lot of* **machinery.**

°**mad** /mad/ *adjective* **(madder, maddest)**
1 having a sick mind: *He behaves very strangely — I think he's* **mad.**
2 very foolish: *You're* **mad** *to drive your car so fast.*
madly *adverb*

madam /mad′ əm/ *noun*
a polite way of speaking or writing to a woman: *I began my letter "Dear* **Madam***".*

made /mād/ see **make**

magazine /mag″ ə zēn′ *or* mag′ ə zēn″/ *noun*
a paper-covered book containing stories, articles, and pictures: **Magazines** *are usually sold weekly or monthly.*

magic[1] /maj′ ik/
noun (no plural)
1 strange or wonderful things that happen by a special power; the power to do strange things: *Some people say they can cure illnesses by* **magic.**
2 clever or strange tricks done to amuse people
magical *adjective: a* **magical** *cure*
magically *adverb*
magician /mə jish′ ən/ *noun* a person who can do magic: *There was a* **magician** *at the party.*

magic[2] *adjective*
about or having magic

magnet /mag′ nit/ *noun*
a piece of iron which draws other pieces of iron toward it: *The* **magnet** *picked up the pins.*
magnetic /mag net′ ik/ *adjective*

magnificent /mag nif′ ə sənt/ *adjective*
very great; very fine: *What a* **magnificent** *building!*
magnificently *adverb*

magnify /mag′ nə fī/ *verb*
(*present participle* **magnifying,** *past* **magnified)**
to make things look larger than they really are: *We use a* **magnifying glass** *to see small objects more clearly; it is an instrument which* **magnifies** *things.*

maid /mād/ *noun*
a woman servant

maiden /mād′ ən/ *noun*
an unmarried woman: *A woman's* **maiden name** *is her name before she is married.*

mail /māl/ *(no plural)*
the letters and parcels sent or brought by post: *The* **mail** *arrived late today.*

main /mān/ *adjective*
chief; most important: *the* **main** *road into town*
mainly *adverb: This train is* **mainly** *for commuters; there are only a few shoppers on it.*

maintain /mān tān'/ *verb*
to support; look after: *He has worked hard to* **maintain** *his family. The car has always been properly* **maintained.**
maintenance /mān' tə nans/ *noun (no plural): He took a course to learn about car* **maintenance.**

°**maize** /māz/
another name for corn plant, especially in British English

majestic /mə jes' tik/ *adjective*
very fine; important-looking: **majestic** *figure*
majestically *adverb*

major[1] /mā' jar/ *adjective*
chief; most important: *a* **major** *city*
majority *noun* the largest part or number: *The* **majority** *of children in our class have brown eyes; only two have blue eyes.*

major[2] *noun*
an officer in the army

°**make** /māk/ *verb* (*present participle* **making,** *past* **made** /mād/)
1 to produce; build: *He* **made** *a model plane out of wood. Who is* **making** *all that noise?*
2 to earn; gain; win: *He* **makes** *a lot of money every week — he's got a good job.*
3 to force someone to do something, or cause something to happen: *I don't like milk, but she* **made** *me drink it. That dress* **makes** *you look very pretty.*
4 (used in some phrases): *He* **made up his mind** (= decided) *to become a doctor. The boy* **made up** *a story; it was not true. She* **made up** *her face* (= put special coloring and powder on it) *to look prettier.*
make up *noun (no plural)* special powder and paint put on the face: *to wear* **make up**

malaria /mə lâr' ē ə/ *noun (no plural)*
an illness in which the person has very high fevers, caused by being bitten by a kind of mosquito (see)

°**male**[1] /māl/ *adjective*
belonging to the sex that does not give birth to young: *A lion is a* **male** *animal; a lioness is a female animal.*

°**male**[2] *noun*
a male person or animal: *Men and boys are* **males.**

malnutrition /mal" nōō trish' ən/ *noun (no plural)*
the unhealthy condition caused by not having enough food

mammal /mam' əl/ *noun*
an animal which is fed on its mother's milk when it is young: *A cow is a* **mammal;** *her calves drink her milk.*

°**man** /man/ *noun*
1 (*plural* **men** /men/) a fully grown human **male**
2 (*plural* **men**) a person; a human being: **Men** *have lived here for thousands of years.*
3 *(no plural)* all humans: **Man** *uses animals in many ways.*
mankind *noun (no plural)* all human beings
man-made *adjective* made by people, not grown or produced naturally: *a* **man-made** *material*

manage /man' ij/ *verb* (*present participle* **managing,** *past* **managed)**
1 to succeed in doing something: *He* **managed** *to avoid an accident.*
2 to handle; have power over someone or something: *The horse was difficult to* **manage.** *He*

managed *the supermarket when the owner was away.*

management *noun* 1 the people who control a business **2** *(no plural)* managing: *A business can't do well without good* **management.**

manager *noun* a person who looks after a business

mane /mān/ *noun*
the long hair on the necks of some animals (picture at **animal** and **horse**)

°**mango** /mang′ gō/ *noun* (*plural* **mangoes**)
a sweet juicy fruit with one large seed from a tree which grows in hot countries

mangrove /mang′ grōv/ *noun*
a tree that grows in water near hot sea coasts and has roots hanging from its branches into the water

manner /man′ ər/ *noun*
the way in which something is done or happens: *Why are you talking in such a strange* **manner? Manners** *are the way you behave. You should have* **good manners** *all the time. You should be* **well-mannered,** *not* **ill-mannered.**

manual /man′ ū əl/ *adjective*
using the hands: **manual** *work*

manually *adverb: The work was done* **manually** (= by people), *not by a machine.*

manufacture¹ /man′ yə fak′ chər/ *verb* (*present participle* **manufacturing,** *past* **manufactured)**
to make things in large numbers, usually by machinery: *to manufacture goods in a factory*

manufacture² *noun (no plural)*
making things in large numbers: *the* **manufacture** *of cars*

°**many** /men′ ē/ **(more, most)**
a lot; a large number of: **How many** *bananas are in the basket? There are not* **many** *there.*

°**map** /map/ *noun*
a flat drawing of a large surface: *In the library there are* **maps** *of towns, countries, and the world.*

map

marble /mär′ bəl/ *noun*
1 *(no plural)* a hard stone which can be made smooth and shiny and is used in making buildings
2 a small glass or stone ball used in a game: *to play* **marbles**

march¹ /märch/ *verb*
to walk with regular steps: *The soldiers* **marched** *along the street.*

march² *noun* (*plural* **marches)**
1 a way of walking with regular steps; the distance of a walk
2 a piece of music to which soldiers march

°**March** *noun*
the third month of the year

margarine /mär′ jə rən/ *noun (no plural)*
a food made from animal or vegetables fats: *We use* **margarine** *in cooking.*

margin /mär′ jin/ *noun*
the space at each edge of a page without writing or printing

°**mark¹** /märk/ *noun*
1 a spot or line on the surface of something: *You have a dirty* **mark** *on your face. The black cat has a white* **mark** *on its ear.*
2 a sign; something written to show

something: *It is dangerous to swim beyond this* **mark.** *The teacher gave me a good* **mark** *for my story.*

°**mark²** *verb*
1 to put a sign on something: *He* **marked** *the floor with chalk. The teacher* **marked** *my examination* (= saw how many questions I had right).
2 to put a spot or line on something: *She* **marked** *her white dress when she sat on the grass.*

°**market** /mär′ kit/ *noun*
a place where people can bring goods to sell

marry /mar′ ē/ *verb* (*present participle* **marrying,** *past* **married)**
1 to take someone as a husband or wife: *I am going to* **marry** *John.*
2 to join as husband and wife: *They were* **married** *by a priest.*
marriage /mar′ ij/ *noun: My sister's* **marriage** *took place at eleven o'clock today.*

marsh /märsh/ *noun* (*plural* **marshes)**
low, wet ground: *When they tried to cross the* **marsh,** *their shoes sank into the soft ground.*

marvelous /mär′ vəl əs/ *adjective*
wonderful: *a* **marvelous** *film*

masculine /mas′ kya lin/ *adjective*
like or of a man

mask /mask/ *noun*
a covering to hide the face: *We all wore* **masks** *at the party and no one knew who we were.*

mask

°**mass** /mas/ *noun* (*plural* **masses)**
1 a large quantity of something with no special shape: *Before the rain, the sky was a* **mass** *of clouds.*
2 a large number of people

massacre¹ /mas′ ə kər/ *verb* (*present participle* **massacring** /mas′ ə kring/, *past* **massacred)**
to kill a large number of people: *They cruelly* **massacred** *all the people in the village.*

massacre² *noun*
the cruel killing of many people

mast /mast/ *noun*
a tall length of wood or metal: *The* **mast** *on a ship holds the flag and sails. A radio or television* **mast** *is a metal post which sends out signals.*

master /mas′ tər/ *noun*
1 the chief person; the person who has power over people who live or work with him: *The dog obeyed his* **master.**
2 a word used in front of a boy's name: *The letter was addressed to "***Master** *Peter Jones".*

°**mat** /mat/ *noun*
a floor covering made of woven straw, wood, etc.

°**match¹** /match/ *noun* (*plural* **matches)**
a small stick with something on the end which burns when it is rubbed or struck: *It is dangerous to play with* **matches;** *you might burn yourself.*

°**match²** *noun* (*plural* **matches)**
a game between two people or two teams: *a boxing* **match**

°**match³** *verb*
to be like something else in size,

shape, etc.: *These shoes do not* **match;** *one is large and the other is small.*

mate[1] /māt/ *noun*
1 a friend: *The people we work with are called* **workmates,** *and our friends at school are called* **classmates.**
2 one of a male and female pair of animals or birds.

mate[2] *verb* (*present participle* **mating,** *past* **mated)**
to join together to have young: *Birds* **mate** *in the spring.*

°**material** /mə tir′ ē əl/ *noun*
1 anything from which something can be made: *Wood and iron are* **materials;** *we can make many things from them.*
2 *(no plural)* cloth: *blue cotton* **material**

mathematics /math″ ə mat′ iks *or* math″ mat′ iks/
plural noun (used with a singular verb)
the study or science of numbers: *In our* **mathematics** *class we study arithmetic, algebra, and geometry.*
math /math/ *is a short way of saying or writing* **mathematics.**
mathematical *adjective*

matron /mā′ trən/ *noun*
1 a married woman; a woman in charge, as in a prison
2 a chief nurse in a hospital

matter[1] /mat′ ər/ *noun*
1 *(no plural)* the substance of which things are made: *Everything we can see and touch is made up of* **matter.**
2 something important; something about which we must talk or think: *I have an important* **matter** *to talk to you about.* **As a matter of fact** (= really; in fact) *I'm only thirty-five, so don't say I'm old.*
3 something wrong; something which troubles us: **What is the matter** *with her? She's crying.*

°**matter**[2] *verb*
to be important: *It doesn't* **matter** *if I miss this bus, I can walk.*

mattress /mat′ rəs/ *noun*
(*plural* **mattresses)**
a large flat bag full of soft material on which we sleep: **Mattresses** *are filled with feathers, cotton, or foam.*

mature /mə chůr′ *or* mə too̅r/
adjective
fully grown: *You are a* **mature** *man now; you are no longer a boy.*

maximum[1] /maks′ sə məm/ *noun*
the largest possible amount, number, or size: *I can swim a* **maximum** *of 1 mile.*

maximum[2] *adjective*
biggest; largest: *"What's the* **maximum** *distance you've swum?"*

°**May** /mā/ *noun*
the fifth month of the year

°**may** *verb*
1 (used to show that something is possible but is not sure to happen): *He* **may** *come tonight, or he* **may** *wait until tomorrow.*
2 be allowed to: *Please,* **may** *we go home now?*
3 (showing a hope that something will happen): **May** *the best team win!*

maybe /mā′ bē/ *adverb*
perhaps; possibly: *Are you coming to the party? —* **Maybe,** *I don't know yet.*

me /mē/ *pronoun*
the person who is speaking, (used in sentences like this): *I need that*

book, so please give it to **me.** *Give* **me** *the book.*

°**meal** /mēl/ *noun*
the food we eat at regular times: *I always enjoy my evening* **meal.**

mean[1] /mēn/ *adjective*
unkind; not wanting to share with or help other people: *Peter's father was very* **mean;** *he never gave Peter any new clothes.*

°**mean**[2] *verb* (*past* **meant** /ment/)
1 to be the same as; have as a meaning: *The word "house"* **means** *a building where people live.*
2 to plan or want to do something: *I* **meant** *to give you this book today, but I forgot.*
meaning *noun* what something is or stands for; what should be understood from something: *If you don't understand a word, look up its* **meaning** *in a dictionary.*

means /mēnz/ *plural noun*
1 something which helps us to do what we want to do: *He climbed the tree* **by means of** *a ladder.*
2 money: *He wants to go to college, but his family doesn't have the* **means** *to help him.*

meanwhile /mēn′ hwil/ *or* **meantime** /mēn′ tīm/ *adverb, noun*
the time before something happens or while something else is happening: *They'll arrive in a few minutes —* **meanwhile,** *we'll have a cup of tea. You get the table ready and* **in the meantime** (= while you are doing it) *I'll cook the fish.*

°**measure**[1] /mezh′ ər/ *noun*
the size, weight, or amount of anything: *A meter is a* **measure** *of length.*

°**measure**[2] *verb* (*present participle* **measuring,** *past* **measured**)
to find out the size, weight, or amount of anything: *Mother* **measured** *me to see what size dress I should have.*
measurement *noun: We take the* **measurements** *of something to see how long, tall, or wide it is.*

°**meat** /mēt/ *noun (no plural)*
the parts of an animal's body used as food: *We always cook* **meat.**

mechanic /mə kan′ ik/ *noun*
a person who has been trained to work with machines
mechanical *adjective* of a machine; done or made by machine
mechanically *adverb*

medal /med′ əl/ *noun*
a piece of metal like a coin given to someone who has done something special

°**medicine** /med′ ə sən/ *noun*
1 *(no plural)* the science of treating and understanding illnesses: *A person who wants to become a doctor has to study* **medicine.**
2 things which we drink or eat when we are ill, to help us to get better
medical /med′ i kəl/ *adjective: He is a* **medical** *student. The doctor gave him a* **medical** *examination.*

medium /mē′ dē əm/ *adjective*
not big or small; of middle size or amount: *She is of* **medium** *height.*

°**meet** /mēt/ *verb* (*past* **met** /met/)
1 to come together: *I* **met** *my teacher in the street today. Let us*

meet *at your house tonight.*
2 to get to know someone: *I would like you to* **meet** *my father.*
meeting *noun: Many people came to the* **meeting** *in the hall.*

melody /mel′ ə dē/ *noun*
(*plural* **melodies**)
a number of musical sounds coming one after the other in a song or tune (see): *I like that song; it has a pleasant* **melody.**

melon /mel′ ən/ *noun*
a large round fruit with watery juice inside

°**melt** /melt/ *verb*
to make or become a liquid by heating: *Iron will* **melt** *when it is made very hot.*

°**member** /mem′ bər/ *noun*
a person who belongs to a group: *I am a* **member** *of our school football team.*
membership *noun (no plural)* belonging to a group or the people who belong to it

°**memory** /mem′ rē *or* mem′ ə rē/ *noun*
(*plural* **memories**)
1 the ability to remember things: *Grandmother* **has a good memory;** *she can remember things which happened many years ago.*
2 a thought about the past; something remembered: *I had happy* **memories** *of my school.*

men /men/ see **man**

menace /men′ is/ *noun*
a danger: *A man who drives fast is a* **menace** *to other people.*

°**mend** /mend/ *verb*
to repair or fix something broken or with a hole in it: *Can you* **mend** *the hole in my shirt?*

mental /men′ təl/ *adjective*
of or done with the mind: *A* **mental** *hospital is for people who have an illness of the mind.*
mentally *adverb: He added the numbers* **mentally;** *he did not need a pencil and paper.*

°**mention** /men′ shən/ *verb*
to speak about in a few words: *On the telephone, he* **mentioned** *that he had been ill.*

menu /men′ ů/ *noun*
a list of food that you can choose to eat, in a restaurant, etc.

merchant /mur′ chənt/ *noun*
a person who buys and sells goods, often buying from and selling to people in other countries: *a* **fruit** *merchant*

mercury /mur′ kya rē/ *noun*
(no plural)
a silver-colored metal

mercy /mur′ sē/ *noun (no plural)*
kindness shown to other people by a person who does not have to be kind: *The soldier showed* **mercy** *to his prisoner and set him free.*
merciful *adjective* showing mercy
mercifully *adverb*
merciless *adjective* cruel; without mercy
mercilessly *adverb*

mere /mēr/ *adjective*
only; not more than: *A* **mere** *child cannot do the work of a man*
merely *adverb: I* **merely** *looked at the chocolate; I did not eat it.*

merit[1] /mer′ it/ *noun (no plural)*
greatness; goodness

merit[1] *verb*
to deserve: *His work* **merits** *a prize.*

merry /mer′ e/ *adjective* **(merrier,**

merriest)
happy; full of laughter: *a* **merry** *expression on her face*

merrily *adverb*

merry-go-round *noun* a big machine that you can ride on for pleasure while it turns around and around

mess[1] /mes/ *noun* (*plural* **messes**)
many things mixed up together, often dirty: *Your room is* **in a mess.** *Please tidy it.*

messy *adjective* **(messier, messiest):** *a* **messy** *room*

mess[2] *verb*
1 to make something dirty or untidy; make something not happen in the right way: *I've just cleaned the floor, and you've* **messed** *it* **up** *again by dropping bits of paper everywhere!*
2 to play instead of working; be silly: *Stop* **messing around** *— finish your work.*

°**message** /mes' ij/ *noun*
news or an order sent from one person to another: *I have sent mother a* **message** *to tell her I shall be home late.*

messenger /mes' ən jər/ *noun* a person who takes a message

met /met/ see **meet**

°**metal**[1] /met' əl/ *noun*
a substance such as iron, tin, gold, etc.

°**metal**[2] *adjective*
made of metal: *a* **metal** *box*

meter /mē' tər/ *noun*
a machine used for measuring: *The electricity* **meter** *in our house shows how much electricity we have used.*

°**meter** *noun*
a measure of length equal to 100 centimeters (see) or 39 inches (see)

metric /met' rik/ *adjective: The* **metric system** *of measurement and counting uses* **meters** *for measuring length,* **grams** *for measuring weight, and* **liters** *for measuring liquid.*

method /meth' əd/ *noun*
the way in which something is done: *Our teacher is showing us a new* **method** *of writing.*

mice /mīs/ see **mouse**

microcomputer
/mī" krō kəm pū'tər/ *noun*
a small computer (see) that you can use at home or at school

microphone
/mī' krə fōn"/
noun
an instrument which carries sounds a long distance or makes sounds louder

°**microscope** /mī' krə skōp"/ *noun*
an instrument which helps us to see very small things by making them look much bigger: *She looked at the insect* **under a microscope.**

midday /mid' dā/ *noun (no plural)*
the middle of the day; 12 o'clock **noon** is another word for **midday.**

°**middle**[1] /mid' əl/ *noun*
the part which is the same distance from the two ends or sides of something: *Please stand* **in the middle** *of the room. I woke* **in the middle** *of the night.*

°**middle**[2] *adjective*
in the center: *Which book do you want? I'll have the* **middle** *one. A* **middle-aged** *person is between forty and sixty years old.*

midnight /mid′ nīt/ *noun*
(no plural)
12 o'clock at night

°**might¹** /mīt/ *verb*
1 past tense of **may:** *I asked if I* **might** *borrow the book.*
2 (used to show that something is possible, but not certain or likely): *Jane* **might** *come later, but I don't think she will.*
3 a very polite way of asking for something: **Might** *I borrow your pen?*

might² *noun (no plural)*
strength; power: *He tried* **with all his might** *to open the door, but it stayed shut.*
mighty *adjective* **(mightier, mightiest):** *He gave it a* **mighty** *push and it opened.*

migrate /mī′ grāt/ *verb (present participle* **migrating,** *past* **migrated)**
1 to move from one place to another: *People* **migrate** *to find work.*
2 to travel at the same time every year from one part of the world to another: *Some birds* **migrate** *to find warmer weather.*
migration *noun*

mild /mīld/ *adjective*
gentle; not rough: *The weather is* **mild** *today; it is neither hot nor cold.*
mildly *adverb*

°**mile** /mīl/ *noun*
a measure of length equal to 1,760 yards or 1.6 kilometers

°**military** /mil′ ə ter″ ē/ *adjective*
of soldiers: *a* **military** *government*

°**milk¹** /milk/ *noun (no plural)*
the white liquid that comes from female animals as food for their young: *We drink cows'* **milk.**
milkman /milk′ man″/ *noun* a person who delivers milk to people's houses

°**milk²** *verb*
to get milk from an animal: *to* **milk** *a cow*

mill /mil/ *noun*
1 a place where corn is made into flour
2 a place where things are made by machinery: *Cotton is made in a cotton* **mill.**

millet /mil′ it/ *noun (no plural)*
a grain plant with small seeds

millimeter /mil′ ə mē″tər/ *noun*
a measure of length; 1/1000 of a meter. **mm** is a short way of writing **millimeter.**

million /mil′ yən/ *noun, adjective*
the number 1,000,000
millionaire /mil″yan âr′/ *noun* a person who is very, very rich

mime /mīm/ *verb*
(present participle **miming,** *past* **mimed)**
to use actions instead of speech to show the meaning of something
mime *noun (no plural)*

mimic /mim′ ik/ *verb*
(present participle **mimicking,** *past* **mimicked)**
to copy someone's speech or actions to make people laugh: *He* **mimicked** *the teacher's voice.*
mimic /mim′ ik/ *noun*

mince¹ /mins/ *verb*
(present participle **mincing,** *past* **minced)**
to cut meat up into very small pieces: *We* **mince** *meat in a machine called a* **mincer.**

°**mind** /mīnd/ *noun*
thoughts; a person's way of

thinking or feeling: *Her* **mind** *is full of dreams about becoming famous. He* **made up his mind** (= decided) *to work hard at school. I was going to buy some chocolate but* **I changed my mind** *and bought some apples instead.*

°**mind**[2] *verb*
1 to look after: *Will you* **mind** *the children while I go out?*
2 to dislike: *Do you* **mind** *if I smoke?*
3 to take notice of: **Mind** *the step! Don't fall over it.*

°**mine**[1] /mīn/ *pronoun*
something that belongs to the person speaking: *That bicycle is* **mine** — *I bought it yesterday.*

°**mine**[2] *noun*
a deep hole in the ground from which people dig out coal, iron, gold, etc.

mine[3] *verb* (*present participle* **mining,** *past* **mined**)
to dig out something from a mine: *They* **were mining** *for silver.*
miner *noun*

°**mineral** /min′ ər əl/ *noun*
a substance like iron, coal, or oil which is dug out of the ground

miniature /min′ ē ə chər *or* min′ ə chər/ *adjective*
very small: *a* **miniature** *railroad*

minimum[1] /min′ ə məm/ *noun* the smallest possible amount, number, or size: *You must get a* **minimum** *of 65 questions right to pass the examination.*

minimum[2] *adjective*
smallest: *The* **minimum** *passing mark is 65 out of 100.*

minister /min′ i stər/ *noun*
1 an important person in a government
2 a Christian priest
ministry *noun* (*plural* **ministries**) a part of government: *the* **Ministry** *of Education in Britain*

minor /mī′ nər/ *adjective*
smaller; not very important: *A* **minor** *illness is not a serious one.*
minority /mə nôr′ ə tē/ *noun (no plural)* the smaller part or number: *Only a* **minority** *of the children were noisy; the majority were quiet.*

minus /mī′ nəs/ *preposition*
less: *10* **minus** *2 is 8* (10 – 2 = 8).

°**minute**[1] /min′ it/ *noun*
a measure of time, of which there are 60 in an hour: *He'll be here* **in a minute** (= soon).

minute[2] /mī nūt′/ *adjective*
very small: **minute** *writing*

miracle /mir′ ə kəl/ *noun*
a wonderful happening which cannot be explained so is thought to be caused by God
miraculous /mə rak′ yə ləs/ *adjective: a* **miraculous** *cure for an illness*
miraculously *adverb*

°**mirror** /mir′ ər/ *noun*
a flat piece of glass with a shiny back in which we can see ourselves: *She looked at herself in the* **mirror.**

misbehave /mis″be hāv′/ *verb* (*present participle* **misbehaving,** *past* **misbehaved**)
to behave badly; do something bad: *The teacher was angry because the children were* **misbehaving.**

mischief /mis′ chif/ *noun (no plural)*
foolish actions which may cause harm or damage: *Those boys have been* **up to mischief** *again; they've put water all over the floor.*
mischievous /mis′ chə vəs/ *adjective:* **mischievous** *children*

misery /miz′ ər ē/ *noun (no plural)*
great unhappiness: *the* **misery** *of the people who had lost their homes in the fire*
miserable /miz′ ər ə bəl/ *adjective: I'm feeling* **miserable;** *I'm tired, cold, and very hungry.*

misfortune /mis fôr′ chən/ *noun*
bad luck; something bad which happens to you: *to suffer a* **misfortune**

°**miss** /mis/ *verb*
1 not to hit or catch something: *He threw the ball to me, but I* **missed** *it and it landed on the ground. I was late because I* **missed** *the bus.*
2 not to be where it should be: *A book is* **missing** *from my desk. When she read the list of names aloud, she* **missed** *my name* (= she did not say it).
3 to feel sad when someone is not there: *We will all* **miss** *you when you go away.*

Miss *noun* (*plural* **Misses**)
the title of a girl or unmarried woman: *We call our teacher* **Miss** *Johnson.*

missile /mis′ əl/ *noun*
something which is thrown or fired to harm or damage: *Spears and arrows are* **missiles.** *Men make rockets* (see) *to use as* **missiles.**

missionary /mish ən er′ ē/ *noun* (*plural* **missionaries**)
a person whose work is to teach others about his religion
mission *noun* the place where missionaries work

mist /mist/ *noun*
a thin cloud near the ground: *We couldn't see through the* **mist.**
misty *adjective* **(mistier, mistiest): misty** *weather*

°**mistake**[1] /mis″ tāk′/ *noun*
a wrong thought or act: *You have* **made a mistake** *here; this 3 should be 5. I took your pen* **by mistake.**

°**mistake**[2] *verb*
(*present participle* **mistaking,** *past tense* **mistook** /mis″ to͝ok′/, *past participle* **mistaken)**
to think or act wrongly: *I am sorry, I* **mistook you for** (= thought that you were) *someone I know.*

mistress /mis′ tris/ *noun*
(*plural* **mistresses)**
a female who has control over others: *The dog obeys its* **mistress.**

°**mix** /miks/ *verb*
to put different things together to make something new; join together: *We* **mix** *flour and water to make bread.*
mixture /miks′ chər/ *noun: A* **mixture** *is what we make by putting different things together.*

moan /mōn/ *verb*
to make a low sound of pain: *The child lay* **moaning** *gently.*
moan *noun*

mock /mok/ *verb*
to laugh unkindly at someone: *You shouldn't* **mock** *the way he walks.*

°**model**[1] /mod′ əl/ *noun*
1 a small copy of something: *a* **model** *of an airplane.*
2 a small object which is going to

be copied in a much larger size: *The builder had a* **model** *of the new house.*

model² *verb*
(*present participle* **modeling,** *past* **modeled)**
to make the shape of something; make a small copy of something: *to* **model** *animals in clay*

model³ *adjective*
made in a small size: *a* **model** *car*

°**moderate** /mod′ ər it/ *adjective*
neither high nor low, fast nor slow, large nor small: *a* **moderate** *speed*
moderately *adverb*

°**modern** /mod′ ərn/ *adjective*
of the present time; not old: **modern** *clothes*/**modern** *music*

modest /mod′ ist/ *adjective*
not making oneself noticed or telling other people about what you do well: *She is very* **modest** *about the prizes she has won.*
modesty *noun (no plural)*

moist /moist/ *adjective*
a little wet; not dry: *His eyes were* **moist** *with tears.*
moisture /moist′ chər/ *noun (no plural* small drops of water; wetness: *The sun dries the* **moisture** *on the ground.*

mold¹ /mōld/ *verb*
to make something into the shape we want it to be: *We* **mold** *clay with our fingers.*

mold² *noun*
a hollow container which shapes whatever we pour into it

mold³ *noun (no plural)*
a greenish-white substance which grows on food and clothes if they are left in warm, wet air
moldy *adjective* **(moldier, moldiest): moldy** *bread*

mole¹ /mōl/
noun
a small animal which makes and lives in holes underground

mole

molehill *noun* a small heap of earth thrown up by a mole when it is digging

mole² *noun*
a small round dark spot on the skin

molecule /mol′ ə kūl″/ *noun*
the smallest part which a substance can be broken up into without changing its form: *A* **molecule** *is made up of atoms* (see).

moment /mō′ mənt/ *noun*
a very short time: *He will be here* **in a moment. At the moment** (= now), *I am working.*

monarch /mon′ ərk/ *noun*
a king or queen
monarchy *noun* (*plural* **monarchies**) a country that has a monarch: *Britain is a* **monarchy.**

monastery /mon′ əs ter″ē/ *noun*
(*plural* **monasteries)**
a place where monks (see) live

°**Monday** /mun′ dā/ *noun*
the second day of the week

°**money** /mun′ ē/ *noun (no plural)*
coins and paper banknotes: *He* **makes a lot of money** *selling clothes.*

monk /mungk/ *noun*
one of a group of men who live together and have given their lives to a religion

°**monkey** /mung′ kē/ *noun*
the animal that is most like a human in shape but which usually has a long tail and lives in trees

monotony /ma not′ ə nē/ *noun (no plural)*
lack of change; being the same all the time: *The* **monotony** *of his voice put me to sleep.*
monotonous *adjective: a* **monotonous** *voice which sent me to sleep*

monsoon /mon so͞on′/ *noun*
a wind to the south of Asia; the rain which comes with the wind in the wet season

monster /mon′ stər/ *noun*
an animal or person with a strange or unusual shape, often very big
monstrous /mon′ strəs/ *adjective* big and ugly

°**month** /munth/ *noun*
one of the twelve periods of time which make a year
monthly *adjective, adverb: A* **monthly** *paper is printed every month. We read it* **monthly.**

monument /mon′ yə mənt/ *noun*
something which is built to help us to remember a person or an event

mood /mo͞od/ *noun*
the way we feel at any one time: *The beautiful sunny morning put me in a happy* **mood.**

°**moon** /mo͞on/ *noun*
the large body in the sky which shines at night: *When we can see all of the moon, we call it a* **full moon.** *When we can only see a small thin part of the moon we call it a* **new moon.**

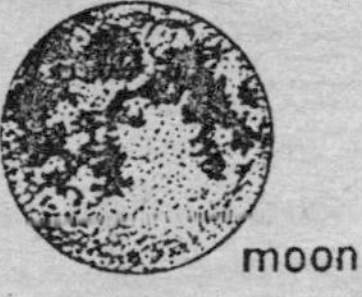
moon

moonlight *noun (no plural)*

moor /môr/ *verb*
to tie up a boat

moral /môr′ əl/ *noun*
a lesson about what is right and wrong which we learn from a story or happening: *The* **moral** *of the story was that we should be kind to other people.*

°**more** /môr/ *adjective, adverb*
1 a larger amount or number: *The other children only have a little bread, but I have* **more.** *I have* **more** *bread than they. I like football* **more** *than swimming. I run* **more** *quickly than Simon.*
2 (used in some phrases): *Next year my brother is going to get a job, so he won't come to school* **any more** (= again). *It is* **more and more** *difficult to find work.*

°**morning** /môr′ ning/ *noun*
the time from when the sun rises to midday

Morse code /môrs′ cōd′/ *noun (no plural)*
a way of sending messages using flashing lights or sounds

Moslem /moz′ ləm/ *noun, adjective*
Muslim

°**mosque** /mosk/ *noun*
a Muslim religious building where people pray

°**mosquito** /məs kē′tō/ *noun* (*plural* **mosquitoes)**
a fly that drinks blood and can carry malaria (see) from one person to another

moss /môs/ *noun (no plural)*
a bright green plant that grows flat on wet ground and stones

°**most** /mōst/ *adjective, noun*
1 the largest amount or number: *You all ate a lot of rice, but David ate* **most.** *He ate* **the most** *of all. I gave him* **(the) most** *rice because he*

was very hungry.

2 very: *You have been* **most** *kind.*

3 (used in some phrases): *It will take you an hour* **at (the) most** (= not more than an hour) *to get to the village.*

mostly *adverb* almost all: *The earth here is* **mostly** *clay.*

moth /môth/ *noun*
an insect with four wings, like a butterfly (see) but usually flying at night

°**mother** /muTH′ ər/ *noun*
a female parent: *the* **mother** *of three sons*

mother-in-law *noun* (*plural* **mothers-in-law**) the mother of your wife or husband

motion /mō′ shən/ *noun (no plural)*
movement: *You must not get out of the car when it is* **in motion.**

motionless *adjective: The cat sat* **motionless** (= not moving).

motive /mō′tiv/ *noun*
the reason for doing something: *His* **motive** *for working so hard is that he needs money.*

°**motor** /mō′tər/
an engine that makes things move or work

motorboat *noun* a small boat with an engine

motorcar *noun* a vehicle on wheels, driven by an engine, that you can travel in; **car** is the usual word for a **motorcar.**

motorcycle *noun*
a big bicycle worked by an engine
motorbike is another word for a **motorcycle.**

motorcycle

motorist *noun* a person who drives a motorcar

motorway *noun* a wide road built for vehicles to travel long distances fast

mound /mound/ *noun*
a heap of earth; a small hill: *Your dog has dug up a* **mound** *of earth.*

mount[1] /mount/ *verb*
to climb up something; to get on a horse or bicycle

mount[2] *noun*
a mountain, usually used in names: **Mount** *Everest*

°**mountain** /moun′ tən/ *noun*
a very high hill: *Mount Everest is the highest* **mountain** *in the world.*

mourn /môrn/ *verb*
to be very sad especially for someone who is dead: *She* **mourned for** *her dead child.*

mourning *noun (no plural): She was* **in mourning** *for her child.*

mouse /mous/ *noun* (*plural* **mice** /mīs/)
a small animal with a long tail which may live in houses and eat stored food

mouse

°**mouth** /mouth/ *noun*
the opening in our faces through which we speak and take in food

mouthful *noun* the amount of food or drink that fills your mouth

°**move** /mōv/ *verb* (*present participle* **moving,** *past* **moved**)

1 to go from one place to another: *The teacher asked Peter to* **move** *to the front of the room. That family* **moved** *last week.*

2 to take something from one place and put it in another: *Who has* **moved** *my book? I left it here.*

movement *noun: She watched the dancer and tried to copy her* **movements** (= how she moved).

mow /mō/ *verb (present participle* **mowing,** *past tense* **mowed,** *past participle* **mown)**
to cut grass: *to* **mow** *the grass*

°**Mr.** /mis' tər/ *noun*
a title put before a man's name: *This is Mr. Brown.*

°**Mrs.** /mis' iz/ *noun*
a title put before a married woman's name: *This is Mrs. Brown.*

°**much** /much/ **(more, most)**
1 a lot; a large amount of: *The baby can't eat* **much** *food. "Did you pay* **much** *for that old bicycle?" "No,* **not much.**" "**How much** *did you pay?" His garden is* **much** *larger than mine.*
2 often: *I don't see her* **much** *because she lives so far away.*
3 (used in some phrases): *Thank you* **very much. How much** *longer can you wait? He talks* **too much.**

°**mud** /mud/ *noun (no plural)*
wet earth
muddy *adjective* **(muddier, muddiest):** *When it rains, the ground becomes very* **muddy.**

muddle[1] /mud'əl/ *noun*
a mixed-up state: *She was in a* **muddle;** *she couldn't even remember what day it was.*

muddle[2] *verb*
(present participle **muddling** /mud' ling/, *past* **muddled)**
to put into disorder; mix up: *If your mind is* **muddled,** *you can't think clearly.*

mug /mug/ *noun*
a big cup with straight sides

mug

mule /mūl/ *noun*
an animal whose parents were a horse and a donkey (see)

multiply /mul' tə plī/ *verb (present participle* **multiplying,** *past* **multiplied)**
to increase by a number of times: *2* **multiplied by** *3 is 6* (2 × 3 = 6).
multiplication /mul' tə plə kā'shən/ *noun (no plural)*

mumble /mum' bəl/ *verb (present participle* **mumbling,** *past* **mumbled)**
to speak in a way that is difficult to hear or understand: *He* **mumbled** *something to me but I could not hear what he said.*

mummy /mum' me/ *noun*
(plural **mummies)**
a preserved dead body

mumps /mumps/ *noun (no plural)*
an illness which causes fever and swellings in the neck and throat

murder[1] /mur' dər/ *verb*
to kill a person when you have decided to do it
murderer *noun* a person who murders someone

murder[2] *noun*
an act of murdering: **Murder** *is a serious crime.*

murmur /mur' mər/ *verb*
to make a soft sound; speak quietly: *The child* **murmured** *in her sleep.*
murmur *noun*

°**muscle** /mus' əl/ *noun*
one of the pieces of stretchy material in the body which can tighten to move parts of the body: *We use our* **muscles** *to bend our arms and legs.*

muscles

museum /mū zē′ əm/ *noun*
a building in which interesting objects are kept and shown to visitors

mushroom /mush′ ro͞om″/ *noun*
a plant which is not green and is a fungus (see) that we can eat

°**music** /mū′ zik/ *noun (no plural)*
1 the pleasant sounds made by voices or by instruments: *to listen to* **music**
2 a written or printed set of musical notes: *a* **sheet of music**
musical *adjective* of music; skilled in music: *She is very* **musical.** *She plays and sings well.*
musician /mū zish′ ən/ *noun* a person who plays an instrument or writes music

°**Muslim** /muz′ lim/ *noun, adjective*
a follower of the religion that believes in the teachings of Mohammed as written in the Koran (see)

°**must** /must/ *verb*
1 (used with another verb to show what is necessary or what has to be done): *I* **must** *shut the door, or the rain will come in. You* **mustn't** (= must not) *be late for school.*
2 (showing what is sure or likely): *It is very late; it* **must** *be nearly 12 o'clock. I can't open the door — somebody* **must have** *locked it.*

mustache /mus′ tash″/ *noun*
the hair that grows above a man's mouth (picture at **beard)**

mustard /mus′ tərd/ *noun*
(no plural)
a yellow powder made from the seeds of a plant, used mixed with water to give a hot taste to food

mutter /mut′ ər/ *verb*
to speak in a low voice: *He was* **muttering** *on the telephone so I asked him to speak more clearly.*

mutton /mut′ ən/ *noun (no plural)*
meat from a sheep eaten as food

°**my** /mī/ *pronoun*
belonging to the person speaking: *I hurt* **my** *knee when I fell off* **my** *bicycle.*

myself /mī self′/ *pronoun*
1 the same person as the one who is speaking: *I looked at* **myself** *in the mirror. I played by myself* (= alone). *I did the arithmetic* **by myself** (= without help).
2 (used to give **I** a stronger meaning): *I made this shirt* **myself.**

mystery /mis′ tər ē/ *noun*
(*plural* **mysteries)**
a strange thing which we cannot explain: *Who had taken the money? It was a* **mystery.**
mysterious /mis′ tir′ e əs/ *adjective*

Nn

°**nail** /nāl/ *noun*
1 a small piece of metal,

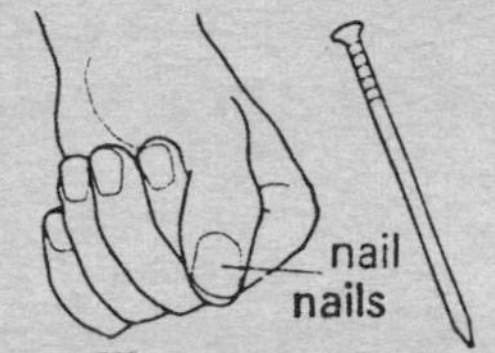

pointed at one end and flat at the other: *He fastened the lid to the box with* **nails.**
2 the hard parts at the end of the fingers and toes: *Sarah cut her* **fingernails,** *but forgot to cut her* **toenails.**

°**nail²** *verb*
to fasten or fix with a nail: *Will you* **nail** *the sign* **on/to** *the door?*

naked /nā' kid/ *adjective*
1 without clothes: *The* **naked** *baby sat in the bath.*
2 not covered: *a* **naked** *flame*

°**name¹** /nāme/ *noun*
the word used in speaking to or about a person or thing: *My* **name** *is Jane Smith. What is the* **name** *of this town?*

°**name²** *verb* (*present participle* **naming,** *past* **named)**
to give a name to someone or something: *They* **named** *the baby Ann.*
namely *adverb* that is: *Ask the smallest girl in the class,* **namely** *Sarah.*

nanny /nan' nē/ *noun*
(*plural* **nannies)**
a woman whose job is to look after children

nap /nap/ *noun*
a short sleep: *to have a* **nap**

napkin /nap' kin/ *noun*
a square of cloth or paper used at meals to keep one's clothes, hands, and mouth clean

°**narrow** /nar' ō/ *adjective*
not wide; small from side to side: *a* **narrow** *path*

nasty /nas' tē/ *adjective* **(nastier, nastiest)**
not pleasant: **nasty** *medicine*

nation /nā' shən/ *noun*
all the people belonging to a country and living under its government: *The whole* **nation** *supported the government.*
national /nash″ nəl' *or* nash″ ə nəl'/ *adjective* of or belonging to a country: *a* **national** *holiday*
nationality /nash″ nal' ə tē *or* nash″ ə nal' ə tē/ *noun* (*plural* **nationalities)** belonging to a country: *Richard is American, John is British — they have different* **nationalities.**

native¹ /nā' tiv/ *noun*
a person born in a certain place: *Mary is a* **native** *of Australia.*

native² *adjective*
belonging to or being the place where one was born

°**nature** /nā' tūr/ *noun*
1 *(no plural)* the world and everything in it which man has not made: *In* **nature** *study, we learn about plants, insects, and animals.*
2 the character of a person or thing: *Peter has a happy* **nature;** *he is a* **good-natured** *boy.*
natural /nach' ə rəl/ *adjective* **1** made by nature: *Rubber in its* **natural** *state is a liquid.* **2** usual: *It is* **natural** *for a cat to catch mice.*
naturally *adverb* **1** by nature: *Her hair is* **naturally** *wavy.* **2** as

you would expect: **Naturally,** *I want to win the race.*

naughty /nô′ te/ *adjective* **(naughtier, naughtiest)**
not well-behaved: *the* **naughtiest** *boy in the class*
naughtily *adverb*

navigate /nav′ ə gāt/ *verb* (*present participle* **navigating**, *past* **navigated**)
1 to decide the way a ship or plane should go: *He* **navigated** *the plane through the low cloud.*
2 to go through or across by sea or air: *He was the first man to* **navigate** *the Atlantic alone.*
navigation *noun (no plural).*

navy /nā′ vē/ *noun* (*plural* **navies**)
the warships of a country; the officers and men of these ships: *My son is in the* **navy.**
naval /nā′ vəl/ *adjective*

°**near** /nēr/ *adjective, adverb, preposition*
not far; close; at a short distance: *Our school is very* **near.** *My aunt lives quite* **near.** *He sat in a chair* **near** *the window.*

nearby /nēr bī′/ *adjective, adverb*
close; not far away: *We swim in a* **nearby** *river. Is the school* **nearby?**

nearly /nēr′ le/ *adverb*
almost: *We have* **nearly** *finished.*

°**neat** /nēt/ *adjective*
clean and well arranged: *She always kept her room* **neat.**
neatly *adverb*

°**necessary** /nes′ ə ser″ ē/ *adjective*
which we must do or must have: *Good food is* **necessary** *to good health.*
necessity /na ses′ə te/ *noun* (*plural* **necessities**) something we need

°**neck** /nek/ *noun*
the part of the body between the head and shoulders

necklace /nek′ lis/ *noun: The girl is wearing a bead* **necklace.**

°**need**[1] /nēd/ *noun*
1 *(no plural)* not having something that is necessary: *The hungry children were* **in need of** *food.*
2 something that is necessary: *The mother looks after all her children's* **needs** — *she gives them food and clothes and other things.*

°**need**[2] *verb*
1 to not have something that is necessary: *I* **need** *a hammer and some nails to repair this chair.*
2 to have to: *You* **needn't** *go home yet — it's only two o'clock.*

°**needle** /nēd′ əl/ *noun*
a thin piece of pointed metal with a hole at one end for thread: *She used a* **needle** *to sew the button onto the shirt.*

negative /neg′ ə tiv/ *noun*
the piece of film from which we make a photograph

neglect[1] /ni glekt′/ *verb*
not to look after someone or something: *The animals were thin and ill because the farmer had* **neglected** *them.*

neglect[2] *noun (no plural)*
the action of neglecting: *The animals were ill because of the farmer's* **neglect.**

Negro /nē grō/ *noun* (*plural* **Negroes**)

a member of the black race of mankind

°**neighbor** /nā′ bər/ *noun*
someone who lives very near you: *My next-door* **neighbor** *lives in the house next to mine.*

neighborhood *noun* the area around a place: *You will find several shops* **in the neighborhood.**

°**neither** /nē THər *or* nī THər/ *pronoun*
not one and not the other of two: **Neither** *boy could swim, but they both wanted to learn.* **Neither** *Peter* **nor** *James can swim. Sarah can't reach the top shelf, and* **neither** *can I* (=I can't reach it either).

nephew /nef′ ū/ *noun*
the son of one's brother or sister

nerve /nurv/ *noun*
a very small part in the body like a thread which carries feelings and messages to and from the brain

nervous *adjective* afraid: *The old woman felt* **nervous** *as she tried to cross the busy road.*

nervously *adverb*

nest /nest/ *noun*
the home built by a bird or by some animals and insects: *The bird laid three eggs in her* **nest.**

°**net** /net/ *noun*
material with open spaces between knotted thread, string, or wire: *The soccer player kicked the ball into the back of the* **net.** *A* **fishing net** *is spread out under water to catch fish.*

° **network** *noun* a large group of lines, wires, etc. which cross or meet each other: *a railroad* **network**

°**never** /nev′ ər/ *adverb*
not at any time; not ever: *I'll never forget her kindness. My brother* **never** *lets me ride his bicycle.* **Never mind** (=don't worry), *you can ride mine.*

nevertheless /nev′ ər THə les′/ *adverb*
but; yet: *He was very tired;* **nevertheless** *he didn't stop working.*

°**new** /nū/ *adjective*
1 not used or worn; not old: *a* **new** *dress.*
2 not seen or known before: *She is learning a* **new** *language. He was* **new to** *the town; he had never been there before.*

newly *adverb* recently; freshly: *The house was* **newly** *built.*

°**news** /nūz/ *pural noun (used with a singular verb)*
things which have just happened: *We listen to the* **news** *on the radio.*

° **newspaper** /nūs′ pā′ pər/ *noun* a paper printed daily or weekly with news, notices, etc. in it **paper** is another word for **newspaper.**

°**next** /nekst/ *adjective, adverb*
1 nearest; without anything between: *Jane sits at the* **next** *desk. My* **next door** *neighbor lives in the house* **next to** *mine.*
2 coming after without anything between: *It was Saturday, so the* **next** *day was Sunday. What did you do* **next?**

nibble /nib′ əl/ *verb* (*present participle* **nibbling,** *past* **nibbled**) to take little bites of food: *Aren't you hungry? You're only* **nibbling** *your food.*

°**nice** /nīs/ *adjective* **(nicer, nicest)**
pleasant; good: *This shop sells* **nice** *fruit.*
nicely *adverb: The child was* **nicely** *dressed.*

nickname /nik′ nām″/ *noun*
a name given to someone which is not his real name: *John's* **nickname** *is "Tiny" because he is very small.*

niece /nēs/ *noun*
the daughter of one's brother or sister

°**night** /nīt/ *noun*
the time when it is dark and the sun cannot be seen: *It rained during the* **night.**

nine /nīn/ *noun, adjective*
the number 9: **Nine** *and one is ten* (9+1=10).
ninth /nīnth/ *noun, adjective*
number 9 in order; 9th: *It's my* **ninth** *birthday today.*

nineteen /nīn′ tēn/ *noun, adjective*
the number 19
nineteenth *noun, adjective*
number 19 in order, 19th

ninety /nīn′ tē/ *noun, adjective*
the number 90
ninetieth *noun, adjective*
number 90 in order; 90th

°**no** /nō/ *adverb, adjective*
1 a word we use to answer a question, to show that something is not true, or that we do not agree with something: *Shall we go for a walk?* — **No,** *I'm busy.*
2 not a; not any: *There are* **no** *children in the classroom.*

noble /nō′ bəl/ *adjective* **(nobler, noblest)**
showing courage to help others; good in character: *It was a* **noble** *act when he saved his friend from drowning.*
nobly *adverb*

°**nobody** /nō′ bod ē/ *or* **no one** /nō′ wun/
not anybody; no person: *I knocked on the door but* **nobody** *opened it.*

nod[1] /nod/ *verb* (*present participle* **nodding,** *past* **nodded)**
to bend the head forward quickly: *She* **nodded** *to show that she agreed with me.*

nod[2] *noun*
an act of nodding: *He greeted me with a* **nod.**

°**noise** /noiz/ *noun*
a loud sound, often unpleasant: *Planes make a lot of* **noise.** *My car's making strange* **noises.**
noisily *adverb*
noisy *adjective* **(noisier, noisiest):** *"What a* **noisy** *class you are!" said the teacher.*

nomad /nō′ mad/ *noun*
a person who travels about with his tribe and who has no fixed home
nomadic *adjective*

°**none** /nun/ *pronoun*
not one; not any: **None** *of the pupils knew the answer. I've eaten all the bread and there is* **none** *left.*

nonsense /non′ sens″/ *noun (no plural)*
something which has no sense or meaning: *She told me that the moon was made of cheese. What* **nonsense!**

noon /nōōn/ *noun (no plural)*
the middle of the day; 12 o'clock: *At* **noon,** *the sun is high in the sky.*

°**no one** /nō′ wun/ *pronoun*
nobody

°**nor** /nôr/
a word used between two choices

after **neither: Neither** *Anna* **nor** *Maria likes cooking.*

normal /nôr′ məl/ *adjective*
usual; not special: *It is* **normal** *to find your lessons difficult sometimes; everybody does.*

normally *adverb:* **Normally** *I get up at seven o'clock, but today I got up at nine o'clock.*

°**north** /nôrth/ *noun, adjective, adverb*
the direction that is on the left when you look towards the rising sun: *We traveled* **north** *for two days. There is a strong* **north** *wind* (=coming from the north).

northern *adjective* in or of the north

northward *adverb* toward the north: *to travel* **northward**

°**nose** /nōz/ *noun*
the part of the face through which we breathe and with which we smell: *She had to* **blow her nose** *to clear it when she had a cold.*

nostril /nos′ tril/ *noun*
one of the two holes in the nose

°**not** /not/ *adverb*
a word that gives the opposite meaning to another word or a sentence: *He is* **not** *at school, because he* **isn't** (=is not) *well.*

°**note**[1] /nōt/ *noun*

notes

1 a single sound in music

2 a short written message: *Mary sent her mother a* **note.**

3 a few words written down to help us remember something: *Please* **make a note** *of my new address.*

4 a piece of paper money: *She collected the money from the bank in new* **notes. Banknote** is sometimes used instead of **note.**

notebook *noun: We used a* **notebook** *to write down things which we must remember.*

°**note**[2] *verb (present participle* **noting,** *past* **noted)**
to look at or listen to carefully so that one can remember: *The pupil* **noted** *what the teacher said.*

°**nothing** /nuth′ ing/ *pronoun*
not any thing: *There is* **nothing** *in this box — it's empty. I got this bicycle* **for nothing** (=free).

°**notice**[1] /nō′ tis/ *noun*
a warning; news in writing that something is going to happen or has happened: *The* **notice** *on the door said that the library was closed.*

°**notice**[2] *verb (present participle* **noticing,** *past* **noticed)**
to see: *The prisoner* **noticed** *that the door was open and ran away.*

noticeable *adjective: The hole in your trousers is not* **noticeable;** *no one will see it.*

°**noun** /noun/ *noun*
a word that is the name of a person, place, animal, or thing: *In the sentence "The boy threw a stone at the dog" "boy" "stone" and "dog" are* **nouns.**

novel /nov′ əl/ *noun*
a long written story usually printed as a book

novelist *noun* a person who writes novels

°**November** /nō vem′ bər/ *noun*
the 11th month of the year

°**now** /nou/ *adverb*
1 at the present time: *We used to*

live in a village, but **now** *we live in a city. I must go* **now** *— I can't wait any longer.*
2 (used to call attention): **Now,** *children, what are you doing?*

nowadays *adverb* in these times: **Nowadays** *people can fly all over the world in planes.*

°**nowhere** /nō′ hwâr/ *adverb*
not anywhere; in, at or to no place: *We look for the key everywhere but it was* **nowhere** *to be found* (=we couldn't find it anywhere).

nuclear /nū′ klē ər/ *adjective*
using the very great power made by splitting an atom (see) or joining atoms: *A* **nuclear bomb** *is the most powerful weapon we have.*

nucleus /nū′ klē əs/ *noun (plural* **nuclei)**
the central part of something round which other parts gather: *A* **nucleus** *is the central part of an atom* (see).

nudge[1] /nuj/ *verb (present participle* **nudging,** *past* **nudged)**
to push someone lightly with the elbow: *He* **nudged** *him to wake him up.*

nudge[2] *noun*
an act of nudging: *He gave him a* **nudge.**

°**nuisance** /nōō′ səns/ *noun (no plural)*
someone or something which troubles us: *What a* **nuisance!** *I've missed my train.*

°**number**[1] /num′ bər/ *noun*
1 words or figures like one, two, and three or 1, 2, and 3
2 more than one person or thing, in a group: *Birds gather in large* **numbers** *beside the river.*

numerous /nōō′ mə rəs/ *adjective: Your work has* **numerous** (=very many) *mistakes in it.*

number[2] *verb*
to give a figure to something: *The pages of the book were* **numbered** *1 to 268.*

numeral /nōōm′ rəl *or* nōō′mər əl/ *noun*
a sign used to represent a number: *3 is a* **numeral.**

nun /nun/ *noun*
one of a group of women who live together and have given their lives to God

°**nurse**[1] /nurs/ *noun*
1 a person who is trained to look after people who are ill: *She works as a* **nurse** *in a hospital.*

°**nurse**[2] *verb (present participle* **nursing,** *past* **nursed)**
to care for sick people: *She* **nursed** *her mother when she was ill.*

°**nut** /nut/ *noun*
1 a fruit of a plant or tree, with a hard shell
2 a shaped piece of metal which we put on the end of a bolt (see)

nylon /nī′ lon/ *noun (no plural)*
a strong thread, made by machines: **Nylon** *is used to make stockings* (see) *and clothes.*

Oo

°**oak** /ōk/ *noun*
a tree with hard wood

oar /ôr/ *noun*
a long bar of wood with a flat blade at the end, used to make a boat move

oasis /ō ā′ sis/ *noun (plural* **oases** /ō ā′ sēz/*)*
a place in the desert where there is water and where trees can grow

oath /ōth/ *noun*
a very serious promise: *In court we* **take an oath** *to tell the truth.*

oats /otz/ *noun*
a grain plant

°**obey** /ō bā′/ *verb*
to do what you are told to do: *You should* **obey** *your teacher.*
obedience /ō bē′ dē əns/ *noun (no plural) The dog has learned* **obedience.** *It obeys its owner.*
obedient /ō bē′ dē ənt/ *adjective*

°**object**[1] /ob′ jikt *or* ob′ jekt″/ *noun*
1 a thing: *What is that big red* **object** *over there?*
2 an aim or purpose

object[2] *noun*
the person or thing that the action of a verb is done to; the noun that usually follows the verb: *In the sentence "Jane bought the bread", bread is the* **object.**
Look at subject.

object[3] /ob jekt′/ *verb*
to say that you do not like or agree with something: *She* **objected to** *our plan.*
objection *noun: She had strong* **objections** *to the plan.*

oblige /əb′ blīj′/ *verb (present participle* **obliging,** *past* **obliged)**
to make someone do something: *It was raining so hard that I was* **obliged** *to stay at home.*
obligation /ob″ lə gā′ shan/ *noun* a duty; something we must do

oblong /ob′ lông″/ *noun, adjective*
a flat shape with four straight sides and four equal angles, that is longer than it is wide

observe /əb zurv′/ *verb (present participle* **observing,** *past* **observed)**
1 to watch something carefully; see and notice something: *The policeman asked if we had* **observed** *anything unusual.*
2 to say
observation /ob″ zər vā′ shən/ *noun (no plural)*
1 watching carefully: *The police kept the man* **under observation.**
2 something said

obstacle /ob′ stə kəl/ *noun*
something that gets in the way; a difficulty: *The truck had to go slowly because of fallen trees and other* **obstacles** *on the road.*

obstinate /ob′ sti nit/ *adjective*
having a strong will; not willing to change easily

obstruct /ob strukt′/ *verb*
to get in the way of something or stop it completely: *The road was* **obstructed** *by a fallen tree.*
obstruction noun: There was an **obstruction** *on the road.*

obtain /ob tān′/ *verb*
to get: *I haven't been able to* **obtain** *that book.*

obvious /ob′ vē əs/ *adjective*
clear and easy to see or understand: *It is* **obvious** *that she is very clever.*
obviously *adverb:* **Obviously** *the thief got in through the door — the lock is broken.*

occasion /ə kā′ zhən/ *noun*
a time when something happens, often something special: *My son's first birthday is an important* **occasion.**
occasional *adjective* happening from time to time
occasionally /ə kā′ zhən ə lē/ *adverb: We go for walks in the fields* **occasionally.**

occupy /ok′ yə pī″/ *verb (present participle* **occupying,** *past* **occupied)**
1 to live or be in a place: *Three families* **occupy** *that big house.*
2 to use time to do something: *While he was waiting, he* **occupied** *himself by reading a book. This work keeps us fully* **occupied** (=busy).
occupation *noun*
1 a job; a way of using time: *What is his* **occupation?** He is a teacher.
2 *(no plural)* being in a certain place or space

occur /ə kər′/ *verb (present participle* **occurring,** *past* **occurred)**
1 to happen, especially of something unexpected: *The accident* **occurred** *at five o'clock.*
2 to come into mind: *That idea has never* **occurred to** *me before.*

ocean /ō′ shən/ *noun*
a very large sea: *the* **Atlantic Ocean**

°**o'clock** /ə klok′/ *adverb*
a word used when saying what hour of the day it is: *What time is it? It's four* **o'clock** *exactly.*

°**October** /ok tō′ bər/ *noun*
the tenth month of the year

octopus /ok′ tə pəs/ *noun (plural* **octopuses)**
a soft sea creature, sometimes very large, which has eight long limbs

octopus

°**odd** /od/ *adjective*
1 strange or unusual: *It's* **odd** *that he hasn't telephoned me.*
2 (of a number) that cannot be divided by two: *7 and 9 are* **odd** *numbers, but 6 and 8 are even numbers.*
3 one of a pair, or not fitting together as a pair: *I've found an* **odd** *shoe — where is the other one? You've got* **odd** *socks on — one's blue and the other is green! In the pantry there's a box full of* **odds and ends** (=different things which are not important).

odor /ō′dər/ *noun*
a smell: *a strange* **odor**

°**of** /uv, ov, *or* əv/ *preposition*
1 belonging to: *a friend* **of** *mine*
2 containing: *a cup* **of** *tea/ a pound* **of** *butter*
3 from among: *I gave my friend some* **of** *my pencils.*
4 made from: *a dress* **of** *cotton*
5 about: *I often think* **of** *you.*
6 (used in some phrases): *Canada is north* **of** *the United States.*

of course /uv, ov, *or* əv kôrs/see **course**

°**off** /ôf *or* of/ *adverb, preposition*
1 away from; from a place: *Take* **off** *that wet shirt, and clean the mud* **off** *your shoes. The car took* **off** *down the road.*
2 not on or not working: *Is the light in the kitchen on or* **off?** *I*

turned it **off.** *Sunday is my only day* **off.** (=when I don't work).
3 at a distance: *My house is not far* **off.**

offend /ə fend'/ *verb*
to make someone feel unhappy or angry: *I* **offended** *him by not answering his letter.*

offense *noun* **1** something that is wrong; a crime: *It is an* **offense** *to ride a bicycle at night without lights.* **2** *(no plural)* making someone angry or unhappy; rudeness: *He* **took offense** *because I didn't answer his letter.*

°**offer¹** /ô' fər/ *verb*
to say or show that we are ready to give or do something: *James* **offered** *me an orange, but I didn't take it. Sarah* **offered** *to carry the box for her mother.*

°**offer²** *noun*
1 when we say we are ready to give or do something: *Thank you for your* **offer** *of help.*
2 the thing we offer: *He would not sell us the car because our* **offer** (=the money we offered) *was too low.*

°**office** /ôf' is/ *noun*
a place where business and paper work is done: *She works in an* **office.**

°**officer** /ôf' ə sər/ *noun*
1 a person who can give orders to other people, in the army, etc.
2 a person who has an important job in the government, a business, etc.: *A policeman is also called a* **police officer.**

offical¹ /ə fish' əl/ *adjective*
of or from the government or someone important: *an* **official** *letter.*

official² *noun*
a person who works in the government: *an* **official** *in the department of health*

°**often** /ôf' ən/ *adverb*
many times: *I* **often** *see her because she lives near me.* **How often** *have you been abroad? Not* **often,** *only twice.*

°**oil¹** /oil/ *noun*
(no plural)
thick liquid that comes from plants or animals, from under the ground or under the sea, used for cooking, burning, or for making machines work smoothly: *An* **oil well** *is a hole made in the ground to get* **oil** *out. The tall machinery above it is called an* **oil rig.**

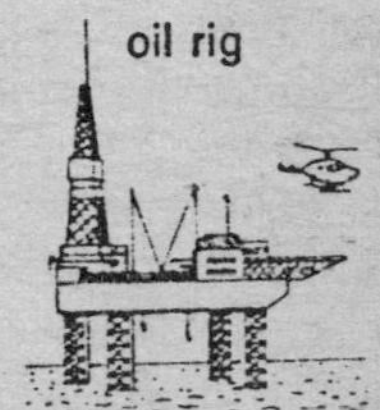
oil rig

°**oil²** *verb*
to put oil on something: *You should* **oil** *that machine often.*

ointment /oint' mənt/ *noun*
(no plural)
smooth oily medicine that can be rubbed on the skin

°**old** /ōld/ *adjective*
1 not young; having lived a long time: *My grandmother is very* **old.**
2 the word we use to show our age: *How* **old** *are you? I am eleven years* **old.**
3 not new: **old** *clothes/an* **old** *building*
4 having lasted for a long time: *We are very* **old** *friends — we've known each other since we were children.*

old-fashioned *adjective* not modern; not common any more: **old-fashioned** *clothes*

olive /ol' iv/ *noun*

a small fruit which is green or black, from the olive tree

olive oil *noun (no plural)* oil made from olives and used for food

omelet /om′ lit/ *noun*
eggs beaten together and cooked in hot fat in a flat pan

omit /ō′ mit/ *verb (present participle* **omitting,** *past* **omitted)**
to leave out; not include: *You have* **omitted** *my name from the list.*

°**on** /on/ *preposition, adverb*
1 (used to show where something is): *I put the glass* **on** *the shelf. There is a list of our lessons* **on** *the wall. The town stands* **on** *the hill.*
2 (used with days or dates, to show when): *The party is* **on** *March 12th. We gave Julie a present* **on** *her birthday.*
3 about: *a lesson* **on** *history*
4 in use; working: *Is the light in the kitchen off or* **on?** *I'll turn it* **on.**
5 continuously; without stopping; further: *I stopped for a rest and James went* **on** *alone.*
6 covering the body: *When I heard the door bell I was in the bath with nothing* **on,** *so I put my clothes* **on** *quickly.*
7 (used in some other ways): *What's* **on** *television tonight?* (=what film or pictures are being shown) **On** *her arrival* (=when she arrived) *she telephoned her mother. Did you come by car or* **on foot?** (=walking)

°**once** /wuns/ *adverb*
1 one time: *I have been to Europe* **once,** *but my friend has been* **more than once.**
2 sometime ago: *My grandmother was* **once** *a teacher in this school.*
3 when: *It was easy* **once** *I learned how to do it.*
4 (used in some phrases): *Go* **at once** (=without waiting), *or you will be late. You can't do three different things* **at once** (=at the same time). *If you can't do it the first time, try* **once more** (=again).

°**one** /wun/ *pronoun*
1 the number 1: *Only* **one** *person came to the meeting.* **One** *and two make three* (1+2=3).
2 a single thing or person: *Have you any books on farming? — I'd like to borrow* **one** (=a book on farming). *That girl has only got* **one** *shoe on, I wonder where the other* **one** *is.*
3 a: *John telephoned me* **one** *day last week.*
4 the same: *They all ran in* **one** *direction.*
5 any person: **One** *should try to help other people. Mary and I like* **one another** (=Mary likes me and I like her).

oneself /wun″ self′/ *pronoun*
the same person as **one** in the sentence: *Sometimes it's nice to sit* **by oneself** (=alone) *and read.*

onion /un′ yən/ *noun*
a round vegetable with a strong smell, which is made up of one skin inside another

onions

°**only** /ōn′ lē/ *adjective, adverb*
1 that is the one person or thing of the same kind or in the same group: *She is the* **only** *girl in her family; all the other children are boys. James is an* **only child** (=his parents have no other children).
2 and nothing more; and no one else: *I don't want to buy anything; I'm* **only** *looking. The sign on the*

door said "Ladies **only".**
3 but: *I'll lend you my book,* **only** *you must take care of it.*
4 (used to make something stronger): **If only** *she would come!* (=I want her to come very much) *They've* **only just** *arrived* (=they arrived a very short time ago).

onto /on' to͞o/ *preposition*
to a place: *He climbed* **onto** *a rock.*

onward /on' ward/ (also **onwards**) *adverb*
forward in time or space: *They hurried* **onward.** *From Monday* **onward** *I shall be in another class.*

ooze /o͞oz/ *verb* (*present participle* **oozing,** *past* **oozed**)
to move or flow slowly: *The blood* **oozed** *out of the meat.*

°**open**[1] /ō' pən/ *adjective*
1 not shut or covered: *She's not asleep; her eyes are* **open.** *There is an* **open** *market in the village.*
2 ready for business: *The bank isn't* **open.**
3 not surrounded by other things: *We drove through* **open** *country, where there were no towns or villages. The party was held* **in the open air** (=outside).

°**open**[2] *verb*
1 to make something open or become open: **Open** *your books at page three. The door* **opened** *and my sister walked in.*
2 to start: *The shop doesn't* **open** *until 10 o'clock.*

opener *noun* an instrument for opening things: *a can-opener*

opening /ō' pən ing/ *noun* a space or a way through something: *He put a gate across the* **opening** *in the fence.*

opera /op' rə *or* op' ə rə/ *noun*
a kind of play which has songs and music instead of spoken words

operate /op' ə rāt/ *verb* (*present participle* **operating,** *past* **operated**)
1 to work or make something work: *Do you know how to* **operate** *this machine?*
2 to cut the body of someone who is ill, to make the unhealthy part better: *The doctors* **operated on** *her stomach.*

operation *noun* **1** *(no plural)* the way a thing works; making something work: *The* **operation** *of a sewing machine is easy.* **2** cutting a part of the body of someone who is ill: *an* **operation** *on her stomach*

operator /op' ə rā" tər/ *noun* **1** a person who makes a machine work: *a telephone* **operator**

°**opinion** /ə pin' yən/ *noun*
what someone thinks about something: *He asked his father's* **opinion** *about his plans.* **In my opinion** (=I think), *you're wrong.*

opponent /ə pō' nənt/ *noun*
someone who is on the opposite side, in playing or fighting: *We beat our* **opponents** *in football.*

opportunity /op' ər too'nə tē/ *noun* (*plural* **opportunities**)
a chance or time to do something: *I have been offered a job. It's a great* **opportunity.**

oppose /ə pōz'/ *verb*
(*present participle* **opposing,** *past* **opposed**)
to be against something; not agree with something: *My mother is* **opposed to** *the new plan.*

opposition /op" ə zish' ən/ *noun:*

opposition *to his plan.*

opposite[1] /op′ ə zit/ *noun*
a person or thing that is as different as possible from another: *High is the* **opposite** *of low.*

°**opposite**[2] *adjective*
1 as different as possible: *The buses went in* **opposite** *directions — one went south and the other went north.*
2 facing: *The library is on the* **opposite** *side of the road from the school.*

°**opposite**[3] *preposition*
facing: *The library is* **opposite** *the school.*

optician /op tish′ ən/ *noun*
a person who makes and sells eyeglasses

option /op′ shən/ *noun*
a choice; the power to choose: *Since the train didn't come, and there was no bus, I had no* **option** *but to wait* (=there was nothing I could do except wait).

optional *adjective* that you can choose: *Is English an* **optional** *lesson, or does everyone have to learn it?*

°**or** /ôr/ *conjunction*
(used when giving a choice): *Will you have tea* **or** *coffee? I don't know where I left my book —* **either** *at school* **or** *on the bus.*

oral /or′ əl *or* ō′ rəl/ *adjective*
spoken, not written: *We're having an* **oral** *test in class this week.*

°**orange**[1] /ôr′ inj/ *noun*
a round sweet juicy fruit from the orange tree

°**orange**[2] *noun, adjective*
(of) the color of the skin of an orange when it is ripe; a mixture of yellow and red

orbit[1] /ôr′ bit/ *noun*
the path of one thing moving around another in space

orbit[2] *verb*
to move in an orbit around something: *The spaceship* **orbited** *the moon.*

orchard /ôr′ chərd/ *noun*
a field where fruit trees grow

orchestra /ôr′ kəs trə/ *noun*
a large group of people who play musical instruments together

orchestra

°**order**[1] /ôr′ dər/ *noun*
1 *(no plural)* being carefully arranged; neatness: *You must try to keep these important papers* **in order.** *The teacher kept the children* **in order** (=made them stay calm and quiet). *The telephone is* **out of order** (=not working).
2 *(no plural)* a special way things are arranged or placed: *The words in this book are in alphabetical* **order** *— so "apple" comes before "banana", and "many" comes before "mend".*
3 something that tells someone what he must do: *Soldiers have to obey* **orders.**
4 (used in some phrases): *He stood on a chair* **in order to** (=so that he could) *reach the top shelf.*

°**order**[2] *verb*
to say that something must be done, made, brought, etc.: *The officer* **ordered** *the soldiers to attack. I* **ordered** *a new suit from the shop.*

°**ordinary** /ôr də ner′ ē/ *adjective*
usual or common; not special: *It was a very* **ordinary** *day today — I got up, went to school, came home, ate a meal, and went to bed.*
ordinarily *adverb*

ore /ôr/ *noun*
a kind of rock or earth in which metal is found: *iron* **ore**

organ /ôr′ gən/ *noun*
1 a part of an animal or a plant that has a special purpose: *The eyes are the* **organs** *of sight.*
2 a musical instrument which has long pipes. Air goes through the pipes to make the sounds.

°**organize** /ôr′ gən iz/ *verb* (*present participle* **organizing,** *past* **organized**)
to arrange in a careful way; put in order; plan: *Jane* **organized** *the party. She asked people to come and bought the food and drinks.*
organization *noun* **1** *(no plural)* arranging or planning: *Good* **organization** *makes your work easier.* **2** a group of people with a special purpose, like a club or a business

origin /ôr′ ə jin/ *noun*
the place or people that someone or something comes from: *Many Americans are Italian* **by origin.**
original /ə rij′ ə nəl/ *adjective* **1** first; earliest: *Who was the* **original** *owner of this house?* **2** new and different: *an* **original** *idea for a game* **3** not copied: *This is the* **original** *painting, and these others are copies.*
originally *adverb* in the beginning: *I live here now, but I wonder who lived here* **originally?**

°**ornament** /ôr′ nə mənt/ *noun*
something which we have because it is beautiful, not because it is useful: *That pot is an* **ornament;** *we don't use it.*
ornamental: ôr″ nə mənt′ əl/ *adjective: an* **ornamental** *pot*

orphan /ôr′ fən/ *noun*
someone whose mother and father are dead
orphanage *noun* a home for orphan children

ostrich /os′ trich/ *noun* (*plural* **ostriches**)
a very large bird, with long legs, that is black and white, and cannot fly

ostrich

°**other** /uTH′ ər/ *adjective*
1 not the same; a different one; *I sleep in this room, and my brother sleeps in the* **other** *room. Alice didn't like that dress, so she asked to see some* **others.**
2 someone or something not mentioned specially: *The blue pen is mine and all the* **others** (=the other pens) *are yours.*

otherwise /uTH′ ər wīz/ *adverb*
1 if not: *You should go now,* **otherwise** *you'll miss the bus.*
2 except for that: *I've got one more page to write;* **otherwise** *I've finished.*
3 differently: *We were going to play football, but it was so hot that we decided to do* **otherwise** (=to do something different).

°**ought** /ôt/ *verb*
(used to show what someone should or must do, or what is right): *He* **ought to** *take care of his children.*

ounce /ouns/ *noun*
a measure of weight equal to 28.35 grams (see): *There are 16* **ounces** *in one pound.* **Oz.** is a short way of writing **ounce.**

°**our** /our/ *adjective*
belonging to us: *We put* **our** *books in* **our** *bags.*

°**ours** /ourz/ *pronoun*
something that belongs to us: *They left their books at school but we took* **ours** *home.*

ourselves /our selvz′/ *pronoun*
the same people as *we* or *us* in the sentence: *We hid* **ourselves** *in the cupboard. We did that* **by ourselves** (=no one helped us). *Our mother never lets us go on the train* **by ourselves** (=without another person).

°**out** /out/ *adverb*
1 not in or inside; away from: *Shut the gate or the dog will get* **out.** *She opened the bag and took* **out** *the money.*
2 not at home or in an office: *My father is* **out** *this morning, but he will be in this afternoon.*
3 not shining or burning: *The lights were* **out** *and the house was dark The fire went* **out.**
4 (used in sentences like this): *When he called* **out** (=loudly) I heard him. I feel tired **out** (=completely tired). *This list is for last year; it's* **out of date** (=old) *now.*

outdoor *adjective* not in a building: *an* **outdoor** *pool*

outdoors *adverb: A farmer works* **outdoors.**

°**outer** *adjective* on the outside or edge of something; far away from the middle: *The* **outer** *walls of the house were made of brick.*

outing *noun* a trip or short journey.

outfit /out′ fit″/ *noun*
a set of clothes, especially for a special purpose: *The football team wore yellow* **outfits.**

outline /out′ līn″/ *noun*
a line showing the shape of something: *He drew the* **outline** *of a house on the paper.*

°**outside**[1] /out″ sīd′/ *noun*
the outer part or surface of something: *The* **outside** *of an orange is bitter, but the inside is sweet.*

°**outside**[2] *preposition, adverb, adjective*
1 to or on the outside of something: **Outside** *the house there was a notice saying "For Sale". The box was red* **outside** *and green inside. The* **outside** *parts of some fruit are not good to eat.*
2 not in a building: *Come* **outside** *and see my bicycle.* **Outside** *the house is a large yard.*

outskirts /out′ skurts″/ *plural noun*
the parts of a town which are not in the center: *We live on the* **outskirts** *of the city.*

outstanding /out″ stan′ ding/ *adjective*
very good: *an* **outstanding** *pupil*

outward /out′ wərd″/ *adverb* (*also* **outwards)**
toward the outside; away from the middle

oval /ō′ vəl/ *noun, adjective*
a round flat shape like an egg

oven /uv′ ən/ *noun*
a box which can be made hot to cook food in

°**over** /ō′ vər/ *preposition, adverb*
1 above: *The lamp is hanging* **over** *the table.*
2 covering: *My father went to sleep with a newspaper* **over** *his face.*
3 across; from one side to the other: *He jumped* **over** *the wall. I can see our neighbor* **over** *the fence.*
4 down to a lying position: *He knocked the bottle* **over** *and the oil ran out.*
5 finished: *When we arrived the film was* **over.**
6 more; more than: *Children* **over** *12 pay full price.*
7 in every part: **All over** *the world, people like music.*
8 from the start to the finish; again: *Think it* **over** *before you decide. We played the songs* **over and over (again)** (=many times).
9 not used: *If there is any food left* **over** *after dinner, keep it for tomorrow.*

overall /ō′ vər ôl″/ *adjective, adverb*
including all things; as a whole: *The* **overall** *cost of the uniform was $50.*

overall overalls

overalls /ō′ vər ôlz″/ *plural noun*
loose trousers with a top part, worn over other clothes to keep them clean

overboard /ō′ vər bôrd″/ *adverb*
over the side of a boat into the water: *He fell* **overboard.**

overcoat /ō′ vər kōt″/ *noun*
a warm coat worn outside when it is cold

overflow /ō″ vər flō′/ *verb*
to flow over the edge of something: *If you put too much water in the pot, it will* **overflow.**

overhead[1] /ō″ vər hed′/ *adverb, adjective*
above our heads; in the sky: *The plane flew* **overhead.** *The cable company uses* **overhead** *wires.*

overhead[2] *noun plural*
fixed cost: *The company's* **overhead** (=cost of rent, heat and light) *is high.*

overlook /ō″ vər lo͝ok′/ *verb*
1 to have or give a sight of something from above: *The house on the hill* **overlooks** *the village.*
2 not to see or notice: *You have* **overlooked** *several of the mistakes in this work.*

overnight /ō″ vər nīt′/ *adjective, adverb*
for the whole night: *We stayed* **overnight** *with my sister.*

overseas /ō″ vər sēz′/ *adverb, adjective*
to, in, or of places across the sea from your own country: *My brother lives* **overseas. Overseas** *trade is important to our country.*

overtake /ō″ vər tāk′/ *verb* (*present participle* **overtaking,** *past tense* **overtook** /ō″ vər to͝ok′/, *past participle* **overtaken**)
to pass another person or vehicle going in the same direction: *The car* **overtook** *the truck.*

°**owe** /ō/ *verb* (*present participle* **owing,** *past* **owed**)
1 to have to give or pay: *The food cost $5, but I only paid $2 so I still* **owe** *$3.*
2 to feel grateful to someone for something: *He* **owes** *his teachers a lot, because he got a very good job*

when he left school.

owing to *preposition* because of: *They could not cross the river* **owing to** *the flood.*

owl /oul/ *noun* a large bird that flies at night and kills small animals for food

owl

°**own**[1] /ōn/ *adjective* belonging to oneself: *I like writing with my* **own** *pen. That bicycle isn't his* **own;** *his brother lent it to him. She lives* **on her own** (=with nobody else).

°**own**[2] *verb*

1 to have something that belongs to you: *Who* **owns** *this house?*

2 (used in sentences like this): *When the teacher asked us who had taken the book, John* **owned up** (=said he had done it).

owner *noun* a person who owns something

°**ox** /oks/ *noun* (*plural* **oxen** /oks′ ən/) a bull (=male bovine)

Pp

pace[1] /pās/ *noun*
a step: *He ran forward ten* **paces.**

pace[2] *verb* (*present participle* **pacing,** *past* **paced)**
to walk with slow regular steps: *The lion was* **pacing** *up and down.*

pack[1] /pak/ *verb*
to put things together in a container: *She* **packed** *(her clothes), as she was going away. I can't* **pack** (=fit) *any more books into the box.*

pack[2] *noun*
1 a container of things packed together: *His clothes were in a* **pack** *on his back. He bought a* **pack** *of cards.*
2 a group of animals that hunt together

package /pak′ ij/ *noun*
a parcel: *a* **package** *of books*

pad /pad/ *noun*
1 a mass of soft material used to protect a part of the body or a wound
2 a number of sheets of paper stuck together at one edge: *a* **pad** *of writing paper*

paddle[1] /pad′ əl/ *noun*
a piece of wood with a broad end used for moving a boat through water (picture at **canoe**)

paddle[2] *verb* (*present participle* **paddling,** *past* **paddled)**
to move a boat through water using a paddle

paddy /pad′ ē/ *or* **paddy field** *noun*
a field for growing rice

padlock
/pad′ lok/
noun
a lock that can be used on doors, boxes, etc.

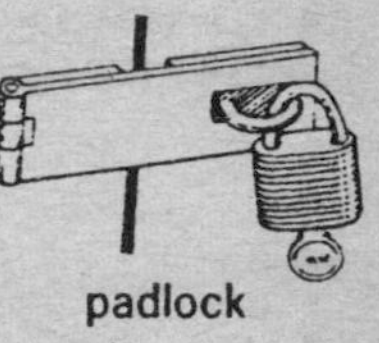
padlock

°**page** /pāj/ *noun*
one of the sheets of paper in a book: *The book has 120* **pages.**

paid /pād/ see **pay**

pail /pāl/ *noun*
a bucket

°**pain** /pān/ *noun*
a feeling of hurting: *He had a* **pain** *in his head.*
painful *adjective: His head was very* **painful** (=hurt a lot).
pains *plural noun: She* **took pains** (=took trouble, tried hard) *to dress nicely.*

°**paint**[1] /pānt/ *noun*
a sticky colored substance that is used to cover walls, or to color pictures: *She brought a box of* **paints** *to school. There's* **paint** *on your clothes.*

°**paint**[2] *verb*
to cover or color with paint: *He* **painted** *the wall yellow. She* **painted** *a (picture of a) boat.*
painter *noun* a person who paints, either pictures or things like houses, as a job
painting *noun* a painted picture: *a* **painting** *of a boat*

°**pair** /pâr/ *noun*
1 two things of the same kind thought of together: *a* **pair of socks**
2 something with two parts joined together: *a* **pair of scissors**

pajamas /pə ja′ məz/ *noun*
a loose shirt and trousers that you wear in bed: *a pair of* **pajamas**

palace /pal′ is/ *noun*
a large building where an important person, like a king, lives

°**pale** /pāl/ *adjective* **(paler, palest)**
light or white in color: *The sky was* **pale** *blue. The baby had* **pale** *skin.*

°**palm¹** /päm/ *noun*
a tree with a long trunk without branches and a group of large leaves at the top: *Coconuts grow on* **palm trees.**

palm

palm² *noun*
the wide part inside the hand: *He put the insect on the* **palm** *of his hand.*

°**pan** /pan/ *noun*
a round metal pot for cooking things over heat: *She fried the eggs in a* **frying pan.** *He heated some milk in a* **saucepan.**

panda /pan′ də/ *noun*
a large black and white animal like a bear (see) which lives in China

pane /pān/ *noun*
a piece of glass used in windows: *Who broke this* **pane** *of glass?*

panel /pan′ əl/ *noun*
a flat piece of wood used in a door or on a wall

panic¹ /pan′ ik/ *noun*
a sudden fear which can spread quickly: *He felt* **panic** *as the wind blew the flames toward his home.*

panic² *verb* (*present participle* **panicking,** *past* **panicked)**
to feel panic: *He* **panicked** *and ran as fast as he could to safety.*

pant /pant/ *verb*
to breathe quickly: *He was* **panting** *when he reached the top of the hill.*

pantomime /pan′ tə mīm/ *noun*
a funny play, usually telling an old story, with songs and dances in it

pantry /pan′ trē/ *noun*
(*plural* **pantries)** a small room in which food is kept

pants /pants/ *plural noun*
trousers

pants

°**paper** /pā′ pər/ *noun*
1 *(no plural)* sheets of thin material used for writing, wrapping, etc.: *These pages are made of* **paper.**
2 a newspaper
3 paper with writing or printing on it: *I left my* **papers** *on my desk.*
paper clip *noun: A* **paper clip** *is used to hold papers together.*

parachute /par′ ə sho͞ot″/ *noun*
a large round piece of cloth that fills with air, and lets someone fall slowly to earth from an airplane

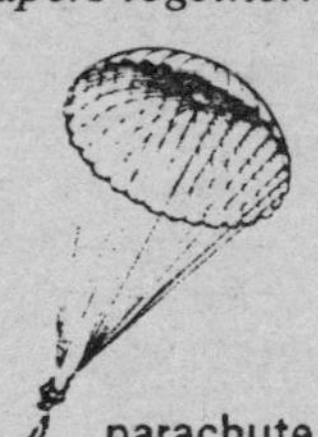
parachute

parade¹ /pə rād′/ *noun*
a number of people walking or marching together to be seen

parade² *verb* (*present participle* **parading,** *past* **paraded)**
to walk in a parade: *The soldiers* **paraded** *through the town.*

paradise /par′ ə dīs″/ *noun*
a place of complete happiness; heaven (see)

paraffin /par′ ə fin/

white, waxy substance used for making candles and wax paper, and to seal jars

paragraph /par′ ə graf″/ *noun*
a piece of writing that begins on a new line: *Read from your book, starting at the second* **paragraph.**

parallel /par′ ə lel/ *adjective*
always the same distance away from each other: **parallel** *lines*

paralyze /par′ ə līz/ *verb* (*present participle* **paralyzing,** *past* **paralyzed**)
to prevent someone from being able to move some or all of his body: *The climber was* **paralyzed** *in a fall, and couldn't walk.*
paralysis /pə″ rəl′ ə sis/ *noun (no plural)* being unable to move

°**parcel** /pär′ səl/ *noun*
something wrapped in paper and tied, for mailing or carrying: *She sent a* **parcel** *(of books) to her brother.*

pardon[1] /pär′ dən/ *noun (no plural)*
forgiveness: *If someone says something that you do not hear, you can say, "I beg your* **pardon?"** or **"Pardon?"** *so they will say it again.*

pardon[2] *verb*
to forgive: **Pardon me** — *I didn't hear what you said.*

°**parent** /pâr′ ənt/ *noun*
a father or mother

parish /par′ ish/ *noun* (*plural* **parishes**)
an area looked after by one Christian priest or served by one church

°**park**[1] /pärk/ *noun*
a large piece of ground in a town used by the public for pleasure: *We were playing in the* **park.**

°**park**[2] *verb*
to leave a car, bus, etc.: *She* **parked** *(the car) near the bank.*

parliament /pär′ lə mənt/ *noun*
a group of people chosen by the people of a country to make laws

parrot /par′ ət/ *noun*
a brightly colored bird with a short curved beak (see)

parrot

°**part**[1] /pärt/ *noun*
1 some of a thing or things: *I ate* **part** *of the apple, and gave the rest to Jane. A day is divided into 24* **parts,** *called hours.*
2 a share in an activity: *We all* **took part in** *the race.*
3 a character in a play or film: *James acted the* **part** *of the soldier in the play.*
partly *adverb: The accident was* **partly** *my fault* (=it was also other people's fault).

part[2] *verb*
to separate; leave one another: *The friends* **parted:** *Jane went home and Mary went to the library.*

participle /pär′ tə sip″ əl/ *noun*
one of two forms of a verb: *The* **past participle** *of "sing" is "sung" and the* **present participle** *is "singing".*

particular /pər tik′ yə lər/ *adjective*
1 special; separate from others: *Have you a* **particular** *reason for choosing this book?*
2 liking things to be just right: *I'm not* **particular** *about my clothes; I don't mind what I wear.*
particularly *adverb: It is* **particularly** *hot today.*

partner /pärt′ nər/ *noun*
a person who is close to another in work, play, etc.: *a dance* **partner**/*a business* **partner**

°**party** /pär′ tē/ *noun* (*plural* **parties**)
1 a meeting of friends to enjoy themselves, eat, drink, etc.: *a birthday* **party**
2 a group of people who have the same interests, aims, etc.: *Our teacher is taking a* **party** *of children to the library.*
3 a group of people with the same opinions in politics (see): *Are you a member of a political* **party?**

°**pass**[1] /pas/ *verb*
to move up to, across, and past: *We* **passed** *a sign saying "Welcome to the city". How much time has* **passed** *since you came to this school? Please* **pass** (=give) *me your books. The government has* **passed** (=agreed to make) *a new law. Seven children* **passed** *the examination* (=got good enough marks in it). *I* **passed the time** (=did something to amuse myself while waiting) *by counting the cars that drove past the school.*

pass[2] *noun* (*plural* **passes**)
1 getting good enough marks in an examination: *In this class there were seven* **passes.**
2 a high mountain road
3 a paper allowing you to go somewhere or have something: *I showed my* **pass** *to the man at the factory gate, and was allowed in.*

passage /pas′ ij/ *noun*
1 a narrow path joining parts of a building: *Sarah's mother used the* **passage** *from the school to the gym.*
2 part of a written work: *He read a* **passage** *on rice farming from the geography book.*

°**passenger** /pas′ ən jər/ *noun*
a person who rides in a car, bus, train, etc., but does not drive it: *There were ten* **passengers** *in the bus. This is a* **passenger** *train, not a freight train.*

passerby /pas′ sər bī/ *noun* (*plural* **passersby**)
someone who goes past, especially in the street: *A* **passerby** *told me the time.*

passion /pash′ ən/ *noun*
a very strong feeling, especially of love or anger: *She spoke with* **passion** *about human rights.*
passionate *adjective* with very strong feelings: *She made a* **passionate** *speech.*

passive /pas′ iv/ *adjective*
having the action done by someone to something or someone else: *In the sentence "The ball was kicked by John", "was kicked" is a* **passive** *verb.*
The opposite of **passive** is **active.**

passport /pas′ pôrt/ *noun*
a little book with your photograph and facts about you in it, which you must have if you are going abroad

°**past**[1] /past/ *noun (no plural)*
all the time which has already gone: **In the past,** *I have always lived in a village; in the future, I shall live in the town.*

°**past**[2] *adjective*
of time, events, etc. in the past: *I've been ill for the* **past** *two weeks.*

°**past**[3] *preposition, adverb*
up to and beyond; by: *Did he drive* **past** *the school? Yes, he drove* **past,** *but he didn't stop. It is* **past** *3 o'clock.*

°**past**[4] *noun, adjective*
talking about an action that has already happened: *The sentence "We saw them yesterday" has the verb in the* **past.** Look at **tense.**

paste /pāst/ *noun (no plural)*
a soft mixture such as that made from flour and water

pastime /pas′ tīm/ *noun*
something that you do for fun: *Swimming is my favorite* **pastime.**

pat[1] /pat/ *verb (present participle* **patting,** *past* **patted)**
to touch lightly with the open hand: *She* **patted** *the baby's cheek.*

pat[2] *noun*
a light touch; patting: *a* **pat** *on the cheek*

patch[1] /patch/ *noun*
a piece of material used for covering a hole in something

patch[2] *verb*
to put a patch on: *You can* **patch** *a bicycle tire with a piece of rubber.*

°**path** /path/ *noun*
a track for walking on: *There was a narrow* **path** *through the forest.*

patient[1] /pā′ shənt/ *adjective*
able to bear something or wait for something calmly: *I know your leg hurts, just be* **patient** *until the doctor arrives.*
patience *noun (no plural): Have* **patience;** *the bus will come soon.*
patiently *adverb: He sat* **patiently** *waiting for the bus.*

patient[2] *noun*
a person who is ill: *The doctor visited his* **patients** *in the hospital.*

patrol[1] /pə trōl′/ *noun*
1 a small group of policemen or soldiers
2 *(no plural)* keeping watch: *The policeman was* **on patrol.**

patrol[2] *verb (present participle* **patrolling,** *past* **patrolled)**
to go around watching for thieves, fires, etc.: *Every hour a policeman* **patrolled** *our street.*

patter /pat′ tər/ *verb*
to make a light knocking noise: *The rain* **pattered** *on the roof.*

°**pattern** /pat′ ərn/ *noun*
1 an ornamental arrangement of shapes and colors: *a* **pattern** *of flowers on dress material*
2 something you copy if you want to make something: *You can make a dress from this paper* **pattern.**

pause[1] /pôz/ *noun*
a short time when you stop what you are doing: *There was a* **pause** *in the talk when Mary came in.*

pause[2] *verb (present participle* **pausing,** *past* **paused)**
to stop for a short time: *When he had run up the hill, he* **paused** *for a minute to rest.*

pavement /pāv′ mənt/ *noun*
a path at the side of a road for people to walk on

paw /pô/ *noun*
the foot of an animal such as a dog or cat

pawpaw /pô′ pô/ *noun*
a large fruit grown in hot places that has a sweet yellow inside

°**pay**[1] /pā/ *verb (present participle* **paying,** *past* **paid)**
to give money to someone in exchange for goods or something done for you: *He* **paid** *$3 for the book. Can you lend me some money — I can* **pay** *you* **back** (=return it) *tomorrow!*
payment *noun: He gave the man $3 in* **payment** *for the book.*

°**pay**[2] *noun (no plural)*
the money received for work

pea /pē/ *noun*
a round seed that is used for food

°**peace** /pēs/ *noun (no plural)*
1 a time when there is no war or fighting: *War started again after six years of* **peace.**
2 quietness; calm: *the* **peace** *of the country*
peaceful *adjective* quiet: *It's* **peaceful** *at home when the children are at school.*

peach /pēch/ *noun (plural* **peaches)**
a juicy fruit with one large seed and a soft skin

peacock /pē′ kok″/ *noun*
a bird with a large brightly colored tail

peak /pēk/ *noun*
1 a pointed hill or mountain
2 the front part of a cap (=sort of hat) which sticks forward over the eyes

peal /pēl/ *noun*
a ringing noise, or loud noise: *the* **peal** *of bells/a* **peal** *of thunder*
peal *verb*

peanut /pē′ nut″/ *noun*
a root plant that bears pods that taste like nuts

pear /pâr/ *noun*
a juicy yellow, brown, or green fruit

pearl /purl/ *noun*
a small round gem, found in the shells of some fish, which is used as an ornament: *Her ring had* **pearls** *on it.*

pebble /peb′ əl/ *noun*
a small stone

peck /pek/ *verb*
to cut or lift with the beak (=bird's mouth): *The hens* **pecked** *at the corn.*

peculiar /pi kūl′ yar/ *adjective*
odd; strange; unusual: *a* **peculiar** *smell*

pedal[1] /ped′ əl/ *noun*
the part of a machine which you move with the foot: *a bicycle* **pedal** (picture at **bicycle**)

pedal[2] *verb (present participle* **pedaling,** *past* **pedaled)**
to move pedals with the feet: *We* **pedaled** *slowly up the hill.*

pedestrian /pə des′ trē ən/ *noun*
a person walking: *This path is only for* **pedestrians.**

peel[1] /pēl/ *noun (no plural)*
the outside part of a fruit or vegetable: *Apples have red or green* **peel.**

peel[2] *verb*
to take the peel off: *Please* **peel** *this banana.*

peep[1] /pēp/ *verb*
to look quickly, and sometimes secretly: *I* **peeped** *through the window to see if she were there.*

peep[2] *noun*
a quick look: *I had a* **peep** *at your new dress.*

peg /peg/ *noun*
a wooden or metal hook for hanging clothes, etc.

°**pen**[1] /pen/ *noun*
an instrument for writing which uses a colored liquid **(ink)** to make marks on paper

pen[2] *noun*
a place for keeping cattle or sheep shut in

penalty /pen′ əl tē/ *noun (plural* **penalties)**
a punishment: *What is the* **penalty** *for dangerous driving?*

°**pencil** /pen′ sil/ *noun*
a writing instrument made of wood with a hard gray substance in it which marks the paper

penetrate /pen′ ə trāt″/ *verb (present participle* **penetrating,** *past* **penetrated)**
to go into or through: *The knife* **penetrated** *her finger and made it bleed.*

penknife /pen′ nīf/ *noun (plural* **penknives** /nīvz/)
a small knife with a folding blade that can be carried in your pocket

penknife

penny /pen′ ē/ *noun (plural* **pennies)**
a coin of many countries that is of very low value

pension /pen′ shən/ *noun*
money given to someone regularly when they leave work when they are old

°**people** /pē′ pəl/ *noun*
the plural noun for **person:** *I saw many* **people** *at the dance.*

°**pepper** /pep′ ər/ *noun*
1 *(no plural)* a powder made from the seeds of some plants and used to give food a hot taste
2 the fruit of pepper plants, which can be eaten raw or used in cooking

peppermint /pep′ ər mint″/ *noun*
1 *(no plural)* oil from a plant which is used to give a taste to foods
2 a candy that tastes of this

per /pur/ *preposition*
for each; during each: *How much do you earn* **per** *week? The fruit cost 30 cents per pound.*
percent /pər sent′/ *noun* out of a hundred: *"Sixty* **percent** *(60%) of the pupils are boys" means that of every hundred pupils, sixty are boys.*

perch /purch/ *verb*
to sit on something narrow: *Birds* **perched** *on the branch.*

°**perfect**[1] /pur′ fikt/ *adjective*
so good that it cannot be made better: *His reading is* **perfect.**
perfectly *adverb* **1** completely: **perfectly** *happy* **2** in a perfect way: *He reads* **perfectly.**

perfect[2] /pur fekt″/ *verb*
to make very good or perfect: *They worked hard to* **perfect** *their dance.*
perfection *noun (no plural)*

perform /pər fôrm′/ *verb*
to act: *The children* **performed** *a play. The singer* **performed** (= sang) *beautifully. I am going to* **perform** (= do) *a difficult job.*
performance *noun: Her* **performance** *in the play was very good. The* **performances** (= times when the play is acted, music is played, etc.) *are on the 5th and 6th of this month.*

perfume /pur′ fūm/ *noun (no plural)*
a sweet smell; liquid that has a sweet smell: *She was wearing a strong* **perfume.**

°**perhaps** /pər haps′/ *adverb*

possibly; it may be: **Perhaps** *our team will win.*

°**period** /pir′ ē əd/ *noun*
a length of time: *the happiest* **period** *of my life*

perish /per′ ish/ *verb*
to die: *The plants all* **perished** *because there was no rain.*

permanent /pur′ mə nənt/ *adjective*
not changing or moving; fixed: *I have a* **permanent** *job here.*
permanently *adverb*

°**permit**[1] /pər mit′/ *verb* (*present participle* **permitting,** *past* **permitted)**
to allow: *Do you* **permit** *your children to use the telephone?*
°**permission** *noun (no plural): You must* **ask permission** *if you want to leave early.*

permit[2] /pur′ mit/ *noun*
a piece of paper saying you are allowed to do something

°**person** /pur′ sən/ *noun* (*plural* **persons)**
a human being; man, woman, or child: *We need a* **person** *to help us.*
personal *adjective* belonging to or for one person; of one's own: *a* **personal** *letter/a* **personal** *friend*
personally *adverb:* **Personally** (= my own opinion is that), *I think he is dishonest, but many people trust him.*

°**persuade** /pər swād′/ *verb* (*present participle* **persuading,** *past* **persuaded)**
to talk with someone until they agree with what you say: *He* **persuaded** *her to go to school, even though she did not want to.*
persuasion /pər swā′ zhən/ *noun (no plural): After a lot of* **persuasion,** *she agreed to go.*

pest /pest/ *noun*
a person or animal that is harmful or annoying: *Insects which eat crops are* **pests.**

pet /pet/ *noun*
1 an animal you look after and keep in your house: *She has two cats as* **pets.**
2 a favorite child: *She's the teacher's* **pet.**

petal /pet′ əl/ *noun*
one of the parts of a flower that are usually brightly colored (picture at **flower)**

petition /pə tish′ ən/ *noun*
a letter to a powerful person asking for something: *The villagers all signed a* **petition** *asking for a hospital to be built.*

philosophy /fi läs′ ə fē/ *noun (no plural)*
the study of life and what it means, how we should live, etc.

phone[1] /fōn/ *noun*
a short way of saying **telephone**

phone[2] *verb* (*present participle* **phoning,** *past* **phoned)**
to telephone: *I* **phoned** *my parents.*

°**photograph**[1] /fō′tə graf″/ *noun*
a picture made by a camera
photo /fō″ tō/ is a short word for **photograph.**

°**photograph**[2] *verb*
to take a photograph of: *We* **photographed** *the school team.*
photographer /fə tog′ rə fər/ *noun* a person who takes photographs.
photography *noun (no plural)* the art or business of producing photographs

phrase /frāz/ *noun*
a group of words that does not make a full sentence: *"Later that*

day" and "on the way home" are **phrases.** Look at **clause.**

physical /fiz′ i kəl/ *adjective*
of or about the natural world or the body: **Physical** *geography is the study of mountains, rivers, seas, and rocks.* **Physical** *fitness is having a strong healthy body.*

physician /fi zish′ ən/ *noun*
a doctor

physics /fiz′ iks″/ *plural noun (used with a singular verb)*
the study of natural forces

physicist *noun* a person who studies physics

piano /pē an′ ō/ *noun*
a musical instrument with strings inside a large wooden frame

piano

pianist /pē′ ə nist/ *noun*
a person who plays a piano

°**pick**[1] /pik/ *verb*
1 to choose: *I* **picked** *a book to read.*
2 to take up or off with the fingers: *We* **picked** *apples (from the tree).* **Pick up** *your coat, it should not be on the floor!*

pick[2] *noun (no plural)*
choice: **Take your pick** (= choose which you want) *of these books.*

pickax /pik′ aks/ *or* **pick** *noun*
a sharp metal tool with a long handle, for making holes in rock or hard ground

picnic /pik′ nik/ *noun*
a meal eaten outside, when you are away from home: *We had a* **picnic** *by the sea.*

°**picture**[1] /pik′ chər/ *noun*
something represented on paper, either as a drawing or painting, or as a photograph: *She drew a* **picture** *of me.*

picture[2] *verb (present participle* **picturing,** *past* **pictured)**
to imagine: *She* **pictured** *herself at school in a foreign country.*

°**piece** /pēs/ *noun*
a part of something, or single thing: *He took a* **piece** *of the cake. This page is a* **piece** *of paper. The plate which I dropped lay* **in pieces** *on the floor.*

pierce /pērs/ *verb (present participle* **piercing,** *past* **pierced)**
to make a hole in: *The needle* **pierced** *the material.*

°**pig** /pig/ *noun*
an animal that is kept for its meat

pigeon /pij′ ən/ *noun*
a bird that is gray or green with short legs and makes a soft noise

piglet /pig′ lət/ *noun*
a young pig (see)

°**pile**[1] /pīl/ *noun*
a number of things put on top of each other: *a* **pile** *of books*

°**pile**[2] *verb (present participle* **piling,** *past* **piled)**
to put in a pile: *She* **piled** *the books on the table.*

pilgrim /pil′ grim/ *noun*
a person who goes to pray at a holy place far away from his home

pilgrimage *noun* a journey to a holy place

pill /pil/ *noun*
a small ball of medicine which you swallow

pillar /pil′ ər/ *noun*
a strong, usually round, stone or metal post: *The roof of the church was supported by stone* **pillars.**

pillow /pil′ ō/ *noun*
a soft thing to put your head on when you are in bed
pillowcase *noun* a cloth bag to keep a pillow clean

pilot /pī′ lət/ *noun*
1 a person who drives an airplane
2 a person who guides ships into harbor or along rivers

pin[1] /pin/ *noun*
a pointed bit of metal used for fastening paper, cloth, etc: *A* **safety pin** *has a metal covering over the pointed end. A* **drawing pin** *is a thin nail with a flat head that is used for fastening papers to a board or wall.*

pins

pin[2] *verb* (*present participle* **pinning,** *past* **pinned**)
to fasten with a pin

pinch[1] /pinch/ *verb*
to take something between the fingers and press it: *She* **pinched** *my arm hard, and it still hurts.*

pinch[2] *noun*
a small amount: *A* **pinch of salt** *is the amount you can pick up between your finger and thumb.*

pine /pīn/ *noun*
a tree that has leaves like needles

pineapple /pīn′ əp″ əl/ *noun*
the large juicy fruit of the pineapple plant

pineapple

°**pink** /pink/ *noun, adjective*
(of) the color made by mixing red and white

pint /pīnt/ *noun*
a measure of liquid, equal to 0.57 liters: *There are eight* **pints** *in a gallon.*

pioneer /pī″ ə nir′/ *noun*
someone who goes somewhere or does something before other people: *His grandfather was one of the* **pioneers** *of flying.*

°**pipe** /pīp/ *noun*
a tube: *The water flows along a* **pipe** *to our houses. The man was smoking a* **pipe** (= a short tube with tobacco (see) in it).

pirate /pī′ rit/ *noun*
a robber of ships

pistol /pis′ təl/ *noun*
a small gun

pit /pit/ *noun*
1 a deep hole in the ground
2 a mine

pitch[1] /pitch/ *noun* (*plural* **pitches**)
1 toss or throw of a ball
2 how high or low a sound is: *a* **high-pitched** *voice*

pitch[2] *verb*
to put up: *The girls* **pitched** *a tent.*

°**pity[1]** /pit′ ē/ *noun*
the sadness that you feel when someone else is hurt, in trouble, etc.: *I felt great* **pity** *for the woman whose baby died.* **It's a pity** (= it makes us sorry) *that you have to go so soon.*

°**pity[2]** *verb* (*present participle* **pitying,** *past* **pitied**)
to feel sadness for someone else: *We all* **pitied** *the woman whose baby died.*

°**place[1]** /plās/ *noun*
1 where something is: *The right* **place** *for the bowl is on the shelf.*
2 space for something: *There are no* **places** *left to sit on the train.*
3 a town, village, etc.: *What is this* **place** *called?*

4 a building: *A school is a* **place** *to learn things.*

°**place²** *verb (present participle* **placing,** *past* **placed)**
to put: *She* **placed** *a book on the table.*

°**plain¹** /plān/ *adjective*
easy to see, hear, or understand; simple: *He made it* **plain** *that he did not like me. She wore a* **plain** *brown dress.*
plainly *adverb: It was* **plainly** (=clearly) *too hot to be working in the sun.*

°**plain²** *noun*
a flat piece of country

plait¹ /plāt/ *verb*
to twist or braid together three or more pieces of rope, hair, etc.

plait²/plāt/ *noun*
a length of something that is braided.

plait

°**plan¹** /plan/ *noun*
1 something you have decided to do, and how to do it: *We listened as he told us his* **plan** *for starting a football team.*
2 a drawing of a new building

°**plan²** *verb (present participle* **planning,** *past* **planned)**
to think about what you are going to do and how to do it: *The government* **plans** *to build a bridge.*

°**plane** /plān/ *noun*
a short word for airplane, hand tool for shaving wood

planet /plan′ it/ *noun*
one of the large masses like the Earth that go round a sun

plank /plank/ *noun*
a long, flat, thin piece of wood

°**plant¹** /plant/ *noun*
something living that is not an animal: *Trees and vegetables are* **plants.**

°**plant²** *verb*
to put in the ground to grow: *Have you* **planted** *any vegetables yet?*
plantation *noun* a large piece of land on which tea, sugar, cotton, or rubber is grown

plaster¹ /plas′ tər/ *noun*
(no plural) a soft white material which is spread on walls and becomes hard and smooth when it is dry

plaster² *verb*
to cover with plaster or other soft material

°**plastic** /plas′ tik/ *adjective, noun*
a strong man-made substance used for strong containers, toys, etc.: *If you drop a* **plastic** *bowl, it will not break.*

°**plate** /plāt/ *noun*
a flat dish: *a* **plate** *of food*

platform /plat′ fôrm/ *noun*
1 a part of a station where you get on and off trains: *The train at* **Platform** *2 goes to the city.*
2 a raised part: *The principal stood on a* **platform** *at one end of the hall.*

°**play¹** /plā/ *verb*
1 to amuse yourself; take part in a game: *The children were* **playing** *with a ball. He* **plays** *football.*
2 to make sounds on a musical instrument: *She* **plays** *the drum.*
player *noun: a football* **player**
playground *noun: All the schoolchildren ran about in the* **playground.**

°**play²** *noun*
1 *(no plural)* amusement: *The*

children were **at play** *in the yard.*
2 a story acted in a theater, as a film, on the radio, etc.: *She is in a* **play** *about a famous singer.*

°**pleasant** /plez′ ənt/ *adjective*
nice; enjoyable: We spent a **pleasant** *day in the country.*
pleasantly *adverb*

°**please**[1] /plēz/ *verb* (*present participle* **pleasing,** *past* **pleased)**
to give happiness or pleasure to: *I am* **pleased** *that you have a new job. He is* **pleased with** *his new job.*
°**pleasure** *noun: It gives me* **pleasure** *to see you looking happy. I will help you* **with pleasure** (= willingly).

°**please**[2]
a word added to a question or an order, to make it polite: **Please** *bring your book to me.*

°**plenty** /plen′ tē/
a lot, enough: *We have* **plenty of** *time to catch the train. She thought there wasn't enough bread, but there was* **plenty.**
plentiful *adjective: Fruit is* **plentiful** *in summer.*

pliers /plī′ ərz/ *plural noun*
a tool like scissors used for cutting wire or for holding things: *Do you have* **a pair of pliers?**

pliers

plot[1] /plot/ *noun*
a small piece of ground, especially for growing vegetables

plot[2] *noun*
1 a secret plan, usually to do something wrong
2 the story of a book, film, etc.: *The film had an exciting* **plot.**

plot[3] *verb* (*present participle* **plotting,** *past* **plotted)**
to plan (something wrong): *We were* **plotting** *to rob a bank.*

plough[1] /plou/ *noun*
an instrument for cutting up and turning over the earth

plough[2] *verb*
to cut up the earth with a plough: *A farmer must* **plough** *the land before planting crops.*

pluck /pluk/ *verb*
to pull off: *When you kill a chicken to eat, you have to* **pluck** *it* (= pull the feathers off).

plug[1] /plug/ *noun*
1 a round piece of rubber, plastic, etc. which stops water running out of a basin
2 a metal and plastic thing joined to an electric wire, which you put into holes called electric sockets (see) in the wall

socket
plugs

plug[2] *verb* (*present participle* **plugging,** *past* **plugged)**
1 to put a plug in something: *How can I* **plug** *the hole in this bucket?*
2 to put an electric plug in a special part **(socket)** in a wall: *to* **plug in** *a lamp*

plum /plum/ *noun*
a sweet juicy red fruit with one large seed

plumbing /plum′ ing/ *noun (no plural)*
all the water pipes, containers, etc. put in a building so that there can be running water: *A* **plumber** /plum′-ər/ *is a person who fits and mends the* **plumbing.**

plump /plump/ *adjective*
nicely fat: *the baby's* **plump** *arms*

plural /plŏŏr′ əl/ *adjective, noun*
more than one: *"Dogs" is the* **plural** *of "dog".* The opposite of **plural** is **singular.**

plus /plus/ *preposition*
added to; and: *Four plus two is six* (4+2=6).

p.m. /pē em/
in the afternoon or evening: *It is 4:30* **p.m.**

°**pocket** /pok′ ət/ *noun*
a piece of material sewn onto clothes to make a little bag to keep things in
pocket money *noun* money for daily expenses such as bus fare

pod /pod/ *noun*
in some plants, a long part in which the seeds grow: *Peas and beans grow in* **pods.**

pod

poem /pō′ əm/ *noun*
writing with regular lines and sounds that expresses something in powerful or beautiful language: *He wrote a* **poem** *about war.*
poet *noun: A* **poet** *writes poems.*
poetry *noun (no plural)* poems

°**point**[1] /point/ *verb*
to show, especially with a finger stretched out: *The signpost* **pointed** *to the school. He* **pointed** *his pen at the student and said "Go on reading".*
pointed adjective sharp at one end; *a* **pointed** *stick*

°**point**[2] *noun*
1 a sharp end: *the* **point** *of a nail*
2 importance; purpose: *I don't see the* **point** *of waiting for her, she is probably not coming.*
3 mark: *Our team scored ten* **points.**
4 time: *At the* **point** *when I left, the teacher was reading a story.*

poison[1] /poi′ zən/ *noun (no plural)*
a substance which kills or harms you if it gets into your body
poisonous *adjective*

poison[2] *verb*
to kill with poison: *The farmer* **poisoned** *the rats.*

poke /pōk/ *verb (present participle* **poking,** *past* **poked)**
to push a pointed thing into someone or something: *He* **poked** *the fire with a stick.*

°**pole**[1] /pōl/ *noun*
a long narrow piece of wood: *A* **pole** *for a flag is called a* **flagpole.**

pole[2] *noun*
one end of the Earth: *The* **North Pole** *is the part of the Earth that is farthest north; the* **South Pole** *is the farthest south.*

°**police** /pə lēs′/ *noun (no plural)*
the people who make sure that everyone obeys the law: **Policemen** *and* **policewomen** *work at a* **police station.**

policy /pol′ ə sē/ *noun (plural* **policies)**
a general plan: *It is the* **policy** *of the government to improve education.*

polish[1] /pol′ ish/ *verb*
to rub something so that it shines: *He* **polished** *the car.*

polish[2] *noun (no plural)*
an oily substance which helps to make things shine

°**polite** /pə līt/ *adjective* **(more polite, most polite)**
having a kind and respectful way of behaving; not rude: *You should be* **polite** *to everyone.*

politics /pol′ ə tiks/ *plural noun*
the study of government; how countries should be governed: *an argument about* **politics**

political /pə lit′ ə kəl/ *adjective*
of or about government: *A* **political party** *is a group of people who agree about politics.*

politician /pol ə tish′ ən/ *noun* a person who takes part, or wants to take part in the government of a country

pond /pond/ *noun*
a pool of water: *a* **pond** *with fish in it*

°**pool** /po͞ol/ *noun*
an area of a liquid: *There were* **pools** *of water in the holes in the road. a* **swimming pool**

°**poor** /po͝or/ *adjective*
1 not having much money: a **poor** *family*
2 needing kindness or help: *The* **poor** *animal hadn't been fed.*
3 not good: *Your writing is* **poor.**

pop[1] /pop/ *noun*
a sudden noise like the sound of the top being pulled out of a bottle

pop[2] *noun (no plural)*
music or songs that many younger people like and dance to: *A* **pop group** *plays* **pop music.**

pope /pōp/ *noun*
the head of the Roman Catholic (see) church

°**popular** /pop′ ya lər/ *adjective*
liked by many people: *She is* **popular** *at school. This dance is* **popular** *with young people.*

popularity /pop″ yə lar′ ə tē/ *noun (no plural)*

population /pop″ yə lā′ shən/ *noun*
the number of people living in a place: *What is the* **population** *of this city?*

pork /pôrk/ *noun (no plural)*
meat from pigs

porridge /pôr′ ij/ *noun (no plural)*
food made by boiling grain in water or milk until it is very soft

°**port** /pôrt/ *noun*
a harbor, or a town with a harbor

porter /pôr′ tər/ *noun*
a person who carries bags and other things for people

portion /pôr shən/ *noun*
a part or share of something:*she only eats a small* **portion** *of food.*

portrait /pôr′ trit *or* pôr′ trāt/ *noun*
a picture of a person: *He painted a* **portrait** *of his daughter.*

°**position** /pə zish′ ən/ *noun*
1 a place where a person or thing is: *The telephone is in a bad* **position** *— I cannot reach it.*
2 a job: *He has an important* **position** *in the company.*
3 the state or condition of a person: *I am not* **in a position to** *lend you money* (= I am unable to).

positive /pos′ ə tiv/ *adjective*
sure: *I am* **positive** *that I gave you his address:*

positively *adverbs: I* **positively** *hate* (= hate very much) *fish.*

possess /pə zes′/ *verb*
to have or own: *She* **possesses** *some interesting pictures.*

possession *noun: He had few* **possessions** (= things he owned).

°**possible** /pos′ ə bəl/ *adjective*
able to happen: *Is it* **possible** *to get to the city by train, or must I take a bus?*

°**possibility** *noun* (*plural* **possibilities**): *Is it a* **possibility** *that you will work abroad?*

possibly *adverb: I can't* **possibly** *eat all that food* (= I cannot do it at all). *You may* **possibly** (= it may happen that) *get a new job.*

°**post**[1] /pōst/ *noun*
a thick bar of wood, metal, or stone fixed in the ground: *The fence was held up by wooden* **posts.**

°**post**[2] *verb*
1 to send a letter or parcel
2 to keep posted, inform one of late news or developments

°**post**[3] *noun (no plural)*
the way of sending letters, etc.; mail (see): *You can send letters* **by post.**

postage /pōst′ ij/ *noun (no plural)* the amount of money paid for something posted: (Postage) **Stamps** *show how much* **postage** *has been paid.*

postcard *noun* a small card which you can write a message on and send by post

postcard

postman *noun* a man who collects and gives out letters and parcels

post office *noun* a place where you can buy stamps, post parcels, etc.

poster /pōs′ tər/ *noun*
a large printed paper advertising something

postpone /pōst pōn′/ *verb* (*present participle* **postponing,** *past* **postponed)**
to change the time of some event to a later time: *We* **postponed** *the game from March 5th to March 19th.*

°**pot** /pot/ *noun*
a container, especially a round one, made of baked clay: *She made a* **pot** *of coffee. The flowers were growing in* **(flower) pots.**

pottery *noun (no plural)* dishes, pots, etc. made of baked clay; the art of making these things

potato /pə tā′ tō/ *noun* (*plural* **potatoes)**
a vegetable found under the ground and cooked before eating

poultry /pōl′ trē/ *noun (no plural)*
hens and other birds kept for eggs or meat

pounce /pouns/ *verb* (*present participle* **pouncing,** *past* **pounced)**
to jump on suddenly: *The cat* **pounced** *on the bird.*

°**pound**[1] /pound/ *noun*
the money used in Britain and some other places: I bought a car for five hundred **pounds** (*£500*).

pound[2]*noun*
a measure of weight equal to 454 kilograms (see): a **pound** *of rice* **lb** is a short way of writing **pound**.

pound[3] *verb*
to crush by hitting hard and often: *She* **pounded** *the corn.*

°**pour** /pôr/ *verb*
to flow or cause to flow: *She* **poured** *the tea (from the teapot into the cups). It was* **pouring** *(with rain).*

poverty /pov′ ər tē/ *noun (no plural)*
the state of being poor: *She has lived* **in poverty** *all her life.*

°**powder** /pou′ dər/ *noun (no plural)*
fine grains like dust: *They washed the clothes with soap* **powder.**

°**power** /pou′ ər/ *(no plural)*
strength or force: *The* **power** *of falling water is used to make*

electricity. The teacher has **power** *over his pupils* (= he can tell them what to do, punish them, etc.).

powerful *adjective: The general is a* **powerful** *man.*

practical /prak′ ti kəl/ *adjective* about or good at doing rather than thinking: *He is very* **practical** *— he can make or repair almost anything.*

practically *adverb* almost: *I've* **practically** *finished — I'll come in a minute.*

°**practice** /prak′ tis/ *noun* *(no plural)* doing something to improve how you do it: *You need more* **practice** *before you can play for our team.*

°**practice** *verb* (*present participle* **practicing,** *past* **practiced**) to go on doing something so as to become better at it: *You won't become a good singer if you don't* **practice.**

°**praise**[1] /prāz/ *verb* (*present participle* **praising,** *past* **praised**) to speak well of; say that you admire: *She* **praised** *her daughter's hard work.*

°**praise**[2] *noun (no plural)* praising; admiration: *He gave a speech in* **praise** *of the school.*

°**pray** /prā/ *verb* to talk to God or a god; ask for something: *She* **prayed** *silently.*

prayer /prāy′ ər/ *noun* praying; words said in praying

preach /prēch/ *verb* to give a religious talk; talk to people about how they should live, etc.

preacher *noun*

precaution /pri kô′ shən/ *noun* something that is done to prevent something else happening: *He took the* **precaution** *of locking his door when he went out.*

precious /presh′ əs/ *adjective* worth a lot of money; very much loved: *a* **precious** *stone*

predict /pri dikt′/ *verb* to say what is going to happen: *The teacher* **predicted** *that we would all pass the examination.*

prediction *noun*

prefer /pri fur′/ *verb* (*present participle* **preferring,** *past* **preferred**) to like better: *Which of these two dresses do you* **prefer?**

preference /pref′ rəns *or* pref′ ər əns/ *noun*

prefix /prē′ fix″/ *noun* (*plural* **prefixes**) letters that can be added to the beginning of another word to change the meaning: *If we add the* **prefix** *"un" to the word "happy", we make the word "unhappy".* Look at **suffix.**

pregnant /preg′ nənt/ *adjective* about to have a child: *A woman is* **pregnant** *for nine months before a child is born.*

prejudice /prej′ ə dis/ *noun* an opinion formed before you know all the facts about something: *Why have you a* **prejudice** *against women drivers? They can drive just as well as men.*

°**prepare** /pri pâr′/ *verb* (*present participle* **preparing,** *past* **prepared**) to make ready: *I* **prepared** *the ground for the seeds.*

preparation *noun*

preposition /prep″ ə zish′ ən/ *noun* a word like *to, for, on, by,* etc.; a word which is put in front of a noun to show where, when, how, etc.: *She sat* **by** *the fire. They went* **to** *town.*

prescription /pri skrip′ shən/ *noun* a paper written by a doctor, ordering medicine for someone: *The doctor wrote me a* **prescription** *for medicine for my cough.*

°**present**[1] /prez′ ənt/ *adjective*
1 here; in this place: *There are twenty children* **present.**
2 now: *What is your* **present** *job?*

°**present**[2] *noun*
this time: **At present,** *he is on vacation.*
presently *adverb* in a short time

°**present**[3] *noun, adjective*
talking about an action that is happening now: *The sentence "We see them every day" has the verb in the* **present.** Look at **tense.**

°**present**[4] *noun*
something given to someone: *He gave his mother a* **present.**

present[5] /pri zent′/ *verb*
to give: *He* **presented** *me with some flowers.*

preserve /pri zurv′/ *verb* (*present participle* **preserving,** *past* **preserved)**
to keep from being damaged, or from going bad: *You can* **preserve** *meat or fish in salt.*
preservation /prez″ ər vā′ shən/ *noun*

president /prez′ ə dənt/ *noun*
1 the head of government in many countries
2 the head of a big company, a club, etc.

°**press**[1] /pres/ *verb*
1 to push steadily on: *He* **pressed** *the doorbell.*
2 to make flat: *I've* **pressed** *your trousers with the iron.*
pressure /presh′ ər/ *noun (no plural): Do not put much* **pressure** *on the handle, it may break.*

press[2] *noun*
1 (*plural* **presses)** a machine for printing
2 *(no plural)* newspapers: *He works for the* **press.**

°**pretend** /pri tend′/ *verb*
to do something to make people believe something untrue: *He* **pretended** *that he was ill so that he could stay at home.*

°**pretty**[1] /prit′ ē/ *adjective* **(prettier, prettiest)**
beautiful: *a* **pretty** *girl*

pretty[2] *adverb*
fairly; quite: *It was a* **pretty** *serious accident.*

°**prevent** /pri′ vent/ *verb*
to stop something happening: *Try to* **prevent** *fires in dry weather.*
prevention *noun (no plural):* **Prevention** *of illness is better than curing it.*

previous /prē′ vē əs/ *adjective*
happening before; coming before in time: *In my* **previous** *job, I used to travel to the city every day.*
previously *adverb*

prey /prā/ *noun (no plural)*
something that is hunted and caught: *The big bird carried its* **prey** *in its claws* (= hooked toes).

°**price** /prīs/ *noun*
the money that you must pay for something: *The* **price** *of that house is high.*

°**prick** /prik/ *verb*
to make a small wound with

something sharp: *The needle* **pricked** *her hand.*

°**prickle** /prik′ əl/ *noun*
a sharp part of a plant or animal
prickly *adjective* **(pricklier, prickliest)** having sharp pieces on it

prickles

°**pride** /prīd/ *noun (no plural)*
the feeling of having a high opinion of yourself or things that are yours; being proud: *She showed us her new home with great* **pride.**

°**priest** /prēst/ *noun*
a religious person whose job is to lead ceremonies, say prayers, and look after the religious part of people's lives

primary /prī′ mer ē/ *adjective*
first: **Primary** *grades are the first grades in a school.*

prime minister /prīm min′ is tər/ *noun*
the head of government in many countries

primitive /prim′ ə tiv/ *adjective*
early in history; simple: **Primitive** *people used* **primitive** *tools.*

prince /prins/ *noun*
1 the son of a king or queen
2 the ruler of a country

princess /prin′ sis/ *noun*
1 the daughter of a king or queen
2 the wife of a prince

principal¹ /prin′ sə pəl/ *adjective*
the most important; chief: *What is your* **principal** *reason for staying here?* **principally** *adverb*

principal² *noun*
the head of a school

principle /prin′ sɔ pəl/ *noun*
a rule for living in a way you think is right: *It is a* **principle** *of mine to help people when I can.*

°**print¹** /print/ *verb*
to press words and pictures on paper or cloth by machine: *You are reading a* **printed** *book.*
printer *noun*

print² *noun*
something printed: *The book was in large* **print** (= had big letters).

°**prison** /priz′ ən/ *noun*
a place where criminals are kept as a punishment: *He was in* **prison** *for ten years.*
prisoner *noun* someone who is kept in prison

private /prī′ vit/ *adjective*
belonging to one person or group; not public: *This is* **private** *land, you can't walk across it. Can I speak to you* **in private** (= with no one else there)?
privately *adverb*

privilege /priv′ lij/ *noun*
a favor allowed to one or only a few people: *I had the* **privilege** *of meeting the president.*

°**prize** /prīz/ *noun*
something that you win: *I won a* **prize** *for running.*

probable /prob′ ə bəl/ *adjective*
likely: *It is* **probable** *that I shall be working here next year.*
probably *adverb: It will* **probably** *rain.*

problem /prob′ ləm/ *noun*
a difficult question; a cause of worry: *The* **problem** *was how to move the heavy machinery.*

proceed /prə sēd'/ *verb*
to go; go on: *After stopping to rest, they* **proceeded** *up the hill.*

process /pros' es/ *noun* (*plural* **processes**)
a number of actions one after another: *Building a car is a long* **process.**

procession /prə sesh' ən/ *noun*
a number of people following one another: *They watched the* **procession** *go by.*

procession

°**produce¹** /prə dōōs'/ *verb* (*present participle* **producing,** *past* **produced**)
to make or bring out: *That factory* **produces** *cars. He* **produced** *some candy from his pocket.*
°**product** /prod' əkt/ *noun: The company sells plastic* **products.**
° **production** /prə duk'shən/ *noun (no plural)* making: the **production** *of cars*

produce² /prō' dōōs/ *noun (no plural)*
something produced by growing or farming: *The farmer's* **produce** *was vegetables and fruit.*

profession /prə fesh' ən/ *noun*
an empoyment which needs special learning: *Teaching is a* **profession.**
professional *adjective: He got* **professional** *advice* (= from someone who has learned the profession) *from his doctor.*

professor /prə fes' ər/ *noun*
a teacher of the highest class in a university (see)

profit /prof' it/ *noun*
money gained when you sell something for more than you paid for it: *The fruit seller made a penny* **profit** *on each orange.*
profitable *adjective: Selling oranges is* **profitable.**

program /prō' gram"/ *noun*
1 a list of things which are planned to happen: *A* **program** *for a play contains a list of the actor's names and other information about the play.*
2 something sent out by radio or television: *We watched a* **program** *about farming.*

progress /prog' res/ *noun (no plural)*
going forward; becoming better: *You have made* **progress** *with your English.*

progress² /prə gres'/ *verb*
to go forward; get better: *Our company cannot* **progress** *until we employ more people.*

project /proj' ekt/ *noun*
a plan for a special thing: *a* **project** *to build a new road*

project /prə jekt'/ *verb*
to put forward: *The ornament* **projected** *from the hood of the car.*

prominent /prom' ə nənt/ *adjective*
1 noticeable, especially because it is tall or large: *a* **prominent** *nose*
2 important: *a* **prominent** *doctor*

°**promise¹** /prom' is/ *verb* (*present participle* **promising,** *past* **promised**)
to say you will do something: *She* **promised** *her brother that she would write to him. She* **promised** *to write to him.*

°**promise²** *noun*
something you have said you will do: *She* **made a promise** *to her brother. He* **broke his promise** *and did not come to see me.*

promote /prə mōt′/ *verb* (*present participle* **promoting,** *past* **promoted**) to give someone a better job: *Our teacher has been* **promoted** *to principal.*

promotion *noun: Our teacher has got a* **promotion.**

prompt /prompt/ *adjective*
quick; without delay: *a* **prompt** *answer*

pronoun /prō′ noun′/ *noun*
a word like *he, she, it, they,* etc., which is used instead of using a noun again: *Instead of saying "Peter went to school" we can use a* **pronoun** *and say "He went to school".*

pronounce /prə nouns′/ *verb* (*present participle* **pronouncing,** *past* **pronounced**)
to speak the sounds of a word: *How do you* **pronounce** *this word?*

pronunciation /prə nun″ sē ā′ shən/ *noun (no plural)* the way of saying words: *What is the* **pronunciation** *of this word?*

°**proof** /pro͞of/ *noun (no plural)*
facts which prove something: *Have you any* **proof** *that he took the money?*

propeller
/prə pel′ ər/ *noun*
a wheel of curved blades which turn quickly to make a ship or airplane move

propeller

proper /prop′ ər/ *adjective*
correct; right for the time and place: *You aren't wearing* **proper** *clothes for this hot weather.*

properly *adverb: You haven't done the job* **properly** *— you'll have to do it again.*

°**property** /prop′ ər tē/ *noun* (*plural* **properties**)
something, usually land or buildings, belonging to someone: *This book is not your* **property.**

prophet /prof′ it/ *noun*
1 someone who says what is going to happen in the future
2 a man who believes that God has told him to teach or lead a special religion: *Mohammed is the* **prophet** *of the Muslims.*

prophecy *noun* (*plural* **prophecies**) what someone says will happen; the words of the prophet

proportion /prə pôr′ shən/ *noun*
the amount of something compared to something else: *The* **proportion** *of girls to boys in the school is about equal.*

propose /prə pōz′/ *verb* (*present participle* **proposing,** *past* **proposed**)
1 to give as an idea: *He* **proposed** *that we should go for a walk.*
2 to ask someone to marry you: *He* **proposed** *to her, and she accepted.*

proposal *noun*

prosper /pros′ pər/ *verb*
to do well; become rich: *His company is* **prospering.**

prosperity /pros per′ ə tē/ *noun (no plural)*

prosperous /pros′ pər əs/ *adjective: a* **prosperous** *family*

°**protect** /prə tekt′/ *verb*
to prevent someone or something from being harmed, damaged, etc.: *The fence is to* **protect** *the farmer's cattle.*

°**protection** *noun (no plural): Her coat gave her* **protection** *from the rain.*

protest¹ /prə test′/ *verb*
to say strongly that you do not agree with something: *The children* **protested** *when they were punished unfairly.*

protest² /prō′ test″/ *noun*
a complaint: *The people made a* **protest** *about the rise in prices.*

Protestant /prot′ is tənt/ *noun, adjective*
(a person) belonging to a Christian church that is not Roman Catholic or Orthodox

°**proud** /proud/ *adjective*
having a high opinion of yourself or of something that is yours: *He is* **proud** *of his daughter's ability to speak four languages. She is too* **proud** *to walk to school with the other children.*
proudly *adverb*

prove /prōōv/ *verb (present participle* **proving,** *past* **proved)**
to show that something is true: *I can* **prove** *that you were in town — James saw you there.*

proverb /prov′ ərb/ *noun*
a short well-known saying

provide /prə vīd′/ *verb (present participle* **providing,** *past* **provided)**
to give: *We* **provided** *food for the hungry children.*
provided (that) if and only if: *You may go out,* **provided (that)** *you come home before dark.*
°**provision** /prə vizh′ ən/ *noun: The* **provision** *of food for all the children was difficult. When I went fishing, I took a day's* **provisions** (= food and drink).

province /prov′ ins/ *noun*
an area of a country, often having its own government for education, hospitals, etc.

provincial /prə vin′ shəl/ *adjective*

°**public¹** /pub′ lik/ *adjective*
open to everyone; for the use of the people in general: *This is a* **public** *park, we can all go into it. I do not want to speak about it* **in public** (= with other people there).

°**public²** *noun (no plural)*
people: **The public** *can use this park.*

publish /pub′ lish/ *verb*
to print and sell: *This company* **publishes** *children's books.*
publication /pub″ lə kā′ shən/ *noun: The* **publication** *of his book will be next month.*
publisher *noun* a person or company that publishes

puff¹ /puf/ *verb*
to breathe quickly: *I was* **puffing** *after swimming so far.*

puff² *noun*
a short burst of air, smoke, etc.: *A* **puff** *of wind blew the papers off the table.*

°**pull¹** /pûl/ *verb*
to move something toward yourself or by going in front of it: *He* **pulled** *his hand out of the hot water. A horse* **pulled** *the cart along the road.*

°**pull²** *noun*
an act of pulling: *He gave a* **pull** *on the rope.*

pullover /pûl′ ōv ər/ *noun*
a sweater that covers the top part of the body, and is pulled over the head

pulse /puls/ *noun*
the beating of your heart: *The doctor* **felt her pulse** *on her wrist.*

°**pump**[1] /pump/ *noun*
a machine for making liquid or gas move: *A bicycle* **pump** *puts air into the tires.*

°**pump**[2] *verb*
to move something with a pump: **Pump up** (= put air into) *your tires before you go.*

pumpkin /pump′ kin/ *noun*
a large round yellow fruit that is used as a vegetable

punch[1] /punch/ *verb*
1 to hit: *He* **punched** *him on the nose.*
2 to make a hole in: *He* **punched** *two holes in the can of oil, and then poured it out.*

punch[2] *noun* (*plural* **punches**)
a blow: *a* **punch** *on the nose*

punctual /pungk′ cho͞o əl/ *adjective*
coming at the right time; not late: *She is always* **punctual,** *but her friend is always late.*
punctually *adverb*

punctuate /pungk′ cho͞o āt/ *verb* (*present participle* **punctuating,** *past* **punctuated)**
to put punctuation (see) into writing

punctuation /pungk″ cho͞o ā′ shan/ *noun (no plural)*
signs like , ; . and ? used to end or break up writing

puncture[1] /pungk′ chər/ *noun*
a hole, especially in a tire

puncture[2] *verb* (*present participle* **puncturing,** *past* **punctured)**
to make a hole in: *The nail* **punctured** *the tire.*

°**punish** /pun′ ish/ *verb*
to make someone do something he does not like because he has done something wrong: *The teacher* **punished** *the noisy children by making them stay after school.*
punishment *noun: They deserved their* **punishment.**

°**pupil** /pū′ pəl/ *noun*
a person being taught, especially at a school

puppet /pup′ it/ *noun*
a small figure of a person or animal which is moved by someone and appears to move and speak

puppy /pup′ ē/ *noun*
(*plural* **puppies)**
a young dog

°**pure** /pūr/ *adjective*
(purer, purest)
without anything mixed with it; clean: *The water in mountain rivers is usually* **pure.**

purple /pur′ pəl/ *noun, adjective*
(of) the color made by mixing red and blue together

°**purpose** /pur′ pəs/ *noun*
a reason for doing something; aim: *He went to town with the* **purpose** *of buying a new television. The girl broke a cup* **on purpose** (= she had planned to do it).

purr /pur/ *verb*
(of cats) to make a soft low noise showing pleasure

purse /purs/ *noun*
a small bag for carrying money

pursue /pər so͞o′/ *verb* (*present participle* **pursuing,** *past* **pursued)**
to go after someone hoping to catch him

°**push**[1] /pu̇sh/ *verb*
to press or lean against, so as to move: *They* **pushed** *the door open.*

°**push²** *noun*
an act of pushing: *She gave a hard* **push,** *and the door opened.*

°**put** /pu̇t/ *verb* (*present participle* **putting,** *past* **put**)
to move to a place; to place: *He* **put** *the cups on the table. The thief was* **put** *in prison.* **Put** *the lights* **on** (= turn them on); *it's too dark to read. He* **put out** *the light* (= turned it off) *and went to sleep.*

puzzle¹ /puz′ əl/ *noun*
1 a difficult question to answer: *It's a* **puzzle** *where all my money goes each week.*
2 a game which is difficult to understand or do: *A jigsaw* **puzzle** *is a picture which has been cut up into bits, and you must make the picture again.*

puzzle² *verb* (*present participle* **puzzling,** *past* **puzzled**)
to be difficult to understand: *The new machine* **puzzled** *me until Sarah explained how it worked.*

pyramid /pir′ ə mid/ *noun*
a solid shape which is square at the base and pointed at the top

Qq

quack /kwak/ *verb*
to make a noise like a duck (see)

qualify /kwäl′ ə fī/ *verb* (*present participle* **qualifying,** *past* **qualified)**
to finish training to do some special work: *He is a* **qualified** *doctor.*

qualification /kwal″ ə fə kā′ shən/ *noun: What* **qualifications** (= special training or knowledge) *have you got to have for this job?*

°**quality** /kwäl′ ə tē/ *noun* (*plural* **qualities)**
how good something is: *We only sell cloth of the finest* **quality.** *Her best* **qualities** (= good things in her character) *are courage and cheerfulness.*

quantity /kwän′ tə tē/ *noun* (*plural* **quantities)**
an amount: *He ate a small* **quantity** *of rice.*

°**quarrel**[1] /kwôr′ əl/ *noun*
an angry argument: *We had a* **quarrel** *about money.*

°**quarrel**[2] *verb* (*present participle* **quarrelling,** *past* **quarrelled)**
to have an argument: *Those children are always* **quarrelling** *over little things.*

quarry /kwôr′ ē/ *noun* (*plural* **quarries)**
a hole in the ground where people dig up stone or sand

quart /kwôrt/ *noun*
a measure of liquid equal to 1.13 liters: *There are two* **pints** *in a* **quart** *and four* **quarts** *in a gallon.*

°**quarter** /kwôr tər/ *noun*
1 one of four equal parts of something, ¼: *There were four of us, so we divided the orange into* **quarters** *and each ate a piece. He was waiting for a* **quarter** *of an hour* (= 15 minutes). *It's* **(a) quarter to** *six* (= 15 minutes before 6 o'clock). *I must leave at* **(a) quarter past** six (= 15 minutes after 6 o'clock).
2 a part of a town

quarters /kwôr′ tərz/ *plural noun*
a place where people live, especially if they live where they work: *The soldiers'* **quarters** *are in that long building over there.*

quay /kē/ *noun*
a place where boats tie up and unload: *The* **quay** *looked like a long stone road going into the sea.*

queen /kwēn/ *noun*
1 the female ruler of a country, especially one who comes from a family of rulers
2 the wife of a king

queer /kwēr/ *adjective*
odd; strange: *He has some* **queer** *opinions on education.*

queerly *adverb*

quench /kwench/ *verb*
to stop thirst or fire: *The cold drink* **quenched** *his thirst.*

query[1] /kwēr′ ē/ *noun* (*plural* **queries)**
a question: *I have several* **queries** *about the work you gave me.*

query[2] *verb* (*present participle* **querying,** *past* **queried** /kwēr′ ēd/)
to ask about something, usually to make sure that it is right: *If you think the price is too high, you should* **query** *it.*

°**question**[1] /kwes′ chən/ *noun*
1 something you ask someone: *You haven't answered my* **question.**

2 something to be talked about; a difficulty: *We talked about the* **question** *of private education. I want to buy the house, but it's a* **question** *of money — I haven't got enough.*

°**question**[2] *verb*
to ask about something: *I* **questioned** *the teacher about the work she had given us. I do not* **question** (= doubt) *his honesty.*

question mark /kwes′ chən märk′/ *noun*
the sign ?, used in writing at the end of a sentence which asks a question: *Where are you going?*

queue[1] /kū/ *noun*
a line of people waiting for something: *a* **queue** *for a bus*

queue

queue[2] *verb* (*present participle* **queuing,** *past* **queued)**
to stand in a line to wait for something: *We* **queued** *for the bus.*

°**quick** /kwik/ *adjective*
fast; not slow; happening in a short time: *We had a* **quick** *meal and then ran to catch the train. This is the* **quickest** *way to get to school.*
quickly *adverb*

°**quiet**[1] /kwī′ et/ *adjective*
1 having or making very little noise: *The streets were* **quiet** *at night. He has a* **quiet** *voice, I cannot hear what he says.*
2 not active: *I had a* **quiet** *day reading at home.*
quietly *adverb*

quiet[2] *noun (no plural)*
silence; a time when there is no noise: *Your brother needs* **peace and quiet** *because he's working.*

quilt /kwilt/ *noun*
a soft, thick covering for a bed

°**quite** /kwīt/ *adverb*
1 completely; perfectly: *I* **quite** *agree with you. That fruit is not* **quite** *ripe.*
2 rather; not very much: *I was* **quite** *busy last week.*

quiver /kwiv′ ər/ *verb*
to shake a little: *The bridge* **quivered** *as the truck crossed it.*

quiver *noun*
a case for holding arrows

quiz /kwiz/ *noun* (*plural* **quizzes**)
a game in which people try to answer questions correctly

quote /kwōt/ *verb* (*present participle* **quoting,** *past* **quoted)**
to say or write something that has been said or written before by someone else: *He* **quoted** *the saying "Every dog has his day", meaning that he would get a chance in life sometime.*
quotation *noun: Which book do these* **quotations** (= things quoted) *come from?*

Rr

rabbit /rab′ it/ *noun*
a small animal with long ears and long back legs which lives in holes under the ground

°**race[1]** /rās/ *noun*
a group of human beings, animals or plants different from other groups in shape, color, size, etc.: *White people are of a different* **race** *from black people.*
racial /rā′ shəl/ *adjective*

°**race[2]** *noun*
a competition to see who can run, swim, walk, etc., fastest: *Jane can run fast — she usually wins* **races.**

°**race[3]** *verb* (*present participle* **racing,** *past* **raced)**
to try to run or go faster than: *Paul* **raced (against)** *John in the one-mile race.*

rack /rak/ *noun*
a frame on which things can be kept: *The bottles were stored in a* **rack.**

racket /rak′ it/ *noun*
an instrument used in games like tennis (see) to hit the ball

radar /rā′ där/ *noun (no plural)*
a way of finding out the position of something by using radio waves: *The airplane could land at night because the pilot* (= driver) *was using* **radar.**

radiator /rā′ dē ā″ tər/ *noun*
1 an instrument for cooling the engine of a car
2 an instrument for sending out heat in a house

°**radio** /rā′ dē ō/ *noun*
1 *(no plural)* sending out or receiving sounds by electrical waves: *Ships send messages to each other* **by radio.**
2 (*plural* **radios**) a machine which receives the waves and plays them to you: *He was listening to music on the* **radio.**

radius /rā′ dē əs/ *noun*
straight line from the center of a circle to its side

raft /raft/ *noun*
large pieces of wood joined together to make a rough flat boat

rag /rag/ *noun*
1 an old torn garment
2 a piece of cloth: *She washed the floor with a* **rag.**

rage /rāg/ *noun*
fierce anger; bad temper: *My father was* **in a rage** *last night.*

raid[1] /rād/ *noun*
a sudden attack

raid[2] *verb*
to attack: *They* **raided** *the village.*

rail /rāl/ *noun*
a fixed metal bar: *Trains run on two* **rails.** *You can hang clothes from a* **rail.**
railing *noun* a rail in a fence: *There were* **railings** *around the park.*

railroad /rāl′ rōd/ *noun*
1 a track made of rails for trains to go on: *We went to the* **railroad station** *to catch a train.*
2 the tracks, stations, etc. used in carrying people and goods by train: *a book about* **railroads**

rain[1] /rān/ *verb*
(of water) to fall from the sky: *It* **rained** *last night.*

rain[2] *noun*
(no plural)
water falling from the sky: *There was* **rain** *in the night.*

rainbow

rainbow /rān′ bō/ *noun* an arch of colors in the sky, especially after rain
raincoat *noun* a coat that keeps out the rain
rainy *adjective: Last week was very* **rainy;** *rain fell every day.*

°**raise** /rāz/ *verb* (*present participle* **raising,** *past* **raised**)
to lift up; make higher: *He* **raised** *his arms above his head. Her wages were* **raised** *last week.*

raisin /rā′ zin/ *noun*
a small dried grape (see)

rake[1] /rāk/
noun
a tool for pulling leaves, etc. together on the ground, and for making ground level

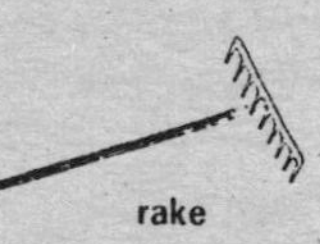
rake

rake[2] *verb* (*present participle* **raking,** *past* **raked**)
to pull a rake over; gather with a rake

ran /ran/ see **run**

ranch /ranch/ *noun*
a large cattle farm

rang /rang/ see **ring**

°**range** /rānj/ *noun*
1 a line of mountains or hills
2 a number of different things: *We sell a wide* **range** *of goods.*
3 the distance something can reach or travel: *What is the* **range** *of your gun* (= how far can you fire it)?

rank /rank/ *noun*
a group or class thought of as higher or lower than other groups: *A general is an army officer with a high* **rank.**

ransom /ran′ səm/ *noun*
money paid so that a prisoner is made free: *The rich man was asked to pay a high* **ransom** *for his daughter who was taken away by criminals.*

rapid /rap′ id/ *adjective*
quick; fast
rapidly *adverb: He talked so* **rapidly** *that I could not understand him.*

rare /râr/ *adjective* **(rarer, rarest)**
not happening often; not often seen: *That bird is very* **rare** *in this country.*
rarely *adverb: She is old and* **rarely** *goes out.*

rascal /ras′ kəl/ *noun*
a bad person; a badly-behaved child

rash[1] /rash/ *adjective*
acting quickly without thinking enough what might happen: *It was* **rash** *to say you would buy it when you haven't any money.*
rashly *adverb*

rash[2] *noun*
red spots on the skin: *With some illnesses, you get a* **rash.**

°**rat** /rat/ *noun*
a small animal like a mouse (see) but larger, which often eats food or grain that is stored

°**rate** /rāt/ *noun*
1 the money paid for a fixed amount of work; the amount

produced, bought, used, etc. in a period of time: *He was paid at the* **rate** *of $5 an hour.*
2 the speed of something: *She learns at a quick* **rate.**

°**rather** /raTH′ ər/
a little: *This shirt is* **rather** *tight; I need a bigger one.*

ration¹ /rash′ ən/ *verb*
to limit the goods that someone can have: *The government had to* **ration** *sugar during the war.*

ration² *noun*
a fixed amount of something that is given or allowed: *Have you used your* **ration** *of gasoline for this week?*

rattle¹ /rat′ əl/ *verb* (*present participle* **rattling,** *past* **rattled**)
to shake, making a noise: *She* **rattled** *some coins in the box.*

rattle² *noun*
a toy which a baby shakes to make a noise

ravine /rə vēn′/ *noun*
a deep narrow area between hills or mountains

°**raw** /rô/ *adjective*
1 not cooked: **raw** *meat*
2 in the natural state; not changed: *Clay and water are the* **raw** *materials used for making pots.*

ray /rā/ *noun*
a line of light: *the* **rays** *of the sun*

razor /rā′ zər/ *noun*
an instrument with a sharp blade, used especially for removing hair from men's faces

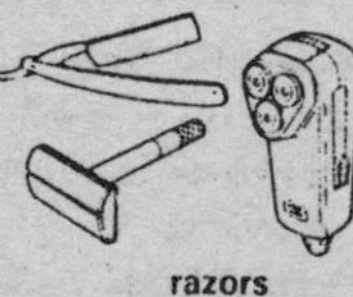
razors

°**reach¹** /rēch/ *verb*
1 to get to a place; arrive at: *I have* **reached** *the age when I can vote.*
2 to stretch out your hand: *I* **reached up** *and took an apple from the tree.*

°**reach²** *noun (no plural)*
the distance that we can reach: *The book was* **within reach** (= I could reach it). *The ball was* **out of reach** (= I couldn't reach it).

react /rē akt′/ *verb*
to act because of something that has happened: *How did your mother* **react to** *the news? She* **reacted** *by getting very angry.*
reaction *noun*

°**read** /rēd/ *verb* (*present participle* **reading,** *past* **read** /red/)
to look at words and understand them: *She* **read** *the newspaper. He* **read** *the story to his son. I like* **reading.**
reader *noun* **1** a person who reads **2** a book for teaching reading

°**ready** /red′ ē/ *adjective*
1 in the right way or order for use; prepared: *I am not* **ready** *to go out yet; I have not got my keys or my money. He got his tools* **ready** *to start the job.*
2 willing: *I'm always* **ready** *to help.*
readily *adverb: I can* **readily** (= easily and willingly) *believe that she is lazy at home — she is very lazy at school.*

°**real** /rēl/ *adjective*
being in fact; not imagined: *That is a* **real** *dog, not a toy.*
really *adverb: I am* **really** (= truly) *worried about my work. He is* **really** (= very) *nice!* **Really,** *Jane, you are behaving badly.*

realize /rē′ əl īz″/ *verb* (*present participle* **realizing,** *past* **realized**)

to know or understand something as true, especially suddenly: *When I heard the noise on the roof, I* **realized** *that it was raining.*
realization *noun*

reap /rēp/ *verb*
to cut a crop and gather it: *They* **reaped** *the corn.*

rear[1] /rēr/ *adjective*
at the back: *the* **rear** *wheels of a car*

rear[2] *noun*
the back part: *We sat at the* **rear** *of the bus.*

rear[3] *verb*
to keep (animals, children, etc.) while they grow up: *to* **rear** *sheep/ to* **rear** *a family*

°**reason[1]** /rē′ zən/ *noun*
1 why something is done or happens: *The* **reason** *she was ill was that she had eaten bad meat.*
2 (no plural) the power of thinking and deciding: *Use your* **reason** *— you can't expect to pass the examination if you don't work!*
reasonable *adjective* **1** having good sense: *Don't be afraid to talk to the teacher, she's very* **reasonable. 2** fair: *a* **reasonable** *price*
reasonably *adverb*

°**reason[2]** *verb*
to argue in a thoughtful way: *He* **reasoned with** *the boy who had run away, and made him see that it was a silly thing to do.*

reassure /rē″ ə shūr′/ *verb* (*present participle* **reassuring,** *past* **reassured)**
to help feel safe and comfortable: *When the child was afraid in the storm, his parents* **reassured** *him.*

rebel[1] /rē bel′ / *verb* (*present participle* **rebelling,** *past* **rebelled)**
to fight against a leader or government: *The students* **rebelled** *against their government.*
rebellion *noun: When a lot of people rebel, there is a* **rebellion.**

rebel[2] /reb′ əl/ *noun*
a person who rebels

°**receive** /ri sēv′/ *verb* (*present participle* **receiving,** *past* **received)**
to get something given to you: *Did you* **receive** *any letters today?*
receipt /ri sēt′/ *noun: When you have paid for something, a* **receipt** (= a piece of paper showing that you have paid) *is given to you.*
receiver *noun: The part of a telephone you speak into and listen at is called a* **receiver.**

receiver

reception /ri sep′ shən/ *noun: A party for a special event is called a* **reception.** *The place where you go to see if there is a room for you in a hotel is called the* **reception desk.**

recent /rē′ sənt/ *adjective*
happening a short time ago: *a* **recent** *visit to the city*
recently *adverb: I have been abroad* **recently.**

recipe /res′ ə pē/ *noun*
a piece of writing telling you how to cook something: *In the* **recipe,** *it says that I must use two eggs.*

reckless /rek′ lis/ *adjective*
careless and dangerous: *His* **reckless** *driving caused a serious accident.*
recklessly *adverb*

reckon /rek′ ən/ *verb*
1 to guess: *I* **reckon** *he must have*

finished eating by now.

2 to add or count: *She* **reckoned** *the money we owed her.*

recognize /rek′ əg nīz″/ *verb* (*present participle* **recognizing,** *past* **recognized)**

1 to know someone or something again: *I* **recognized** *Peter although I hadn't seen him for 10 years. I don't* **recognize** *this word — what does it mean?*

2 to know as true: *Everyone* **recognizes** *that Richard is the best player in the team.*

recognition /rek″ əg nish′ ən/ *noun*

recommend /rek″ ə mend′/ *verb*

1 to tell someone that a person or thing is good, useful, etc.: *If you are going to the city, I* **recommend** *the new hotel — it is very nice.*

2 to advise: *I* **recommended** *him to finish school before getting a job.*

recommendation *noun: I went to the new hotel on your* **recommendation.**

record¹ /ri kôrd′/ *verb*

1 to write the story of, or make pictures of: *The newspapers* **recorded** *the interesting news story.*

2 to store sounds electrically so that they can be listened to: *The songs were* **recorded** *by the radio company.*

recording *noun: We made a* **(tape) recording** *of the songs.*

record² /rek′ ərd/ *noun*

1 a round thin flat piece of plastic that stores sounds, and which we play on a machine (a **record player**) to hear the sounds

record player

2 information that is written down and kept: *The doctor keeps a* **record** *of all the serious illnesses in the village.*

3 something done better, quicker, etc. than anyone else has done it: *He holds the world* **record** *for the high jump. Can anyone* **break his record** (= do better)?

recover /ri kuv′ ər/ *verb*

to get better, or get back to a usual state: *She has had a bad illness, but she is* **recovering** *now. I* **recovered** (= got back) *the money I had lost.*

recovery *noun: She made a quick* **recovery** *after her illness.*

recreation /rek″ rē ā′ shən/ *noun*

rest or play after you have been working: *Football is the boys' usual* **recreation** *after school.*

recruit¹ /ri kro͞ot′/ *noun*

a new member of a group, especially of the armed forces

recruit² *verb*

to find or get someone as a recruit: *to* **recruit** *new police officers*

rectangle /rek′ tang″ gəl/ *noun*

a flat shape with four straight sides and four equal angles, the opposite sides of which are parallel

rectangular /rek′ tang″ ū lər/ *adjective: a* **rectangular** *table*

°**red** /red/ *noun, adjective* **(redder, reddest)**

(of) the color of blood: *The sticks in the fire became* **red** *as they burnt. She was dressed* **in red.**

reduce /rē do͞os/ *verb* (*present participle* **reducing,** *past* **reduced)**

to get or make smaller or less: *They've* **reduced** *the prices in the*

shop, so it's a good time to buy.
reduction /ri dukt′ shən/ *noun*

reed /rēd/ *noun*
a tall plant like grass, which grows in or near water

reel /rēl/ *noun*
a round thing on which thread, film, etc. can be wound: *a* **reel** *of cotton*

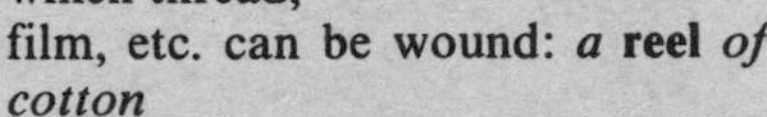

refer /ri fur′/ *verb* (*present participle* **referring,** *past* **referred)**
1 to go to a person, book, etc., to get a piece of knowledge: *I* **referred to** *the dictionary to find out the meaning of the word.*
2 to speak about: *The teacher* **referred to** *Jane's good work when she spoke to her parents.*
reference /ref′ rəns *or* ref′ ər əns/ *noun: A dictionary is a* **reference book** (= a book that you can refer to if you want to know things). *When I was looking for a job, I asked my head teacher to give me a* **reference** (= to write about me to people who might employ me).

referee /ref″ ə rē′/ *noun*
a person who is in charge of a game to see that the rules are followed

reflect /ri flekt′/ *verb*
1 to throw back light, heat, a picture, etc.: *A mirror* **reflects** *a picture of you when you look in it.*
2 to think: *He* **reflected** *before answering my question.*
reflection *noun* **1** throwing back light, heat, etc.
2 what we see in a mirror: *He saw his* **reflection** *in the mirror.*
3 *(no plural)* thinking: *After a minute's* **reflection,** *he answered.*

refresh /ri fresh′/ *verb*
to make someone feel better, less tired, etc.: *A cool drink* **refreshed** *me after my long walk. I had a* **refreshing** *drink.*
refreshments *plural noun* food and drink: *We bought* **refreshments** *at the football game.*

refrigerator /ri frij′ ə rā″tər/ *noun*
a machine for keeping food cold and fresh: *We have a* **refrigerator** *in our kitchen.*

refuge /ref′ ūj/ *noun*
somewhere safe: *He* **took refuge** *from the storm in a hut.*
refugee /ref′ ū jē″/ *noun* a person who has to leave his own country because he is in danger

refuse /ri fūz′/ *verb* (*present participle* **refusing,** *past* **refused)**
not to allow; not to agree or accept: *She* **refused** *to let me help.*
refusal *noun: her* **refusal** *of my help*

regard¹ /ri gärd′/ *verb*
to think of or see: *We* **regard** *him as our best student.*
regarding *preposition* about: *I wrote a letter* **regarding** *my daughter's school examinations.*

regard² *noun (no plural)*
care: *He always says what he thinks, without* **regard** *for other people's feelings.*
regardless *adverb: He says what he thinks,* **regardless** *of other people's feelings.*
regards *plural noun* best wishes: *Give my* **regards** *to your parents.*

regiment /rej′ ə mənt/ *noun*
a large group of soldiers; part of an army

region /rē′ jən/ *noun*
an area: *This is a farming* **region.**

register[1] /rej′ is tər/ *noun*
a list: *The county kept a* **register** *of the names of the voters.*

register[2] *verb*
1 to have your name put on a list: *He* **registered** *the birth of his child.* **2** to show: *The machine* **registered** *how fast we were going.*
registration *noun*

regret[1] /ri gret′/ *verb*
(*present participle* **regretting,** *past* **regretted)**
to be sorry about something: *I* **regret** *spending so much money on a car. I* **regret** *to say I cannot come.*

regret[2] *noun*
a feeling of being sorry: *He told me* **with regret** *that he could not come to the party.*

°**regular** /reg′ yə lər/ *adjective*
1 happening or being at fixed times: *He is a* **regular** *visitor — he comes every Sunday.*
2 ordinary; usual: *Is he your* **regular** *doctor?*
regularity /reg″ yə lər′ i te/ *noun (no plural): The clock ticked with great* **regularity.**
regularly *adverb: Take the medicine* **regularly** *three times a day.*

regulation /reg′ yə lā′ shən/ *noun*
a rule: *It is a* **regulation** *of the football team that smoking is prohibited.*

rehearse /ri hurs′/ *verb* (*present participle* **rehearsing,** *past* **rehearsed)**
to do or say again and again, to make it as good as possible: *He* **rehearsed** *his speech last night.*
rehearsal *noun: All the children in the play must come to the* **rehearsal.**

reign[1] /rān/ *verb*
to be king or queen

reign[2] *noun*
the time when a king or queen reigns: *He has had a long* **reign.**

rein /rān/ *noun*
a long narrow piece of leather used to handle a horse: *The rider pulled on the* **reins,** *and the horse stopped.*

reject /ri jekt′/ *verb*
to decide not to have; throw away: *We* **rejected** *his idea for a music club, and decided to have an art club instead.*

rejoice /ri jois′/ *verb* (*present participle* **rejoicing,** *past* **rejoiced)**
to be very happy

relate /ri lāt′/ *verb* (*present participle* **relating,** *past* **related)** .
1 to have a connection with: *This film* **relates to** *what we were learning about metals last week.*
2 to tell: *I* **related** *my adventure to my family.*
related *adjective* connected; of the same family: *I am* **related to** *him — he's my uncle.*
relation *noun* a member of the same family: *Some of my* **relations,** *my mother's aunt and uncle, live in Germany.*
relationship *noun* **1** being related: *"Do you know her* **relationship** *to that girl?" "She's her sister."* **2** feelings between people: *The teacher has a very good* **relationship** *with her students.*

°**relative** /rel′ ə tiv/ *noun* a relation

relax /ri lax′/ *verb*
to become less worried, angry, tight, etc.: *Don't worry about it, just try to* **relax.**
relaxation *noun (no plural)*

release[1] /ri lēs′/ *verb* (*present participle* **releasing,** *past* **released)**
to let go: *I* **released** *(my hold on) the horse and it ran away. Four prisoners were* **released.**

release[2] *noun*
letting go: *After their* **release,** *the prisoners came home.*

relieve /ri lēv′/ *verb* (*present participle* **relieving,** *past* **relieved)**
to make pain or trouble less: *The medicine* **relieved** *his headache. I was* **relieved** *when he arrived home safely.*
relief *noun (no plural): I felt great* **relief** *when I heard I had passed the examination.*

°**religion** /ri lij′ ən/ *noun*
1 *(no plural)* belief in one or more gods: *Almost every country has some form of* **religion.**
2 a special set of beliefs in one or more gods: *Hinduism and Buddhism are Eastern* **religions.**
religious *adjective*

reluctant /ri luk′tənt/ *adjective*
not willing: *The child was* **reluctant** *to leave her mother.*

rely /ri lī′/ *verb* (*present participle* **relying,** *past* **relied)**
to trust in: *You can* **rely on** *me to help you.*
reliable *adjective: He is a* **reliable** *person; if he says he will do something, he will do it.*

remain /ri mān′/ *verb*
to stay: *I went to the city, but my brother* **remained** *at home. We* **remained** *friends for many years.*
remainder *noun* the rest; what is left: *I will go ahead with three of you, and the* **remainder** *(of the group) can wait here.*
remains *plural noun* parts which are left: *We found the* **remains** *of a meal on the table.*

remark[1] /ri märk′/ *noun*
something said: *He made a rude* **remark** *about the person who passed us.*

remark[2] *verb*
to say; notice: *"That is where Jane lives," she* **remarked.**
remarkable *adjective* unusual, usually in a good way: *Your work has been* **remarkable** *this week.*
remarkably *adverb*

remedy /rem′ ə dē/ *noun* (*plural* **remedies)**
a way of making something better: *a* **remedy** *for an illness*

°**remember** /ri mem′ bər/ *verb*
to keep in the mind; not to forget: *Did you* **remember** *to feed the animals?*

°**remind** /ri mīnd′/ *verb*
to make someone remember: **Remind** *me to write to my uncle. That man* **reminds** *me* **of** (= is lke) *my teacher.*

remote /ri mōt′/ *adjective*
far away; far from where people live: *They have a* **remote** *farm in the hills.*
remotely *adverb: He is not* **remotely** (= not in any way) **like me.**

remove /ri mo͞ov′/ *verb* (*present participle* **removing,** *past* **removed)**
to take and move to somewhere

else: *Will you* **remove** *your books from my desk?*

removal *noun:* The citizens demanded the removal of the trash from the park.

renew /ri nū′/ *verb*
1 to get or give a new thing or a thing of the same sort: *He* **renewed** *his car license* (= document saying that he was allowed to keep a car).
2 to start again: *The soldiers* **renewed** *their attack on the town.*

rent[1] /rent/ *noun*
money paid regularly for the use of a house, office, etc.: *He pays $100 a week* **rent.**

rent[2] *verb*
to have the use of or let someone use a house, etc. in return for rent: *My father* **rents** *an office in the city.*

°**repair**[1] /ri pâr′/ *verb*
to make something that is broken or old good again; mend: *Have you* **repaired** *the bicycle yet?*

°**repair**[2] *noun*
recondition: *I haven't paid for the* **repairs** *to my bicycle.*

repay /ri pā′/ *verb* (*present participle* **repaying,** *past* **repaid)**
to give money back to someone: *I will* **repay** *you tomorrow.*

repeat /ri pēt′/ *verb*
to say or do again: *Could you* **repeat** *the question?*

repetition /rep″ ə tish′ ən/ *noun: I want no* **repetition** *of your bad behavior.*

replace /ri plās′/ *verb* (*present participle* **replacing,** *past* **replaced)**
1 to put something back in its place: *When you have finished using the ax, please* **replace** *it.*
2 to put a new or different thing in place of something: *The man who sold me the radio said he would* **replace** *it if it didn't work.*

replacement *noun: This radio does not work; I must get a* **replacement.**

reply[1] /ri plī′/ *verb* (*present participle* **replying,** *past* **replied)**
to give an answer: *I asked him how he was, and he* **replied** *that he was well. "I'm well," he* **replied.**

reply[2] *noun* (*plural* **replies)**
an answer: *His* **reply** *was, "I'm very well, thank you."*

report[1] /ri pôrt′/ *verb*
to give the story of; tell about the facts of: *The newspaper* **reported** *that there had been a fire in the village. We* **reported** *the robbery to the police.*

report[2] *noun*
facts told or written: *The newspaper* **report** *was on the front page.*

reporter *noun* a person who writes reports in newspapers or tells news stories on television or radio

°**represent** /rep″ ri zent′/ *verb*
1 to act for: *Mr. Johnson* **represented** *his company at the meeting.*
2 to be a sign of: *The sign "&"* **represents** *the word "and".*

representative /rep″ ri zent′ tə tiv/ *noun: a* **representative** *of a company*

reproach /ri″ prōch′/ *verb*
to blame someone in a sad way, not an angry way: *Do not* **reproach** *yourself, it was not your fault.*

reproduce /rē″ prə dōōs′/ *verb* (*present participle* **reproducing,** *past* **reproduced)**

1 to produce young: *Cats often* **reproduce** *twice a year.*
2 to make a copy of: *I* **reproduced** *the drawing I had seen.*

reproduction /rē″ prə dukt′ shən/ *noun* **1** *(no plural)* producing young ones: *human* **reproduction**
2 a copy: *a* **reproduction** *of a famous picture*

reptile /rep′ təl *or* rep′ tīl″/ *noun* a cold-blooded animal such as a snake

republic /ri pub′ lik/ *noun* a form of government in which people elect their representatives.

reputation /rep″ yə tā′ shən/ *noun* the opinion that people have about someone or something: *This hotel has the best* **reputation** *in the city.*

°**request**[1] /ri kwest′/ *verb* to ask: *May I* **request** *you to be quiet in the hospital?*

°**request**[2] *noun* something that you ask: *She* **made a request** *for some water.*

require /ri kwīr′/ *verb (present participle* **requiring,** *past* **required)** to need: *I* **require** *two children to help me.*

requirement *noun: If you have any* **requirements** (= if you need anything), *ask me.*

rescue[1] /res′ kū/ *verb (present participle* **rescuing,** *past* **rescued)** to save: *We* **rescued** *the boy who fell into the river.*

rescue[2] *noun* saying: *We* **came to his rescue** *and pulled him out of the river.*

research[1] /rē′ surch/ *noun (no plural)* careful study, especially to find out something new: *scientific* **research/** *medical* **research**

research[2] /ri surch′/ *verb* to study something to find out new things: *to* **research** *into the causes of an illness*

resemble /ri zem′bəl/ *verb (present participle* **resembling,** *past* **resembled)** to be like: *She* **resembles** *her mother in the way she moves her hands when she talks.*

resemblance *noun: There is no* **resemblance** *between the two brothers.*

resent /ri zent′/ *verb* to feel angry with someone: *I* **resent** *what you said about me — it's not true.*

resentment *noun (no plural)*

reserve[1] /ri zurv′/ *verb (present participle* **reserving,** *past* **reserved)** to keep something for someone: *I have* **reserved** *a room for you at the hotel.*

reservation /rez″ ər va′ shən/ *noun: If you want to go to the concert, you'll have to make a* **reservation,** *or there will be no tickets.*

reserve[2] *noun*
1 an amount of something that has been stored: *We have large* **reserves** *of oil.*
2 a place where wild animals live and are protected: *Africa has many* **game reserves.**

reservoir /rez′ ər vwär″/ *noun* a place where a lot of water is stored: *This* **reservoir** *gives water to the whole city.*

residence /rez′ ə dəns/ *noun*
1 a house: *a* **residence** *in the country*
2 *(no plural)* having your home in a place: *to* **take up residence** *in a town*
residential /rez″ ə den′ shəl/ *adjective: a* **residential** *area of a town* (= where people live)

resign /ri sīn′/ *verb*
1 to leave your job: *to* **resign** *from a job*
2 to accept something unpleasant calmly: *I* **resigned myself to** *a long wait.*
resignation /rez″ ig nā′ shən/ *noun* 1 a letter saying you are leaving your job: *I sent in my* **resignation** *last week.* 2 *(no plural)* accepting

resist /ri zist′/ *verb*
1 to refuse to do or accept something: *I can't* **resist** *eating chocolates.*
2 to be strong against: *Will this new wall* **resist** *the force of the sea?*
resistance *noun*

resolve /ri zolv′/ *verb* (*present participle* **resolving,** *past* **resolved)**
to decide: *I* **resolved** *to work hard until the examination.*
resolution /rez″ ə lo͞o′ shən/ *noun: I made a* **resolution** *to work hard.*

resource /ri sôrs′ *or* rē′ sôrs″/ *noun*
1 a source of help: *This book is a good* **resource.**
2 a form of wealth: *The nation's major* **resources** *were lumber and fish.*

°**respect**[1] /ri spekt′/ *noun*
1 *(no plural)* a good opinion of someone: *He has great* **respect** *for his parents.*
2 way: *In some* **respects,** *he is like his father.*
respectable *adjective: a* **respectable** *young man* (of good character)

°**respect**[2] *verb*
to feel respect for: *All the children* **respected** *their teacher.*

respond /ri spänd′/ *verb*
to answer: *How did she* **respond to** *your question? She* **responded by** *laughing.*
response *noun: I've had no* **response** *to my letter.*

responsible /ri spän′ sə bəl/ *adjective*
taking care of someone or something, and taking the blame if anything goes wrong: *I am* **responsible** *for my sister until she gets a job. Simon is a* **responsible** *boy; we can leave him to look after the smaller children.*
responsibility /ri spän″ sə bil′ ə tē/ *noun* (*plural* **responsibilities**): *My children are my* **responsibility.**

°**rest**[1] /rest/ *noun*
1 a time of quiet away from work or play: *I had an hour's* **rest** *after work.*
2 *(no plural)* that or those left behind: *Have you seen* **the rest** *of the children?*

°**rest**[2] *verb*
1 to have a quiet time away from work or play: *I* **rested** *for an hour before I went out.*
2 to put or be placed: *I* **rested** *my elbows on the table.*

restaurant /res′ tər ənt/ *noun*
a place where you can buy and eat food

restore /ri stôr′/ *verb* (*present participle* **restoring,** *past* **restored)**
1 to repair, so that it looks new: *to*

restore *an old building*
2 to give back

restrain /ri strān′/ *verb*
to stop or hold back: *I can't* **restrain** *my anger when I hear of people being cruel to animals.*

restrict /ri strikt′/ *verb*
to keep within a limit: *Swimming is* **restricted** *to this part of the river only — the rest is dangerous.*

°**result**[1] /ri zult′/ *noun*
what happens because something else has happened: *What was the* **result** *of your examination — did you pass or fail?*

°**result**[2] *verb*
to happen as a result; have as a result: *The accident* **resulted in** *three people being killed.*

resume /ri zoom′/ *verb* (*present participle* **resuming,** *past* **resumed)**
to start again: *We shall* **resume** *our work in a quarter of an hour.*

retain /ri tān′/ *verb*
to keep; keep in: *I have* **retained** *my job for a year.*

retire /ri tīr′/ *verb* (*present participle* **retiring,** *past* **retired)**
to stop work because of old age or illness: *He* **retired** *from the business when he was 65.*
retirement *noun: She plans to spend her* **retirement** *traveling.*

retreat[1] /ri trēt′/ *verb*
to go back or away from something or someone: *The soldiers had to* **retreat** *when they were beaten in battle.*

retreat[2] *noun*
retreating

°**return**[1] /ri turn′/ *verb*
1 to come or go back: *I was* **returning** *from school when I saw him.*
2 to give back: *Could you* **return** *the book I lent you?*

°**return**[2] *noun*
coming or going back: *On my* **return** *from work, I saw the door was open. I would like a* **return ticket** (= to go to a place and come back from it).

reveal /ri vēl′/ *verb*
to say or show something that was covered up or secret before: *I lifted the cloth to* **reveal** *a bicycle.*

revenge /ri venj′/ *noun*
(no plural)
doing something bad to someone who has done something bad to you: *I broke Mary's pen by accident, and* **in revenge** *she tore up my school work.*

reverend /rev′ rənd/ *noun*
a title for a religious leader: *We say the* **Reverend** *Richard Jones, but we write* **Rev.** *Richard Jones.*

reverse[1] /ri vurs′/ *verb* (*present participle* **reversing,** *past* **reversed)**
1 to turn over or around: *If you* **reverse** *this sentence, you read it from the end to the beginning.*
2 to make something go backwards: *The driver* **reversed** *the truck into the narrow road.*

reverse[2] *noun*
the opposite: *You think I gave him the fruit, but the* **reverse** *is true: he gave it to me.*

review[1] /ri vū′/ *noun*
a piece of writing telling you about a book, film, etc.

review[2] *verb*
to look at books, films, etc. and say what you think about them

revise /ri vīs′/ *verb* (*present participle* **revising,** *past* **revised)**
1 to look through again and change

things where needed: *He was* **revising** *what he had written.*
2 to learn and practice things, especially for an examination: *I've been* **revising** *all week.*
revision /rē vizh′ ən/ *noun*

revive /rē vīv′/ *verb*
(*present participle* **reviving,** *past* **revived)**
to come or bring back to strength or life: *He managed to* **revive** *the woman he saved from the river.*

revolt[1] /ri vōlt′/ *verb*
1 to fight in a mass against leaders or government: *The soldiers* **revolted** *against their officers.*
2 to make someone feel ill, by being very unpleasant: *I was* **revolted** *by the bad smell.*
revolting *adjective: What a* **revolting** *smell!*

revolt[2] *noun*
when a lot of people fight against their leaders or government: *The army officers led a* **revolt** *against the king.*

revolve /ri volv′/ *verb* (*present participle* **revolving,** *past* **revolved)**
to go around and around: *The wheels* **revolved** *quickly. The earth* **revolves** *around the sun.*
revolution /rev″ ə lo͞o′ shən/ *noun* **1** a great change, especially in the government of a country: *The army officers led a* **revolution** *against the king.* **2** going around like a wheel

reward[1] /ri wôrd/ *noun*
something given in return for good work, kindness, bravery, etc.: *He has had a hard life, and if he is rich now, it is a fair* **reward.**

reward[2] *verb*
to give a reward to: *The police said they would* **reward** *anyone who found the stolen car.*

rhinoceros /rī nos′ ər əs/ *noun* (*plural* **rhinoceroses)**
a large wild animal with a hard skin and two horns on its nose, which lives in Africa and Asia
rino /rī′ nō/ is a short way of saying and writing **rhinoceros.**

rhyme[1] /rīm/ *noun*
1 words with the same sounds, like "pot", "lot", and "got"
2 a short thing you say or sing which has rhymes in it

rhyme[2] *verb* (*present participle* **rhyming,** *past* **rhymed)**
(of words) to end with the same sound: *Weigh* **rhymes with** *play.*

rhythm /riTH′ əm/ *noun*
a regular sound like a drum in music: *I can't dance to music without a good* **rhythm.**

rib /rib/ *noun*
one of the narrow bones which go round your chest

ribbon /rib′ ən/ *noun*
a long narrow piece of material used for tying things: **ribbons** *in her hair*

°**rice** /rīs/ *noun (no plural)*
a grain plant grown in hot countries with seeds which are used as food

°**rich** /rich/ *adjective*
1 having a lot of money
2 cooked with a lot of oil, sugar, etc. *I don't like* **rich** *food.*
riches *plural noun* money and goods; things that cost a lot of money: *She gave away all her* **riches.**

°**rid** /rid/ *preposition*
free of: *We* **got rid of** *the insects by killing them.*

riddle /rid′ əl/ *noun*
a question which is a trick, which makes people laugh: *Here is a* **riddle** *for you: "Why is 'smiles' the longest word in the world? Because it is made of two s's with a 'mile' between them."*

°**ride**[1] /rīd/ *verb (present participle* **riding,** *past tense* **rode** /rōd/, *past participle* **ridden** /rid′ ən/)
to go along on or in something: *She was* **riding** *a bicycle. They* **rode** *in the back seat of the bus.*
rider *noun: The bicycle* **rider** *was hurt in the accident.*

°**ride**[2] *noun*
an act of riding: *He went for a* **ride** *in his car.*

ridge /ridj/ *noun*
a long narrow raised part of something, such as the top of a hill: *The waves had pushed the sand into little* **ridges.**

ridiculous /ri dik′ yə ləs/ *adjective*
not reasonable; silly: *Don't be* **ridiculous** *— you can't play outside in the storm.*

rifle /rī′ fəl/ *noun*
a long gun fired from the shoulder

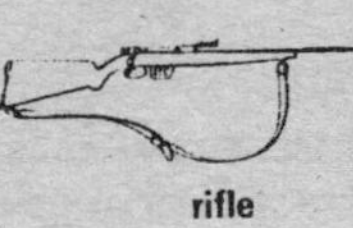
rifle

°**right**[1] /rīt/ *adjective*
1 correct; good: *He showed us the* **right** *way to build a boat. It is* **right** *that everyone should go to school. This is the* **right** *time to ask her.*
2 the opposite of left
right-handed *adjective: If you do most things with your right hand, you are* **right-handed.**

°**right**[2] *noun*
1 *(no plural)* what is fair and good: *You must learn the difference between* **right** *and wrong.*
2 what is or should be allowed by law: *We must work for equal* **rights** *for everyone.*
3 the side opposite to the left side: *The school is on the left of the road, and his house is on the* **right.**

°**right**[3] *adverb*
1 correctly: *I did all my work* **right.**
2 toward the right side: *Turn* **right** *at the corner.*
3 completely; all the way: *I read* **right** *to the end of the book.*
4 directly; straight: *That's our house,* **right** *in front of you.*

rim /rim/ *noun*
the edge of something: *a pattern around the* **rim** *of a plate*

rind /rīnd/ *noun*
the hard outer part of fruit, cheese, etc.; skin

°**ring**[1] /ring/ *noun*
1 a round shape: *The children sat in a* **ring** *around the teacher.*
2 something round: *She wore a gold ring on her finger. He hung the keys on a* **ring.**

°**ring**[2] *verb (present participle* **ringing,** *past tense* **rang** /rang/, *past participle* **rung** /rung/)
1 to make a sound like a bell: *He heard the telephone* **ringing.** *He* **rang** *the bell but no one came to the door.*
2 to speak to on the telephone: *I* **rang** *Peter to see if he could come to dinner. I* **gave him a ring.**

rinse /rins/ *verb (present participle* **rinsing,** *past* **rinsed)**
to wash the soap out of: *I* **rinsed** *the clothes I had washed.*

riot[1] /ri′ət/ *noun*
fighting against something by an angry crowd of people: *There was*

a **riot** *when the workers were told they had lost their jobs.*

riot[2] *verb*
to fight in an angry crowd: *They* **rioted** *in the streets.*

rip /rip/ *verb* (*present participle* **ripping,** *past* **ripped)**
to tear: *When Paul was climbing over the fence, he* **ripped** *his trousers on a nail.*

°**ripe** /rīp/ *adjective*
full-grown and ready to eat: *This fruit isn't* **ripe** *yet — we can't eat it.*

ripple[1] /rip′əl/ *noun*
a little wave: *There were* **ripples** *on the pool as the wind grew stronger.*

ripple[2] *verb* (*present participle* **rippling,** *past* **rippled)**
to move in little waves: *The water* **rippled** *as the bird swam along.*

°**rise**[1] /rīz/ *verb* (*present participle* **rising,** *past tense* **rose** /rōz/, *past participle* **risen** /riz′ən/)
to come or get up: *The sun* **rose** *at seven o'clock. The land* **rises** *steeply from the river.*

rise[2] *noun*
an increase: *a* **rise** *in prices*

°**risk**[1] /risk/ *noun*
the chance of being in danger: *He took a* **risk** *when he crossed the old bridge* (= there was a chance it might fall down).

°**risk**[2] *verb*
to take a chance of something bad happening; put in danger: *He* **risked** *his life when he saved the child from the fire.*

rival /ri′ vəl/ *noun*
a person who tries to do better than another: *She and I are* **rivals** *for the swimming medal.*
rivalry *noun: There is great* **rivalry** *between the two sisters.*

°**river** /riv′ ər/ *noun*
a continuous flow of water along a course to the sea: *The longest* **river** *in Africa is the Nile.*

°**road** /rōd/ *noun*
a hard, wide tract that people and traffic can use: *Do you like to travel* **by road** *or by rail* (= by bus, car, etc., or by train)?

roam /rōm/ *verb*
to wander: *The visitors* **roamed** *around the town.*

roar[1] /rôr/ *verb*
to make a deep, angry noise, like a lion

roar[2] *noun*
a sound of roaring: *The lion gave a loud* **roar.**

roast /rōst/ *verb*
to cook in an oven (see) without water, or over a fire: *The meat is* **roasting.**

°**rob** /rob/ *verb* (*present participle* **robbing,** *past* **robbed)**
to take money, good, etc. from a person or place, when it is not yours; steal from: *While he was away, his house was* **robbed.**
robber *noun* a person who robs
robbery *noun* (*plural* **robberies**): *a bank* **robbery**

robe /rōb/ *noun*
a long loose piece of clothing that covers much of the body

robot /rō′ bot/ *noun*
a machine that does some of the work a person can do

°**rock**[1] /rok/ *noun*
1 *(no plural)* stone: *Mountains are made of* **rock.**
2 a large piece of stone
rocky *adjective* **(rockier, rockiest)** *a* **rocky** *shore*

rock² *verb*
to move from side to side: *When I stepped onto the side of the boat, it* **rocked.**

rocket /rok′ ət/ *noun*
1 a thing driven into the air by burning gas, used to lift a weapon or a spaceship from the ground
2 a firework (= toy which bursts with a loud noise and pretty lights) which goes up into the air

rod /rod/ *noun*
a thin bar: *You catch fish with a* **fishing rod.**

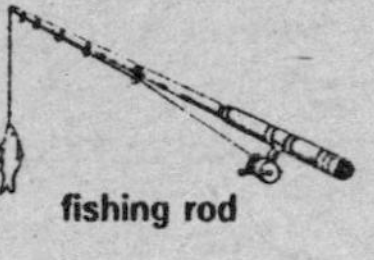
fishing rod

rode /rōd/ see **ride**

rogue /rōg/ *noun*
a bad or dishonest person

role /rōl/ *noun*
a character in a play or film: *He played the* **role** *of the old king in our school play.*

°**roll¹** /rōl/ *verb*
1 to move along by turning over and over: *The ball* **rolled** *under the table.*
2 to make a rounded shape by turning something over and over: **Roll** *the picture* **up** *so that it does not get damaged.*
3 to make flat by passing something over and over: *She* **rolled out** *the flour and water mixture to make bread.*
4 to make a long loud noise: *We heard the drums* **roll.**

°**roll²** *noun*
1 something rolled up into a long round shape: *a* **roll** *of cloth*
2 a small round piece of bread
3 a list of names, such as children in a class
4 a long steady sound of drums

Roman Catholic /rō′ mən kath′ lik/ *or* **Catholic** *noun, adjective*
(a Christian) belonging to the church whose head is the Pope

°**romance** /rō mans′ *or* rō′ mans/ *noun*
1 *being in love: a* **romance** *between a king and a poor girl*
2 a story about love
romantic *adjective*

°**roof** /ro͝of *or* ro͞of/ *noun*
the top covering of a building, car, etc.: *There is a cat on our* **roof.**

°**room** /ro͝om *or* ro͞om/ *noun*
1 one of the parts of a house separated by walls and doors: *We sleep in the* **bedroom,** *and wash in the* **bathroom.**
2 *(no plural)* space; enough space: *There isn't* **room** *for anyone else in the car. This desk takes up a lot of* **room.**

°**root** /ro͝ot *or* ro͞ot/ *noun*
the part of a plant which grows downwards, and is usually below the ground (picture at **flower**)

°**rope** /rōp/ *noun*
a very thick string

rose¹ /rōz/ see **rise**

rose² *noun*
a beautiful and sweet-smelling flower

rot /rot/ *verb* (*present participle* **rotting,** *past* **rotted**)
to go bad and soft because it is old or wet: *The ripe fruit began to* **rot** *when no one came to pick it.*
rotten *adjective: The fish is* **rotten;** *you must not eat it.*

rotate /rō′ tāt/ *verb* (*present participle* **rotating,** *past* **rotated**)
to go around like a wheel: *The*

Earth **rotates,** *around the sun.*
rotation *noun: The* **rotation** *of the Earth around the sun takes one year.*

°**rough** /ruf/ *adjective*
1 not smooth; uneven: *a* **rough** *surface*
2 not calm or gentle; wild: *The sea was* **rough** *in the storm.*
3 not finished: *a* **rough** *drawing*
roughly *adverb* 1 about: *I had* **roughly** *four miles to go.* 2 wildly: *He played* **roughly** *with the baby.*

°**round**[1] /round/ *adjective*
like a ring or circle: *A ball is* **round.**

roundabout /round′ ə bout′/ *adjective*
not direct or straightforward: *He gave a* **roundabout** *answer to the question.*
a place where traffic goes in a circle and where roads cross each other

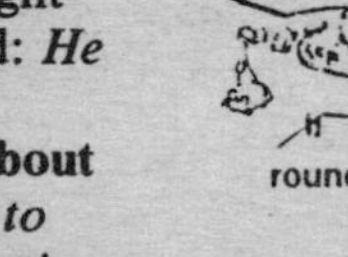
roundabouts

route /ro͞ot *or* rout/ *noun*
a way to a place: *We came by a longer* **route** *than usual.*

routine /ro͞o tēn′/ *noun*
a set way of doing things: *I arrive at nine o'clock, teach until twelve-thirty and then have a meal: that is my morning* **routine.**

°**row**[1] /rō/ *noun*
a line: *a* **row** *of pots on a shelf*

row[2] /rou/ *noun*
a quarrel; a loud noise: *The two men were having a* **row.**

row[3] /rō/ *verb*
to move oars (see) through water to make a boat move

royal /roi′ əl/ *adjective*
of, belonging to, or like a king or queen: *the* **royal** *family*
royalty *noun (no plural)* a member of a king or queen's family

°**rub** /rub/ *verb (present participle* **rubbing,** *past* **rubbed)**
to move something back and forward over something else: *She* **rubbed** *her shoes with a cloth to make them shine. He* **rubbed out** *the writing* (= used an eraser to rub the writing off the paper).

°**rubber** /rub ′ər/ *noun*
1 *(no plural)* a soft material from a tree that can be stretched and that goes back into shape when it is let go: *Tires are made of* **rubber.**
2 a piece of this material used for getting rid of pencil marks
rubber band *noun* a piece of rubber in a ring shape that is used to fasten things together

rubbish /rub′ ish/ *noun (no plural)*
1 things which you do not want and will throw away: *The cellar was full of old papers, broken toys, and other* **rubbish.**
2 anything silly: *I thought that story was* **rubbish.**

°**rude** /rūd/ *adjective* **(ruder, rudest)**
not polite or kind; saying unpleasant things: *He was punished because he was* **rude** *to his teacher.*

rug /rug/ *noun*
a thick floor mat

rugged /rug′ id/ *adjective*
rough and wild; full of rocks: **rugged** *country*

ruin[1] /ro͞on/ *verb*
to destroy: *She poured water all over my painting, and* **ruined** *it.*

ruin² *noun*
a building that has been destroyed: *We saw the* **ruins** *of the church.*

°**rule¹** /rōōl/ *verb* (*present participle* **ruling,** *past* **ruled**)
1 to be the king or most powerful person of: *Who* **rules** *this country?*
2 to make a straight line: *He* **ruled** *a line under his name.*

ruler *noun*
1 someone who governs a country
2 a piece of wood, plastic, or metal with a straight edge to help you measure and draw lines

ruler

°**rule²** *noun*
1 a law; thing that you must or must not do: *The school* **rules** *must be obeyed.*
2 (no plural) government

rum /rum/ *noun (no plural)*
a strong alcoholic drink made from sugar

rumble /rum′ bəl/ *verb* (*present participle* **rumbling,** *past* **rumbled**)
to make a long low noise, like thunder in the distance

rumor /rōō′ mər/ *noun*
something that people tell each other but that may not be true: *I heard a* **rumor** *that the principal is leaving.*

°**run¹** /run/ *verb* (*present participle* **running,** *past tense* **ran** /ran/, *past participle* **run**)
1 to move on your feet very quickly: *He* **ran** *across the road.*
2 to work or make work: *This machine is not* **running** *correctly. She is* **running** *a school in the city.*
3 to make a journey: *Trains* **run** *every hour.*
4 (used in sentences like these): *The river has* **run dry** (= become dry). *The wall* **runs** (= goes) *around the village. We have* **run out of** (= we have no more of) *sugar. A dog was* **run over** (= a car or bus went over the dog) *outside our school. He stole the fruit and then* **ran away** (= escaped quickly).

°**run²** *noun*
1 a time of running: *to go for a run*
2 a journey: *There are no stops on the* **run** *to the coast.*
3 a score in the game of baseball

rung¹ /rung/ see **ring**

rung² *noun*
one of the bars in a ladder (picture at **ladder**)

rural /rŭr′ əl/ *adjective*
in, of, or belonging to the country; not of the town: *Crops are grown in* **rural** *areas.*

rush¹ /rush/ *verb*
to hurry; go fast: *She* **rushed** *into the room to tell us the news.*

rush² *noun (no plural)*
hurry: *I can't stop; I'm* **in a rush.**

rust¹ /rust/ *noun (no plural)*
red-brown substance that forms on iron when it has been wet: *an old car with a lot of* **rust**

rusty *adjective* (**rustier, rustiest**)
covered with rust: *a* **rusty** *car*

rust² *verb*
to become covered with rust: *If you leave your metal tools outside in the rain, they will* **rust.**

rustle¹ /rus′ əl/ *verb* (*present participle* **rustling,** *past* **rustled**)
to make a light sound like paper being moved: *The leaves* **rustled** *in the wind.*

rustle[2] *noun (no plural)*
a light sound of rustling: *the* **rustle** *of paper*

rut /rut/ *noun*
a deep narrow track made by a wheel in soft ground

Ss

sack /sak/ *noun*
a large bag made of strong material: *a* **sack** *of rice*

sacred /sā′ krid/ *adjective*
religious; holy: *a* **sacred** *building*/ **sacred** *writings*

sacrifice[1] /sak′ rə fīs″/ *noun*
1 something killed and offered to a god
2 something important to you that you give up for some good purpose: *Her parents made many* **sacrifices** *so that she could study abroad.*

sacrifice[2] *verb* (*present participle* **sacrificing,** *past* **sacrificed)**
1 to offer to a god: *They* **sacrificed** *a goat.*
2 to give up: *She* **sacrificed** *her job so that she could help her parents.*

°**sad** /sad/ *adjective*
(sadder, saddest)
not happy; feeling sorrow: *I am very* **sad** *to hear that your father has died.*
sadly *adverb*

saddle /sad′ əl/ *noun*
a seat for the rider of a horse

safari /sə fär′ ē/ *noun*
a journey to hunt or look at wild animals, especially in Africa

°**safe**[1] /sāf/ *adjective*
not in danger; not dangerous: *It is good to be* **safe** *at home on a night like this. The bridge is* **safe** *to walk on.*
safely *adverb*
safety *noun (no plural)* a safe place: *They ran to* **safety,** *away from the fire. A* **safety pin** *has a cover over its point.*

safe[2] *noun*
a strong box that can be locked, for keeping things safely

sag /sag/ *verb* (*present participle* **sagging,** *past* **sagged)**
to hang down heavily: *The bed* **sags** *in the middle and is uncomfortable.*

said /sed/ see **say**

sail[1] /sāl/ *noun*
a large cloth used to catch the wind and move a boat

sail[2] *verb*
1 to travel on water: *His ship* **sails** *today.*
2 to direct a boat with sails: *She* **sailed** *the boat without any help.*
sailor *noun* a person who works on a ship

saint /sānt/ *noun*
a person who has lived a very good and religious life
St. /sānt/ *is a short way of writing* **saint: St.** *Peter's Church*

sake /sāk/ *noun*
used with **for,** to show purpose or reason: *Your sister is trying to read; please be quiet* **for her sake.** *I stopped smoking* **for the sake of** *my health. Oh,* **for goodness' sake,** *hurry up!*

salad /sal′ əd/ *noun*
a dish of cold, usually raw vegetables

salary /sal′ rē/ *noun*
(*plural* **salaries)**
a fixed amount of money paid to someone regularly for the work done

°**sale** /sāl/ *noun*
1 selling: *He got $40 from the* **sale** *of his drawing. That house is* **for sale** (= waiting to be sold).
2 a time when prices are low: *The shoe shop is having a* **sale** *this week.*
salesman /sālz′ mən/ *noun* (*plural* **salesmen**) *or* **saleswoman** /sālz′ woom″ən/ (*plural* **saleswomen**) a person whose job is to sell goods

salmon /sam′ ən/ *noun* (*plural* **salmon**)
a large river and sea fish

°**salt** /sôlt/ *noun (no plural)*
a white chemical found in seawater, rocks, etc., which we add to our food to make it taste better
salty *adjective* **(saltier, saltiest)** having a lot of salt

salute[1] /sə lo͞ot′/ *noun*
a mark of respect to someone, done by holding your right hand to your forehead

salute[2] *verb* (*present participle* **saluting,** *past* **saluted)**
to hold up your hand as a salute: *The soldier* **saluted** *his officer.*

°**same** /sām/ *adjective*
1 not different; alike in one or more ways: *Your pen is* **the same** *as mine.*
2 being one person or thing; not another: *We go to* **the same** *school.*

sample[1] /sam′ pəl/ *noun*
a single piece taken as an example of what something is like: *a* **sample** *of his work*

sample[2] *verb* (*present participle* **sampling,** *past* **sampled)**
to try: *I have* **sampled** *all the cakes and I like Jane's best.*

°**sand** /sand/ *noun (no plural)*
fine powder, usually white or yellow, made of rock, often found next to the sea and in deserts
sands *plural noun* places covered with sand
sandy *adjective* **(sandier, sandiest):** *a* **sandy** *shore*

sandal /san′ dəl/ *noun*
an open shoe that can be put on easily

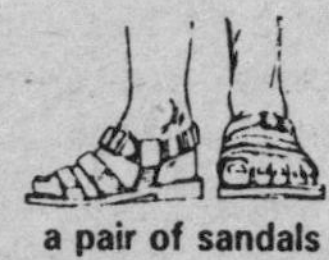
a pair of sandals

sandwich /sand′ wich/ *noun* (*plural* **sandwiches)**
two pieces of bread put together with something else in between them: *I made a chicken* **sandwich.**

sane /sān/ *adjective* **(saner, sanest)**
not mad; reasonable: *I don't think a* **sane** *person would drive as dangerously as he did.*

sang /sang/ see **sing**

sank /sank/ see **sink**

sap /sap/ *noun (no plural)*
the liquid inside a plant which feeds it

sardine /sär dēn′/ *noun*
a small fish that is usually put into cans and used for food

sat /sat/ see **sit**

satellite /sat′ ə līt/ *noun*
something which moves around the earth or another planet (= mass like the earth which goes around the sun): *They receive television pictures by* **satellite** (= pictures sent out in one part of the world, which hit a man-made satellite and come back to earth in a different place).

satisfy /sat′ is fī/ *verb* (*present participle* **satisfying,** *past* **satisfied**)
1 to be enough or good enough for: *This work does not* **satisfy** *me.*
2 to make sure: *I* **satisfied** *my employer that I had finished.*
satisfaction /sat″ is fak′ shən/ *noun (no plural)* being satisfied; pleasure: *He looked at his work with a smile of* **satisfaction.**
°**satisfactory** *adjective* enough or good enough

°**Saturday** /sat′ ər dā/ *noun*
the seventh day of the week

sauce /sôs/ *noun*
a liquid that we put on or eat with food to improve its taste

saucepan /sôs′ pan/ *noun*
a pan with a handle for cooking things over heat

saucer /sô′ sər/ *noun*
a small plate that a cup stands on (picture at **cup**)

sausage /sô′ sij/ *noun*
finely chopped meat cooked inside a thin skin

sausages

savage /sav′ ij/ *adjective*
wild and fierce: *a* **savage** *animal*

°**save** /sāv/ *verb* (*present participle* **saving,** *past* **saved**)
1 to help someone or something to be safe: *I* **saved** *the animals from the flood.*
2 to keep something until it is wanted: *If you* **save** *(money) now, you will be able to buy a car soon.*
3 to use less: *We should* **save** *oil, or else there won't be any left in the world.*
savings *plural noun* money that you keep without spending: *He used his* **savings** *to buy the bicycle.*

savior /sav′ yər/ *noun*
someone who saves others from danger or evil

saw[1] /sô/ see **see**

saw[2] *noun*
a tool with a blade with metal teeth, used for cutting through wood or metal

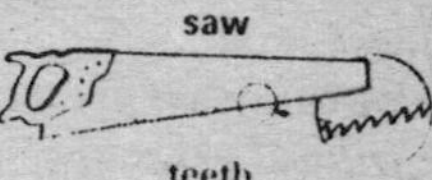

saw[3] *verb* (*present participle* **sawing,** *past tense* **sawed,** *past participle* **sawed** *or* **sawn**)
to use a saw to cut something: *He* **sawed** *the wood into three pieces.*

°**say** /sā/ *verb* (*present participle* **saying,** *past* **said** /sed/)
to speak something: *He* **said** *(that) he wanted to go to town. "I'm going to town," he* **said.**
saying *noun* a wise statement that is often said: *"Every dog has his day" is a* **saying,** *meaning that everyone gets his chance of doing well.*

scab /skab/ *noun*
a hard covering which grows over a wound

scaffold /skaf′ əld *or* skaf′ ōld″/ *noun*
(no plural)
a framework of bars fixed to a building for the builders to stand on while they work

scald /skôld/ *verb*
to burn with steam or boiling water

scale /skāl/ *noun*
1 marks on a measuring instrument: *A machine for weighing people has a* **scale** *from one pound to 300 pounds on it.*
2 the way distances or sizes are

shown on a map, a model, etc.: *The* **scale** *of this map is one centimeter to the kilometer* (= on this map, every centimeter represents one kilometer of distance).
3 a set of musical notes going up or down in order
4 a round shiny part of the skin: *Fish have* **scales.** (picture at **fish**)

scales /skālz/ *plural noun*
a machine for for weighing things or people

scalp /skalp/ *noun*
the skin and hair of the head

scamper /skam′ pər/ *verb*
to run lightly and quickly: *The dog* **scampered** *along the road.*

scandal /skan′ dəl/ *noun*
something which causes a lot of people to talk and show that they do not approve: *There was a great* **scandal** *when we found out that the doctor had been sent to prison for stealing.*

scar¹ /skär/ *noun*
a mark left on the skin where a wound has been

scar² *verb* (*present participle* **scarring,** *past* **scarred)**
to make a scar: *His face was badly* **scarred** *after the car accident.*

scarce /skârs/ *adjective*
not often seen or found; uncommon: *The bird has become* **scarce** *in this country.*
scarcely *adverb: There is* **scarcely** (= almost not) *enough food.*

scare¹ /skâr/ *verb* (*present participle* **scaring,** *past* **scared)**
to make someone afraid: *I was* **scared of** *the big dog.*
scarecrow *noun* a wooden figure dressed in old clothes and put in a field of crops to frighten birds away

scare² *noun*
something that makes you afraid

scarf /skärf/ *noun* (*plural* **scarves)**
a piece of cloth worn around the neck or head

scarlet /skär′ lit/ *noun, adjective*
bright red: **scarlet** *drops of blood*

°**scatter** /skat′ ər/ *verb*
to go or make things or people go in different directions: *The farmer* **scattered** *the corn in the yard for the hens.*

°**scene** /sēn/ *noun*
1 what we see in a special place: *The teacher saw a busy* **scene** *as she entered the classroom.*
2 the place where something happens: *a crowd at the* **scene** *of the accident*
3 a short part of a play: *This play is divided into three acts, and each act has three* **scenes.**
scenery *noun (no plural)* **1** what we see of the country: *The* **scenery** *in the mountains is very beautiful.*
2 the painted pictures at the back of a stage

scent /sent/ *noun*
a nice smell: *the* **scent** *of flowers*

schedule /skej o͞ol *or* skej ūl/ *noun*
a list of times when buses or trains should come or when things are to be done: *The next thing on our* **schedule** *is to telephone our friends.*

scheme¹ /skēm/ *noun*
a plan: *He thought of a* **scheme** *to get some money.*

scheme² *verb* (*present participle* **scheming,** *past* **schemed)**
to make plans, especially dishonest ones

scholar /skol′ ər/ *noun*
a person who has studied and knows a lot about a special thing
scholarship *noun* money given to a clever student so that he or she can continue to study

°**school** /sko͞ol/ *noun*
a place where children go to learn: *Children who go to* **school** *are* **schoolchildren.**

°**science** /sī′ əns/ *noun*
the study of nature and the way things in the world are made, behave, etc.: *The chief* **sciences** *are chemistry, physics* (see), *and biology* (see).
°**scientific** *adjective* of or about science: **scientific** *studies*
scientist *noun* a person who studies or practices science

°**scissors** /siz′ ərz/ *plural noun*
an instrument for cutting with two blades joined together: *Have you got a* **(pair of) scissors?**

a pair of scissors

°**scold** /skōld/ *verb*
to tell someone angrily that they have done wrong: *My mother* **scolded** *me when I dropped the plates.*

scoop /sko͞op/ *verb*
to take out with the hands or a spoon: *She* **scooped** *flour out of the bag.*

scorch /skôrch/ *verb*
to burn lightly, usually so that there is a brown mark: *I* **scorched** *my dress with the iron.*

score[1] /skôr/ *noun*
the marks or points you get in a game or test: *The* **score** *in the football game was 14 to 7* (fourteen to one team, seven to the other).

score[2] *verb* (*present participle* **scoring,** *past* **scored**)
1 to win: *to* **score** *a point*
2 to keep a note of the score: *Will you* **score** *for us when we play?*

scorn[1] /skôrn/ *verb*
to think that someone or something is worthless; not to respect

scorn[2] *noun (no plural)*
lack of respect: *He showed his* **scorn** *for my question by saying he would not answer it.*

scorpion /skôr′ pe ən/ *noun*
a small creature which stings with its tail

scorpion

scowl[1] /skoul/ *verb*
to look angry, especially by pulling the eyebrows (= hairy lines above the eyes) down

scowl[2] *noun*
an angry look on the face: *a* **scowl** *on his face*

scramble /skram′ bəl/ *verb* (*present participle* **scrambling,** *past* **scrambled**)
to climb on hands and knees: *The children* **scrambled** *up the hill.*

scrap /skrap/ *noun*
a small piece: *a* **scrap** *of paper*

scrape /skrāp/ *verb* (*present participle* **scraping,** *past* **scraped**)
to rub with a sharp instrument such as a knife: **Scrape** *the mud off your shoes with his knife.*

scratch[1] /skrach/ *verb*
to make marks with something

pointed: *The stick* **scratched** *the side of the car. He* **scratched** *the insect bite on his leg (with his nails).*

scratch[2] *noun* (*plural* **scratches**)
a mark or small wound made by scratching: *a* **scratch** *on her hand*

scream /skrēm/ *verb*
to give a loud high cry: *She* **screamed** *with fear.*
scream *noun*

screech /skrēch/ *verb*
to give a loud high noise: *The car tires* **screeched** *on the road as it turned too fast.*
screech *noun*

screen /skrēn/ *noun*
1 a flat, square surface on which pictures can be shown: *a television* **screen**
2 a covered frame used to stop someone being seen, protect from the cold, etc.

°**screw**[1] /skrōō/ *noun*
a thing like a nail which can be pushed into something by being turned around and around

screwdriver *noun: You turn the screws around and around with a* **screwdriver.**

°**screw**[2] *verb*
to turn around and around; fix or fasten with screws, or by turning around and around: *She* **screwed** *the top onto the bottle. He* **screwed** *the mirror onto the wall.*

scribble /skrib′ əl/ *verb* (*present participle* **scribbling,** *past* **scribbled**)
to write quickly or carelessly

scripture /skrip′ chər/ *noun*
1 an old religious writing
2 learning about religion

scrub /skrub/ *verb*
(*present participle* **scrubbing,** *past* **scrubbed**)
to rub with a hard brush

sculptor /skulp′ tər/ *noun*
a person who cuts shapes from wood, stone, or metal
sculpture /skulp′ chər/ *noun* a figure made from wood, stone, etc.; the art of making these figures

°**sea** /sē/ *noun*
a large mass of salt water that surrounds the land
seashell *noun* the shell of a small sea animal
seashore *noun: We are going to the* **seashore** *for our vacation.*

seal[1] /sēl/ *noun*
an animal with a thick coat and flat limbs for swimming which lives on cold sea coasts

seal[2] *verb*
to close firmly so that it cannot open by mistake: *We* **seal** *the back of envelopes* (= paper covers for letters).

seam /sēm/ *noun*
a line of sewing where two pieces of cloth are joined together

°**search**[1] /surch/ *verb*
to look for: *I* **searched** *everywhere for the book.*

°**search**[2] *noun* (*plural* **searches**)
an act of searching: *After a long* **search,** *they found the lost child.*

°**season** /sē′ zən/ *noun*
one of the four parts of the year; a special time of year: *Summer is the hottest* **season.**

°**seat** /sēt/ *noun*
a place to sit, or a thing to sit on: *I*

could not find a **seat** *on the bus. Please* **take a seat** (= sit down).

°**second**[1] /sek′ ənd/ *noun*
a very short length of time; there are 60 seconds in a minute

°**second**[2]
the one after the first; 2nd: *This is the* **second** *time I have met him. I came* **second** *in the race.*

secondary school /sek′ ən der″ e/ *noun*
another name for high school

°**secret** /sē krit/ *noun, adjective*
something that has not been told to other people: *Don't tell anyone about our plan,* **keep it a secret** *— it's a secret plan.*

°**secretary** /sek′ rə ter″ ē/ *noun* (*plural* **secretaries**)
1 a person who does office work, writes letters, arranges journeys, etc. for an employer
2 in some countries, a government officer

section /sek′ shən/ *noun*
a part: *One* **section** *of the class was reading and the other* **section** *was writing.*

secure /si kūr′/ *adjective*
1 safe: *I don't feel* **secure** *when I am alone in the house.*
2 strong and fixed firmly: *This lock is* **secure.**
security *noun (no plural): The government looks after the* **security** *of the country.*

°**see** /sē/ *verb* (*present participle* **seeing,** *past tense* **saw** /sô/, *past participle* **seen** /sēn/)
1 to use the eyes to know something: *I can* **see** *two ships in the harbor.*
2 to understand: *I don't* **see** *what you mean.*
3 (used in sentences like these): *Please* **see** *who is at the door* (= go and look). *She* **sees** (= meets) *him after work. I'll* **see** *if I can help you* (= I will think about it and act if possible). **See to** (= Do what is needed about) *the dinner, will you?*

°**seed** /sēd/ *noun*
a small grain from which a plant grows

seek /sēk/ *verb*
(*present participle* **seeking,** *past* **sought** /sôt/)
to look for: *We* **sought** *an answer to the question, but couldn't find one.*

°**seem** /sēm/ *verb*
to appear as or to: *The man* **seemed** *to be ill.*

seep /sēp/ *verb*
(of a liquid) to flow slowly from or through: *Rain* **seeped** *through the roof.*

seesaw /sē′ sô″/ *noun*
a long piece of wood or metal balanced in the middle, so that when persons sit at each end, they can swing up and down

seesaw

seize /sēz/ *verb* (*present participle* **seizing,** *past* **seized**)
to take hold of quickly and firmly or roughly

seldom /sel′ dəm/ *adverb*
only a few times; not often: *The children are* **seldom** *ill.*

select /si lekt′/ *verb*
to choose: *I was* **selected** *for the team.*
selection *noun (no plural)* some

examples: *Here is a* **selection** *of our books.*

°**self** /self/ *noun* (*plural* **selves**)
your own person: *Have you got* **yourself** *a job? I cut* **myself** *on a knife. He can look after* **himself.**
selfish *adjective* always thinking of yourself and not other people: *Don't be* **selfish.**
selfishly *adverb*
selfishness *noun (no plural)*

°**sell** /sel/ *verb* (*present participle* **selling,** *past* **sold** /sōld/)
to give in exchange for money: *She* **sold** *her old bicycle to me.*
seller *noun*

semicircle /sem′ ē sur″kəl/ *noun*
half a circle: *Halfway between new moon and full moon, the moon is a* **semicircle.**

semicolon /sem′ ē kō″lən/ *noun*
the sign **;** used in writing to separate parts of a sentence: *It was a long walk; I'm very tired.*

senate /sen′ it/ *noun*
one of the groups which make up the government in some countries
senator *noun* a member of a senate

°**send** /send/ *verb* (*present participle* **sending,** *past* **sent)**
to cause a person or thing to go somewhere: *She* **sent** *me a present.* **Send** *him to me when he gets in. She* **sent for** *the doctor* (= asked the doctor to come).

senior /sēn yər/ *adjective*
older: *She teaches a* **senior** *class.*
2 higher in position or importance: *She used to be a junior manager, but now she has a* **senior** *position in the company.*

°**sense¹** /sens/ *noun*
1 hearing, seeing, tasting, feeling, and smelling are the five senses: *He has a good* **sense** *of smell.*
2 *(no plural)* good understanding and reasonable ideas: *What she is saying doesn't* **make sense.**
sensation *noun* **1** feeling: *a* **sensation** *of pain* **2** excited interest: *Her strange clothes caused a* **sensation** *in the village.*
sensible *adjective* reasonable: *If you are* **sensible** *you will study for another year.*
sensitive *adjective: She is* **sensitive to** *what people think of her* (= she worries about what people think).

sense² *verb* (*present participle* **sensing,** *past* **sensed)**
to know through the senses; feel: *The dog* **sensed** *that I was afraid.*

°**sentence** /sen′ təns/ *noun*
a group of words which makes a statement and contains a verb: *This is a* **sentence.**

°**separate¹** /sep′ rit/ *adjective*
different: *They have gone to* **separate** *places.*

°**separate²** /sep′ ə rāt/ *verb* (*present participle* **separating,** *past* **separated)**
1 to go in different directions: *The two children* **separated** *at the end of the road.*
2 to make, become, or keep in different places: *A fence* **separated** *the cows from the pigs.*
separation *noun* time away from each other

°**September** /sep tem′ bər/ *noun*
the ninth month of the year

sergeant /sär′ jənt/ *noun*
an officer in the army or police force

serial /sir′ ē əl/ *noun*
a story which is told or written in parts

series /sir′ ēz/ *noun* (**plural series**)
a number of things coming one after the other: *He saw a* **series** *of white arrows painted on the road.*

°**serious** /sir′ ē əs/ *adjective*
1 not cheerful or full of fun: *He is a* **serious** *boy. Be* **serious** *for a minute and listen to me.*
2 important: *How to stop people dying of hunger is a* **serious** *question.*
seriously *adverb*

sermon /sur′ mən/ *noun*
a talk given by a clergyman

serve /surv/ *verb* (*present participle* **serving,** *past* **served**)
1 to do work for other people; be useful to; sell things to: *The girl in the shop* **served** *me.*
2 to give food to: *Please* **serve yourselves** (= take what food you want)! *The chicken was* **served** *with rice.*
servant *noun* a person who works for someone in his house

service /sur′ vis/ *noun*
1 something that you do for others: *We need the* **services** *of a doctor.*
2 selling in a shop: *The* **service** *in this shop is always slow; the girls are very lazy.*
3 something that people can use to help them: *The train* **service** *to the capital is very good.*
4 a church ceremony: *Morning* **service** *will be at 11 o'clock.*

session /sesh′ ən/ *noun*
a meeting of people for some purpose: *a dancing* **session**

°**set¹** /set/ *noun*
1 a group of things thought of together: *I have bought a* **set** *of shelves for the kitchen.*

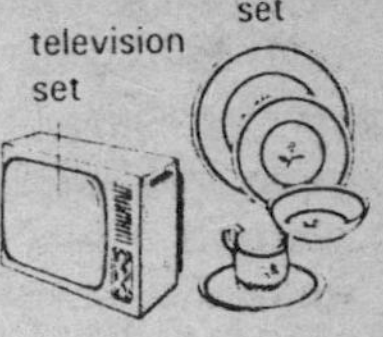

2 an electrical instrument, especially a radio or television

°**set²** *verb* (*present participle* **setting,** *past* **set**)
1 to put: *I* **set** *the flowers on the table.*
2 to make something happen: *I* **set fire to** (= made burn) *the paper.*
3 to go down in the sky: *The sun was* **setting.**
4 to go: *He* **set off/set out** *on his journey.*
5 to put ready: *I* **set** *the table for dinner.*

settle /set′ əl/ *verb* (*present participle* **settling,** *past* **settled**)
1 to go and live in a place: *My son has* **settled** *happily in Kansas.*
2 to make comfortable or calm: *He settled (himself) down with a book.*
3 to rest on something: *The insect* **settled** *on a leaf.*
4 to decide something: *We have* **settled** *who will pay for the meal.*
settlement *noun: We reached a* **settlement** *about which of us should pay for the meal. The* **settlement** *of Africa by white people started 500 years ago.*
settler *noun: The first white* **settlers** *in Africa were farmers.*

seven /sev′ ən/ *noun, adjective*
the number 7
seventh *noun, adjective* number 7 in order; 7th

seventeen /sev′ ən tēn/ *noun, adjective*
the number 17

seventeenth *noun, adjective* number 17 in order; 17th

seventy /sev′ ən tē/ *noun, adjective* the number 70

seventieth *noun, adjective* number 70 in order; 70th

°**several** /sev′ rəl/ *adjective* more than two, but not many: *She has* **several** *friends in the town.*

°**severe** /sə vir′/ *adjective* **(severer, severest)** hard; hard to bear: *a* **severe** *punishment* / *a* **severe** *pain*

severely *adverb*

°**sew** /sō/ *verb* (*present participle* **sewing,** *past tense* **sewed,** *past participle* **sewn)** to mend or make by using a needle and thread: *I like* **sewing.** *He* **sewed** *a button onto his shirt.*

sewing *noun* something being sewn

sewing machine *noun: A* **sewing machine** *helps us to sew things quickly.*

sewing machine

°**sex** /sex/ *noun* being male or female: *Which* **sex** *is your cat?*

shabby /shab′ ē/ *adjective* rather old, cheap, or dirty: **shabby** *clothes*

°**shade**[1] /shād/ *noun*

1 *(no plural)* shelter from the sun or other light: *They sat in the* **shade** *(of a tree).*

2 a sort of color: *I want a darker* **shade** *of blue; this* **shade** *is too light.*

shady *adjective* **(shadier, shadiest):** *It's cool and* **shady** *under the tree.*

°**shade**[2] *verb* (*present participle* **shading,** *past* **shaded)** to shelter from light: *I* **shaded** *my eyes with my hand.*

°**shadow** /shad′ ō/ *noun* a dark shape made by something when it blocks the light: *The* **shadows** *of the trees grew longer as the afternoon went on.*

shaft /shaft/ *noun*

1 a long thin pole: *the* **shaft** *of an arrow*

2 a long hole leading to a mine

°**shake** /shāk/ *verb* (*present participle* **shaking,** *past tense* **shook** /sho͝ok/ *past participle* **shaken)** to move quickly from side to side, up and down, etc.: *The house* **shook** *as the heavy truck went past. She* **shook** *the box to see if there was any money in it. I asked her if she wanted me, but she* **shook her head** (= meaning "no").

°**shall** /shal/ *verb*

1 (a word used instead of **will** with **I** and **we** to say that something is going to happen): *I* **shall** *work tomorrow.*

2 (used with **I** and **we** in questions when asking or offering to do something): **Shall** *we all go to the film tonight?*

Look at **will** and **should**.

shallow /shal′ ō/ *adjective* not deep: *The sea is* **shallow** *here.*

°**shame** /shām/ *noun* the feeling you have when you have done something wrong or silly: *When his teacher told his parents about his behavior, he felt great* **shame. What a shame** (= I'm sorry) *that you can't come to dinner tomorrow!*

shampoo¹ /sham po͞o′/ *noun*
a special soap for washing the hair

shampoo² *verb*
to wash with shampoo

°**shape¹** /shāp/ *noun*
the form of something: *What is the* **shape** *of a coin? It is round.*

shape² *verb* (*present participle* **shaping,** *past* **shaped**)
to make into a certain shape: *He* **shaped** *a pot out of the clay.*

°**share¹** /shâr/ *verb* (*present participle* **sharing,** *past* **shared**)
to divide something so that two or more people can have some: *We* **shared** *the candy.*

°**share²** *noun*
a part that has been divided: *We gave each of the five children an equal* **share.**

shark /shärk/ *noun*
a large fierce fish

shark

°**sharp** /shärp/ *adjective*
1 pointed or having a cutting edge: *a* **sharp** *knife/a needle with a* **sharp** *point*
2 sudden or quick: *There is a* **sharp** *bend in the road. He said something* **sharp** *to the little girl* (= sudden and angry) *and she started to cry.*
3 able to see things far away or very small: **sharp** *eyes*
sharply *adverb*

sharpen /shärp′ ən/ *verb*
to make sharp: *to* **sharpen** *a knife*

shatter /shat′ ər/ *verb*
to break into many pieces: *The glass* **shattered** *when I dropped it.*

shave¹ /shāv/ *verb* (*present participle* **shaving,** *past* **shaved**)
by cutting it very close: *My father* **shaves** *every day.*

shave² *noun*
an act of shaving: *He had a* **shave** *before he went out. When an accident nearly happens, we say it is* **a close shave.**

shawl /shôl/ *noun*
a long piece of cloth worn around the shoulders and head

°**she** /shē/ (*plural* **they**) *pronoun*
the female person or animal that the sentence is about: **She** *is my sister* — **she's** (= she is) *nine and* **she's** (= she has) *got brown eyes. That's a good cow* — **she** gives a lot of milk.

shear /shēr/ *verb*
to cut wool from a sheep or goat
shears *plural noun* large scissors for shearing, for cutting plants, etc.

shed¹ /shed/ *noun*
a small wooden hut

shed² *verb* (*present participle* **shedding,** *past* **shed**)
to let fall: *Some trees* **shed** *their leaves in cold weather.*

°**sheep** /shēp/ *noun* (*plural* **sheep**)
an animal that is kept for meat and for the wool from its thick coat

sheep

sheer /shēr/ *adjective*
straight down; very steep: *There was a* **sheer** *drop from where we stood to the sea below us.*

sheet /shēt/ *noun*
a large flat piece of something: *Everyone had two* **sheets** *of paper to draw on. There are* **sheets** (= pieces of thin cloth) *on our beds.*

°**shelf** /shelf/ *noun* (*plural* **shelves**)
a board fixed to a wall or in a pantry for putting things on: *He took the cup off the* **shelf.**

°**shell** /shel/ *noun*
the hard outside covering of some fish, fruit, or of eggs: **Shellfish** *are good to eat.*

shells

°**shelter¹** /shel′ tər/ *noun*
somewhere you can be protected from the weather, war, etc.: *He stood in the* **shelter** *at the bus stop. We took* **shelter** *under the trees when it rained.*

°**shelter²** *verb*
to protect: *We* **sheltered** *under the tree.*

shepherd /shep′ ərd/ *noun*
someone who looks after sheep

shield¹ /shēld/ *noun*
a piece of wood or metal that soldiers used to hold in front of them to protect their bodies in battle

shield² *verb*
to protect by holding something over or in front of: *He* **shielded** *his eyes from the sun.*

shift¹ /shift/ *verb*
to move: *Shall I* **shift** *the chairs?*

shift² *noun*
1 a set of people who work together at one time: *Peter is on the* **day shift** *and I am on the* **night shift.**
2 the length of time that one group works

°**shine** /shīn/ *verb* (*present participle* **shining,** *past* **shone** /shōn/)
to give out light, or throw back light: *The sun* **shines.** *The water* **shone** *in the sunlight.*
shiny *adjective* **(shinier, shiniest):** **shiny** *shoes*

°**ship** /ship/ *noun*
a large boat that goes on the sea
shipping *noun (no plural)*

°**shirt** /shurt/ *noun*
a piece of clothing that covers the upper part of the body and the arms

shirt
sleeve

shiver /shiv′ ər/ *verb*
to shake with cold or fear: *He* **shivered** *as he heard the strange noise in the night.*
shiver *noun*

°**shock¹** /shok/ *noun*
1 the feeling caused by an unpleasant surprise; something causing this feeling: *It was a great* **shock** *for him when his wife died.*
2 a pain caused by electricity going through you: *An electric* **shock** *can kill you.*

°**shock²** *verb*
to give a shock: *I was* **shocked** *when I heard about your accident.*

°**shoe** /sho͞o/ *noun*
a covering for the foot with a hard bottom part to walk on: **a pair of shoes**
shoelace *noun* a string used to fasten a shoe

shone /shōn/ see **shine**

shook /sho͝ok/ see **shake**

shoot¹ /sho͞ot/ *verb*
(*present participle* **shooting,** *past* **shot** /shot/)
1 to fire at and hit: *He* **shot** *the bird with his gun.*

2 to move quickly: *He* **shot** *out of school when the bell rang.*

shoot² *noun*
part of a plant that leaves will grow from

°**shop¹** /shop/ *noun*
a place where you can go and buy things
shopkeeper *noun* a person who runs a shop

shop² *verb* (*present participle* **shopping,** *past* **shopped)**
to buy things: *We often* **shop** *in the village.*
shopping *noun (no plural)* **1** buying things: the shopping has to be done this morning.

°**shore** /shôr/ *noun*
the flat land at the edge of the sea or a large area of water: *We walked along the* **seashore.**

°**short** /shôrt/ *adjective*
not very tall; not long: *It's a* **short** *distance to school. Mary is much* **shorter** *than her mother. Are you* **short of** (= do you need) *money?*
shortage *noun* not enough: *a* **shortage** *of water*

shorten /shôrt′ən/ *verb*
to make shorter: *to* **shorten** *a dress*

shorts /shôrts/ *plural noun*
trousers which stop above the knee: **(a pair of) shorts**

shorts

shot¹ /shot/ see **shoot**

shot² *noun*
1 the sound of a bullet (= hard thing) fired from a gun: *There was a* **shot,** *and the bird fell dead.*
2 a try: *He's* **having a shot at** *cooking the dinner.*

°**should** /shůd/ *verb*
1 ought to; have a duty to; would be wise to: *You* **should** go home now, or your mother will be angry. You **shouldn't** *stay here anyway.*
2 (the word for **shall** in the past): *I told my mother I* **should** *be late coming home.*
3 (used in sentences with **if**): *If you* **should** *find my pen, please send it to me.*

°**shoulder** /shōl′ dər/ *noun*
the top part of the body where the arms join it

°**shout¹** /shout/ *verb*
to speak in a loud voice: *He is far away, but if you* **shout,** *he may hear you.*

shout² *noun*
an act or sound of shouting: *to give a* **shout**

shovel¹ /shuv′ əl/ *noun*
a wide piece of metal or plastic on a handle, used for moving things like earth or coal

shovel

shovel² *verb* (*present participle* **shovelling,** *past* **shovelled)**
to move with a shovel

°**show¹** /shō/ *verb* (*present participle* **showing,** *past tense* **showed,** *past participle* **shown)**
1 to let someone see something: *He* **showed** *me this new radio. Can you* **show** *me the way to Gabriel's house? Her dress was torn, but it didn't* **show** (= people couldn't see it). *The girl* **showed off** (= let people see) *her new dress. That child* **shows off** (= wants people to notice him, so behaves in a loud or silly way).

2 to explain; make clear: *The teacher* **showed** *us how to draw.*

°**show²** *noun*
1 a lot of things gathered together for people to see: *Many people went to see the flower* **show.**
2 something that people like to go and watch, especially a play, singing, etc.

shred /shred/ *noun*
a small piece torn off: *The cat tore the paper* **to shreds.**

shrewd /shro͞od/ *adjective*
clever, especially about business

shriek /shrēk/ *verb*
to make a high loud cry: *She* **shrieked** *in fear.*
shriek *noun*

shrill /shril/ *adjective*
having a loud, high sound that seems to go through your head: *a* **shrill** *voice*

shrine /shrīn/ *noun*
a holy place

shrink /shrink/ *verb*
(*present participle* **shrinking,** *past tense* **shrank** /shrank/, *past participle* **shrunk** /shrunk/)
to get smaller: *The dress* **shrank** *when I washed it.*

shrub /shrub/ *noun*
a small low tree

shrug /shrug/ *verb* (*present participle* **shrugging,** *past* **shrugged)**
to lift and drop the shoulders to show that you do not know or do not care: *She* **shrugged (her shoulders)** *and said "I don't know."*

shudder /shud′ ər/ *verb*
to shake with fear, dislike, etc.: *He* **shuddered** *when he saw the dead animal.*
shudder *noun.*

°**shut** /shut/ *verb* (*present participle* **shutting,** *past* **shut)**
to move something so that it is not open; close: *Please will you* **shut** *the door? He decided to* **shut down** (= close for ever) *the shop.* **Shut up!** (= a rather rude way of saying Be quiet!)
shutter *noun* a cover for a window to keep out the light

shy /shī/ *adjective* **(shier, shiest)**
afraid to be with other people: *The child was* **shy** *and hid behind his mother.*
shyly *adverb*

sick /sik/ *adjective*
1 bringing or wanting to bring food up from the stomach: *She feels* **sick** *in buses.*
2 ill: *My father is a very* **sick** *man.*
sickness *noun* illness; disease

°**side** /sīd/ *noun*
1 one of the parts of something that is not the top, bottom, back, or front: *He went around to the* **side** *of the house. I have a pain in my left* **side** (= the left part of my body). *The chair had arms at the* **sides.** *You have only written on one* **side** *of your paper, why don't you write on* **both sides?**
2 a team: *Which side do you want to win?*
°**sideways** *adverb* **1** to one side: *He stepped* **sideways** *off the path to let met pass.* **2** turned so that the side is at the front or on top: *We turned the table* **sideways** *to get it into the room.*

sigh¹ /sī/ *verb*
to breathe once deeply, as when you are tired, sad, etc.

sigh² *noun*
an act or sound of sighing: *"I wish*

I had finished this work," she said with a **sigh.**

°**sight** /sīt/ *noun*
1 *(no plural)* the power to see: *She lost her* **sight** *in an accident.*
2 a thing seen: *The fire was a frightening* **sight.** *The visitors to the town went* **sightseeing** (= looking at all the interesting things to see).
3 *(no plural)* seeing: *I* **caught sight of** (= saw) *an empty seat at the back of the bus. When he came* **into sight** (= was seen), *I waved.*

°**sign**[1] /sīn/ *noun*
a movement, mark, or words which have a message for the person who sees it or them: *He made a* **sign** *for me to follow him. The* **sign** *by the road said "No Parking"* (= you cannot leave your car here).
signpost *noun*

TO THE HOSPITAL

signpost

°**sign**[2] *verb*
to write your name
signature /sig′ nə chər/ *noun* a name written in the usual way

°**signal**[1] /sig′ nəl/ *noun*
a movement or thing which tells you what to do: *The railroad* **signal** *showed that the train could pass.*

°**signal**[2] *verb (present participle* **signalling,** *past* **signalled)**
to give a signal: *The teacher* **signalled** *to the boy to begin.*

significant /sig nif′ i kənt/ *adjective*
having a special meaning: *It is* **significant** *that the animals are excited: I think a storm is coming.*
significance *noun (no plural)* meaning: *What is the* **significance** *of this speech?*

°**silence** /sī′lens/ *noun (no plural)*
complete quiet: *They worked* **in silence.**
°**silent** *adjective* without any noise; completely quiet
silently *adverb: The children worked* **silently.**

silk /silk/ *noun (no plural)*
a fine cloth made from the threads that come from a silkworm (see)

silkworm /silk′ wurm″/ *noun*
a caterpillar (see) that makes the soft threads from which the material called silk can be made

°**silly** /sil′ ē/ *adjective* **(sillier, silliest)**
not reasonable or clever: *Don't be* **silly,** *that insect can't hurt you.*

silver /sil′ vər/ *noun (no plural)*
1 a soft shiny gray white metal used for ornaments, old coins, etc.
2 the color of this metal

similar /sim′ ə lər/ *adjective*
like: *My new dress is* **similar to** *the one you have. Our dresses are* **similar.**
similarity /sim″ ə lär′ ə tē/ *noun (plural* **similarities)** likeness: *a* **similarity** *between the sisters*

°**simple** /sim′ pəl/ *adjective* **(simpler, simplest)**
1 easy to understand: *a* **simple** *question*
2 not ornamented; plain: **simple** *clothes*/**simple** *food*
simply *adverb*

simplify /sim′ plə fī″/ *verb (present participle* **simplifying,** *past* **simplified)**
to make simple: *The language in this story has been* **simplified** *to make it easier to understand.*

sin /sin/ *noun*
something people think is a very

bad act; something your religion teaches you is wrong: *It's a sin to tell lies.*

°**since** /sins/
between a time in the past and now; after: *He came to school last week, but I haven't seen him* **since.** *She has been ill* **since** *Christmas. It is six years* **since** *we first met. We have been friends* **ever since** *(then).*

°**sincere** /sin sēr'/ *adjective*
true and real; not pretending: *He was* **sincere** *in his wish to help us.*
sincerely *adverb: You can end a letter to someone you know with* **"Yours sincerely"** *and then write your name.*

°**sing** /sing/ *verb (present participle* **singing,** *past tense* **sang** /sang/ *past participle* **sung** /sung/)
to make music with the voice: *She* **sang** *as she worked. She* **sang** *a song.*
singer *noun* someone who sings

°**single** /sing' əl/ *adjective*
one only: *There is a* **single** *name on the blackboard — whose is it? A* **single** *person is one without a husband or wife. I would like a* **single ticket** (= for one journey only, not a return ticket). A **single** *bed is made for one person.*

singular /sing' gyə lər/ *adjective, noun*
only one: *"Dog" is the* **singular** *of "dogs".* The opposite of **singular** is **plural.**

sink[1] /sink/ *noun*
a large basin for washing clothes or dishes

°**sink**[2] *verb (present participle* **sinking,** *past tense* **sank** /sank/ *past participle* **sunk** /sunk/)
1 to go down: *The sun* **sank** *behind the mountain.*
2 to go down, or make go down in the water: *The ship is* **sinking.**

sip[1] /sip/ *verb (present participle* **sipping,** *past* **sipped)**
to drink in very small amounts: *She* **sipped** *the hot tea.*

sip[2] *noun*
an act of sipping; a very small amount: *I had a* **sip** *of his drink.*

sir /sir/ *noun*
1 a polite way of speaking or writing to a man: *I began my letter "Dear* **Sir***".*
2 the title of a knight (see)

siren /sī' rən/ *noun*
something which makes a loud long warning sound

°**sister** /sis' tər/ *noun*
1 a girl who has the same parents as you: *She is my* **sister.** *We are* **sisters.**
2 a nun (see)
sister-in-law *noun (plural* **sisters-in-law)** the sister of your wife or husband, or the wife of your brother

°**sit** /sit/ *verb (present participle* **sitting,** *past* **sat** /sat/)
to rest on the bottom of the back: *He* **sat** *in a chair. Please* **sit down.**

site /sīt/ *noun*
a place where a building is, was, or will be: *The* **site** *of the new hotel is by the sea.*

situate /sitch' o͞o āt"/ *verb (present participle* **situating,** *past* **situated)**
to put; place: *The house is* **situated** *on a hill.*
situation *noun* **1** position **2** state of events: *This* **situation** *is very*

difficult. I want to take the job but I don't like the employer.

six /siks/ *noun, adjective*
the number 6: *I want* **six** *oranges.*
sixth *noun, adjective* number 6 in order; 6th

sixteen /siks′ tēn/ *noun, adjective* the number 16
sixteenth *noun, adjective* number 16 in order; 16th

sixty /siks tē/ *noun, adjective* the number 60
sixtieth *noun, adjective* number 60 in order; 60th

°**size** /sīz/ *noun*
how big something or someone is: *What* **size** *is your house? The two books were the same* **size.** *These shoes are* **size** *5.*

skate¹ /skāt/ *verb* (*present participle* **skating,** *past* **skated)**
to move smoothly over ice or on wheels over the ground: *She* **skated** *over the ice towards us. He loves* **roller skating.**

skate² *noun*
a special shoe with wheels or a blade fixed under it: **roller skates/ice skates.**

skeleton /skel′ ə tən/ *noun*
the bones of a whole animal or person

sketch¹ /sketch/ *noun* (*plural* **sketches)**
a quick drawing

sketch² *verb*
to draw: *He* **sketched** *the cat.*

skid /skid/ *verb* (*present participle* **skidding,** *past* **skidded)**
to slip sideways on a wet surface: *The car* **skidded** *on a pool of oil and ran into the fence.*

skill /skil/ *noun*
the ability to do something well; something you do well: *He has great* **skill** *in drawing.*
°**skillful** *adjective* having or showing skill: a **skillful** *piece of work.*
skillfully *adverb*

°**skin** /skin/ *noun*
the outside of a person, animal, vegetable, or fruit: *You can make shoes from the* **skins** *of animals.*

skinny /skin′ ē/ *adjective* **(skinnier, skinniest)** very thin: *a* **skinny** *child*

skip /skip/ *verb* (*present participle* **skipping,** *past* **skipped)**
to jump with short light steps, especially over a rope **(skipping rope)** which is made to swing over the head and under the feet.

°**skirt** /skurt/ *noun*
a piece of woman's clothing that hangs from the waist.

skull /skul/ *noun*
the bones of the head (picture at **skeleton)**

°**sky** /skī/ *noun* (*plural* **skies)**
the space above the Earth which we can see if we look up: *The* **sky** *was blue and clear.*

skyscraper /ski′ skrā″ pər/ *noun*
a very tall building

slab /slab/ *noun*
a large flat block: *a* **slab** *of stone*

slack /slak/ *adjective*
1 loose: *The string around the parcel was* **slack.**
2 not lively: *Business is* **slack** *this season.*

slam /slam/ *verb* (*present participle* **slamming,** *past* **slammed**)
to shut or put down with a loud noise: *He* **slammed** *the door angrily. She* **slammed** *the books down on the table.*

slang /slang/ *noun (no plural)*
language you use in ordinary talk, but which is not always suitable or correct: *"Shut up" is* **slang;** *it sounds more polite to say "Please be quiet".*

slant /slant/ *verb*
to lean or slope

slap¹ /slap/ *verb* (*present participle* **slapping,** *past* **slapped**)
to hit with the flat inside of the hand

slap² *noun*
a hit: *I gave the dog a* **slap.**

slaughter¹ /slô′ tər/ *noun (no plural)*
killing, especially of animals or large numbers of people: *the* **slaughter** *of cattle for food*

slaughter² *verb*
to kill animals or people in large numbers

slave /slāv/ *noun*
a person who is owned by another person and has to work for him and has no freedom: *In ancient times conquered people were held as* **slaves.**
slavery *noun (no plural)* **1** being a slave: *to live in* **slavery** **2** having slaves: **Slavery** *was abolished* (= not allowed by law) *a long time ago.*

°**sleep¹** /slēp/ *noun (no plural)*
the state of not being awake; a time when we are in this state: *He had a long* **sleep.** *He* **went to sleep** *at two o'clock.*

°**sleep²** *verb* (*past* **slept** /slept/)
to be in sleep; not be awake: *He* **slept** *for two hours.*
sleepy *adjective* (**sleepier, sleepiest**) wanting to sleep: *I felt* **sleepy** *all day.*

sleeve /slēv/ *noun*
part of a piece of clothing which covers the arm: *His shirt had short* **sleeves.** (picture at **shirt**)

slender /slen′dər/ *adjective*
thin, in a pleasant way: *a* **slender** *figure*

slice¹ /slīs/ *noun*
a flat piece cut from something: *a* **slice** *of meat/of bread*

slice² *verb* (*present participle* **slicing,** *past* **sliced**)
to cut into thin flat pieces: *I* **sliced** *the bread.*

°**slide¹** /slīd/ *verb* (*present participle* **sliding,** *past* **slid** /slid/) to move smoothly over a surface: *She fell over and* **slid** *across the shiny floor.*

slide² *noun*
a thing which you can sit on and slide down a slope

slide

°**slight** /slīt/ *adjective*
small; of no importance: *I have a* **slight** *headache.*
slightly *adverb: Paul is* **slightly** *taller than John.*

slim¹ /slim/ *adjective* (**slimmer, slimmest**)
thin: *He is not* **slim** *enough to wear these tight trousers.*

slim² *verb* (*present participle* **slimming,** *past* **slimmed**) to get thinner: *He will have to* **slim** *down if he wants to wear the trousers.*

sling¹ /sling/ *noun*
a piece of cloth passed round something to support it: *He had to keep his broken arm in a sling.*

sling² *verb* (*present participle* **slinging,** *past* **slung** /slung/)
to throw

°**slip¹** /slip/ *verb* (*present participle* **slipping,** *past* **slipped)**
1 to move smoothly on something by mistake: *She* **slipped** *on the shiny floor and fell.*
2 to move quickly, smoothly, or quietly: *He* **slipped** *the money into his pocket. She* **slipped out** of the room, and no one noticed.

slip² *noun*
1 a mistake: *to make a* **slip**
2 a small piece (of paper)

slipper /slip′ ər/ *noun*
a soft shoe, worn in the house: (a pair of) **slippers**

°**slippery** /slip′ rē/ *adjective*
smooth; likely to slide: *a* **slippery** *floor*

slit¹ /slit/ *noun*
a long narrow opening: *He put the letter through a* **slit** *in the door.*

slit² *verb* (*present participle* **slitting,** *past* **slit)**
to cut in a thin line: *I* **slit open** *the letter with a knife.*

°**slope¹** /slōp/ *noun*
a surface which is higher on one side than the other: *He ran up the* **slope** *to the top of the hill.*

°**slope²** *verb* (*present participle* **sloping,** *past* **sloped)**
to lie or move in a slope: *The hill* **slopes** *steeply down to the town.*

slot /slot/ *noun*
a narrow opening: *If you put a coin in the* **slot** *of this machine, stamps come out of another* **slot.**

°**slow** /slō/ *adjective*
taking a long time; not fast: *The bus is very* **slow.** *The clock is (a minute)* **slow** (= it shows a time which is earlier than the real time).
slowly *adverb*

slug /slug/ *noun*
a soft creature without bones or legs that lives on land and eats plants

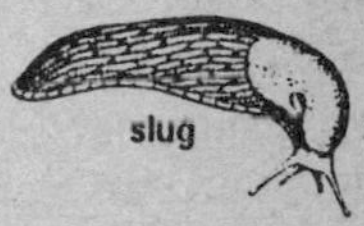

sly /slī/ *adjective* (**slier, sliest)**
clever in deceiving: *The fruit seller was* **sly** *— he put his best fruit in front but gave people bad ones from behind.*
slyly *adverb*

smack¹ /smak/ *verb*
to hit with the open hand: *He* **smacked** *the naughty child.*

smack² *noun*
an act of smacking; a hit: *Don't do that or you'll get a* **smack.**

°**small** /smôl/ *adjective*
little; not large: *Insects are much* **smaller** *than people. He has a* **small** *farm.*

smart /smärt/ *adjective*
1 dressed in new-looking, good, clean clothes: *My sister always looks* **smart.** *She always wears* **smart** *clothes.*
2 clever: *He's a* **smart** *businessman.*

smash /smash/ *noun*
to break into pieces: *She* **smashed** *a cup.*

smear¹ /smēr/ *noun*
to leave a sticky, dirty, or oily mark on: *The child's face was* **smeared** *with chocolate.*

smear² *noun*
a mark left by smearing

°**smell¹** /smel/ *verb*
(*present participle* **smelling,** *past* **smelled** *or* **smelt** */smelt/*)
1 to discover by taking in air through the nose: *He* **smelled** *the flowers.*
2 to give off something that we discover in this way: *The flowers* **smell** *(very sweet).*

°**smell²** *noun*
something that we discover through the nose: *There is a* **smell** *of fried chicken in this room.*

°**smile¹** /smīl/ *verb* (*present participle* **smiling,** *past* **smiled**)
to turn up the corners of your mouth to show pleasure, approval, etc.: *She* **smiled** *when she saw me.*

°**smile²** *noun*
a smiling expression: *a* **smile** *on his face*

°**smoke¹** /smōk/ *noun (no plural)*
cloud of gas and bits of ash that come out of a fire

°**smoke²** *verb* (*present participle* **smoking,** *past* **smoked**)
1 to give out smoke: *Why is the fire* **smoking** *so much?*
2 to use cigarettes, a pipe, etc.: *Do you* **smoke?**

smolder /smōl′ dər/ *verb*
to burn slowly without a flame: *The mat was* **smoldering** *where the burning log had fallen.*

°**smooth** /smo͞oth/ *adjective*
having a flat even surface; not rough: **smooth** *skin*
smoothly *adverb*

smother /smuTH′ ər/ *verb*
to stop air from reaching a person or thing: *Don't put that cloth over the baby's face, you'll* **smother** *him!*

smuggle /smug′ əl/ *verb*
(*present participle* **smuggling,** *past* **smuggled**)
to bring things into a country secretly without paying the money that should be paid: *He was caught* **smuggling** *cameras into the country.*
smuggler *noun*

snail /snāl/ *noun*
a soft creature without bones or legs, but with a round shell on its back, which eats plants

°**snake** /snāk/ *noun*
an animal that has a hard skin and a long body without legs and may have a dangerous bite (picture at **reptile**)

snap¹ /snap/ *verb* (*present participle* **snapping,** *past* **snapped**)
1 to break with a sharp noise: *The branch* **snapped** *under his foot.*
2 to try to bite: *Your dog* **snapped** **at** *me.*

snap² *noun*
a sharp sound of something breaking

snarl /snärl/ *verb*
to make an angry noise, or talk in an angry way: *The two dogs* **snarled** *at each other, and then started fighting.*

snatch /snach/ *verb*
to take quickly and, usually, roughly: *She* **snatched** *the book from my hands.*

sneer /snēr/ *verb*
to show you have a low opinion of a person or thing by laughing at him or it, or making him or it seem bad or stupid: *James* **sneered at** *my old bicycle. He has a new one.*

sneeze /snēz/ *verb* (*present participle* **sneezing,** *past* **sneezed**)
to push air out of the lungs (see) suddenly, making a noise through your mouth and nose: *When you have a cold, you* **sneeze** *often.*
sneeze *noun*

sniff /snif/ *verb*
to take air in through the nose in short breaths; to see what the air smells of: *When she had stopped crying, she* **sniffed** *and dried her eyes.*
sniff *noun*

snore /snôr/ *verb* (*present participle* **snoring,** *past* **snored**)
to make a noise in your nose or throat when you are asleep: *Grandfather was* **snoring.**
snore *noun*

snort /snôrt/ *verb*
to make an angry noise in the nose
snort *noun*

snow[1] /snō/ *noun (no plural)*
very cold rain, which falls in soft white flakes (= pieces)

snow[2] *verb*
(of snow) to come down from the sky: *It's* **snowing!**

°**so** /sō/ *adverb*
1 in such a way; to such a point: *I was* **so** *tired that I fell asleep on the bus. I have read 20 pages* **so far** (= up to this time).
2 also: *Ann was there, and* **so** *was Mary.*
3 very; very much: *You have been* **so** *kind to me.*
4 therefore: *I promised to send him a letter,* **so** *I'll write it now.*
5 in order that: *We got up early* **so (that)** *we could go for a swim.*
6 the same; that same thing: *How do you know? Peter told me* **so.**
7 (used to show agreement): *"Look, it's raining!"* "**So** *it is!"*

soak /sōk/ *verb*
1 to leave in a liquid: *She* **soaked** *the dirty clothes in water.*
2 *to make very wet: The rain* **soaked** *us. Our clothes were* **soaking (wet).**

°**soap** /sōp/ *noun*
a substance that cleans things when it is put with water: *She washed her hands with* **soap.**

soar /sôr/ *verb*
1 to fly high in the air
2 to become very high: *Prices are* **soaring** *again.*

sob /sob/ *verb* (*present participle* **sobbing,** *past* **sobbed**)
to make the noise of crying: *The child* **sobbed** *loudly.*
sob *noun*

sober /sō′ ber/ *adjective*
not drunk (= not having drunk too much alcoholic drink)

soccer /sok′ ər/ *noun (no plural)*
football: *a* **soccer** *team*

society /sə sī′ ə tē/ *noun* (*plural* **societies**)
1 a group of people who live together with shared ideas about how to live: **Society** *makes laws to protect people.*

2 a club; group of people with special interests: *a music* **society**

social /sō′ shəl/ *adjective: Man is a* **social** *animal* (= he lives in a group of people). **Social studies** *is the study of how man lives in societies.*

sock /sok/ *noun*
a soft covering for the foot and ankle

a pair of socks

socket /sok′ ət/ *noun*
a hole or set of holes for something to fit into: *an electric* **socket** *in a wall* (picture at **plug**)

sofa /sō′ fə/ *noun*
a long chair for two or more people to sit on

°**soft** /sôft/ *adjective*
1 not hard; moving inward when it is pressed: *This orange is* **soft.**
2 feeling smooth and pleasant: **soft** *skin*
3 not loud or noisy: *a* **soft** *voice*
soft drink *noun* a drink with no alcohol in it
soften /sôf′ ən/ *verb* to become or make soft: *The rain* **softened** *the earth.*

softly *adverb: He speaks* **softly,** *so it is difficult to hear what he says.*

soil[1] /soil/ *noun (no plural)*
earth: *This* **soil** *is very sandy.*

soil[2] *verb*
to make dirty

solar /sō′ lər/ *adjective*
of or using the sun: **solar** *heat*

sold /sōld/ *see* **sell**

°**soldier** /sōl′ jər/ *noun*
a person in the army

sole /sōl/ *noun*
the under part of your foot or shoe

solemn /sol′ əm/ *adjective*
serious: a **solemn** *face/a* **solemn** *ceremony* **solemnly** *adverb*

°**solid**[1] /sol′ id/ *adjective*
1 hard; not liquid or gas: *Gold is* **solid,** *but when you heat it, it becomes liquid.*
2 made of one material all the way through; not hollow: *This table is* **solid** *wood.*

°**solid**[2] *noun*
not a liquid or gas: *Iron is a* **solid.**

solitary /sol′ ə ter ē/ *adjective*
being the only one; alone: *There was a* **solitary** *sheep in the field.*

solo /sōlō/ *noun, adjective*
something done by one person alone: *She sang a* **solo.**

solution /sə loo′ shən/ *noun*
the answer: *What is the* **solution** *to your trouble?*

solve /solv/ *verb (present participle* **solving,** *past* **solved)**
to find the answer to: *to* **solve** *a crime*

°**some** /sum/
1 an amount of; a number of; not all: *She had a big piece of chocolate and she gave me* **some.** *Would you like* **some** *bananas? We asked all the class to the party but only* **some** *of them came.*
2 (used when speaking about people or things without saying exactly which ones): **Some** *girls are dancing, others are talking.*

somebody /sum′ bud″ ē/ *pronoun or* **someone**
1 any person: *If you don't know the answer, ask* **somebody.**
2 some unknown person, or a

person the speaker does not name: *There is* **somebody** *knocking at the door. I know* **somebody** *who lives near you.*

°**somehow** /sum′ hou″/ *adverb*
in some way: *The bridge is broken, but we must cross the river* **somehow.**

°**someone** /sum′ wun″/ *pronoun*
see **somebody**

somersault /sum′ ər sôlt″/ *noun*
jumping and turning upside down at the same time: *to do a* **somersault**

somersault

something /sum′ thing/ *pronoun*
a thing, either known or unknown: *I want to tell you* **something.** *She bought* **something** *to eat.*

sometime /sum′ tīm/ *adverb*
at some time in the past or the future: *I hope I'll see you again* **sometime.**

°**sometimes** /sum′ tīmz/ *adverb*
at times; now and then: **Sometimes** *I help my mother in the house.*

°**somewhere** /sum′ hwâr″/ *adverb*
in, to, or at some place: *At last he found* **somewhere** *to park the car.*

°**son** /sun/ *noun*
a male child: *I have a* **son** *and a daughter.*

°**song** /sông/ *noun*
a piece of music with words that are sung

°**soon** /so͞on/ *adverb*
1 in a short time: *Dinner will be ready soon.*
2 early: I made the coffee **too soon** *and now it is cold. Give me the book* **as soon as** *you can.*

soot /su̇t/ *noun (no plural)*
black powder left by smoke

soothe /so͞oTH/ *verb (present participle* **soothing,** *past* **soothed)**
to make calm: *She* **soothed** *the child who was afraid.*

°**sore**[1] /sôr/ *adjective*
hurting; painful: *My leg is* **sore,** *it hurts.*

°**sore**[2] *noun*
a painful place on the body, especially where the skin is broken: *He had a* **sore** *on his foot.*

°**sorrow** /sor′ ō/ *noun*
sadness: *He told me with* **sorrow** *that his mother was very ill.*

°**sorry** /sôr′ ē/ *adjective*
a polite way of saying that you are a little sad, or that you cannot do what is wanted: *Did I stand on your foot?* **Sorry!** *I was* **sorry** *to hear about your illness. I'm* **sorry,** *I can't come to your party.*

°**sort**[1] /sôrt/ *noun*
kind; type: *A hammer is a* **sort** *of tool.*

sort[2] *verb*
to put in order; to put things that are alike together: *I* **sorted (out)** *the books into big ones and small ones.*

sought /sôt/ see **seek**

soul /sōl/ *noun*
the part of you that is not body, and that some people think does not die with your body

°**sound**[1] /sound/ *noun*
something you hear: *the* **sound** *of birds singing*

°**sound²** *verb*
1 to seem, when you hear it: *Your idea* **sounds** *good to me.*
2 to make a sound: *When the bell* **sounds,** *you must come in.*

sound³ *adjective*
1 healthy or strong: *I've repaired the roof and it's quite* **sound** *now.*
2 (of sleep) deep: *He's in a* **sound** *sleep.*

°**soup** /so͞op/ *noun*
liquid food made from meat, fish, or vegetables: *I had a bowl of chicken* **soup.**

°**sour** /sour/ *adjective*
tasting sharp, like an orange that is not ripe: *The fruit was too* **sour** *to eat. If you leave milk in the sun, it goes* **sour** *quickly.*

source /sôrs/ *noun*
where something comes from: *The river is the* **source** *of all our water. Bad food is a* **source** *of illness.*

°**south** /south/
noun, adjective, adverb
the direction that is on the right when you look at the rising sun: *We travelled* **south** *for two days. There is a strong* **south** *wind* (= coming from the south).
southern /suTH' ərn/ *adjective* in or of the south
southward *adverb* towards the south: *to travel* **southward**

souvenir /so͞o' və nēr/ *noun*
a thing that is kept to remember a place or an event

sovereign /sov' rən/ *noun*
a king or queen

sow /sō/ *verb (past tense* **sowed,** *past participle* **sown)**
to put seeds in the ground so that they will grow into plants

°**space** /spās/ *noun*
1 *(no plural)* the empty area that surrounds the sun, the Earth, etc: *People have traveled through* **space** *to the moon.*
2 an empty place: *There is no* **space** *for another chair in this room.*
spaceman *noun (plural* **spacemen**): *The first man on the moon was an American* **spaceman.**
spaceship *noun: People who travel in space go in* **spaceships.**
space shuttle *noun* a type of rocket (see) which can return to earth like an airplane

°**spade** /spād/ *noun*
an instrument used for digging (picture at **dig**)

spare¹ spâr/ *adjective*
kept in addition to what you have, in case it is needed: *If you have a* **spare** *bed, may I stay tonight? Have you any* **spare** *time to help me?*

spare² *verb (present participle* **sparing,** *past* **spared)**
to be able to give or lend something: *Can you* **spare** *me some money? I need to buy food.*

spark /spärk/ *noun*
a small piece of burning material: **Sparks** *flew up from the fire.*

sparkle /spärk' əl/ *verb (present participle* **sparkling,** *past* **sparkled)**
to give out bright points of light: *Drops of water* **sparkled** *in the sun.*

sparrow /spar' ō/ *noun*
a small brownish-gray bird

spat /spat/ see **spit**

°**speak** /spēk/ *verb*
(present participle **speaking,** *past tense* **spoke** /spōk/, *past participle* **spoken** /spōk' ən/)
to say works aloud: *Can your child*

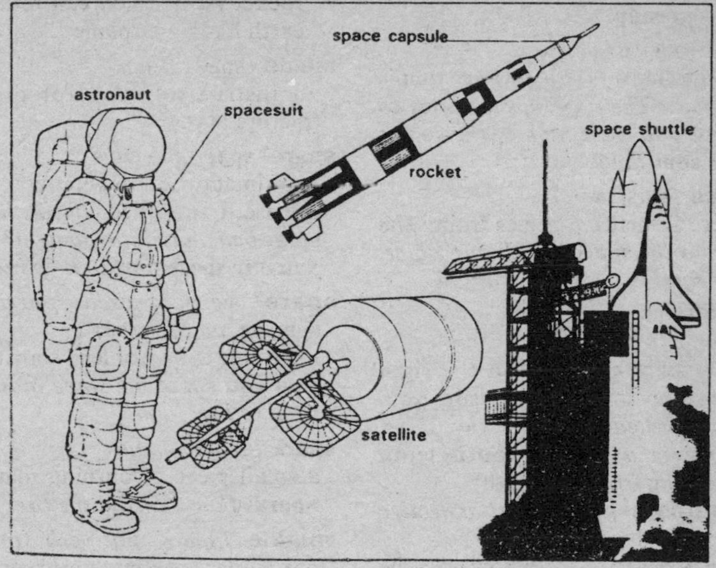

The *earth* is a *planet.* It moves around the *sun* in an *orbit,* once a year. The sun is a *star.* There are millions of stars in the sky, but all the others are much farther away from us than the sun is, so they look much smaller. We can see them only at night, when the sun is not in the sky.

The *moon* moves around the earth. If the moon moves between the earth and the sun it blocks out the sun's light. This is called an *eclipse* of the sun, and it does not happen very often.

A *comet* is a mass with a long tail which moves around the sun, and can sometimes be seen in the sky at night.

speak *yet? Have you* **spoken** *to her about the money? She can* **speak** *three languages.*
speaker *noun*

°**spear** /spēr/
noun
a long thin weapon with a pointed end

spear

°**special** /spesh′ əl/ *adjective*
not usual; important for a reason: *He has a* **special** *car because he cannot walk. This is a* **special** *day in the history of our country.*
specialist *noun* a person who specializes in something
specially *adverb* **1** for one purpose: *I came here* **specially** *to ask you a question.* **2** unusually: *He is not* **specially** *clever, but he works hard.*

specialize /spesh′ əl īz/ *verb* (*present participle* **specializing,** *past* **specialized**)
to study one special thing: *That doctor* **specializes in** *children's illnesses.*

species /spē shēz *or* spē′ sēz/ *noun* (*Plural* **species**)
sort; type: *a* **species** *of animal*

specific /spi sif′ ik/ *adjective*
exact; fixed; clear in meaning: *I want a* **specific** *answer.*

specimen /spes′ ə mən/ *noun*
an example; typical thing: *The doctor took a* **specimen** *of blood from his arm.*

speck /spek/ *noun*
a small piece of something: *a* **speck** *of paint/ of dust*

spectacles /spek′ tə kəls/ *plural noun*
glasses for the eyes, set in a frame which rests on the nose and ears: *She wears* **spectacles** (picture at **glasses**)

spectator /spek′ tā tər/ *noun*
someone who watches a sport or show

°**speech** /spēch/ *noun*
1 *(no plural)* the ability to speak: **Speech** *is learned in the first years of life.*
2 *(plural* **speeches)** a long set of words spoken for people to listen to: *to make a* **speech**

°**speed** /spēd/ *noun*
how fast something moves: *The* **speed** *of the car was frightening. He works at a slow* **speed.**
speedily *adverb*

°**spell** /spel/ *verb* (*past* **spelled)**
to say the letters that make up a word: *You* **spell** *dog, D-O-G.*
spelling *noun: His* **spelling** *is better than his brother's.*

°**spend** /spend/ *verb* (*present participle* **spending,** *past* **spent)**
1 to give out money: *How much money do you* **spend** *each week?*
2 to pass or use time: *I* **spent** *an hour reading.*

sphere /sfer/ *noun*
a solid round shape, like a ball
spherical *adjective*

spice /spīs/ *noun*
a seed, root, or other part of a plant used to give a strong or hot taste to food: *Pepper is a* **spice.**
spicy *adjective* **(spicier, spiciest)**

spider /spī dər/ *noun*
a creature with eight legs, which

uses threads from its body to catch insects in a web (picture at **web**)

spike /spīk/ *noun*
a sharp piece of metal: *There are* **spikes** *on the bottom of shoes used for running.*

spill /spil/ *verb* (*present participle* **spilling,** *past* **spilled)**
to let fall; to pour out by mistake: *I* **spilled** *the coffee — it* **spilled** *all over my book.*

°**spin** /spin/ *verb* (*present participle* **spinning,** *past* **spun** /spun/)
1 to go around and around fast: *The wheels of the car were* **spinning** *(around).*
2 to make thread by twisting cotton, wool, etc.
3 to make thread: *Spiders* (see) **spin** *threads.*

spine /spīn/ *noun*
the long row of bones in your back

spiral /spī′ rəl/ *noun, adjective*
a shape that goes around and around as it goes up: *A spring* (see) *is a* **spiral.**

°**spirit** /spir′ it/ *noun*
1 the part of you that is not body, and that some people think does not die with your body
2 state of mind: *The children were* **in high spirits** (= feeling happy).
3 strong alcoholic drink: *"Rum" is a* **spirit** *made from sugar.*

spit /spit/ *verb* (*present participle* **spitting,** *past* **spat** /spat/)
to throw water with the mouth; to throw something out of the mouth: *He* **spat** *into the river. The child* **spat out** *its food.*

°**spite** /spīt/ *noun (no plural)*
dislike; wanting to hurt or annoy another person: *He took my best toy just out of* **spite!**
in spite of even though something else happens: *I went out* **in spite of** *the rain.*

splash[1] /splash/ *noun*
the sound made by something falling into a liquid: *She jumped into the river with a* **splash.**

splash[2] *verb*
to make liquid fall in drops: *The children* **splashed** *(about) in the pool. Don't* **splash** *me: I don't want to get wet.*

splendid /splen′ did/ *adjective*
very great or fine

splinter /splin′ tər/ *noun*
a thin sharp piece of wood or metal: *I have got a* **splinter** *in my finger.*

°**split**[1] /split/ *verb* (*present participle* **splitting,** *past* **split)**
1 to break, especially from one end to the other: *We* **split** *the wood into long thin pieces. My trousers* **split** *when I sat down.*
2 to share: *We* **split** *the work between us.*

split[2] *noun*
a break: *a* **split** *in my trousers*

°**spoil** /spoil/ *verb* (*present participle* **spoiling,** *past* **spoiled)**
to damage something so that it becomes useless: *The rain has* **spoiled** *my painting.*
spoiled *adjective* given everything, so that you become selfish: *a* **spoiled** *child*

spoke[1] /spōk/ see **speak**

spoke[2] *noun*
one of the bars joining the outer

ring of a wheel to the center (picture at **bicycle**)

spoken /spōk′ ən/ see **speak:** *Her* **spoken** *English is very good.*

sponge /spunj/ *noun*
a soft sea creature like a piece of rubber with many holes; this or a substance like it, used for cleaning

sponge

spool /spo͞ol/ *noun*
a round thing for winding thread, wire, etc.

°**spoon** /spo͞on/ *noun*
an instrument with a rounded part used for eating liquids, mixing in cooking, etc.

spoonful *noun* (*plural* **spoonfuls** *or* **spoonsful**) the amount a spoon holds: *You must take three* **spoonfuls** *of medicine.*

°**sport** /spôrt/ *noun*
games and exercises done for pleasure: *Football and running are* **sports.**

°**spot** /spot/ *noun*
1 a small mark: *She had* **spots** *on her face when she was ill. A* **spot** *of blood fell on the floor.*
2 a place: *This is a nice* **spot** *for a house.*

spout /spout/ *noun*
part of a container through which liquid is poured

sprain /sprān/ *verb*
to damage a joint of your body by turning it suddenly: *He* **sprained** *his ankle when he fell.*

spray¹ /sprāy/ *verb*
to make wet with small drops: *He* **sprayed** *water over the flowers. He* **sprayed** *the flowers with water.*

spray² *noun*
liquid in small drops: *a* **spray** *of water*

°**spread** /spred/ *verb* (*present participle* **spreading,** *past* **spread)**
1 to cover thinly: *She* **spread** *the bread with butter* (see).
2 to open out: *The bird* **spread** *its wings.*
3 to move over an area: *The illness* **spread** *through the village.*

spring¹ /spring/ *noun*
1 a river coming up from the ground
2 a twisted round piece of metal wire which goes back into shape if you pull it

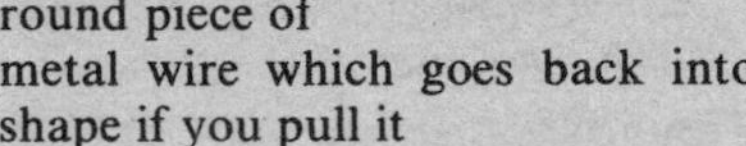
spring

spring² *verb*
(*present participle* **springing,** *past tense* **sprang** /sprang/, *past participle* **sprung** /sprung/)
to jump: *She* **sprang** *out of her chair to greet her father.*

spring³ *noun, adjective*
the season after winter, in cool countries, when plants start to grow again: **spring** *flowers*

sprinkle /spring′ kəl/ *verb*
(*present participle* **sprinkling,** *past* **sprinkled)**
to scatter: *She* **sprinkled** *sugar on the cakes.*

sprout /sprout/ *verb*
to start to grow: *These seeds have* **sprouted** *— you can see little green leaves above the earth.*

spun /spun/ see **spin**

spy[1] /spī/ *noun* (*plural* **spies**)
a person whose job is to find out secret information, usually about another country

spy[2] *verb* (*present participle* **spying,** *past* **spied**)
to look at and find out things, especially secretly: *Have you been* **spying on** *me?*

squabble /skwab′ əl/ *verb* (*present participle* **squabbling,** *past* **squabbled**)
to quarrel about small things: *The children were* **squabbling** *about who had won the game.*
squabble *noun*

°**square[1]** /skwâr/ *noun*
1 a shape with four equal sides
2 an open place in a town: *There was a* **square** *with trees and grass in it in the center of the city.*

°**square[2]** *adjective*
having four equal sides: *The window was* **square.**

squash[1] /skwäsh/ *noun*
a vegetable that grows on a vine

squash[2] *verb*
to press; hurt or damage by pressing: *We all* **squashed** *into the car. The fruit at the bottom of the box had been* **squashed.**

squeak /skwēk/ *verb*
to make a high, thin sound: *Rats* **squeak.**
squeak *noun*

squeal /skwēl/ *verb*
to make a loud high cry: *Pigs* **squeal.**
squeal *noun*

squeeze /skwēz/ *verb* (*present participle* **squeezing,** *past* **squeezed**)
to press sideways: *He* **squeezed** *an orange to get the juice out. The children* **squeezed** *together to make room for me to sit down.*

squirrel /skwur′əl/ *noun*
a small animal that has a brown or gray hairy coat and a thick tail and usually lives in trees

stab /stab/ *verb* (*present participle* **stabbing,** *past* **stabbed**)
to wound with a pointed weapon: *He* **stabbed** *the woman with a knife and she died.*

stable[1] /stā′ bəl/ *noun*
a building in which horses are kept

stable[2] /adjective
firm; steady; not easily moved or changed: *Is that ladder* **stable?**

stack[1] /stak/ *noun*
a large pile: *a* **stack** *of books*

stack[2] *verb*
to put in a stack: *to* **stack** *books*

stack

stadium /stā′ dē əm/ *noun*
an open place where games and races are held

staff /staf/ *noun (no plural)*
a group of people working under a leader: *the* **staff** *of a school* (= all the teachers)

°**stage** /stāj/ *noun*
1 a time or step in a long event: *When a book has been written, the next* **stage** *is printing.*
2 a raised floor: *The play was acted upon a* **stage.**

stagger /stag′ ər/ *verb*
to walk in an unsteady way: *The wounded man* **staggered** *along.*

stain[1] /stān/ *verb*
to make a mark that cannot be taken away: *The coffee* **stained** *his shirt brown.*

stain[2] *noun*
a mark: *a coffee* **stain**

°**stairs** /stârz/ *plural noun*
a set of steps leading up and down inside a building: *The principal's room is* **upstairs,** *but to get to the library you must go* **downstairs.**

stake /stāk/ *noun*
a pointed post in the ground

stale /stāl/ *adjective*
(staler, stalest)
not fresh; tasting old and dry: **stale** *bread*

stalk /stôk/ *noun*
the main upright part of a plant that is not a tree; the long part that supports leaves or flowers (picture at **grain**)

stall /stôl/ *noun*
a small open shop, especially one in a market: *a fruit* **stall**

stammer /stam′ ər/ *verb*
to speak with difficulty, repeating the same sounds: *"Th-th-thank you," he* **stammered.**

°**stamp**[1]
/stamp/
noun **1** a small piece of special paper that you stick on letters and parcels to show how much you have paid to send them: *He collects* **(postage) stamps.**
2 an instrument used to make marks with ink on paper

°**stamp**[2] *verb*
1 to put a stamp on
2 to bring your foot down hard: *He* **stamped** *on the insect.*

°**stand**[1] /stand/ *verb*
(*present participle* **standing,** *past* **stood** /stůd/)
1 to be on your feet: *We* **stood** *outside the shop.* **Stand up** (= get to your feet), *please.*
2 to be: *The house* **stands** *at the top of the hill.*
3 to mean: *The letters P.J. on his bag* **stand for** *Peter Johnson.*

stand[2] *noun*
a place for people to watch sports

°**standard** /stan′ dərd/
noun, adjective
(of) a fixed weight, length, cost, or quality by which things are compared: *Your work is of a low* **standard.** *It is not* **up to standard** (= as good as we expect).

stank /stangk/ see **stink**

°**star** /stär/ *noun*
1 a small point of light that can be seen in the sky at night
2 a five-pointed shape (★)

stare /stâr/ *verb* (*present participle* **staring,** *past* **stared)**
to look steadily for a long time: *He* **stared** *at the word trying to remember what it meant.*

°**start**[1] /stärt/ *verb*
to begin: *If you are ready, you may* **start** *you work. The children* **started** *singing.*

°**start**[2] *noun*
an act of starting: *We made an early* **start** *in the morning.*

startle /stär′ təl/ *verb* (*present participle* **startling,** *past* **startled)**
to surprise; give a shock to: *You* **startled** *me when you shouted.*

starve /stärv/ *verb* (*present participle* **starving,** *past* **starved**)
to die of hunger: *People* **starve** *because there is not enough for everyone to eat.*
starvation *noun (no plural)*
starving *adjective* **1** dying of hunger: **starving** *children* **2** very hungry: *I'm* **starving** *— is dinner ready yet?*

°**state**[1] /stāt/ *verb* (*present participle* **stating,** *past* **stated**)
to say: *He* **stated** *that he had never seen the criminal before.*
statement *noun* something that is said: *The man made a* **statement** *to the police.*

°**state**[2] *noun*
1 the condition of something; how good, bad, etc., it is: *This book is in a very bad* **state.** *She is in a worried* **state** *of mind.*
2 (a part of) a country, which governs itself: *Mississippi is one of the 50* **states** *in the United* **States** *of America.*
3 a country and its government: *In Britain, the railroads are owned by the* **state.**
statesman *noun* (*plural* **statesmen**) a government leader

°**station** /stā′ shən/ *noun*
1 a place where buses or trains stop: *a* **railway station**/*a* **bus station**
2 a building for some special work: *Policemen work at a* **police station.**

stationary /stā′ shən er″ ē/ *adjective*
not moving; still: *Wait until the bus is* **stationary** *before you get off.*

stationery /stā′ shən er″ ē/ *noun (no plural)*
paper, pens, pencils, notebooks, etc.: *We can buy writing paper at a* **stationery** *store.*

statue /stach′ o͞o/ *noun*
a figure of a person or animal made of stone, metal, or wood: *There is a* **statue** *of a famous soldier in the park.*

statue

°**stay** /stā/ *verb*
to continue to be: **Stay** *in your classroom until it is time to go home. He* **stayed** *with his father while he was ill.*

°**steady** /sted′ e/ *adjective, adverb* (**steadier, steadiest**)
1 firm; not moving: *Hold the chair* **steady** *while I stand on it.*
2 regular: *a* **steady** *job*/ *a* **steady** *speed*
steadily *adverb: We drove* **steadily** *at 30 miles an hour.*

steak /stāk/ *noun*
a thick, flat piece of meat or fish

°**steal** /stēl/ *verb* (*present participle* **stealing,** *past tense* **stole** /stol/, *past participle* **stolen**)
1 to take something that does not belong to you, without asking for it: *Who* **stole** *my money?*
2 to move quietly: *She* **stole** *out of the room.*

°**steam**[1] /stēm/ *noun (no plural)*
the gas that water becomes when it boils: *There was* **steam** *coming from the kettle.*
steam engine *noun* an engine that works by the pressure of steam inside it
steamer *or* **steamship** *noun* a ship driven by a steam engine

°**steam**[2] *verb*
1 to give off steam: *The hot water was* **steaming.**
2 to cook by putting in steam

°**steel** /stēl/ *noun (no plural)*
a hard metal made of specially treated iron, used for knives, machines, etc.

°**steep** /stēp/ *adjective*
having a sharp slope: *a* **steep** *hill*
steeply *adverb*

steer /stēr/ *verb*
to direct or guide a vehicle: *He* **steered** *the ship carefully between the rocks.*

°**stem** /stem/ *noun*
the central part of a plant from which the leaves or flowers grow (picture at **flower**)

°**step**[1] /step/ *verb (present participle* **stepping,** *past* **stepped**)
to move the foot in walking or running: *He* **stepped** *over the dog.*

°**step**[2] *noun*
1 a movement with the foot; the sound of this: *He took a* **step** *toward the door. There was the sound of a* **step** *outside the door.*
2 a flat edge in a set of stairs: *There are two* **steps** *up onto the bus.*
3 an event in a set of events: *The first* **step** *in changing a car tire is to loosen the wheel. He showed us how to repair the tire* **step by step.**

stepfather /step′ fä″ THər/ *noun*
a man who marries your mother but is not your father

stepmother /step′ muTH″ ər/ *noun*
a woman who marries your father but is not your mother: *The children of a* **stepfather** *or* **stepmother** *are your* **stepbrothers** *or* **stepsisters.**

stern /sturn/ *adjective*
firm and serious: *a* **stern** *teacher*

stew[1] /sto͞o/ *noun*
meat or fish and vegetables, cooked together in liquid

stew[2] *verb*
to cook slowly in liquid: *You can* **stew** *fruit in water and sugar.*

steward /sto͞o′ ərd/ *noun*
a man who looks after passengers on a boat or plane
stewardess *noun* a female steward

°**stick**[1] /stik/ *noun*
a long thin piece of wood: *We made the fire out of dry* **sticks.** *The old man walked leaning on a* **stick.**

°**stick**[2] *verb (present participle* **sticking,** *past* **stuck** /stuk/)
1 to fix with a special substance (glue): *I* **stuck** *a stamp on the letter.*
2 to put something pointed into: *I* **stuck** a needle into the cloth.
3 to stay fixed: *The wheels of the car* **stuck** *in the mud and we could not go on.*
sticky *adjective* **(stickier, stickiest)** able to hold things together: *a* **sticky** *candy*

°**stiff** /stif/ *adjective*
1 not able to move or bend easily: *The cards were made of* **stiff** *paper.*
2 difficult: *a* **stiff** *examination*
stiffly *adverb: to walk* **stiffly**

°**still**[1] /stil/ *adverb*
1 up to this or that time: *My father* **still** *remembers his first day at school.*
2 even: *The car was very fast, but the plane was faster* **still.**
3 even so: *It was raining, but she* **still** *went out.*

°**still**[2] *adjective*
not moving; quiet: *The sea was calm and* **still.** *Keep* **still** *while I comb your hair.*

°**sting**[1] /sting/ *verb*
(*present participle* **stinging,** *past* **stung** /stung/)
to hurt by pricking the skin: *The bee* **stung** *her leg.*

°**sting**[2] *noun*
1 the part of an insect which stings
2 the pain or wound of a sting: *The red spot on his arm is a* **sting.**

stink[1] /stink/ *verb* (*present participle* **stinking,** *past tense* **stank** /stank/, *past participle* **stunk** /stunk/)
to smell very unpleasant

stink[2] *noun*
a very unpleasant smell

stir /stur/ *verb* (*present participle* **stirring,** *past* **stirred**)
1 to mix about with a spoon: *He put sugar in his tea and* **stirred** *it.*
2 to move a little: *The leaves* **stirred** *in the wind.*

°**stitch**[1] /stich/ *noun* (*plural* **stitches**)
1 the movement of a needle and thread through cloth and out again: *The dress was sewn with small* **stitches.**
2 a turn of wool round a needle in knitting (see)

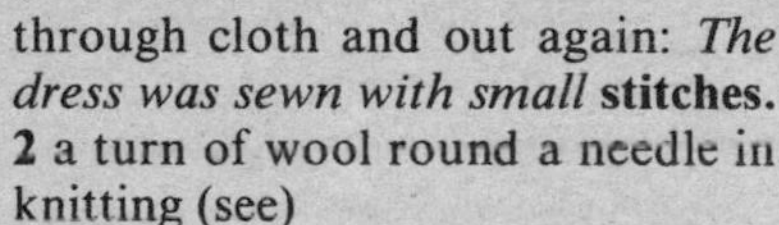
stitches

°**stitch**[2] *verb*
to sew: *to* **stitch** *a button onto a shirt*

stock[1] /stok/ *noun*
a store of goods in a shop: *We have a large* **stock** *of canned fruit.*

stock[2] *verb*
to have for sale in a shop: *They do not* **stock** *flowers, only fruit.*

stocking /stok′ ing/ *noun*
one of a pair of coverings for the legs and feet: *She wore nylon* (= very thin material) **stockings.**

stole /stōl/ see **steal**

stolen /stō′ lən/ see **steal**

°**stomach** /stum′ ək/ *noun*
the part of the body into which the food goes when it is swallowed

°**stone** /stōn/ *noun*
1 a small piece of rock
2 rock: *This is a* **stone** *building.*
3 a gem or mineral of great value that is used as an ornament: *A diamond* (see) *is a* **precious stone.**

stood /sto͝od/ see **stand**

stool /sto͞ol/ *noun*
a chair without a back or sides

stoop /sto͞op/ *verb*
to bend the body over forwards: *He* **stooped** *to look under the table.*

°**stop**[1] /stop/ *verb* (*present participle* **stopping,** *past* **stopped**)
1 to end; make an end to: *We* **stopped** *eating.*
2 to prevent something happening, moving, etc.: *They* **stopped** *me going out of the door. The driver* **stopped** *the car and got out.*
3 to finish moving: *The bus* **stopped.**

stopper *noun*
something which closes an opening, especially of a bottle

°**stop**[2] *noun*
a place where a bus or train stops: *We waited at the* **bus stop.**

°**store**[1] /stôr/ *verb* (*present participle* **storing,** *past* **stored**)
to put away or keep for use later: *I* **stored** *all the apples from our trees.*

°**store²** *noun*
1 things kept for future use: *a* **store** *of apples*
2 a large shop
3 a place for keeping things: *a* **store** *for furniture*

°**storm** /stôrm/ *noun*
a time of high winds and sometimes thunder and rain
stormy *adjective* **(stormier, stormiest): stormy** *weather*

°**story** /stôr′ ē/ *noun* (*plural* **stories**)
1 a book about something imaginary that happened: *Please read us a* **story!**
2 a telling of events: *What is the* **story** *of your accident?*

stove /stōv/ *noun*
a metal or brick container which is heated and used for cooking or heating: *My mother has a gas* **stove** *for cooking.*

°**straight¹** /strāt/ *adjective*
1 not bending or curved: *This road is* **straight.**
2 level: *The picture is not* **straight,** *you must move the left side up.*
3 in order

°**straight²** *adverb*
1 in a straight line: *The car went* **straight** *down the road.*
2 without waiting; directly; without going anywhere else or doing anything else: *He went* **straight** *to his friend to ask for help. I must see you* **straight away** (= now).
straighten *verb* to make or become straight: *She* **straightened** *the picture on the wall.*

strain /strān/ *verb*
1 to pull against: *They* **strained** *on the rope to pull the boat in.*
2 to damage a part of the body by pulling or using it wrongly: *I* **strained** *my back when I lifted the box.*
3 to take the lumps out of something by putting it through an instrument with small holes in it: *There are tea leaves in my cup — you haven't* **strained** *the tea.*

strait /strāt/ *noun*
a narrow piece of water between two pieces of land

°**strange** /strānj/ *adjective* **(stranger, strangest)**
1 odd; unusual: *a* **strange** *sound*
2 not what you are used to: *a* **strange** *city*
strangely *adverb: He acted* **strangely** *when he was ill.*
stranger *noun* a person you do not know

strangle /strang′ gəl/ *verb* (*present participle* **strangling,** *past* **strangled**)
to kill by pressing around the throat

strap¹ /strap/ *noun*
a narrow piece of leather, plastic, cloth, etc. used for fastening something

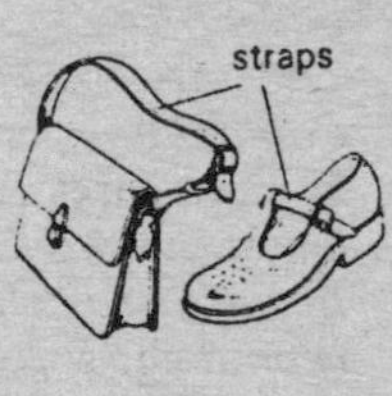

strap² *verb* (*present participle* **strapping,** *past* **strapped**)
to fasten with a strap: *He* **strapped** *the bag onto his bicycle.*

straw /strô/ *noun*
1 *(no plural)* dry stems of wheat, rice, etc.: *a bag made of* **straw**
2 a dry stem
3 a thin tube for drinking through: *He drank the milk through a* **straw.**

stray¹ /strā/ *adjective*
(of animals) not owned by anyone: *a* **stray** *dog*

stray[2] *verb*
to wander away from home or from the right way: *She* **strayed** *from the road and got lost.*

streak /strēk/ *noun*
a long mark: *a* **streak** *of paint on the wall*

°**stream** /strēm/ *noun*
1 a small river
2 a flow: *a* **stream** *of cars*

°**street** /strēt/ *noun*
a road in a town: *Across the* **street** *from the school is the library. He lives on Park* **Street.**

°**strength** /strengkth/ *noun (no plural)*
being strong: *I haven't the* **strength** *to lift this table.*

strengthen /strengkth′ən/ *verb*
to make stronger: *The fence was* **strengthened** *with wire.*

stress[1] /stres/ *noun*
1 *(no plural)* a state of difficulty: *The* **stress** *of studying for the examinations made him ill.*
2 (*plural* **stresses**) saying a word or a part of a word with special force: *In the word "chemistry" the* **stress** *is on the first part of the word.*

stress[2] *verb*
to say with special force: *We* **stress** *the first part of the word "chemistry". I must* **stress** *that we haven't much time.*

°**stretch** /strech/ *verb*
1 to make or become larger or longer by pulling; pull tightly: *She* **stretched** *the material. Rubber* **stretches.**
2 to make as long as possible: *He* **stretched** *his legs in front of him.*
3 to try and reach: *I* **stretched out** *my hand towards the book.*

stretcher /strech′ər/ *noun*
a framework on which an ill person can be carried

stretcher

strict /strikt/ *adjective*
severe, especially about behavior: *Our teacher is* **strict;** *we have to do what she says.*
strictly *adverb* **1** severely. **2** exactly: *What he says is not* **strictly** *true.*

stride[1] /strīd/ *verb*
(*present participle* **striding,** *past tense* **strode** /strōd/, *past participle* **stridden** /strid′ən/)
to walk with large steps: *He* **strode** *angrily into the classroom.*

stride[2] *noun*
a large step: *With two* **strides** *he crossed the room.*

strike[1] /strīk/ *verb*
(*present participle* **striking,** *past* **struck** /struk/)
1 to hit: *He* **struck** *me with a stick.*
2 to refuse to work: *The workers were* **striking** *because they wanted more money.*
3 to seem to: **It struck me** *that the room looked different.*

strike[2] *noun*
refusing to work: *There is a* **strike** *at the factory. The workers are* **on strike.**

°**string** /string/ *noun*
1 *(no plural)* thin rope used for fastening things: *The package was tied with* **string.**
2 a fine piece of wire used in some musical instruments: *A violin* (see) *has* **strings.**

strip[1] /strip/ *noun*
a long narrow piece of something:

a **strip** *of paper*

strip[2] *verb*
1 to pull off an outer covering: *He* **stripped** *the paper off the wall.*
2 to take off clothes: *John* **stripped off** *his shirt.*

stripe /strīp/ *noun*
a long, thin line: *A tiger has* **stripes.**

striped *adjective: a* **striped** *dress*

°**stroke**[1] /strōk/ *noun*
a blow: *With one* **stroke** *of his ax, he had cut the tree down.*

stroke[2] *verb* (*present participle* **stroking,** *past* **stroked)**
to move the hand over gently: *He* **stroked** *the baby's head.*

stroll /strōl/ *verb*
to walk slowly: *We* **strolled** *through the park.*
stroll *noun*

°**strong** /strông/ *adjective*
1 having power or force: *He is a* **strong** *man. She is a* **strong** *swimmer. a* **strong** *smell of cats*
2 firm: *a* **strong** *fence*
3 having a powerful result: **Strong** *drink can make you feel ill.*

struck /struk/ see **strike**

structure /struk′ chər/ *noun*
1 a building or framework: *The builders had put up a tall* **structure** *between the shops.*
2 the way something is made: *We learned about the* **structure** *of the brain today.*

struggle[1] /strug′ əl/ *verb* (*present participle* **struggling,** *past* **struggled)**
to fight: *I* **struggled** *to get free.*

struggle[2] *noun*
a fight: *We had a* **struggle** *to stop the criminal.*

stubborn /stub′ ərn/ *adjective*
not changing your mind or doing what others want: *She won't do what I ask — she's very* **stubborn.**
stubbornly *adverb*

stuck /stuk/ see **stick**

°**student** /sto͞o′ dənt/ *noun*
a person who is learning, especially at a college or university (see): *He is a* **student** *of history.*

studio /sto͞o′ dē ō/ *noun*
1 a workroom: *a painter's* **studio**
2 a room in which movies or radio or television shows are made

°**study**[1] /stud′ ē/ *verb* (*present participle* **studying,** *past* **studied)**
to learn about: *I am* **studying** *art.*

°**study**[2] *noun* (*plural* **studies)**
1 learning: *He will finish his* **studies** *next year.*
2 a room for working in

stuff[1] /stuf/ *noun (no plural)*
any substance or material: *There's some white* **stuff** *on this plate.*

stuff[2] *verb*
to fill: *The bed was* **stuffed** *with cotton so it was very soft. He* **stuffed** *himself full of food.*
stuffy *adjective* **(stuffier, stuffiest)** with no clean air: *This room seems* **stuffy** *— open a window.*

stumble /stum′ bəl/ *verb* (*present participle* **stumbling,** *past* **stumbled)**
to walk unsteadily, so that you seem to be falling: *He* **stumbled** *along the road. I* **stumbled** *over a stone and fell.*

stump /stump/ *noun* what is left when something is cut down: *He sat on a tree* **stump.**

tree stump

stung /stung/ see **sting**

stunk /stunk/ see **stink**

°**stupid** /sto͞o′ pid/ *adjective* not clever; not intelligent: *a* **stupid** *question/a* **stupid** *person*
°**stupidity** *noun (no plural)*
stupidly *adverb*

sturdy /stur′ dē/ *adjective* **(sturdier, sturdiest)** strong and firm: *The child had* **sturdy** *legs.*

sty /stī/ *noun* (*plural* **sties**) a place for pigs to live in

°**style** /stīl/ *noun*
1 a way of doing something: *a hair* **style**
2 the way of dressing that everyone likes at a special time: *That dress is in the latest* **style.**
3 a sort or type: *a new* **style** *of car*

subject[1] /sub′ jikt/ *noun*
1 something studied: *English is one of our school* **subjects.**
2 something talked about: *I was the* **subject** *of their talk.*
3 a person who belongs to a country: *She is a British* **subject.**

subject[2] *noun* the person or thing that does the action of a verb; the noun that usually goes in front of the verb: *In the sentence "Jane bought the bread", Jane is the* **subject.** Look at **object.**

submarine /sub′ mə rīn″/ *noun* a ship that can go along under the water

submarine

submit /sub mit′/ *verb* (*present participle* **submitting,** *past* **submitted)**
1 to agree to obey
2 to give: *I* **submitted** *my papers to the examiner.*

°**substance** /sub′ stans/ *noun* a sort of material: *Salt is a* **substance** *we use in cooking.*

subtract /sub trakt′/ *verb* to take away one number from another: *If you* **subtract** *3 from 5, you get 2.*
subtraction *noun*

suburb /sub′ ərb/ *noun* an outer part of a town: *He lives in the* **suburb** *of Greenfield, and works in the city.*

succeed /sək sēd′/ *verb* to do well; get what you wanted: *He* **succeeded** *in the examination. His business has* **succeeded,** *and is making a lot of money.*

success /sək ses′/ *noun*
1 *(no plural)* succeeding: *his* **success** *in the examination*
2 (*plural* **successes**) a thing which succeeds: *Her party was a* **success;** *everyone enjoyed it.*
successful *adjective*
successfully *adverb*

such /such/ *pronoun*
1 of this or that kind: *Don't play with knives or matches;* **such** *things are not toys.*
2 so unusual in some way: *I have never seen* **such a** *wide river.*

3 (used in some phrases): *They wanted some juicy fruit* **such as** (= like) *oranges, but there was* **no such** *fruit* (= no fruit of that kind) *in the market.*

suck /suk/ *verb*
to draw liquid into the mouth: *The baby was* **sucking** *milk from its bottle.*

°**sudden** /sud′ ən/ *adjective*
happening or done unexpectedly: *Her illness was very* **sudden** *— she was well yesterday. a* **sudden illness**
suddenly *adverb:* **Suddenly,** *I heard a loud bang.*

suffer /suf′ ər/ *verb*
to be in pain or trouble: *She was* **suffering** *from a headache.*
suffering *noun*

sufficient /sə fish′ ənt/ *adjective*
enough: *Have you had* **sufficient** *sleep?*

suffix /suf′ iks/ *noun*
(*plural* **suffixes**)
letters that are added to the end of a word, to change the meaning: *If we add the* **suffix** *"ful" to the word "hope", we make the word "hopeful".* Look at **prefix.**

°**sugar** /shůg′ ər/ *noun (no plural)*
a substance made from some plants, used to make food sweet

suggest /səg jest′/ *verb*
to say to someone that something is a good idea: *I* **suggested** *that it would be quicker to travel by train.*
suggestion *noun: He made the* **suggestion** *that we go by train.*

°**suit**[1] /so͞ot/ *verb*
to be right for; look nice when worn: *It* **suits** *me if you come to work at eight o'clock. That dress* **suits** *you.*
suitable *adjective: This toy is not* **suitable** *for young children.*

°**suit**[2] *noun*
a set of clothes made from the same material: *His* **suit** *was made up of a jacket* (see) *and trousers.*

suitcase /soot′ cās″/ *noun*
a large bag that you put things in when you travel

suitcase

sulk /sulk/ *verb*
to feel angry for a long time, usually silently: *When we told her she couldn't come with us, she went and* **sulked** *in her room.*

sultan /sul′ tən/ *noun*
a Muslim leader

°**sum** /sum/ *noun* the answer
an exercise in using numbers: *The* **sum** *of 4 and 7 is 11.*

°**summer** /sum′ ər/ *noun, adjective*
the season, in cool countries, when it is warmest: *a* **summer** *vacation*

summit /sum′ it/ *noun*
the top: *a mountain* **summit**

summon /sum′ ən/ *verb*
to call for someone to come to you: *The teacher* **summoned** *all the children to the room.*

°**sun** /sun/ *noun*
the large ball of fire in the sky which gives light and heat: *The* **sun** *rose at six o'clock. Sit in the* **sun** *and get warm.*
sunlight *noun (no plural): The* **sunlight** *was very bright.*
sunny *adjective* **(sunnier, sunniest):** *The day was bright and* **sunny.**
sunrise *noun: At* **sunrise,** *the sun looks as if it is coming up.*

sunset *noun: At* **sunset,** *the sun looks as if it is going down.*
sunshine *noun (no plural): The children played in the* **sunshine.**

sunbathe /sun′ bāTH″/ *verb* (*present participle* **sunbathing,** *past* **sunbathed)**
to lie in the sun

°**Sunday** /sun′ dā/ *noun*
the first day of the week; the day on which Christians go to church

sung /sung/ see **sing**

sunk /sunk/ see **sink**

super /so͞o′ pər/ *adjective*
very nice or exciting: *We had a* **super** *day at the beach.*

superb /sə purb′/ *adjective*
very fine: *Her dancing is* **superb.**

superior /sə pir′ e ər/ *adjective*
better or higher

superlative /sə pur′ lə tiv/ *noun, adjective*
a word or a form of a word that shows that something is the best, worst, biggest, smallest, etc. of its kind: *This pen is quite good, that one is better, but Peter's pen is* **the best** *of all. "Best" is a* **superlative.** Look at **comparative.**

supermarket /so͞o′ pər mär′ kit/ *noun*
a big shop where you choose what you want and pay as you go out

supersonic /so͞o″ pər son′ ik/ *adjective*
faster than sound: *a* **supersonic** *plane*

superstition /so͞o″ pər stish′ ən/ *noun*
something that people believe that cannot be proved, and is probably not true: *Some people think that the number four is unlucky, but that is just a* **superstition.**

supervise /so͞o′ pər vīz″/ *verb* (*present participle* **supervising,** *past* **supervised)**
to watch over people while they work, to see that they are doing the right thing: *The teacher* **supervised** *our drawing class.*

supervision /so͞o″ pər vizh′ ən/ *noun (no plural): We worked under the teacher's* **supervision.**

supper /sup′ ər/ *noun*
an evening meal

supply[1] /sə plī′/ *noun* (*plural* **supplies)**
a store which can be used; and amount: *We keep a large* **supply** *of food in the house. Our* **supplies** (= the things we need) *for this month are in the pantry.*

supply[2] *verb* (*present participle* **supplying,** *past* **supplied)**
to give or sell what is needed: *That company* **supplies** *paper to the printers.*

°**support**[1] /sə port′/ *verb*
1 to hold up: *These posts* **support** *the roof.*
2 to help, especially with money: *She* **supports** *her husband on the money she earns from teaching.*
3 to be on the side of: *Which football team do you* **support?**

°**support**[2] *noun*
something that holds up: *There are two large wooden* **supports** *that hold up the roof.*

suppose /sə poz′/ *verb* (*present participle* **supposing,** *past* **supposed)**
1 to think: *What do you* **suppose** *you will do after school?*

2 to be expected to; ought to: *What are you* **supposed to** *be doing when you have finished your work? You* **aren't supposed to** *drink alcohol* (= you are not allowed to).

supposing if: **Supposing** *(that) you catch the next bus, you'll be home before 10 o'clock.*

supreme /sə prēm'/ *adjective*
highest; best: *The most important law court* (see) *is called the* **Supreme Court.**

°**sure** /shůr/ *adjective*
without doubt: *I am* **sure** *that I put the money in the box. Please* **make sure** *that the house is locked before you leave.*

surely *adverb:* **Surely** *you locked the door? I would be surprised if you hadn't.*

surf /surf/ *noun*
(no plural)
white bubbles (= water filled with air) on waves when they come onto land

surf

°**surface** /sur' fis/ *noun*
the outside, flat part or top of something: *The table had a shiny* **surface,** *but underneath it was dull and rough.*

surgeon /sur' jən/ *noun*
a doctor who cuts into people's bodies to help cure them

surgery /sur' jər ē/ *noun*
(*plural* **surgeries**)
(no plural) when a doctor cuts a part of a person's body to cure him

surname /sur' nām/ *noun*
a name that is used by a family, usually written last: *He is called Peter Brown. Brown is his* **surname.**

°**surprise**[1] /sə prīz' *or* sər prīz'/ *noun*
an unexpected event; a feeling caused by this event: *Don't tell him about the present — it's a* **surprise.** *I looked at him* **in surprise** *— I didn't expect to see him again.*

°**surprise**[2] *verb* (*present participle* **surprising,** *past* **surprised**)
to cause the feeling of surprise: *His anger* **surprised** *me — I had thought he was a calm person.*

surrender /sə ren' dər/ *verb*
to stop fighting and give yourself to the people you are fighting

°**surround** /sə round'/ *verb*
to be or go all around something: *The fence* **surrounds** *the school.*

surroundings *plural noun* the area around something: *The house is in beautiful* **surroundings.**

survive /sər vīv'/ *verb* (*present participle* **surviving,** *past* **survived**)
to go on living: *The man was very ill, but he* **survived.**

survival *noun (no plural): The man's* **survival** *was surprising, as the doctors thought he would die. We need food and water for* **survival.**

suspect[1] /sə spekt'/ *verb*
to think that something is true, though you do not know: *He seems poor, but I* **suspect** *that he has quite a lot of money.*

suspicious /sə spish' əs/ *adjective* feeling that something is wrong: *I am* **suspicious** *of that woman — I think she may have stolen something from our shop.*

suspect[2] *noun*
someone who is thought to have done wrong: *The police have taken the* **suspect** *to the police station.*

suspend /sə spend′/ *verb*
1 to hang: *The lamp was* **suspended** *from the ceiling.*
2 to delay: *We* **suspended** *the building work during the rain.*
suspense *noun (no plural)* delay which frightens or excites people: *Please tell us what happened, we're all waiting in* **suspense.**

°**swallow¹** /swäl′ ō/ *verb*
to take food or drink down the throat and into the stomach: *She* **swallowed** *some milk.*

swallow² *noun*
a small bird with a tail divided into two parts

swam /swam/ see **swim**

swamp /swämp/ *noun*
land which is always soft and wet

swan /swän/ *noun*
a large white water bird with a long curved neck

swarm¹ /swôrm/ *noun*
a large group, especially of insects: *a* **swarm** *of bees*

swarm

swarm² *verb*
to move in a large group

sway /swā/ *verb*
to move from side to side: *The trees* **swayed** *in the wind.*

swear /swâr/ *verb*
(*present participle* **swearing,** *past tense* **swore** /swôr/, *past participle* **sworn** /swôrn/)
1 to use very bad words: *He was so angry that he* **swore** *at his friend.*
2 to promise: *I* **swear** *I won't tell anyone your secret.*

sweat¹ /swet/ *noun (no plural)*
water which comes out of your skin: **Sweat** *poured down his face as he ran.*

sweat² *verb*
to give off water through the skin: *She was* **sweating** *as she reached the top of the hill.*

sweater /swet′ ər/ *noun*
a thick garment for the top of the body

°**sweep** /swēp/ *verb*
(*present participle* **sweeping,** *past* **swept** /swept/)
1 to clean with a brush: *I* **swept** *the floor.*
2 to move quickly: *The sea* **swept away** (= moved over and carried away) *the huts.*

°**sweet¹** /swēt/ *adjective*
1 like sugar or ripe fruit to taste. *I don't like* **sweet** *coffee; I like it better without sugar in it.*
2 pleasant or loving: *What a* **sweet** *smile she has!*

°**swell** /swel/ *verb* (*present participle* **swelling,** *past tense* **swelled,** *past participle* **swollen** /swō′ lən/)
to become larger: *A bee has stung my hand and it is* **swelling up.** *After the rain, the river* **swelled.**
swelling *noun: The bee sting has left a* **swelling** *on my hand.*

swerve /swurv/ *verb* (*present participle* **swerving,** *past* **swerved**)
to move suddenly to one side when you are moving along: *The car* **swerved** *to avoid the dog.*

swift /swift/ *adjective*
fast: *a* **swift** *runner*

°**swim¹** /swim/ *verb*
(*present participle* **swimming,** *past tense* **swam** /swam/, *past participle* **swum** /swum/)
to move through the water by using

your legs and arms: *He* **swam** *across the river.*
swimmer *noun*
swimming *noun (no plural): He had some* **swimming** *lessons, and now he is good at* **swimming.**
swimming pool *noun* a pool built for people to swim in

swim² *noun*
an act or time of swimming: *to go for a* **swim**

°**swing¹** /swing/ *verb* (*present participle* **swinging,** *past* **swung** /swung/)
to move freely from a fixed point: *The boy* **swung** *on the rope tied to a tree. The door was* **swinging** *in the wind.*

swing² *noun*
a seat hanging on ropes or chains

swing

switch¹ /swich/ *noun* (*plural* **switches**)
an instrument for turning something on and off: *There is a* **switch** *on the wall for turning on the lights.*

switch² *verb*
1 to turn on or off with a switch: *Please* **switch off** *the lights. She* **switched on** *the radio.*
2 to change: *I used to cook on electricity, but I've* **switched** *to gas.*

swollen /swō'lən/ see **swell**

swoop /swo͞op/ *verb*
to fly down very quickly: *The bird* **swooped** *down to the lake.*

sword /sôrd/ *noun*
a sharp, pointed weapon like a long knife

swore /swôr/ see **swear**
sworn /swôrn/ see **swear**
swum /swum/ see **swim**

syllable /sil'ə bəl/ *noun*
part of a word which can be said by itself: *The word surface has two* **syllables,** *"sur" and "face".*

symbol /sim' bəl/ *noun*
a sign that stands for something: *The* **symbol** = *means "equals".*

sympathy /sim'pə thē/ *noun* (*plural* **sympathies**)
a feeling of kind understanding of another person; a feeling of sharing someone's unhappiness: *I have been a prisoner, so I have a lot of* **sympathy** *for other people in prison.*
sympathetic /sim" pə thet' ik/ *adjective: When I told her why I was worried, she was very* **sympathetic.**

symptom /sim' təm/ *noun*
a sign of something, especially an illness: *Fever is a* **symptom** *of many illnesses.*

syringe /sir inj'/ *noun*
an instrument with a needle at one end for giving injections (medicine through the skin)

needle
syringe

syrup /sir' əp/ *noun (no plural)*
sugar boiled in water or fruit juice

system /sis' təm/ *noun*
a group of things or ideas working together in one arrangement: *We have a large* **system** *of railroads. What* **system** *of government do you have in your country?*

Tt

°**table** /tā′ bəl/ *noun*
a piece of furniture with a flat top and legs: *We eat our meals at a* **table.**
tablecloth *noun* a cloth spread over a table
table tennis *noun (no plural)* a game in which you hit a small ball over a net across a table with a small wooden bat
Ping-pong is another word for **table tennis.**

tablet /tab′ lit/ *noun*
a hard flat piece or block of something: *The doctor gave me small white* **tablets** *to take when I have a headache.*

tack /tak/ *noun*
a small nail with a large head on it

tackle /tak′ əl/ *verb* (*present participle* **tackling,** *past* **tackled**)
1 to begin work on something: *I must* **tackle** *the work this evening.*
2 to try to stop someone: *He* **tackled** *the other player.*

tact /takt/ *noun (no plural)*
the ability to do or say the right thing at the right time: *Ann was sad because she had failed her examination, so her friend used her* **tact** *and talked about something else.*
tactful *adjective: She is very* **tactful;** *she always says the right things to people.*
tactfully *adverb*
tactless *adjective: If you are* **tactless** *you will make people feel hurt or angry.*

tag /tag/ *noun*
a small piece of paper or material fixed to something: *Look for a name* **tag** *on the coat to see to whom it belongs.*

°**tail** /tāl/ *noun*
the part of an animal which sticks out at the end of its back (picture at **bird** and **horse**)

tailor /tā′ lər/ *noun*
a person who makes suits, coats, etc.

°**take** /tāk/ *verb* (*present participle* **taking,** *past tense* **took** /tůk/, *past participle* **taken**)
1 to get hold of something: *The mother* **took** *her child by the hand.*
2 to carry something or go with someone to another place: **Take** *this shopping home. Who has* **taken** *my chocolate? Will you* **take** *me to town today?*
3 to swallow something: *I* **took** *the medicine.*
4 to travel in a vehicle: *to* **take** *a train*
5 to need: *I will* **take** *an hour to cook the dinner.*
6 (used in sentences like these): **Take down** (= write) *this sentence.* **Take off** *your clothes; they're very wet. The plane* **took off** (= left the ground) *at three o'clock.*
takeoff *noun: The plane crashed five minutes after* **takeoff** (= after it left the ground).

tale /tāl/ *noun*
a story

talent /tal′ ənt/ *noun*
the ability to do something well:

My sister has a **talent** *for singing.*
talented *adjective*

°**talk**[1] /tôk/ *verb*
to speak or be able to speak: *The two men were* **talking.** *That child is too young to* **talk.**
talkative /tôk′ ə tiv/ *adjective* liking to talk a lot

°**talk**[2] *noun*
spoken words: *We had a long* **talk.** *A doctor came to give our school a* **talk** *about his work.*

°**tall** /tôl/ *adjective*
1 higher than other people or other things: *James is* **taller** *than Paul, but Richard is the* **tallest.**
2 having a height: *He is 4 feet 7 inches* **tall.**

tame[1] /tām/ *adjective* **(tamer, tamest)**
trained to live with man; not wild: *a* **tame** *monkey*

tame[2] *verb* (*present participle* **taming,** *past* **tamed**)
to make a wild animal tame

tangerine /tan″ jə rēn′/ *noun*
a fruit like an orange, but with a skin that is easy to take off

tangle /tang′ gəl/ *noun*
a mixed-up and knotted mass of string, hair, or thread: *The string was* **in a tangle.**
tangled *adjective*

tank /tangk/ *noun*
1 a container to hold liquids or gas: *The gas* **tank** *in our car is empty.*
2 a heavy vehicle with guns on it, used in battle
tanker *noun* a truck with a tank or a ship with tanks on it for carrying oil or other liquids

tanker

tap[1] /tap/ *verb* (*present participle* **tapping,** *past* **tapped**)
to strike lightly: *He* **tapped** *on the door.*
tap *noun*

tap[2] *noun*
an instrument on the end of a pipe which can be turned to let liquid or gas out (picture at **sink**)

tape /tāpe/ *noun*
a narrow piece of cloth or other material: *We used adhesive* **tape** *to keep the bandage on.*
tape measure *noun* a narrow band of cloth, plastic, etc. used for measuring
tape recorder *noun: A* **tape recorder** *is an instrument that can put sound onto long plastic tapes, and play it again so that we can hear it.*

tar /tär/ *noun (no plural)*
a thick black liquid made from coal or wood: *We use* **tar** *to make roads.*

target /tär′ git/ *noun*
something we try to hit with a gun or an arrow: *The hunter's* **target** *was a wild animal.*

tart /tärt/ *noun*
a piece of pastry with fruit or jam (see) cooked on top of it

task /task/ *noun*
a piece of work which must be done: *Washing the dishes is a* **task** *I do not enjoy.*

°**taste**[1] /tāst/ *noun*
1 the special sense by which we know one food from another: *My sense of* **taste** *isn't very good; I have a cold.*
2 what food is like when it is in the mouth: *Chocolate has a sweet* **taste.**
3 the ability to see the goodness or

badness of something: *She has good* **taste** *in clothes.*

°**taste**² *verb* (*present participle* **tasting,** *past* **tasted)**
1 to try food or drink by taking a little into the mouth: *Can I* **taste** *your drink?*
2 to have a feeling in the mouth: *This tea* **tastes** *sweet.*

tattoo /ta to͞o′/ *verb* to make a pattern on the skin by pricking it and putting coloring substances on it
tattoo *noun*

taught /tôt/ see **teach**

°**tax**¹ /taks/ *noun* (*plural* **taxes)** money which must be paid to the government: *I pay* **tax** *out of my wages every week.*

°**tax**² *verb* *to make people pay taxes*
taxation *noun (no plural)*

°**taxi** /tak′ sē/ *noun* a car with a driver who will take you somewhere if you pay him: *to take a* **taxi** *to the station*

°**tea** /tē/ *noun*
1 *(no plural)* the dried leaves of a plant which we use to make the hot drink called tea: *a cup of* **tea**
2 a small meal in the late afternoon
3 a cup of tea: *Two* **teas,** *please.*
teaspoon *noun* a small spoon

°**teach** /tēch/ *verb* (*present participle* **teaching,** *past* **taught** /tôt/) to help a person to learn: *Who* **taught** *you to ride a bicycle?*
teacher *noun* someone who helps people to learn

°**team** /tēm/ *noun*
1 a group of people who play games against other groups: *a football* **team**
2 two or more animals which work together: *a* **team** *of oxen*

°**tear**¹ /tēr/ *noun* a drop of water from the eye: **Tears** *come to your eyes when you cry.*

°**tear**² /târ/ *verb* (*past tense* **tore** /tôr/, *past participle* **torn** /tôrn/) to pull into pieces; make a hole in: *She* **tore** *a page out of the book. He* **tore** *his trousers.*

tear³ *noun* a place in something which is torn: *a* **tear** *in his trousers*

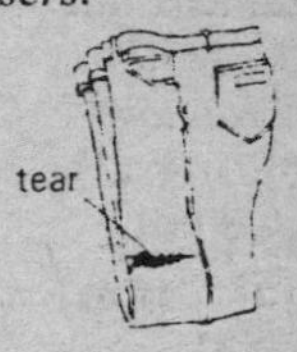

tease /tēs/ *verb* (*present participle* **teasing,** *past* **teased)** to make fun of a person playfully or unkindly: *You must not* **tease** *your little sister.*

technical /tek′ ni kəl/ *adjective*
1 having to do with machines: *a* **technical** *job*
2 having to do with special kinds of ability: *To build this machine, you must have* **technical** *ability.*
technician /tek nish′ ən/ *noun* a person who works with machines or instruments: *Anne is training to be a* **technician.**

technology /tek nol′ ə jē/ *noun* *(no plural)* using the knowledge we get through science to make things in factories, build things, etc.: *the* **new technology** *of micro* (= very small) *computers*

teeth /tēth/ see **tooth**

telegraph /tel′ ə graf″/ *noun (no plural)*
a way of sending messages quickly by electric wire or radio
telegram /tel′ ə gram/ *noun* a message sent by telegraph

°**telephone**[1] /tel′ ə fōn″/ *or* **phone** /fōn/ *noun*
1 *(no plural)* a way of carrying the sound of a person's voice by electricity over a wire or by radio: *We told him the news by* **telephone.**
2 the instrument used to carry the sounds: *Please* **answer the telephone** (= pick it up when it rings and speak into it).
telephone booth *noun* a small building or room with a telephone
telephone directory *noun* a large book with people's names and telephone numbers in it

°**telephone**[2] *verb* (*present participle* **telephoning,** *past* **telephoned**)
to speak to someone by telephone: *I* **telephoned** *my sister last night.*

telescope /tel′ ə skōp″/ *noun*
an instrument which we look through to see objects which are far from us

telescope

°**television** /tel′ ə vizh″ ən/ *noun*
1 *(no plural)* the sending and receiving of pictures by radio; the pictures which are sent out: *to watch* **television**
2 a large box-shaped apparatus on which these pictures appear: *Do you have a* **television? T.V.** is a short way of saying and writing **television.**

°**tell** /tel/ *verb* (*present participle* **telling,** *past* **told** /tōld/)
to speak to or advise someone: **Tell** *me what happened. I* **told** *you not to do it.*

°**temper** /tem′ pər/ *noun*
the way we feel: *Jane is* **good-tempered;** *she never gets angry. He* **lost his temper** (= became angry).

temperature /tem′ pər chur *or* tem′ prə chər/ *noun*
the amount of heat or cold: *In hot weather the* **temperature** *gets very high. When I was ill, I* **had a high temperature;** *I felt very hot.*

temple[1] /tem′ pəl/ *noun*
a holy building

temple[2] *noun*
the part of the head above and in front of the ear

temporary /tem′ pə rer″ ē/ *adjective*
lasting or meant to last for a short time: *a* **temporary** *job*
temporarily /tem′ pə rer″ ə lē/ *adverb*

tempt /tempt/ *verb*
1 to try to make someone do something wrong
2 to make someone want to do something: *Can I* **tempt** *you to eat some more of this cake?*

ten /ten/ *noun, adjective*
the number 10
tenth *noun, adjective* number 10 in order; 10th: *her* **tenth** *birthday*

tenant /ten′ ənt/ *noun*
a person who pays money to use a house or land

tend /tend/ *verb*
to be likely to; usually do something: *I* **tend** *to get tired in the evening.*
tendency /ten′ dən sē/ *noun* (*plural* **tendencies**): *Milk has a*

tendency *to go sour in hot weather.*

°**tender** /ten′ dər/ *adjective*
1 easy to eat: *This meat is* **tender.**
2 easily damaged or hurt: *My finger is* **tender** *because I cut it yesterday.*
3 kind and gentle: *a* **tender** *expression on her face*
tenderly *adverb*

tennis /ten′ is/ *noun (no plural)*
a game played by two or four people in which you hit a ball over a net

tense[1] /tens/ *adjective*
1 full of excitement: *The players were* **tense** *at the start of the game.*
2 tightly stretched: **tense** *muscles* (see)

tense[2] *noun*
the form of a verb that shows when the action of the verb happens: *"I look" and "I am looking" are* **present tenses;** *"I looked", "I was looking" and "I have looked" are* **past tenses;** *"I will look" and "I am going to look" are* **future tenses.**

tent /tent/ *noun*
a shelter made of thick cloth spread over poles

term /turm/ *noun*
1 a fixed length of time: *He was made captain of the football team for a* **term** *of one year.*
2 a part of the school year: *There are three* **terms** *in a school year.*
terms *plural noun* the things you are asking for: *If you agree to my* **terms** *— free meals and good wages — I will work for you.*

terrace /ter′ is/ *noun*
1 a level area cut out from the side of a hill
2 a flat area outside a house: *We sat on the* **terrace** *in the evening.*

terrible /ter′ ə bəl/ *adjective*
1 causing fear: *We saw a* **terrible** *storm.*
2 very bad: *Your writing is* **terrible.**
terribly *adverb: It is* **terribly** (= very) *hot.*

terrify /ter′ ə fī/ *verb*
(*present participle* **terrifying,** *past* **terrified**)
to fill with fear: *The animals were* **terrified** *by the storm.*
terror /ter′ ər/ *noun (no plural)*
great fear: *a feeling of* **terror**

territory /ter′ ə tôr ē/ *noun*
(*plural* **territories**)
1 land ruled by one government: *This island is British* **territory.**
2 an area belonging to one person or animal: *Wild animals will not allow other animals to enter their* **territory.**

°**test**[1] /test/ *verb*
1 to look at something to see if it is correct or will work properly: *Before he bought the car, he drove it to* **test** *it.*
2 to ask someone questions: *The teacher* **tested** *the children on their homework.*

°**test**[2] *noun*
an examination: *I passed my* **driving test** *today.*
test tube *noun*
a small thin glass tube: *We put chemicals in* **test tubes** *in our chemistry class.*

test tube

text /tekst/ *noun*
1 the words used in a book
2 a few words from a book
textbook *noun: A* **textbook** *is a book we use to learn about something.*

°**than** /THan *or* THən/
(used when we compare things, in sentences like these): *My brother is older* **than** *me. Mary sings better* **than** *anyone else in the class.*

°**thank** /thangks/ *verb*
to say we are grateful to someone: *I* **thanked** *her for the present she sent me.* **Thank you** *for the present you sent me.* **No, thank you,** *I don't want any more tea.*
thankful *adjective* very glad; grateful
thanks *plural noun* words used to show that we are grateful: **Thanks** *for helping me. It was* **thanks to** *John* (= because of him) *that we won the game.*

°**that** /THat *or* THət/
1 /THat/ (*plural* **those** /THōz/) the one over there; the one further away than this one: *This is my bowl;* **that** *bowl is yours.*
2 /THat/ (*plural* **those**) (used to point out someone or something; used to mean the one known or mentioned already): *Did you bring* **that** *photograph? We played football, and* **after that** (= next) *we went home.*
3 (used instead of **which**): *It's the blue bike* **that** *is mine.*
4 (used to join two parts of a sentence): *I think* **that** *it will rain.*
5 /THat/ so: *Please slow down — I can't walk* **that** *fast!*
6 (used to show the result of something: *The box was* **so** *heavy* **that** *I dropped it.*
7 (used to show why something is done): *Their father took them to the pool* **so that** *they could swim.*

thatch /thach/ *noun* *(no plural)* roof covering made of dry grass or other plants

thatched *adjective: a* **thatched** *cottage*

thaw /thô/ *verb*
to make or become soft or liquid, after something has been very cold and hard: *The sun* **thawed** *the ice and melted the snow.*

°**the** /THē/ *or* /THə/
1 (a word used before another, when it is clear who or what is meant): *There's a boy outside; it's* **the** *boy from* **the** *house across* **the** *road.*
2 (used in front of names of seas, rivers, deserts, etc.): **the** *Mediterranean Sea*
3 (used to talk about a class or group of people or things): **The** *cow is a useful animal* (= all cows are useful).

theater /thē′ ə tər/ *noun*
a building where plays are acted

theft /theft/ *noun*
1 *(no plural)* the crime of stealing: *He was put in prison for* **theft.**
2 an act of stealing: *When she discovered the* **theft** *of her bag, she went to the police.*

°**their** /THâr/ *pronoun*
belonging to them: *The children carried* **their** *bags to school.*

theirs /THârz/ *pronoun*
something belonging to them: *They looked at our pictures, but they didn't show us* **theirs.**

°**them** /THem/ *or* /THəm/ *pronoun*
(the word we use instead of **they** in sentences like this): *We gave* **them** *some food. We gave it to* **them.** *Did you have to wait for* **them?**

theme /thēm/ *noun*
what we think, speak, or write about: *Stamp collecting was the* **theme** *of his talk.*

themselves /THem selvz'/ *or* /THəm selvz'/ *pronoun*
1 (the same people, animals, or things as the sentence is about; the same as **they** in a sentence): *The travelers washed* **themselves** *in the river. They made a meal for* **themselves** (= without help). *They never go out* **by themselves** (= without another person).
2 (used to give **they** a stronger meaning): *They read us the stories which they* **themselves** *had written.*

°**then** /THən/ *adverb*
1 at another time; not now: *She lived in a village* **then,** *but now she lives in a town.*
2 afterwards; next: *I cooked the meat and* **then** *I washed the pot.*
3 if that is true: *"I have lost my ticket."* "**Then** *you must pay again."*

theory /thir' ē/ *noun*
(*plural* **theories**)
an idea that tries to explain something: *One* **theory** *about the moon is that it is a piece broken off the earth.*

°**there** /THâr/ *adverb*
1 at or to that place: *Don't sit* **there** *by the door; come and sit here.*
2 (used with **be, seem,** and other verbs, in sentences like this): **There seems to be** *a big crowd in the street.* **Is there** *a fair today?*

therefore /THar' fôr"/ *adverb*
for that reason: *He has broken his leg and* **therefore** *he can't walk.*

thermometer
/thər mom' ə tər/
noun
an instrument that measures heat and cold: *The doctor put a* **thermometer** *in my mouth to see if I had a fever.*

thermometer

°**these** /THēz/ *pronoun*
the ones here; the ones nearer than that one or those: *I don't like* **these** *candies; those are better.*

°**they** /THā/ *pronoun*
those people, animals, or things: *My friends are playing football, and* **they** *want us to play too.* **They're** (= they are) *playing behind the houses.* **They've** (= they have) *got two teams.*

°**thick** /thik/ *adjective*
1 wide: *This piece of wood is* **thicker** *than that.*
2 close together: *a* **thick** *forest*
3 difficult to see through: **thick** *smoke*
4 not flowing easily: *This soup is too* **thick.**
thickly *adverb*

°**thief** /thēf/ *noun* (*plural* **thieves**)
a person who steals: *The* **thief** *was sent to prison.*

thigh /thī/ *noun*
the part of the leg above the knee

thimble /thim′ bəl/ *noun* a hard covering for the top of a finger which you use when sewing

thimble

°**thin** /thin/ *adjective*
1 not wide; not thick: *This string is too* **thin,** *I need a thicker piece. Grandfather's hair is very* **thin.**
2 not fat: *You should eat more; you're too* **thin.**
3 flowing easily: **thin** *oil*
thinly *adverb: Spread the butter* **thinly.**

°**thing** /thing/ *noun*
an object; act or event: *What is that* **thing** *you are carrying? That was a good* **thing** *to do.*
things *plural noun* **1** belongings: *They packed all their* **things** *for the journey.* **2** conditions: *There used to be a lot of fighting in this area, but* **things** *are better now.*

°**think** /thingk/ *verb*
(*past* **thought** /thôt/)
1 to use the mind: *Have you* **thought** *about what job you are going to do?*
2 to have an opinion; believe something: *What do you* **think** *of my singing? I* **think** *it will be hot today. I couldn't* **think of** (= remember) *his name.*

°**third** /thurd/ *noun, adjective*
1 number 3 in order; 3rd: *This is the* **third** *time I've asked you to be quiet!*
2 one of three equal parts of something; $^{1}/_{3}$

°**thirst** /thurst/ *noun (no plural)*
the feeling of wanting or needing to drink something
thirsty *adjective* **(thirstier, thirstiest):** *I often feel* **thirsty** *when it's very hot.*

thirteen /thur″ tēn′/ *noun, adjective*
the number 13
thirteenth *noun, adjective* number 13 in order; 13th

thirty /thur′ tē/ *noun, adjective*
the number 30
thirtieth *noun, adjective* number 30 in order; 30th

°**this** /THis/ *pronoun*
(*plural* **these** /THēz/) the one here; the one nearer than that one: **This** *is my bowl; that bowl is yours.*
2 the thing the speaker is talking about: **This** *is what I want to do.*
3 present; nearest to the present time: *Shall we go out* **this** *afternoon, or wait till tomorrow?* **This** *is the 12th of May.*

thistle /this′ əl/ *noun*
a plant with sharp pointed leaves

thorn /thôrn/ *noun*
a sharp or pointed part of a plant

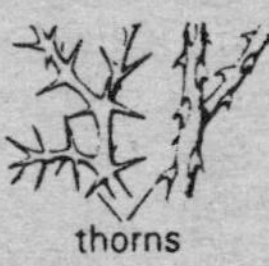
thorns

°**thorough** /thur′ ō/ *adjective*
with nothing missed; complete; careful: *They made a* **thorough** *search for the lost ring, but didn't find it.*
thoroughly *adverb* completely; carefully: *He always does his work* **thoroughly.**

°**those** /THōz/ *pronoun*
the ones over there; the ones further away than this one or these ones: *I don't like these candies;* **those** *are better.*

though /THō/
even if; in spite of: **Though** *he was*

poor, he was happy. The animal was walking **as though** (= as if) *it had hurt its leg.*

thought¹ /thôt/ see **think**

°**thought²** *noun*
1 *(no plural)* the act of thinking: *After much* **thought** *he decided not to buy the car.*
2 something we think: *She's a quiet girl and doesn't share her* **thoughts.**

thousand /thou' zənd/ *noun, adjective*
the number 1,000
thousandth *noun, adjective*
number 1,000 in order; 1,000th

°**thread¹** /thred/ *noun*
a long single piece of cotton, silk, or other material used in weaving or sewing

thread² *verb*
to put a thread through a needle

threaten /thret' ən/ *verb*
to say that you will hurt another person if he does not do what you want: *His father* **threatened** *to scold the boy if he stole again.*
°**threat** /thret/ *noun: He took no notice of his father's* **threat.**

three /thrē/ *noun, adjective*
the number 3: *I've got* **three** *sisters.*

threw /thrōō/ see **throw**

thrill¹ /thril/ *verb*
to fill with excitement: *The traveler (or traveller)* **thrilled** *us with his stories.*

thrill² *noun*
an excited feeling: *It* **gave me a thrill** *to know I had passed the examination.*

°**throat** /thrōt/ *noun*
1 the front part of the neck
2 the inside of the neck: *Food passes through our* **throats** *and down into our stomachs.*

throb /throb/ *verb* (*present participle* **throbbed)**
to beat strongly: *Her heart was* **throbbing** *after the race.*

throne /thrōn/ *noun*
the special chair of a king or queen

°**through** /thrōō/ *preposition, adjective, adverb*
1 from one side or end of something to the other: *The nail went* **through** *the wood. We walked* **through** *the market to the zoo.*
2 by way of: *The thief got in* **through** *the window.*
3 because of: *I failed my examination* **through** *laziness!*
4 among; between: *She searched* **through** *the coats to find hers.*

throughout /thrōō out'/ *preposition*
through every part of: *He is famous* **throughout** *the world. It rained* **throughout** *the night.*

°**throw¹** /thrō/ *verb* (*present participle* **throwing,** *past tense* **threw** /thrōō/, *past participle* **thrown)**

throw

1 to send something through the air by moving your arm: *He* **threw** *the ball to me, and I caught it.*
2 to move one's body or part of one's body suddenly: *He* **threw** *his arms up. Don't* **throw away** *your old shoes, give them to me.*

°**throw²** *noun*
an act of throwing

thrust /thrust/ *verb* (*present participle* **thrusting,** *past* **thrust)**
to push suddenly and hard: *We*

thrust *our way through the mass of people.*
thrust *noun*

thud /thud/ *noun*
a sound made by something heavy and soft falling: *He fell out of the tree and landed on the ground with a* **thud.**
thud *verb*

thumb /thum/ *noun*
the short, thick finger on the hand which is separate from the others

°**thunder** /thun′ dər/ *noun (no plural)*
the loud sound heard in the sky during a storm
thunderstorm *noun* a storm with heavy rain, thunder, and lightning

°**Thursday** /thurz′ dā″/ *noun*
the fifth day of the week

thus /THus/ *adverb*
1 in this way: *He sold his farm and* **thus** *he had enough money for his journey.*
2 with this result; so: *There has been no rain —* **thus,** *the crops are dying.*

tick[1] /tik/ *noun*
1 the sound made by a watch or clock
2 a mark (✓): *All the correct answers had* **ticks** *beside them.*

tick[2] *verb*
1 to make the sound a clock makes
2 to make a mark (✓)

°**ticket** /tik′ it/ *noun*
a small piece of paper or card which shows we have paid for something: *We buy a* **ticket** *to get a seat on a bus, train, or airplane.*

tickle /tik′ əl/ *verb (present participle* **tickling,** *past* **tickled)**
to touch a person lightly and make him laugh: *I* **tickled** *him under his arms.*

tide /tīd/ *noun*
the rise and fall of the sea twice every day: *At* **high tide** *the sea covers the rocks, but at* **low tide** *it uncovers them.*

°**tidy**[1] /tī′ dē/ *adjective*
(tidier, tidiest)
in good order; neat: *a* **tidy** *room*

°**tidy**[2] *verb (present participle* **tidying,** *past* **tidied)**
to make something neat

tie[1] /tī/ *noun*
a narrow band of cloth worn around the neck

tie

°**tie**[2] *verb*
(present participle **tying,** *past* **tie)** to fasten something with string or rope: *Can you* **tie up** *this parcel for me?*

tiger /tī′ gər/ *noun*
a large fierce animal, one of the big cats, which has yellow fur with black stripes (= thin lines)

°**tight** /tīt/ *adjective*
1 pulled or drawn closely together: *The string is tied in a* **tight** *knot.*
2 not loose: **Tight** *shoes can hurt your feet.*
tightly *adverb*

tighten /tīt′ ən/ *verb*
to make or become tight: *Will you* **tighten** *this screw; it's very loose.*

tile /tīl/ *noun*
a flat piece of baked clay: *We use* **tiles** *to cover roofs and sometimes floors and walls.*

till[1] /til/ *noun*
a container or drawer for money in a shop

till^{2} see **until**

tilt /tilt/ *verb*
to move or cause something to move so that it is not level: *I* **tilted** *the cup to drink out of it.*

timber /tim′ bər/ *noun (no plural)*
wood prepared for building; trees to be used for building

°**time**^{1} /tīm/ *noun*
1 *(no plural)* minutes, hours, days, weeks, months, years: *How do you spend your* **time** *at home?*
2 *(no plural)* a special number of minutes, hours, etc.: *I hadn't* **time** *to finish my homework.*
3 a period or event: *How many* **times** *have you read this book?*
4 a special hour or day: *What* **time** *is it? She was* **in time** *for work; she was not late. The train arrived* **on time** (= not early and not late).
timetable *noun* a list of the times when things will happen: *A school* **timetable** *tells us when different classes begin.*

time^{2} *verb (present participle* **timing,** *past* **timed)**
to measure how long it takes to do something

°**tin** /tin/ *noun*
1 *(no plural)* a soft, white metal
2 a container made of this metal

tinkle /ting′ kəl/ *verb (present participle* **tinkling,** *past* **tinkled)**
to make a sound like small bells: *The glasses* **tinkled** *as he carried them.*

tiny /tī′ nē/ *adjective*
(tinier, tiniest)
very small

tip^{1} /tip/ *noun*
the pointed end of something: *the* **tip** *of a finger*

tip^{2} *noun*
1 a small amount of money given to someone who has done something for you: *I gave a* **tip** *to the man who carried my cases.*
2 a useful piece of advice

tip^{3} *verb (present participle* **tipping,** *past* **tipped)**
to give a small amount of money to someone

tip^{4} *verb (present participle* **tipping,** *past* **tipped)**
1 to lean or cause to lean at an angle: *I* **tipped** *the table and the glasses fell off it.*
2 to turn over to cause something to turn over: *I* **tipped** *the bottle over and it broke.*

tip

tiptoe^{1} /tip′ tō″/ *verb (present participle* **tiptoeing,** *past* **tiptoed)**
to walk on one's toes: *I* **tiptoed** *past the sleeping child.*

tiptoe^{2} *noun*
on one's toes: *to walk* **on tiptoe**

°**tire** /tīr/ *verb (present participle* **tiring,** *past* **tired)**
to make someone feel that he needs rest: *Digging* **tires** *me.*
tired *adjective* needing rest or sleep: *I felt* **tired** *after work. Father is* **tired out** (= completely tired) *at the end of the day.*

tire *noun*
rubber, air-filled part of wheel of car, bicycle, etc. which cushions ride

tissue /tish′ ū/ *noun*
very thin cloth or paper: *She used paper* **tissues** *to blow her nose.*

°**title** /tīt′əl/ *noun*
1 the name of a story, a book, a film, etc.
2 a word used in front of a person's name: *A doctor has the* **title** *"Dr." in front of his name.*

°**to** /to͞o/
preposition, adverb
1 in the direction of: *He pointed* **to** *the clock. He sent a letter* **to** *his parents. We are driving* **to** *town.*
2 as far as: *When we got* **to** *the river, we sat down.*
3 on or against: *He fixed the shelf* **to** *the wall.*
4 until: *She works from two o'clock* **to** *ten o'clock. It is ten (minutes)* **to** *nine.*
5 (used to show why): *She worked hard* **to** *earn some money.*

toad /tōd/
noun
a small jumping animal like a large frog

toad

tobacco /tə bak′ ō/ *noun*
(no plural)
the dried leaves of a plant used for smoking in pipes and cigarettes

°**today** /tə dā′/ *noun, adverb*
1 (on) this day: **Today** *is Monday.*
2 modern times: *Many people use computers* **today.**

°**toe** /tō/ *noun*
1 one of the five end parts of the foot
2 the part of a shoe or sock that covers this end of the foot: *There is a hole in the* **toe** *of my sock.*

toffee /tof′ ē/ *noun*
a hard brown candy

°**together** /tə geTH′ ər/ *adverb*
1 one with another; in a group: *The children played* **together** *in the street. I stuck the two pieces of paper* **together.**
2 at the same time: *Don't all speak* **together!**

toilet[1] /toi′ lit/ *noun*
a container joined to a waste pipe, used for passing body waste

toilet[2] *adjective*
of using the toilet: **toilet** *paper*

token /tō′ kən/ *noun*
a sign: *We shook hands as a* **token** *of our friendship.*

told /tōld/ see **tell**

tomato /tə mā′ tō *or* tə mä′ tō/
noun
(*plural* **tomatoes**)
a red, juicy fruit that we eat raw or cooked

tomb /to͞om/ *noun*
a hole in the ground where a dead person is put; a grave (see)
tombstone *noun* a piece of stone put over a tomb, often with the name of the dead person on it

tomorrow /tə mor′ ō/
noun, adverb
1 (on) the day after this day: **Tomorrow** *will be Tuesday. It's my brother's birthday* **tomorrow.**
2 the future: *What will the cars of* **tomorrow** *look like?*

ton /tun/ *noun*
1 a measure of weight equal to 2,000 pounds
2 a measure of weight equal to 1,000 kilos: *1,000 kilograms is a* **metric ton.**

tone /tōn/ *noun*
the sound of a voice or of a musical instrument, etc.: *Her voice has a pleasant* **tone.**

tongs /tôngz *or* tongs/ *plural noun*
an instrument used for picking things up: *He picked up the hot metal with* **a pair of tongs.**

°**tongue** /tung/ *noun*
the part inside the mouth that moves: *Our* **tongue** *helps us to talk and to taste things.*

°**tonight** /tə nīt'/ *noun, adverb*
the night of today; on or during the night of today: *We are going to a party* **tonight.** *I hope that* **tonight** *will be dry.*

°**too** /to͞o/ *adverb*
1 also: *I like bananas, but I like oranges,* **too.**
2 more than is needed or wanted: *He drives* **too** *fast.*

took /to͝ok/ see **take**

°**tool** /to͞ol/ *noun*
an instrument which helps us to do work

tools

°**tooth** /to͞oth/ *noun*
(*plural* **teeth** /tēth/)
1 one of the white bony objects which grow in the mouth: The children **brush their teeth** *after every meal.*
2 something which is shaped like this: *The sharp parts of a comb or a saw are called* **teeth.** (picture at **comb**)

toothache /to͞oth' āk/ *noun (no plural)* a pain in a tooth: *I've had a* **toothache** *all day.*

toothbrush *noun* (*plural* **toothbrushes**) a small brush for cleaning the teeth (picture at **brush**)

toothpaste *noun (no plural)* a substance used for cleaning the teeth

°**top** /top/ *noun*
1 the highest part of something: *He climbed to the* **top** *of the hill.*
2 the lid or cover of something: *He took the* **top** *off the box. I wear shoes* **on top of** (= over) *my socks.*

top² *adjective*
highest: *Put it in the* **top** *drawer.*

top³ *noun*
a toy which spins very quickly on a point

topic /top' ik/ *noun*
something about which we talk or write

topple /top' əl/ *verb* (*present participle* **toppling,** *past* **toppled**)
to make or become unsteady and fall down: *The pile of books* **toppled** *onto the floor.*

tore /tôr/ see **tear**

tornado /tôr nā' dō/ *noun*
(*plural* **tornadoes** *or* **tornados**)
a storm with a strong wind which spins very fast

torpedo /tôr pē' dō/ *noun*
(*plural* **torpedoes**)
a weapon which is fired through the water from a ship to destroy another ship

torrent /tôr' ənt/ *noun*
a fast flow of water: *The river was a* **torrent** *after the storm.*

torrential /tə ren' shəl/ *adjective* like a torrent: *The rain was* **torrential** *last night.*

tortoise /tôr' təs/ *noun*
an animal with a body covered by a round hard shell

tortoise

torture /tôr' chər/ *verb*
(*present participle* **torturing,** *past* **tortured**)

to cause great pain to someone on purpose **torture** *noun*

toss /tôs/ *verb*
1 to throw: *They* **tossed** *the ball to each other.*
2 to move about or up and down: *The horse* **tossed** *its head in the air.*

°**total**[1] /tōt′ əl/ *noun*
everything added together: *Add up these numbers and tell me the* **total.**

°**total**[2] *adjective*
complete; whole: *"I want* **total** *silence," said the teacher. "No one must talk."*
totally *adverb*

°**touch**[1] /tuch/ *verb*
1 to put the hand or another part of the body on or against something: *Don't* **touch** *that pot; it's very hot.*
2 to bring, put, or be on or against something: *The branches of the tree* **touched** *the water.*

°**touch**[2] *noun*
1 (*plural* **touches**) putting part of the body on or against something: *I felt the* **touch** *of his hand.*
2 *(no plural)* the sense which lets us feel the hardness, softness, etc. of something

tough /tuf/ *adjective*
1 hard; not easy to bite or tear: *This meat is* **tough.** *Leather is a* **tough** *material.*
2 strong and brave

tour[1] /to͝or/ *noun*
1 a journey during which several places are visited: *They have gone* **on a tour.**
2 a trip to or through a place: *We went* **on a tour** *of the city.*

tour[2] *verb*
to make a tour

tourist *noun* a person who travels for pleasure

tow /tō/ *verb*
a pull something along by a rope or chain: *We* **towed** *the car to the garage.*

°**toward** /tôrd/ *also* **towards** *preposition*
1 in the direction of: *She walked* **toward** *the door.*
2 facing: *He stood with his back* **toward** *us.*
3 near in time: **Toward** *evening, the day became cooler.*

towel /toul/ *noun*
a piece of cloth for drying skin, dishes, etc.

tower /tou′ ər/ *noun*
a tall narrow building or part of a building: *a church* **tower**

°**town** /toun/ *noun*
a large group of houses and other buildings where people live and work
town hall *noun: A* **town hall** *is a building with offices for the government of the area around the town and with rooms for public meetings.*

°**toy** /toi/ *noun*
something that children play with

trace[1] /trās/ *noun*
a mark or sign left behind by someone or something: *They searched the building but did not find any* **trace** *of the criminal.*

trace[2] *verb* (*present participle* **tracing,** *past* **traced)**
1 to copy a picture, plan, etc. by drawing on a thin piece of paper put over it.
2 to try to find someone or something by looking for signs they

have left behind: *They* **traced** *the criminal to a house in the city.*

°**track**[1] /trak/ *noun*
1 a rough path
2 marks on the ground left by an animal or person: *The hunter followed the animal's* **tracks.**
3 a special path for races

°**track**[2] *verb*
to follow an animal's track

tractor /trak′ tər/ *noun*
a machine used for pulling heavy vehicles and farm machinery

tractor

°**trade**[1] /trād/ *noun*
1 *(no plural)* the buying and selling of goods: **Trade** *with other countries is important.*
2 a kind of business: *the building trades*
3 a job that needs special teaching: *She's a dressmaker* **by trade.**

trade[2] *verb* (*present participle* **trading,** *past* **traded)**
to buy and sell goods: *We* **trade** *with other countries.*
trader *noun* a person who buys and sells goods
tradesman *noun* (*plural* **tradesmen)** a person who buys and sells goods, especially a shopkeeper

tradition /trə dish′ ən/ *noun*
old customs or knowledge passed on from parents to their children: *It is a* **tradition** *that the young look after the old in their family.*
traditional *adjective*

°**traffic** /traf′ ik/ *noun (no plural)*
the movement of cars and people in the streets, or of ships or planes: *The city streets are full of* **traffic.**
traffic lights *plural noun* lights which direct traffic: *A driver must stop when the* **traffic lights** *are red.*

tragedy /traj′ ə dē/ *noun* (*plural* **tragedies)**
1 something sad that happens: *Her son's death was a* **tragedy.**
2 a serious play
tragic /traj′ ik/ *adjective: a* **tragic** *accident*
tragically *adverb*

trail /trāl/ *noun*
1 the marks left by a person or animal: The wounded animal left a **trail** *of blood behind it.*
2 a path across rough country

trailer /trāl′ ər/ *noun*
a two-wheeled vehicle pulled by a car, etc.

°**train**[1] /trān/ *noun*
a number of cars for people or freight pulled along by an engine on a railroad: *Are you traveling* **by train?**

train

°**train**[2] *verb*
to make oneself, or someone or something else ready to do something difficult: *I* **am training** *for the race. She* **is training** *to become a nurse.*
training *noun (no plural): Nurses have several years of* **training.**

traitor /trā′ tər/ *noun*
a person who helps people who are

not friends of his country: *The* **traitor** *was sent to prison.*

tramp /tramp/ *noun*
a person with no home or job who wanders from place to place begging for food or money

trample /tram′ pəl/ *verb*
(*present participle* **trampling,** *past* **trampled**)
to walk heavily on something: *Don't* **trample on** *the flowers when you play in the garden.*

transfer[1] /trans′ fər *or* trans fur′/ *verb*
to move people or things from one place to another: *His employer* **transferred** *him to another office.*

transfer[2] *noun*
the act of transferring a person: *Can I have a* **transfer** *to a new office?*

transform /trans fôrm′/ *verb*
to change completely in appearance or nature: *She* **transformed** *the room by painting it.*

transistor /tran zis′ tər/ *noun*
a small radio: *a* **transistor radio**

transitive /trans′ zə tiv/
noun, adjective
a verb whose action is done to something or somebody; a verb that takes an object (see): *I gave the book to Jane. "Gave" is a* **transitive** *verb.* Look at **intransitive.**

translate /trans′ lāt/ *verb*
(*present participle translating, past* **translated**)
to give the meaning of words of one language in another language: *He* **translated** *the speech from Spanish into English.*
translation *noun* the act of translating; something that has been translated

transparent /trans pâr′ ənt/
adjective
that we can see through: *Glass is a* **transparent** *material.*

transport[1] /trans pôrt′/ *verb*
to carry from one place to another: *The goods were* **transported** *by train.*

transport[2] /trans′ pôrt/ *noun*
the act of transporting or of being transported: *the* **transport** *of goods by air*

trap[1] /trap/ *noun*
1 an instrument for catching an animal
2 a plan to catch a person; a position which you cannot escape from: *The police* **set a trap** *for the thieves.*

trap[2] *verb* (*present participle* **trapping,** *past* **trapped**)
to catch in a trap: *The police* **trapped** *the thieves. She was* **trapped** *in the burning house.*

°**travel** /trav′ əl/ *verb* (*present participle* **traveling,** *past* **traveled**)
1 to go from place to place: *to* **travel** *round the world*
2 to move: *At what speed is he* **traveling?**
traveler *noun* a person on a journey

trawler /trôl′ ər/ *noun*
a boat for fishing

tray /trā/ *noun*
a flat piece of wood, metal, etc. on which things can be carried

tread /tred/ *verb* (*present participle* **treading,** *past tense* **trod** /trod/, *past participle* **trodden**)
1 to stand on: *I* **trod** *on his foot by accident.*
2 to crush with the feet: *They get the juice out of the fruit by* **treading** *it.*

treason /trē′ zən/ *noun (no plural)*
an action which harms one's country or its government: *The man was sent to prison for* **treason** *when he sold secrets to the enemy.*

treasure /trezh′ ər/ *noun (no plural)*
a collection of gold, silver, etc.: *The* **treasure** *dug out of the earth was a box of gold coins.*
treasury *noun* (*plural* **treasuries**): *The* **Treasury** *is the part of the government which collects and pays out the government's money.*

treat[1] /trēt/ *noun*
something which gives pleasure: *Her birthday* **treat** *was a visit to the theater.*

°**treat**[2] *verb*
1 to behave toward: *He* **treated** *the animal cruelly.*
2 to handle: *Glass must be* **treated** *carefully.*
3 to give medicine as a doctor: *to* **treat** *an illness*
treatment *noun: His* **treatment** *of the animal was cruel. The doctor's* **treatment** *cured him.*

treaty /trē′ tē/ *noun*
(*plural* **treaties**)
an agreement between two or more countries: *a peace* **treaty**

°**tree** /trē/ *noun*
a large plant with a trunk, branches, and leaves

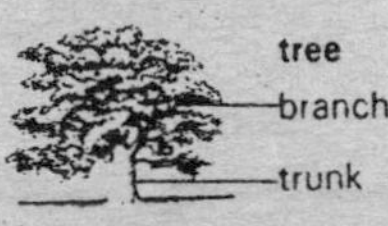

tremble /trem′ bəl/ *verb* (*present participle* **trembling,** *past* **trembled**)
to shake: *to* **tremble** *with fear*

tremendous /tri men′ dəs/ *adjective*
1 very large; very great
2 wonderful: *We went to a* **tremendous** *party.*
tremendously *adverb*

trench /trench/ *noun*
(*plural* **trenches**)
a long narrow hole dug in the earth

trespass /tres′ pas″ *or* tres′ pas/ *verb*
to go on someone else's land without permission: The farmer said we were **trespassing.**
trespasser *noun*

trial /trī′ əl/ *noun*
1 when people in a court (see) of law decide whether a person is guilty of a crime: *The man was* **on trial** *for killing somebody.*
2 a test to see if something is good or bad

triangle /trī′ ang″ gəl/ *noun*
a flat shape with three straight sides and three angles
triangular *adjective* shaped like a triangle

°**tribe** /trīb/ *noun*
a group of people of the same race, language, customs, etc.
tribal *adjective*

tributary /trib′ yə ter″ ē/ *noun*
(*plural* **tributaries**)
a small stream or river that joins a larger river

tribute /trib′ ūt/ *noun*
something done, said, or given to show respect or admiration for someone: *The doctor* **paid tribute to** *his nurses by praising their work.*

°**trick¹** /trik/ *noun*
1 an action meant to deceive someone: *He got the money from me by a* **trick.**
2 a clever act done to amuse people: *I can do magic* **tricks.**
3 something done to someone to make him look stupid and to amuse others: *The children* **played a trick** *on their teacher.*

°**trick²** *verb*
to decieve or cheat someone: *He* **tricked** *me into giving him the money.*

trickle /trik′ əl/ *verb* (*present participle* **trickling,** *past* **trickled)**
to flow in a thin stream: *Blood* **trickled** *from the wound.*
trickle *noun*

tricycle /trī′ sik əl/ *noun*
a cycle with three wheels

tricycle

tried /trīd/ see **try**

trigger /trig′ ər/ *noun*
a small part of a gun which you pull with your finger to fire it

trim /trim/ *verb* (*present participle* **trimming,** *past* **trimmed)**
to make neat by cutting: *She* **trimmed** *his hair.*

°**trip¹** /trip/ *noun*
a short journey: *a* **trip** *to town*

°**trip²** *verb* (*present participle* **tripping,** *past* **tripped)**
to hit one's foot against something: *I* **tripped over** *the box on the floor and fell.*

triumph /trī′ əmf/ *noun*
being successful; a feeling of happiness when you are successful: *It was a great* **triumph** *when our team won the race.*

trod /trod/ see **tread**

trodden /trod′ ən/ see **tread**

troops /tro͞ops/ *plural noun*
soldiers

trophy /trō′ fē/ *noun*
(*plural* **trophies)**
a prize given to a person who has won a game or race

tropics /trop′ iks/ *plural noun*
the hottest parts of the earth: *This plant only grows in* **the tropics.**
tropical *adjective* **1** of the tropics: *a* **tropical** *plant* **2** very hot: **tropical** *weather*

trot /trot/ *verb* (*present participle* **trotting,** *past* **trotted)**
to run with short steps: *The horse* **trotted** *along the road.*
trot *noun*

°**trouble¹** /trub′ əl/ *noun*
a state of anxiety or unhappiness; pain: *The boy caused a lot of* **trouble** *to his parents; he was always* **in trouble** (= doing bad things).

°**trouble²** *verb* (*present participle* **troubling,** *past* **troubled)**
1 to cause someone unhappiness, anxiety, or pain: *Her child's bad behavior* **troubled** *her.*
2 to annoy someone; give someone extra work: *Can I* **trouble** *you to shut the door?*

trough /trôf/ *noun*
a long narrow wooden or metal container: *A* **trough** *is filled with food or water for animals.*

°**trousers** /trou′ zərz/ *plural noun*
a piece of clothing which covers the lower part of the body and the legs

a pair of trousers

trowel /trou′ əl/ *noun*
a small tool used for digging small holes, taking plants out of the ground, etc.

truant /tro͞o′ ənt/ *noun*
a child who stays away from school without a good reason.

truck /truk/ *noun*
a motor vehicle used to carry heavy loads.

°**true** /tro͞o/ *adjective* **(truer, truest)**
1 correct: *Is it* **true** *that you are rich?*
2 real: *What I am saying now will* **come true** (= will happen).
truly *adverb* really: *I am* **truly** *grateful for all your help.*

trumpet /trum′ pit/ *noun*
a brass instrument played by blowing through it

trumpet

°**trunk** /trungk/ *noun*
1 the main stem of a tree (picture at **tree)**
2 the human body without the head and limbs
3 a large box used for clothes when traveling
4 the long round nose of an elephant

trunks /trungks/ *plural noun*
a piece of clothing like very short trousers worn by men for swimming

°**trust**[1] /trust/ *verb*
1 to believe that someone is honest or good: *Don't* **trust** *him — he's not telling the truth.*
2 to be sure that someone will do something: *Can I* **trust** *you to do this work well?*
trustworthy *adjective: A* **trustworthy** *person is someone that you can trust.*

°**trust**[2] *noun (no plural)*
believing that someone is good or honest; being sure that someone or something will do something: *Don't* **put your trust in** *that man: he may trick you.*

°**truth** /tro͞oth/ *noun (no plural)*
what is true; the correct facts: *You should always* **tell the truth.**
truthful *adjective: He is very* **truthful** *— he never lies*

°**try**[1] /trī/ *verb* (*present participle* **trying,** *past* **tried)**
1 to do one's best to do something: *He* **tried** *to climb the tree, but he could not.*
2 to test something: *Have you* **tried** *this chocolate? She* **tried on** *the dress to see if it would fit.*

try[2] *noun* (*plural* **tries)**
an act of trying: *If you can't open the box, can I* **have a try?**

tub /tub/ *noun*
a round wooden or metal container for holding liquid: *She washed the clothes in a* **tub.**

°**tube** /to͞ob/ *noun*
1 a hollow pipe made of metal, plastic, glass, or rubber, usually used for liquids
2 a soft metal or plastic container with a cap: *a* **tube** *of toothpaste*

tubes

tuck /tuk/ *verb*
to push or put something into or under something else: **Tuck** *your shirt into your trousers. She* **tucked in** *the covers on the bed.*

°**Tuesday** /to͞oz′ dā″/ *noun*
the third day of the week

tuft /tuft/ *noun*
a group of hairs, grass, etc. growing together: *The baby only had a few* **tufts** *of hair on its head.*

tug¹ /tug/ *verb* (*present participle* **tugging,** *past* **tugged**)
to pull hard: *The child* **tugged** *at my hand to make me go with her.*

tug² *noun*
a sudden strong pull: *I gave the loose tooth a* **tug.**

tug³ *or* **tugboat** *noun*
a small powerful boat used for guiding large ships into and out of a port

tumble /tum′ bəl/ *verb* (*present participle* **tumbling,** *past* **tumbled**)
to fall suddenly: *She* **tumbled** *downstairs.*

tumbler /tum′ blər/ *noun*
a drinking glass with a flat bottom

tune¹ /to͞on/ *noun*
a number of musical notes put together to make a pleasant sound: *Can you sing this* **tune?**

tune² *verb* (*present participle* **tuning,** *past* **tuned**)
to set the strings of a musical instrument so that it gives the right notes: *to* **tune** *a piano* (see)

tunnel¹ /tun′ əl/ *noun*
a large hole dug for a road or railway through a hill or under a river, town, or mountain

tunnel

tunnel² *verb* (*present participle* **tunneling,** *past* **tunneled**)
to make a tunnel: *They* **tunneled** *for weeks before they reached the other side of the hill.*

turban /tur′ bən/ *noun*
a length of cloth wound tightly round the head

turkey /tur′ kē/ *noun*
a large farm bird that is used for food

°**turn¹** /turn/ *verb*
1 to go or make something go around and around: *The wheels were* **turning.** *Will you* **turn** *the wheel to the right?*
2 to change or make something change position or direction: *She* **turned** *left at the end of the road. He* **was turning** *the pages of the book. She* **turned around** *to look at the boy behind her. She* **turned** (= changed) *her house* **into** *a shop. He* **turned down** (= said he didn't want) *the job.*

°**turn²** *noun*
1 an act or turning: *the* **turn** *of a wheel*
2 a change of direction: *a* **turn** *in the road*
3 a chance to do something: *It's my* **turn** *to play.*
turning *noun* a place where one road branches off from another

turtle /tur′ təl/ *noun*
an animal which has a hard round shell over its body, and lives mainly in the sea

tusk /tusk/ *noun*
a long pointed tooth which grows outside the mouths of some animals

tutor¹ /to͞o′ tər/ *noun*
a person who teaches one pupil or a very small class: *Her* **tutor** *teaches her at home.*

tutor² *verb*
to teach: *He* **tutored** *me in English.*

T.V. /tē vē/ see **television**

tweezers /twēz′ zəs/ *plural noun*
an instrument made of two narrow pieces of metal joined at one end, used for picking up very small objects

a pair of tweezers

twelve /twelv/ *noun, adjective*
the number 12
twelfth *noun, adjective* number 12 in order; 12th

twenty /twen′ tē/ *noun, adjective*
the number 20
twentieth *noun, adjective* number 20 in order; 20th

°**twice** /twīs/ *adverb*
two times: *You've asked me that question* **twice.**

twig /twig/ *noun*
a small branch from a tree

twin /twin/ *noun*
one of two children born of the same mother at the same time

twinkle /twing′ kəl/ *verb* (*present participle* **twinkling,** *past* **twinkled)**
to shine with an unsteady light: *The stars* **twinkled** *in the sky.*

°**twist¹** /twist/ *verb*
1 to wind threads together or around something else: *String is made of threads* **twisted** *together. She* **twisted** *her hair around her fingers.*
2 to turn: **Twist** *the lid to open it.*
3 to turn in several directions: *The path* **twisted** *up the hill.*

°**twist²** *noun*
1 something made by twisting: *a* **twist** *in a piece of rope*
2 an act of twisting: *He gave the cap a* **twist** *to open the jar.*
3 a bend: *a road full of* **twists** *and turns*

twitch /twich/ *verb*
to move suddenly and quickly without control: *The horse* **twitched** *its ears.*
twitch *noun*

two /to͞o/ *noun, adjective*
the number 2

°**type¹** /tīp/ *noun*
a special class or kind: *Cotton is a* **type** *of material.*
typical *adjective* the same as other people or things of the same kind: *He is a* **typical** *pupil; he is like most of the other pupils.*

type² *verb* (*present participle* **typing,** *past* **typed)**
to use a machine to print letters on paper: *to* **type** *a letter*
typewriter *noun* a machine used to type letters
typist *noun* a person whose job is to use a typewriter

typewriter

typhoon /tī′ fo͞on′/ *noun*
a great storm

tyrant /tī rənt′/ *noun*
a person with complete power who uses it cruelly
tyranny /tir′ ə nē/ *noun (no plural)* the rule of a tyrant

Uu

°**ugly** /ug′ lē/ *adjective* **(uglier, ugliest)**
not beautiful to look at: *an* **ugly** *face*

umbrella /əm brel′ ə/ *noun*
a piece of cloth or plastic stretched over a frame, which you can hold over yourself to keep off the rain

umbrella

umpire /um′ pīr/ *noun*
a person who decides about rules in a game

unable /ən ā′ bəl/ *adjective*
not able to do something: *I am* **unable** *to come to school today.*

unanimous /ū nan′ ə məs/ *adjective*
agreed by everyone: *There was a* **unanimous** *decision to go home.*

uncertain /ən sur′ tən/ *adjective*
not sure: *I am* **uncertain** *what to do.*

°**uncle** /un′ kəl/ *noun*
the brother of one of your parents, or the husband of the sister of one of your parents

uncomfortable /ən kum′ fər tə bəl/ *adjective*
not comfortable

uncommon /ən kam′ ən/ *adjective*
not usual: *an* **uncommon** *plant*

unconscious /ən kon′ shəs/ *adjective*
not knowing what is happening or feeling anything: *After she hit her head she was* **unconscious** *for several minutes.*

uncover /ən kuv′ ər/ *verb*
1 to take something from on top of: *He* **uncovered** *the dish and showed us the food.*
2 to find out: *The police* **uncovered** *a plan to steal some money.*

°**under** /un′ dər/ *preposition, adverb*
1 in or to a lower place; below: *She sat in the shade* **under** *a tree. The dog crept* **under** *the bed.*
2 less than: *My shirt cost* **under** *five dollars. All the children are* **under** *twelve (years old).*
3 working for or obeying: *The children worked well* **under** *the kind teacher.*

undergo /un″ dər gō′/ *verb (present participle* **undergoing,** *past tense* **underwent** /un″ dər went′/, *past participle* **undergone** /un″ dər gon′/)
to bear; have done to you: *These people have* **undergone** *many difficulties to get here.*

undergraduate /un″ dər graj′ o͞o it/ *noun*
a student at a college

underground[1] /un′ dər ground″/ *adjective, adverb*
under the ground: *There is an* **underground** *room in the old house. They went* **underground.**

undergrowth /un′ dər grōth″/ *noun (no plural)*
thickly growing plants underneath trees: *They pushed their way through the* **undergrowth.**

underline /un′ dər līn″/ *verb (present participle* **underlining,** *past* **underlined)**
to put a line under a word or words: *This sentence is* **underlined.**

underneath /un″ dər nēth′/ *preposition, adverb*
under: *She sat* **underneath** *the tree in the shade. They looked down from the bridge at the water* **underneath.**

°**understand** /un″ dər stand′/ *verb* (*present participle* **understanding,** *past* **understood** /un″ dər stŏŏd/)
to know the meaning of: *Do you* **understand** *every word on this page?*
understanding *noun (no plural): His* **understanding** *of English is very good.*

undertake /un″ dər tāk′/ *verb* (*present participle* **undertaking,** *past tense* **undertook** /un″ dər tŏŏk′/, *past participle* **undertaken)**
to promise; say that you will do: *I* **undertook** *to teach the children English.*

underwear /un′ dər wâr″/ *noun (no plural)*
clothes worn next to the skin, under your shirt, trousers, dress, etc.: *She* **changes her underwear** (= puts on clean underwear) *every day.*

°**undo** /ən dōō′/ *verb* (*present participle* **undoing,** *past tense* **undid** /ən did′/, *past participle* **undone** /ən dun′/)
to untie or unfasten: *He* **undid** *the string round the parcel. Her buttons were* **undone.**

undoubtedly /ən dout′ id lē/ *adverb*
for sure; surely: *He is* **undoubtedly** *too busy to write me a letter.*

undress /ən dres′/ *verb*
to take clothes off

uneasy /ən ē′ zē/ *adjective* **(uneasier, uneasiest)**
a little afraid: *I had an* **uneasy** *feeling that someone was watching me.*
uneasily *adverb*

unemployed /un″ im ploid′/ *adjective*
having no paid work: *He was* **unemployed** *for two months after leaving college.*
unemployment *noun (no plural): There is high* **unemployment** (= many people without work) *in this town since the factory closed.*

uneven /ən ē′ ven/ *adjective*
not level or flat: *an* **uneven** *road*

unexpected /un″ ik spek′ tid/ *adjective*
not expected
unexpectedly *adverb: She arrived* **unexpectedly** *early.*

unfair /ən fâr′/ *adjective*
not fair; not just: *It's* **unfair** *to punish Peter and not James — they were both behaving badly.*
unfairly *adverb*

unfasten /ən fas′ ən/ *verb*
to stop being fastened; undo: *She* **unfastened** *her belt.*

unfold /ən fōld′/ *verb*
to open out: *She* **unfolded** *the cloth.*

unfortunate /ən fôr′ chə nit/ *adjective*
having bad luck; unlucky
unfortunately *adverb:* **Unfortunately,** *I can't come to your party.*

unfriendly /ən frend′ lē/ *adjective*
not friendly: *Why is she so* **unfriendly?**

ungrateful /ən grāt′ fəl/ *adjective*
not grateful: *The* **ungrateful** *child took her present and ran off without saying anything.*

unhappy /ən hap′ ē/ *adjective* **(unhappier, unhappiest)**
not happy; sad: *She looked* **unhappy** *after she read the letter.*

unhealthy /ən hel′thē/ *adjective* **(unhealthier, unhealthiest)**
not healthy; not good for health: *She looks* **unhealthy**. *This is an* **unhealthy** *place to live.*

uniform /ū′nə fôrm/ *noun*
clothes worn for a special job or for school: *The soldiers were wearing* **uniforms.**

uniform

union /ūn′ yən/ *noun*
1 *(no plural)* coming or joining together: *the* **union** *of states to form a country*
2 a group of people joined for a special reason: *A* **trade union** *is a group of workers such as miners or teachers, who have joined together.*

unique /ū nēk′/ *adjective*
being the only one: *That building is* **unique** *because all the others like it were destroyed.*

unit /ū′nit/ *noun*
1 one complete thing or set: *This lesson is divided into four* **units** *— speaking practice, writing practice, new words, and a word game.*
2 an amount or sum: *We measure distance in* **units** *called kilometers.*

unite /ū nīt′/ *verb* (*present participle* **uniting,** *past* **united)**
to join together: *We are* **united** *in what we believe, the* **United** *States of America*

universe /ū′ nə vurs″/ *noun*
all the stars, space, etc. that we know about
universal *adjective* of or for everyone: *Microcomputers are of* **universal** *interest; everyone is learning how to use them.*

university /ū″ nə vur′ sə tē/ *noun* (*plural* **universities**)
a place where you can study for a higher degree in such fields as medicine, mathematics, law, etc.

unjust /ən just′/ *adjective*
not just; unfair: *an* **unjust** *punishment*
unjustly *adverb*

unkind /ən kīnd′/ *adjective*
not kind; rather cruel: *That was an* **unkind** *thing to say!*

unknown /ən nōn′/ *adjective*
not known: *An* **unknown** *person wrote this story.*

unless /ən les′/
1 if not: **Unless** *you go at once you will be late.*
2 except when: *My baby sister never cries* **unless** *she is hungry.*

unlike /ən līk′/ *preposition*
not like; not the same as: *She is* **unlike** *her mother; she is tall and her mother is very short.*
unlikely *adjective* not expected: *They are* **unlikely to** *come since the weather is so bad.*

unload /ən lōd′/ *verb*
to take something off a vehicle, from a person, etc.: *Two men* **unloaded** *the truck.*

unlock /ən lok′/ *verb*
to open with a key: *to* **unlock** *a door*

unlucky /ən luk′ ē/ *adjective* **(unluckier, unluckiest)**
not having or giving good luck:

Some people think that 13 is an **unlucky** *number. I was* **unlucky** *— I missed the bus by just one minute.*

unnecessary /ən nes′ ə ser″ ē/ *adjective*
not necessary: *All those clothes are* **unnecessary** *on such a hot day.*

unpack /ən pak′/ *verb*
to take things out of boxes, baskets, etc. where they have been stored: *She* **unpacked** *(her clothes) when she arrived home from her vacation.*

unpleasant /ən plez′ ənt/ *adjective*
not nice or pleasant: *That drink has an* **unpleasant** *taste; I don't like it.*
unpleasantly *adverb*

unreasonable /ən rēz′ nə bəl/ *adjective*
not reasonable: *He's being* **unreasonable** *— he wants more money and more free time.*

unreliable /un″ ri lī′ə bəl/ *adjective*
that you cannot depend on: *I wouldn't ask him to help — he's very* **unreliable.**

unsafe /ən sāf′/ *adjective*
not safe

unsatisfactory /un sat is fak′trē/ *adjective*
not good enough: **unsatisfactory** *work*

unsteady /ən sted′ ē/ *adjective*
not safe or sure: *This chair is* **unsteady,** *will you hold it while I stand on it?*
unsteadily *adverb: The old woman walked* **unsteadily** *down the stairs.*

unsuitable /ən so͞ot′ə bəl/ *adjective*
not suitable: *Her light coat was* **unsuitable** *for the weather.*

untidy /ən tī′ dē/ *adjective* **(untidier, untidiest)**
not tidy: *Her room was* **untidy** *— there were clothes all over the floor.*
untidily *adverb*

untie /ən tī′/ *verb (present participle* **untying,** *past* **untied)**
to undo string, a knot, etc.: *She* **untied** *the package and looked inside.*

°**until** /ən til′/ *or* **till** /til/
up to the time when something happens: *We can't go* **until** *Thursday. I couldn't sew* **until** *I was six.*

untrue /ən tro͞o′/ *adjective*
not true

unusual /ən ū′ zho͞o əl/ *adjective*
not usual; strange: *an* **unusual** *hat*
unusually *adverb: She is* **unusually** *quiet.*

unwell /ən wel′/ *adjective*
not well; ill: *He has been* **unwell** *since Sunday.*

unwilling /ən wil′ ing/ *adjective*
not willing: *I was* **unwilling** *to leave the party but I had to go home.*
unwillingly *adverb*

unwind /ən wīnd′/ *verb (present participle* **unwinding,** *past* **unwound** /ən wound′/)
to undo (something that has been wound): *She* **unwound** *the wool from the ball.*

unwise /ən wīz′/ *adjective*
not reasonable or wise: *It is* **unwise** *to go out in this cold weather.*

°**up** /up/
adverb, preposition, adjective
1 to or in a higher place; to or in a standing position: *The boy climbed* **up** *the tree. The village is high* **up**

in the hills. Is Maria **up** *yet, or is she still in bed? Stand* **up** *so that I can see how tall you are.*
2 (used in some phrases, often to make the meaning stronger): *Before you go out,* **lock up** *the house. The boy* **ate up** *all his dinner. Go and see what those children* **are up to** (= are doing).

up-to-date *adjective* modern; having the latest information: *I like wearing* **up-to-date** *clothes. I keep* **up to date** *with the news by listening to the radio.*

upward *adverb* from a lower to a higher place; toward the sky or top of anything: *The plane flew* **upward.** *The people were all looking* **upward.**

uphill /up′ hil′/ see **hill**

upon /ə pon′/ *preposition*
on: *The village stands* **upon** *a hill.*

°**upper** /up′ ər/ *adjective*
in a higher position; further up: *The* **upper** *part of your arm is the part above your elbow.*

upright /up′ rīt/ *adjective*
straight up and down: *Put the bottle* **upright,** *not on its side.*

upset /əp set′/ *verb*
(*present participle* **upsetting,** *past* **upset)**
1 to knock over: *I* **upset** *the soup all over the table.*
2 to make unhappy or worried: *James was* **upset** *because he had lost his ticket.*
3 to spoil something that was planned: *The storm* **upset** *our plans for a party outside.*

°**upside down** *or* **upside-down** /əp′ sīd/ see **down**

upstairs /əp′ stärz′/ see **stairs**

urge[1] /urj/ *verb* (*present participle* **urging,** *past* **urged)**
to try and make someone do something: *He* **urged** *her to rest.*

urge[2] *noun*
a strong wish: *I had an* **urge** *to see him.*

urgent /urj′ ənt/ *adjective*
needing to be done without delay; very important: *I must mail this letter; it's* **urgent.**

urgently *adverb*

°**us** /us/
the person who is speaking and some other person or people, used in sentences like this: *The teacher told* **us** *to be quiet. Please give the book to* **us.**

°**use**[1] /ūz/ *verb* (*present participle* **using,** *past* **used)**
to do something with; have a purpose for: *How do you* **use** *a telephone? What do you* **use** *this thing for?*

used *adjective* not new: **used** *cars*

°**use**[2] /ūs/ *noun*
a purpose; being used; using: *What is the* **use** *of waiting for her? The earth is ready for* **use.** *I was given the* **use** *of their swimming pool.*

useful *adjective* having a good purpose; helpful: *That is a* **useful** *knife.*

usefully *adverb*

useless *adjective* having no good purpose: *This is a* **useless** *knife — the handle has broken!*

uselessly *adverb*

used to[1] /ūst′ too′/ *adjective*
knowing what something or someone is like, so that it does not seem strange or unusual or difficult: *He* **is used to** *traffic because he*

often drives in town. He **is used to** *driving in town.*

used to[2] *verb*
(used with another verb to show that something was done often in the past; but is not done now): *He* **used to** *play football every Saturday when he was young. My father* **didn't use to** *smoke, but now he does.*

°**usual** /ū′ zhōō əl/ *adjective*
done or happening regularly; by custom: *Are you coming home at the* **usual** *time? Yes, I shall leave the office at the same time as* **usual.** *My* **usual** *chair had been moved from its* **usual** *place.*

usually *adverb: I'm* **usually** *at school early, but today I was late.*

utensil /ū ten′ səl/ *noun*
an instrument or container used in everyday activities: *cooking* **utensils**

utmost /ut′ mōst/ *adjective, noun*
the most possible: *He* **did his utmost** *to stop his sister marrying that man.*

utter[1] /ut′ ər/ *verb*
to say: *He looked at me without* **uttering** *a word.*

utter[2] *adjective*
complete: *What he is doing is* **utter** *stupidity!*

utterly *adverb*

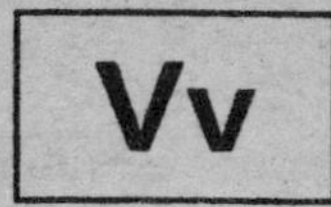

vacant /vā′ kənt/ *adjective*
empty: *a* **vacant** *seat on the bus*
vacancy *noun* (*plural* **vacancies**) an unfilled place or job: *The hotel has no* **vacancies** *— it's full.*

vacation /vā ka′ shən/ *noun*
time spent for rest or amusement away from normal activity: *She is* **on vacation.**

vacuum /vak′ ūm/ *noun*
a space with no air in it: *A* **vacuum flask** *or thermos keeps liquid hot or cold for a long time. A* **vacuum cleaner** *cleans things by sucking the dirt into a* **vacuum.**

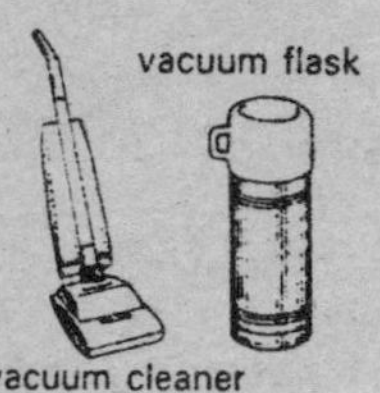

vague /vāg/ *adjective*
not clear: *I have only a* **vague** *idea where the house is.*
vaguely *adverb*

vain /vān/ *adjective*
too proud of yourself, especially of what you look like: *She is very* **vain** *— she's always looking at herself in the mirror.*
vanity /van′ ə tē/ *noun (no plural): What* **vanity** *— he thinks all the girls like him!*

valley /val′ ē/ *noun*
low ground between two hills or mountains

°**value**[1] /val′ ū/ *noun*
what something is worth: *What is the* **value** *of your house? Your help has been of great* **value.**
valuable *adjective: This house is very* **valuable;** *it would cost you a lot of money.*

value[2] *verb* (*present participle* **valuing,** *past* **valued)**
1 to think that something is worth a lot: *I* **value** *your advice.*
2 to say how much something is worth: *He* **valued** *the ring at $300.*

van /van/ *noun*
a small covered truck for carrying goods or passengers

vanish /van′ ish/ *verb*
to go from where you could see it: *I thought it would rain, but the clouds have* **vanished** *and it's a fine day.*

vapor /vā′ pôr/ *noun (no plural)*
a gaslike form of a liquid, like steam

varnish[1] /vär′ nish/ *noun*
a hard, shiny, clear covering that you put on wood, metal, etc.: *The* **varnish** *protected the table from being damaged.*

varnish[3] *verb*
to put varnish on something

vary /vâr′ē/ *verb* (*present participle* **varying,** *past* **varied)**
to change: *The weather* **varies** *from day to day.*
variety /və rī′ ə tē/ *noun* a lot of different things: *At school we learn a* **variety** *of things.*
various /vâr′ ē əs/ *adjective: There are* **various** *colors to choose from — which do you like best?*

vase /vās *or* vāz/ *noun*
a pot for putting cut flowers in

vast /vast/ *adjective*
very big: *The city is* **vast** *compared to our village.*
vastly *adverb*

vault[1] /vôlt/ *noun*
a strongly built room: *The money was kept in the bank's* **vault.**

vault[2] *verb*
to jump over: *He* **vaulted** *the fence.*

°**vegetable**[1] /vej′ tə bəl/ *noun*
a plant that people eat

°**vegetable**[2] *adjective*
of or from plants: *We use* **vegetable** *oil for cooking.*

°**vehicle** /vē′ ə kəl/ *noun*
something which carries people or goods: *Cars and trucks are* **vehicles.**

veil[1] /vāl/ *noun*
a covering for the head and (part of) the face: *In many Muslim countries, the women wear* **veils.**

veil[2] *verb*
to put a veil on or over: *She* **veiled** *her face before she went out.*

vein /vān/ *noun*
one of the tubes in your body that carries blood to the heart

velvet /vel′ vit/ *noun (no plural)*
a type of cloth with a soft surface

verandah /və rən′ də/ *noun*
a roofed area built onto a house, with no outside wall

verb /vurb/ *noun*
a word or words that tells us what someone or something does or is: *In the sentence "We are going home", "are going" is a* **verb.**

verdict /vur′ dikt/ *noun*
what is decided, especially by a law court (see): *The* **verdict** *was that the prisoner was guilty.*

verse /vurs/ *noun*
1 lines of writing which have a rhythm (= musical beat) and often a rhyme (= the words at the end of the lines sound alike)
2 a few lines of this from a longer piece (called a poem)
3 a small part of the Bible (= Jewish and Christian religious book) or Koran (= Muslim religious book)

version /vur′ zhən/ *noun*
a story told by one person compared with the same story told by another: *I have heard two* **versions** *of the accident.*

versus /vur′ səs/ *preposition*
against: *a football game* **versus** *Ohio State In lists,* **versus** *is usually written* **vs.**: *Ohio State* **vs.** *Michigan.*

vertical /vur′ ti kəl/ *adjective*
standing upright; at right angles to: *Walls are usually* **vertical.**

°**very**[1] /ver′ ē/ *adverb*
1 (used to make another word stronger): *It is* **very** *hot in this room. I am* **very** *well, thank you.*
2 (used with **not** like this): *The boy is* **not very** *big* (= he is rather small). *They did* **not** *stay* **very** *long* (= they stayed a short time).

very[2] *adjective*
the same; the one that is right: *I found the* **very** *thing I had been looking for.*

vessel /ves′ əl/ *noun*
1 a container: *A pot is a* **vessel** *for holding food.*
2 a ship or boat: *There were many* **vessels** *in the harbor today.*

veterinarian /vet″ rə nâr′ē ən/ *adjective*
treating animals: *A* **veterinarian** (*or* **vet**) *is an animal doctor.*

via /vī′ə *or* vē′ ə/ *preposition*
traveling through: *I went to New York* **via** *Baltimore.*

vibrate /vī′ brāt″/ *verb* (*present participle* **vibrating,** *past* **vibrated**)
to shake quickly backwards and forwards: *The bus* **vibrated** *when the driver started the engine.*
vibration *noun*

vice- /vīs/
a word used with a title, to mean that the person is next below the person with the title: *The* **vice-president** *is the next person in importance below the president.*

vicinity /vi sin′ ə tē/ *noun (no plural)*
surrounding area: *The market is* **in the vicinity of** (= near) *the school.*

victim /vik′ təm/ *noun*
someone who suffers from an illness or action: *She was the* **victim** *of a road accident.*

victorious /vik tôr′ē əs/ *adjective*
winning: *a* **victorious** *team*

victory /vik′tər ē *or* vik′tre/ *noun* (*plural* **victories**)
winning a fight or a game: *The school football team has had three* **victories** *this month against other schools.*

video /vid′ ē ō″/ *noun*
1 film for showing on a television set: *You can copy the football game from the television onto* **video tape** *by using the* **video recorder.**
2 a machine for copying plays, sport, etc. from the television **video recorder** is another name for **video.**

view /vū/ *noun*
1 something you see: *The house has a* **view** *over the sea.*
2 an opinion: *What is your* **view** *on school punishments?*

vigorous /vig′ər əs/ *adjective*
very active or strong: *The* **vigorous** *young plants grew fast.*

vile /vīl/ *adjective* (**viler, vilest**)
very unpleasant: *a* **vile** *smell*

°**village** /vil′ ij/ *noun*
a small place where people live, not so large as a town

villager *noun*
someone who lives in a village

villain /vil′ ən/ *noun*
the chief bad character in a play or movie

vine /vīn/ *noun*
a name given to some plants with climbing stems, like a **grape vine**

vinegar /vin′ ə gər/ *noun (no plural)*
a very sour liquid used in cooking

violent /vī′ə lənt/ *adjective*
having great force: *a* **violent** *storm*
violence *noun (no plural)*

violet /vī′ ə lit/ *noun*
1 a small flower with a sweet smell
2 the color of the violet, which is a mixture of blue and red

violin /vī″ ə lin′/ *noun*
a musical instrument with four strings, played with a bow (= tightly stretched threads which are drawn across the strings to make a sound)

bow
violin

viper /vī′ pər/ *or* **adder** *noun*
a snake with a dangerous bite

virtue /vur′ cho͞o/ *noun*
a good quality of someone's character: *Honesty is a* **virtue.**

visible /viz′ ə bəl/ *adjective*
able to be seen: *The smoke from the fire was* **visible** *from the road.*
vision /vizh′ ən/ *noun* 1 *(no plural)* sight: *She has good* **vision** *— she can see well.* 2 something we imagine; dream: *He had a* **vision** *of himself as a rich businessman.*

°**visit**[1] /viz′ it/ *verb*
to go and see: *We* **visited** *our friends in town.*

°**visit**[2] *noun*
an act of visiting: *We had a* **visit** *from your teacher. She* **paid us a visit.**
visitor *noun*

vital /vī′ təl/ *adjective*
necessary for life; very important: *a* **vital** *examination*

vivid /viv′ id/ *adjective*
1 bright: *a* **vivid** *color*
2 clear and lifelike: *She gave the police a* **vivid** *description of the accident.*

vocabulary /vō kab′ yə lâr″ ē/ *noun* (*plural* **vocabularies**)
1 all the words you know: *He has a very large* **vocabulary.**
2 a list of words in a book: *The* **vocabulary** *used in the course book is printed at the back.*

°**voice** /vois/ *noun*
the sounds you make when you speak or sing: *a high* **voice**/ *a loud* **voice**

volcano /vol kā′ nō/ *noun* (*plural* **volcanoes**)
a mountain from which burning and melted rock sometimes comes

volleyball /vol′ ē bəl″/ *noun* *(no plural)*
a game in which a large ball is knocked back and forth across a net, by hand

volt /vōlt/ *noun*
a measure of electricity

volume /vol′ yəm *or* vol′ ūm/ *noun*
1 *(no plural)* the space something contains or takes up: *What is the* **volume** *of this box?*
2 the amount of sound that something makes: *She turned down the* **volume** *on the radio.*
3 a book, especially one of a set

volunteer[1] /vol′ ən tēr/ *noun*
a person who offers to do something: *We want some* **volunteers** *to help paint the house.*
voluntary /vol′ ən tar ē/ *adjective* acting or done willingly, without payment: *She is a* **voluntary** *worker at the hospital.*

volunteer[2] *verb*
to offer to do something: *We all* **volunteered** *to paint the house.*

vomit /vom′ it/ *verb*
to bring food up from the stomach: *The child* **vomited** *after eating the bad meat.*

vote[1] /vōt/ *verb* (*present participle* **voting,** *past* **voted)**
to state a choice from among several, especially to choose someone secretly during an election (see): *Three people* **voted for** *a music club, but ten people* **voted for** *a science club, so we started a science club.*
voter *noun* someone who votes

vote[2] *noun*
a choice made by voting: *He won the election* (see) *because he got most* **votes.**

vow¹ /vou/ *verb*
to promise something important: *He* **vowed** *to look after his mother when his father died.*

vow² *noun*
a very important promise

vowel /vou′ əl/ *noun*
a written letter, or the sound of a letter, which is one of *a, e, i, o,* or *u.* Look at **consonant.**

voyage /voi′ ij/ *noun*
a long journey, often by sea

vulgar /vul′ gər/ *adjective*
rude or rough in behavior, taste, etc.

wade /wād/ *verb (present participle* **wading,** *past* **waded)**
to walk through water: *We* **waded** *across the river, because there was no bridge.*

wag /wag/ *verb (present participle* **wagging,** *past* **wagged)**
to move or cause to move from side to side or up and down: *The dog* **wagged** *his tail.*

°**wage** /wāj/ *noun*
money given to us for the work we do: *He earns a low* **wage.** *He gets his* **wages** *on Fridays.*

wagon /wag′ ən/ *noun*
a vehicle: *The horses pulled the* **wagon.**

wail /wāl/ *verb*
to make a long cry showing sadness or pain: *The child was* **wailing** *uhappily.*
wail *noun*

waist /wāst/ *noun*
the narrow part of the body between the chest and the legs: *Ann wore a belt around her* **waist.**

°**wait**[1] /wāt/ *verb*
to stay somewhere until someone comes or something happens: *Please* **wait** *here until I come back. I* **was waiting** *for the bus.*
waiter *or* **waitress** *noun* a person who brings food to people eating at a table
waiting room *noun* a room for people who are waiting: *a doctor's* **waiting room**

wait[2] *noun*
a time of waiting: *He had a long* **wait** *for the train, as it was late.*

°**wake** /wāk/ *verb*
(present participle **waking,** *past tense* **woke** /wōk/ *or* **waked,** *past participle* **woken** *or* **waked)**
to stop or make someone stop sleeping: *I* **woke** *early this morning. Be quiet, or you* **will wake** *the baby. Please* **wake** *me* **up** *at 8 o'clock.*

°**walk**[1] /wôk/ *verb*
to move on the feet at the usual speed: *We* **walk** *to school each day.*

°**walk**[2] *noun*
a journey on foot: *Shall we go for a* **walk** *this afternoon? It is a long* **walk** *to the town.*

°**wall** /wôl/ *noun*
1 something built especially of bricks or stone which goes around a house, town, field, etc.: *There was a* **wall** *around the park.*
2 one of the sides of a building or room: *We have painted all the* **walls** *white.*
wallpaper *noun (no plural)* special paper used to cover the walls of a room

wallet /wäl′it/ *noun*
a small flat case for papers or money, usually carried in a pocket

wallet

°**wander** /wän′ dər/ *verb*
to move about without purpose: *The children* **wandered (about)** *in the woods.*

°**want**[1] /wänt/ *verb*
1 to wish to have something: *I* **want** *a bicycle for my birthday.*

2 to need: *I* **want** *someone to help me.*

want² *noun (no plural)*
need; lack; not having something necessary: *The children were* **in want of** *food. The corn was dying* **from want of** *rain.*

°**war** /wôr/ *noun*
fighting between nations: *The two countries were* **at war** *for two years. One country* **declared war on** (= said they were going to fight) *another.*

warfare /wôr fār/ *noun (no plural)* the fighting which happens in a war

warship *noun* a ship used for war

ward /wôrd/ *noun*
a room in a hospital

warden /wôr′ dən/ *noun*
a person who looks after a large building where people live, a public place, etc.: *Where is the* **warden** *of the prison?*

wardrobe /wôrd′ rōb″/ *noun*
a closet in which clothes are hung up

warehouse /wâr′ hous″/ *noun*
a large building for storing things

wares /wârz/ *plural noun*
goods for selling: *The man spread his* **wares** *on the table.*

°**warm¹** /wôrm/ *adjective*
1 not cold but not hot: **warm** *water*
2 able to keep out the cold: **warm** *clothes*

warmth *noun (no plural): the* **warmth** *of the sun/the* **warmth** *of her welcome*

°**warm²** *verb*
to make or become warm: *The hot drink* **warmed** *him. He* **warmed** *himself by the fire.*

°**warn** /wôrn/ *verb*
to tell someone of something bad which might happen: *She* **warned** *me about the dangerous road, so I crossed it carefully.*

warning *noun: Because of her* **warning,** *I was careful.*

warrant /wôr′ ənt/ *noun*
a document saying that one may do something: *The police must have a* **search warrant** *to search a house.*

was /wuz/ *verb*
past tense of the verb **be** that we use with **I, he, she,** and **it:** *The sun* **was** *shining but it* **wasn't** (= was not) *too hot.*

°**wash¹** /wäsh/ *verb*
1 to make clean with water: *Have you* **washed** *your shirt? Will you* **wash up?** (= clean the dishes after a meal)
2 to flow over continually or carry in a flow of water: *The bridge was* **washed away** *in the storm.*

washing *noun (no plural)* clothes to be washed or already washed

washing machine *noun* a machine for washing clothes

°**wash²** *noun*
1 an act of washing or being washed: *a car* **wash**
2 things to be washed or being washed: *My shirt is in the* **wash.**

washbasin /wäsh′ bās″ ən/ *noun*
a large bowl or basin, often fixed to a wall, for washing

washbasin

wasp /wasp/ *noun*
a flying insect like a bee

°**waste**[1] /wāst/ *verb (present participle* **wasting,** *past* **wasted)**
to use something wrongly or use too much of something: *Don't* **waste** *the flour; there isn't much.*

°**waste**[2] *noun*
1 an act of wasting: *It is a* **waste** *to throw away good food.*
2 used, damaged, or unwanted things: *The* **waste** *from the factory was taken away in trucks.*

°**watch**[1] /wach/ *noun (plural* **watches)**

1 a small clock worn on the wrist or carried in a pocket
2 a person or people told to keep their eyes on a place or a person: *The police* **kept watch on** *the criminal's house.*

watchman *noun (plural* **watchmen)** a guard, especially of a building

°**watch**[2] *verb*
1 to look at; keep on'e eyes on: **Watch out** *for the cars when you cross the road.*
2 to look after: *Will you* **watch** *the baby?*

°**water**[1] /wô' tər/ *noun (no plural)*
the liquid in rivers, lakes, and seas, which animals and people drink

waterfall *noun* a place where water falls over rocks from a high place to a lower place

waterproof *adjective* which does not allow water to go through: *a* **waterproof** *coat*

water[2] *verb*
to put water onto land or plants

watt /wät/ *noun*
a measure of electrical power: *a 60* **watt** *electric bulb*

°**wave**[1] /wāv/ *noun*
1 one of curving lines of water on the surface of the sea which rise and fall
2 a movement of the hand from side to side: *She gave a* **wave** *as she left the house.*

°**wave**[2] *verb (present participle* **waving,** *past* **waved)**
to move or cause to move from side to side or up and down: *She* **waved** *her hand to say goodbye.*

wax /waks/ *noun (no plural)*
a solid substance made of fats or oil which melts when it is heated: *Candles* (see) *are made from* **wax.**

°**way** /wā/ *noun*
1 direction: *Which is the* **way** *to the station? Look both* **ways** *before you cross the road.*
2 distance: *We have to go a long* **way** *to school. I fell* **on the way** (= while I was going) *to school.*
3 a path: *I can't see because you are* **in my way** (= where I want to see).
4 how a thing is done or works: *Show me the* **way** *to use this camera, please.*

°**we** /wē/
the person who is speaking and some other person or people: *When my friend comes to see me,* **we** *play football.* **We're** (= we are) *all in the same class at school. Next year,* **we'll** (= we shall *or* we will) *be in a higher class. My sister and I didn't go to the movie because* **we'd** (= we had) *seen it before. The hill was so steep we thought* **we'd** (= we should or we would) *never get to the top. I've got a bicycle and my friend has one, too —* **we've** (= we have) *each got a bicycle.*

°**weak** /wēk/ *adjective*
not strong in body or character: *She was* **weak** *after her illness.*
weakness *noun* (*plural* **weaknesses**) being weak; a fault: *Spending too much money is her* **weakness.**

weaken /wē′ kən/ *verb*
to make or become less strong

wealth /welth/ *noun (no plural)*
riches; owning a lot of houses, land, etc.: *The father passed on the family's* **wealth** *to his son.*
wealthy *adjective* **(wealthier, wealthiest)** rich: *a* **wealthy** *family*

°**weapon** /wep′ ən/ *noun*
a thing with which we fight: *A gun is a* **weapon.**

°**wear** /wâr/ *verb* (*past tense* **wore** /wôr/, *past participle* **worn** /wôrn/)
1 to have or carry on the body: *She* **wore** *a pretty dress.*
2 to change because of continual use: *My shoes are* **worn out;** *they are full of holes. You've* **worn** *a hole in your sock.*
3 to last; remain unchanged: *This dress has* **worn** *well; it is three years old and it still looks new.*

weary /wir′ ē/ *adjective* **(wearier, weariest)**
tired: *I felt* **weary** *after work.*
wearily *adverb*

°**weather** /weTH′ ər/ *noun (no plural)*
the state of the wind, rain, sunshine, etc.: *I don't like cold* **weather.** *The* **weather** *has been dry this week.*

°**weave** /wēv/ *verb* (*present participle* **weaving,** *past tense* **wove** /wōv/, *past participle* **woven**)
1 to make threads into cloth, by moving a thread over and under a set of longer threads on a loom (see): *The boy learned how to* **weave.**
2 to make something in this way: *I* **wove** *a mat.*
weaving *noun (no plural): She is very good at* **weaving;** *the cloth she makes is beautiful.*

web /web/ *noun*
a net of thin threads spun by a spider

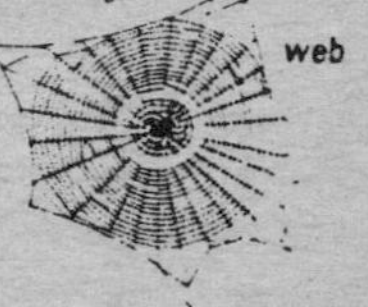

wedding /wed′ ing/ *noun*
the ceremony when people get married: *I'm going to my brother's* **wedding** *tomorrow.*

°**Wednesday** /wenz′ dā/ *noun*
the fourth day of the week

weed[1] /wēd/ *noun*
a wild plant which grows where it is not wanted

weed[2] *verb*
to remove weeds from the ground: *They* **were weeding** *the field.*

°**week** /wēk/ *noun*
a period of seven days, especially from Sunday to Saturday: *I play tennis twice a* **week.** *Will you come and see us next* **week?**
weekday *noun* any day except Sunday
weekend *noun* Saturday and Sunday: *I don't work* **on the weekend.**
weekly *adjective, adverb: This is a* **weekly** *paper; it is printed every Friday. It is printed* **weekly.**

weep /wēp/ *verb* (*past* **wept** /wept/)
to cry: *She* **wept** *when she heard the bad news.*

°**weigh** /wāy/ *verb*
1 to measure how heavy a thing is:

He **weighed** *the fish.*
2 to have a weight of: *The fish* **weighed** *two pounds*
weight *noun (no plural)* the heaviness of anything: *The baby's* **weight** *was 12 pounds.*

weird /wērd/ *adjective*
strange; unusual: **weird** *clothes*

°**welcome¹** /wel′ kəm/ *adjective*
wanted; happily accepted: *You are always* **welcome** *in my home.*

°**welcome** *verb (present participle* **welcoming,** *past* **welcomed)**
to greet someone with pleasure: *My aunt* **welcomed** *me.*

°**welcome³** *noun*
a greeting when someone arrives: *Mother gave our visitor a kind* **welcome.**

°**well¹** /wel/ *adjective*
in good health; not ill: *I hope you are* **well.** *I had a fever, but now I am better, thank you.*

°**well²** *adverb*
(better /bet′ ər/, **best** /best/)
1 in a good or satisfactory way: *Mary can read very* **well. "Well done!"** *the teacher said, when I did my problem correctly.*
2 completely; thoroughly: *Wash your hands* **well** *before you eat.*
3 (used with other words to mean completely, fully, much): *If the room is* **well lighted,** *it's easier to read. That writer is* **well known.**

°**well³** *noun*
a deep hole in the ground from which we take out water or oil

went /went/ see **go**

wept /wept/ see **weep**

were /wur/ *verb*
past tense of the verb **be** that we use with **you, we,** and **they:** *You* **were** *born in this town, but your brothers* **weren't** (= were not).

°**west** /west/
noun, adjective, adverb
the direction in which the sun goes down: *We traveled* **west** *for two days. There is a* **west** *wind* (= coming from the west).
western *adjective* in or of the west
westward *adverb* towards the west: *to travel* **westward**

°**wet¹** /wet/ *adjective*
(wetter, wettest)
1 covered with or containing liquid; not dry: *My hair is* **wet.** *Don't touch the* **wet** *paint.*
2 rainy: *a* **wet** *day*

wet² *verb (present participle* **wetting,** *past* **wet** *or* **wetted)**
to make something wet

whale /hwāl/ *noun*
a very large animal that lives in the sea; it is not a fish but feeds its young with milk

wharf /hwôrf/
noun (plural **wharfs** *or* **wharves** /hwôrvz/)
a place built on the edge of water where ships load and unload

wharf

°**what** /hwat/
1 which thing or things: **What** *is your name?* **What** *did you say?*
2 which: **What** *time is it?* **What** *tools do I need for this job?*
3 (used in sentences like this): *She told me* **what** *to do. I didn't know* **what** *had happened. "***What** *are you using those scissors* **for?***" "To cut paper."*

4 (used to show surprise or other strong feelings): "**What a** *silly thing to do!*"

whatever /hwat″ ev′ ər/
anything at all that; no matter what: *You may do* **whatever** *you want to do.* **Whatever** *you do, I won't tell you my secret.*

°**wheat** /hwēt/ *noun (no plural)*
a grass plant with grain seeds that are made into flour

°**wheel** /hwēl/ *noun*
an object made of a larger circle which turns around a smaller circle, to which it is joined: **Wheels** *make cars, trucks, and bicycles move.* (picture at **bicycle**)
wheelbarrow *noun* a vehicle with a wheel at the front and two handles at the back

°**when** /hwen/
1 at what time: **When** *will the bus come?*
2 at the time at which: *I lived in this village* **when** *I was a boy.*

whenever /hwen″ ev′ər/
1 at any time at all that; every time: *Please come to see me* **whenever** *you can.* **Whenever** *I see him I speak to him.*
2 (used to make **when** stronger): **Whenever** *did you have time to do all that work?*

°**where** /hwâr/
1 at or to what place: **Where** *is that train going? He doesn't know* **where** *his friends are.*
2 (used to tell what place, like this): *The house* **where** *I live has a green door.*

wherever /hwâr″ ev′ər/
1 at or to any place at all that: *I will drive you* **wherever** *you want to go.*
2 (used to make **where** stronger): *You are very late;* **wherever** *have you been?*

°**whether** /hweTH′ ər/
if: *I don't know* **whether** *he'll come or not.*

°**which** /hwich/
1 what person or thing: **Which** *child knows the answer?* **Which** *of you is bigger, Mary or Jane?*
2 that: *The book* **which** *I like best is the one* **which** *you gave me.*

°**while** /hwīl/
all the time that; during the time that: *I met her* **while** *I was at school.* **While** *the child played, her mother worked.*

whine /hwīn/ *verb (present participle* **whining,** *past* **whined)**
to make a high sad sound: *the dog* **whined** *at the door.*
whine *noun*

°**whip**[1] /hwip/ *noun*
a long piece of leather or rope fastened to a handle, used for hitting animals.

°**whip**[2] *verb (present participle* **whipping,** *past* **whipped)**
to beat with a whip: *He* **whipped** *the horse to make it run faster.*

whirl /hwurl/ *verb*
to move or make something move around and around very fast: *The wind* **whirled** *the leaves into the air.*
whirl *noun*

whisker /hwis′ kər/ *noun*
1 hair growing on the sides of a man's face
2 one of the long stiff hairs that grow near the mouth of dogs, cats, rats, etc.

°**whisper**[1] /hwis′ pər/ *verb*
to speak very quietly: *The two girls* **were whispering** *in the library.*

°**whisper²** *noun*
words which are whispered: *She spoke* **in a whisper,** *so I could not hear what she said.*

°**whistle¹**

/hwis′ əl/ *noun*
1 an instrument which makes a high sound when one blows through it: *The teacher blew a* **whistle** *to start the race.*
2 a thin high sound made by putting the lips together and blowing through them or by blowing through an instrument: *When he gave a* **whistle,** *his dog ran to him.*

°**whistle²** *verb (present participle* **whistling,** *past* **whistled)**
1 to make the sound of a whistle: *He* **whistled** *to his dog.*
2 to make music by doing this: *He* **whistled** *the song.*

°**white¹** /hwīt/ *adjective*
1 of the color of the paper in this book; very light: *a* **white** *dress*
2 with light-colored skin: *Some of the children were* **white,** *the others were* **black.**

°**white²** *noun*
1 *(no plural)* white color: *She was dressed* **in white.**
2 a person with light-colored skin
3 the white part of the eye, or of an egg (picture at **egg**)

°**who** /ho͞o/
1 what person or people: **Who** *gave you that book?* **Who** *are those people?*
2 that: *The man* **who** *lives in that house is my uncle.*

whoever /ho͞o″ ev′ ər/
1 any person that; no matter who: **Whoever** *wants a banana may have one.* **Whoever** *those people are, I don't want to see them.*
2 (used to make **who** stronger): **Whoever** *told you that silly story?*

°**whole¹** /hōl/ *adjective*
complete; total: *They told me the* **whole** *story.*
wholly *adverb*

°**whole²** *noun (no plural)*
the complete amount or thing: *Two halves make a* **whole.** *The weather this month has been good* **on the whole** (= most days were fine).

whom /ho͞om/
(used instead of **who,** in sentences like this): **Whom** *did you speak to at the market today? The boy* **whom** *we called Tom is really called Thomas.*

whose /ho͞oz/
of who or whom; belonging to who or whom: **Whose** *coat is that? It's my coat. This is the woman* **whose** *little boy was ill.*

°**why** /hwī/
for what reason: **Why** *is she crying? I can't tell you* **why** *she is crying. No one knows* **why.**

wicked /wik′ id/ *adjective*
very bad: *a* **wicked** *person*
wickedly *adverb*

°**wide¹** /wīd/ *adjective*
(wider, widest)
1 large from side to side; broad
2 fully or completely open: **wide** *eyes*
width /width/ *noun* the distance from one side of something to the other; how wide something is: *What is the* **width** *of this material?*

°**wide²** *adverb*
completely: *The door was* **wide** *open. He stood with his legs* **wide** **apart.**

widow /wid′ ō/ *noun*
a woman whose husband is dead

widower /wid′ ō ər/ *noun*
a man whose wife is dead

°**wife** /wīf/ *noun*
(*plural* **wives** /wīvz/)
the woman to whom a man is married

wig /wig/ *noun*
a covering for the head, made of hair from other people or animals

°**wild** /wīld/ *adjective*
1 not trained to live with man: **wild** *animals*
2 living in the natural state: *We picked the* **wild** *flowers in the woods.*
wildly *adverb*

°**will**[1] /wil/ *verb*
1 (used with other verbs to show that something is going to happen): *Peter* **will** *carry the books, and* **we'll** (= we will) *carry the paper and pens. We* **won't** (= will not) *be late getting home.*
2 (used in questions when asking to do something or used when offering to do something): **Will** *you help me, please? Yes, I* **will** *help you.*
Look at **would, shall,** and **should.**

°**will**[2] *noun*
power in the mind or character; what we want to do: *She has a strong* **will,** *and she does what she wants no matter what people say.*

will[3] *noun*
a document that says who will have a person's belongings after he is dead: *The man left his farm to his son in his* **will** (= his will said that his son should have his farm).

°**willing** /wil′ ing/ *adjective*
1 ready: *Are you* **willing** *to help?*
2 given or done gladly: **willing** *help*
willingly *adverb: I will* **willingly** *help you.*

°**win** /win/ *verb* (*present participle* **winning,** *past* **won** /wun/)
1 to be first or do best in a competition, race, or fight: *Who* **won** *the race? I* **won** *but David came second.*
2 to be given something because one has done well in a race or competition: *He* **won** *the first prize in the competition.*
winner *noun*

°**wind**[1] /wīnd/ *verb*
(*past* **wound** /wound/)
1 to turn around and around: *He* **wound** *the handle. He* **wound up** (= turned the handle on) *the clock because it had stopped.*
2 to make into a ball or twist around something: *She* **wound** *the rope around her arm.*
3 to bend and turn: *The path* **wound** *along the side of the river.*

°**wind**[2] /wind/ *noun*
air moving quickly: *The* **wind** *blew the leaves off the trees.*
windmill *noun* a building containing a machine which is turned by the force of the wind: *A* **windmill** *is used to crush grain into flour.*
windshield *noun* the piece of glass across the front of a car
windy *adjective* **(windier, windiest)** with a lot of wind

windmills

°**window** /win′ dō/ *noun*
an opening in the wall of a building to allow light and air to enter: *Please shut the* **window.**

windowsill *noun* a flat shelf below a window

wine /wīn/ *noun (no plural)*
an alcoholic drink made from a small, round, juicy fruit **(grape)**

°**wing** /wing/ *noun*
one of the two limbs of a bird (see) or insect with which it flies

wink /wingk/ *verb*
to close and open one eye quickly: *He* **winked** *at me.*
wink *noun*

°**winter** /win′ tər/ *noun, adjective*
the season in cool countries when it is cold and plants do not grow

wipe[1] /wīp/ *verb (present participle* **wiping,** *past* **wiped)**
to make dry or clean with a cloth: *Will you* **wipe** *the table? She* **wiped** *the marks* **off** *the table.*

wipe[2] *noun*
a wiping movement: *She gave the table a* **wipe.**

°**wire** /wīr/ *noun*
1 *(no plural)* thin metal thread: *a* **wire** *fence*
2 pieces of wire: *electric* **wires**

wireless /wīr′ lis/ *noun*
(*plural* **wirelesses)** former name for a radio

°**wise** /wīz/ *adjective*
(wiser, wisest)
having or showing good sense and cleverness: **wise** *advice*
wisdom /wiz′ dəm/ *noun (no plural)*
wisely *adverb: to act* **wisely**

°**wish**[1] /wish/ *verb*
1 to want what is not possible: *I* **wish** *I could fly.*
2 to want: *I* **wish** *to see you now!*
3 to hope that someone has something: *We* **wish** *you success in your new job.*

°**wish**[2] *noun* (*plural* **wishes)**
1 a feeling of wanting especially what is not possible: *She had a* **wish** *to see the future.*
2 what is wished for: *It was my mother's* **wish** *that I should go.*

wit /wit/ *noun (no plural)*
1 cleverness; quickness of the mind: *He had the* **wit** *to telephone the police.*
2 the ability to talk in a clever and amusing way
witty *adjective* **(wittier, wittiest)**
clever and amusing: *a* **witty** *person*
wittily *adverb*

witch /wich/ *noun* (*plural* **witches)**
a woman who is believed to have magic (see) powers

°**with** /wiTH *or* with/
1 in the company of: *She comes to school* **with** *her sister.*
2 using: *He opened the door* **with** *his key. Simon filled the bucket* **with** *water.*
3 having: *a white dress* **with** *red spots*
4 because of: *They smiled* **with** *pleasure.*
5 (used in sentences like these): *I don't agree* **with** *you. She quarrelled* **with** *her friend.*

withdraw /wiTH drô′/ *verb*
(*past tense* **withdrew** /wiTH droo͞′/, *past participle* **withdrawn)**
1 to take away or back: *She* **withdrew** *all her money from the bank.*
2 to move or make something move away or back: *The soldiers* **withdrew.**

wither /wiTH′ er/ *verb*
to make or become dry or colorless: *The plants* **withered** *in the dry weather.*

within /wiTH in′/ *preposition, adverb*
1 in less than: *He learned to speak English* **within** *six months!*
2 in; inside: **Within** *these old walls there was once a town.*

°**without** /wiTH out′/ *preposition*
1 not having: *You can't see the film* **without** *a ticket.*
2 (used in sentences like these): *Can you carry these glasses* **without** *dropping them* (= and not drop them)? *Why did you go out* **without** *telling me?*

witness /wit′ nis/ *noun* (*plural* **witnesses**)
a person who sees something happen: *She was a* **witness** *at the accident.*

wives /wīvz/ see **wife**

wobble /wob′ bəl/ *verb* (*present participle* **wobbling,** *past* **wobbled**)
to move or make something move unsteadily: *The table* **is wobbling.**

woke /wōk/ see **wake**

woken /wōk ən/ see **wake**

°**woman** /wům′ ən/ *noun* (*plural* **women** /wim′ in/)
a fully grown human female

won /wun/ see **win**

°**wonder[1]** /wun′ dər/ *verb*
1 to express a wish to know: *I* **wonder** *why James is always late for school.*
2 to be surprised: *We all* **wondered** *at his rudeness.*

°**wonder[2]** *noun*
1 *(no plural)* a feeling of surprise and admiration: *They were filled with* **wonder** *when they saw the spaceship.* **No wonder** (= it is no surprise) *he is not hungry; he has been eating candy all day.*
2 something or someone causing this feeling
wonderful *adjective* unusually good: **wonderful** *news*
wonderfully *adverb*

won't /wōnt/ see **will**

°**wood** /wůd/ *noun*
1 *(no plural)* the material of which trunks and branches of trees are made
2 a small forest: *He was lost in the* **wood.**
wooden *adjective* made of wood: **wooden** *furniture*

°**wool** /wůl/ *noun* *(no plural)*
1 the soft thick hair of sheep and some goats
2 the thread or material made from this hair: *The dress was made of* **wool.**
woolen *adjective: a* **woolen** *dress*

wool

°**word** /wurd/ *noun*
1 a letter or letters, a sound or sounds which together make something we can understand: *Home is the* **word** *for the place we live. She* **had a word** *with me* (= talked to me).
2 *(no plural)* a message: *Send me* **word** *as soon as you get home.*
3 *(no plural)* a promise: *I* **give** *you* **my word** *that I will return.*

wore /wôr/ see **wear**

°**work[1]** /wurk/ *verb*
1 to do an activity, especially as employment: *He* **works** *in a factory.*

Are you **working** *or playing, children?*
2 to be active; move or go properly: *Does this light* **work?**
3 to make someone or something do something: *Can you* **work** *this machine? She* **worked out** (= found an answer to) *the problem.*

°**work²** *noun (no plural)*
1 activity: *It takes a lot of* **work** *to build a house.*
2 a job or business: *to go to* **work**
3 what is produced by work: *He sells his* **work** *in the market.*
worker *noun*
workman *noun* (*plural* **workmen**) a person who works with his hands, especially in a trade
works *plural noun* **1** the moving parts of a machine **2** a factory: *the steel* **works**

°**world** /wurld/ *noun*
1 the earth: *This car is used all over the* **world.**
2 all human beings thought of together

°**worm** /wurm/ *noun*
a long thin creature with a soft body without bones or legs

worm

worn /wôrn/ see **wear**

°**worry** /wur' ē/ *verb* (*present participle* **worrying,** *past* **worried)**
to feel or make someone feel anxious: *My parents* **worry** *(about me) if I come home late. The news of the fighting* **worried** *us.*
worried *adjective*

°**worry²** *noun*
1 *(no plural)* a feeling of anxiety: *The* **worry** *showed on her face.*
2 (*plural* **worries**) someone or something that makes us feel worried: *My father has a lot of* **worries.**

°**worse** /wurs/ *adjective, adverb*
1 more bad: *My writing is bad, but your is* **worse.** *She was ill yesterday, but today she's* **worse** (= more ill).
2 more badly: *My brother sings* **worse** *than my sister.*

worship¹ /wur' ship/ *verb* (*present participle* **worshiping** *or* **worshipping,** *past* **worshiped** *or* **worshipped)**
to pray to and show great respect to: *Many people* **worship** *God.*

worship² *noun (no plural)*
worshipping: *A church is a place of* **worship.**

°**worst** /wurst/
adjective, adverb, noun
1 most bad: *Your spelling is the* **worst** *(spelling) I've seen.*
2 most badly: *They were all very bad, but you behaved* **worst** *of all.*

worth¹ /wurth/ *preposition*
with a value of: *How much is this bicycle* **worth?** *It's* **worth** *$100.*

°**worth²** *noun (no plural)*
value: *When she was in trouble, she discovered the* **worth** *of her friends* (= how good they were).
worthless *adjective* without worth; useless
worthy /wur' TH̶ē/ *adjective* **(worthier, worthiest)** deserving: *He is* **worthy of** *our praise.*

°**would** /wủd/
1 (the word for **will** in the past): *They said they* **would** *play football on Saturday, and* **they'd** (= they would) *win the game, but I said they* **wouldn't** (= would not) *win.*
2 (used when we are not sure enough to say **will**): *It's pretty, but*

would *it be big enough?*
3 (used as a polite way of asking someone something) **Would** *you like a cup of tea?* **I'd** (= I would) *rather have coffee, please.*

wound¹ /wound/ see **wind**

°**wound²** /wōōnd/ *verb*
to cause harm to the body: *The soldier was* **wounded** *in the arm.*

°**wound³** *noun*
a damaged place in the body

wove /wōv/ see **weave**

woven /wov′ ən/ see **weave**

°**wrap** /rap/ *verb (present participle* **wrapping,** *past* **wrapped)**
to put something all round an object: *I* **wrapped** *the book in paper and mailed it.*

wreath
/rēth/ *noun*
a ring of flowers and leaves

wreath

°**wreck¹** /rek/ *noun*
a ship, car, building, etc. which has been partly destroyed
wreckage *noun (no plural)* broken parts: *the* **wreckage** *of the plane after the crash*

°**wreck²** *verb*
to destroy or cause to destroy: *The ship was* **wrecked** *on the rocks.*

wrench /rench/ *verb*
to pull or turn suddenly and with force: *He* **wrenched** *the door open.*
wrench *noun* tool for turning nuts

wrestle /res′ əl/ *verb (present participle* **wrestling,** *past* **wrestled)**
to fight a person and try to throw him to the ground
wrestler *noun* a person who wrestles as a sport
wrestling *noun (no plural)*

wriggle /rig′ əl/ *verb (present participle* **wriggling,** *past* **wriggled)**
to twist from side to side: *He* **wriggled** *on the hard chair. The snake* **wriggled** *through the grass.*

wring /ring/ *verb*
(past **wrung** /rang/)
to twist; remove water by twisting: *She* **wrung** *the wet clothes.*

wrinkle /ring′ kəl/ *noun*
a line or fold on a surface: *Grandfather has many* **wrinkles** *on his face.*

°**wrist** /rist/ *noun*
the joint between the hand and the lower part of the arm
wristwatch *noun* a watch which fastens around the wrist

°**write** /rīt/ *verb (present participle* **writing,** *past tense* **wrote** /rōt/, *past participle* **written** /rit′ ən/)
1 to make letters or words on paper, using a pen or pencil: **Write** *your name and then* **write down** (= put onto paper) *this sentence.*
2 to produce and send a letter: *He* **writes** *to me every day.*
writer *noun* a person who writes books
writing *noun (no plural)* **1** the activity of writing: *I enjoy* **writing.**
2 the way someone writes: *What beautiful* **writing! Handwriting** is another word for **writing.**

°**wrong¹** /rông/ *adjective*
1 not good: *Telling lies is* **wrong.**
2 not correct: *I gave the* **wrong** *answer.*
3 not suitable: *This is the* **wrong** *time to visit her.*
wrongly *adverb: I wrote your name* **wrongly.**

°**wrong**[2] *adverb*
incorrectly: *You've spelled the word* **wrong.**

°**wrong**[3] *noun (no plural)*
something bad: *Small children do not know right from* **wrong.**

wrung /rung/ see **wring**

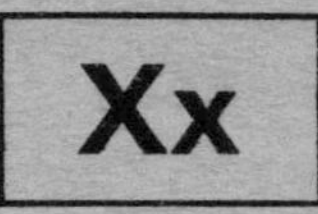

x-ray[1] /eks′ rā/ *noun*
a photograph of the inside of your body, taken with a special unseen light: *The* **x-ray** *showed that the boy's leg was broken.*

x-ray[2] *verb*
to photograph by x-ray

yacht /yät/ *noun*
a boat driven by sails or motor (= large pieces of cloth which catch the wind and make it move)

°**yard** /yärd/ *noun*
1 a piece of ground next to a building with a wall or fence round it: *the school* **yard**
2 a measure of length, the same as three feet; nearly a meter

yawn /yôn/ *verb*
to open the mouth wide and breathe deeply as if tired: *I felt so sleepy I couldn't stop* **yawning.**

°**year** /yēr/ *noun*
a measure of time, 365 days (or 12 months, or 52 weeks): *She is seven* **years** *old. On January 1st, the* **New Year** *begins.*
yearly *adjective, adverb* every year; once a year

yeast /yēst/ *noun (no plural)*
a living substance which is added to flour and water to make bread rise

yell /yel/ *verb*
to shout or cry very loudly

°**yellow** /yel′ ō/ *adjective, noun*
(of) the color of the sun, or the middle part of an egg

°**yes** /yes/
a word we use to answer a question, to show that something is true or that we agree with something: *Can you read this?* — **Yes,** *I can.*

°**yesterday** /yes′ tə dā/
noun, adverb
(on) the day before this day: *It was very hot* **yesterday.**

°**yet** /yet/
1 up to now: *Has he come* **yet?** *No, not* **yet.**
2 but: *He was poor,* **yet** *happy.*

yield /yēld/ *verb*
1 to give way when force is used: *The army* **yielded** *when it was attacked.*
2 to give fruit, etc.: *The trees* **yielded** *a large crop of fruit.*

yogurt *or* **yoghurt** /yō′ gərt/ *noun (no plural)*
milk treated in a special way to make it thick and a bit sour but not bad

yoke /yōk/ *noun*
a piece of wood put across the necks of cattle when pulling carts

yolk /yōk/ *noun*
the yellow part inside an egg (picture at **egg**)

°**you** /ū/ (*plural* **you**)
the person or people that the speaker is talking to: **You** *can swim fast.* **You're** (= you are) *a good swimmer. If I watch* **you,** *I'll learn to swim too. I hope that* **you'll** (= you will) *teach me.* **You've** (= you have) *got a lot of books.* **You'd** (= you had) *already gone when I arrived — I thought that* **you'd** (= you would) *still be there.*

°**young**[1] /yung/ *adjective*
not having lived very long; not old: *His children are* **young** *— four and two years old.*

young[2] *plural noun*
young people or animals: *She teaches the* **young.** *Animals protect their* **young.**

°**your** /yôr *or* ūr/
belonging to you: *Put* **your** *books on* **your** *desks.*

°**yours** /yôrz *or* ūrz/
something belonging to you: *Are all these pencils* **yours?**

°**yourself** /yôr self *or* ūr′ self/ (*plural* **yourselves** /yôr′ selvz *or* ūr′ selvz/)
1 the same person as the one that the speaker is talking to: *Look at* **yourself** *in the mirror. You can't lift that* **by yourself** (= without help). *Why are you playing* **by yourself** (= alone)?
2 (used to make **you** have a stronger meaning): *You told me the story* **yourself.**

youth /ūth/ *noun*
1 *(no plural)* the time when a person is young: *In his* **youth** *he was a soldier.*
2 (*plural* **youths** /ūTHz/) a young man
3 *(no plural)* young people: *the* **youth** *of this country*

Zz

zebra /zē′ brə/ *noun*
(*plural* **zebra** *or* **zebras**)
an African wild animal like a horse which has brown and white lines all over its body

zero /zir′ ō/ *noun*
(*plural* **zeros** *or* **zeroes**)
the number 0

zigzag /zig′ zag″/ *noun*
a z-shaped pattern

zigzag

zinc /zingk/ *(no plural)*
a white metal often mixed with other metals

zip *verb* (*present participle* **zipping,** *past* **zipped**)

zipper /zip′ ər/ *noun*
a fastener that is often used on clothes, and has two sets of teeth which can be joined together

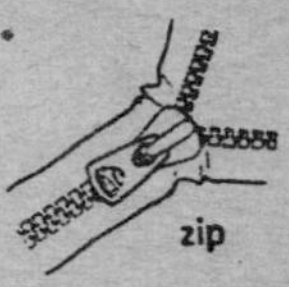

to shut with a zip: *She* **zipped up** *her dress.*

zone /zōn/ *noun*
an area

zoo /zo͞o/ *noun*
a place where different animals are kept for people to look at

Irregular verbs

verb	past tense	past participle
abide	abided	abided
arise	arose	arisen
awake	awoke, awakened	awoken
baby-sit	baby-sat	baby-sat
be	*see dictionary entry*	
bear	bore	borne, born
beat	beat	beaten
become	became	become
befall	befell	befallen
beget	begot (*also* begat *bibl*)	begotten
begin	began	begun
behold	beheld	beheld
bend	bent	bent
beseech	besought, beseeched	besought, beseeched
beset	beset	beset
bet	bet	bet
bid	bade, bid	bidden, bid
bind	bound	bound
bite	bit	bitten
bleed	bled	bled
bless	blessed, blest	blessed, blest
blow	blew	blown
break	broke	broken
breed	bred	bred
bring	brought	brought
broadcast	broadcast	broadcast
build	built	built
burn	burned, burnt	burned, burnt
burst	burst	burst
buy	bought	bought
cast	cast	cast
catch	caught	caught
chide	chided, chid	chid, chidden
choose	chose	chosen
cleave	cleaved, cleft, clove	cleaved, cleft, cloven
cling	clung	clung
come	came	come
cost	cost	cost
creep	crept	crept
cut	cut	cut
deal	dealt	dealt
dig	dug	dug
dive	dived, dove	dived
do	did	done
draw	drew	drawn
dream	dreamed, dreamt	dreamed, dreamt
drink	drank	drunk
drive	drove	driven
dwell	dwelt, dwelled	dwelt, dwelled
eat	ate	eaten
fall	fell	fallen
feed	fed	fed
feel	felt	felt

verb	past tense	past participle
fight	fought	fought
find	found	found
flee	fled	fled
fling	flung	flung
fly	flew	flown
forbear	forbore	forborne
forbid	forbade, forbad	forbidden
forecast	forecast, forecasted	forecast, forecasted
foresee	foresaw	foreseen
foretell	foretold	foretold
forget	forgot	forgotten
forgive	forgave	forgiven
forgo	forwent	forgone
forsake	forsook	forsaken
freeze	froze	frozen
get	got	got, gotten
give	gave	given
go	went	gone
grind	ground	ground
grow	grew	grown
hang	hung, hanged	hung, hanged
have	had	had
hear	heard	heard
heave	heaved, hove	heaved, hove
hew	hewed	hewed, hewn
hide	hid	hidden, hid
hit	hit	hit
hold	held	held
hurt	hurt	hurt
keep	kept	kept
kneel	kneeled, knelt	kneeled, knelt
knit	knitted, knit	knitted, knit
know	knew	known
lay	laid	laid
lead	led	led
lean	leaned	leaned
leap	leaped, leapt	leaped, leapt
learn	learned	learned
leave	left	left
lend	lent	lent
let	let	let
lie	lay	lain
light	lighted, lit	lighted, lit
lose	lost	lost
make	made	made
mean	meant	meant
meet	met	met
miscast	miscast	miscast
mislay	mislaid	mislaid
mislead	misled	misled
misspell	misspelled	misspelled
misspend	misspent	misspent
mistake	mistook	mistaken
misunderstand	misunderstood	misunderstood
mow	mowed	mowed, mown
outdo	outdid	outdone

verb	past tense	past participle
outgrow	outgrew	outgrown
outshine	outshone	outshone
overcome	overcame	overcome
overdo	overdid	overdone
overhang	overhung	overhung
overload	overloaded	overloaded
overrun	overran	overrun
oversee	oversaw	overseen
oversleep	overslept	overslept
overtake	overtook	overtaken
overthrow	overthrew	overthrown
partake	partook	partaken
pay	paid	paid
prove	proved	proved, proven
put	put	put
read	read	read
repay	repaid	repaid
rethink	rethought	rethought
rid	rid	rid
ride	rode	ridden
ring	rang	rung
rise	rose	risen
run	ran	run
saw	sawed	sawed, sawn
say	said	said
see	saw	seen
seek	sought	sought
sell	sold	sold
send	sent	sent
set	set	set
saw	sewed	sewed, sewn
shake	shook	shaken
shear	sheared	sheared, shorn
shed	shed	shed
shine	shone, shined	shone, shined
shoe	shod	shod
shoot	shot	shot
show	showed	shown, showed
shrink	shrank, shrunk	shrunk, shrunken
shut	shut	shut
sing	sang	sung
sink	sank, sunk	sunk
sit	sat	sat
slay	slew	slain
sleep	slept	slept
slide	slid	slid
sling	slung	slung
slink	slunk	slunk
slit	slit	slit
smell	smelled, smelt	smelled, smelt
sow	sowed	sowed, sown
speak	spoke	spoken
speed	sped, speeded	sped, speeded
spell	spelled	spelled
spend	spent	spent
spill	spilled, spilt	spilled, spilt

verb	past tense	past participle
spin	spun	spun
spit	spit, spat	spit, spat
split	split	split
spoil	spoiled, spoilt	spoiled, spoilt
spread	spread	spread
spring	sprang, sprung	sprung
stand	stood	stood
steal	stole	stolen
stick	stuck	stuck
sting	stung	stung
stink	stank, stunk	stunk
strew	strewed	strewed, strewn
stride	strode	stridden
strike	struck	struck
string	strung	strung
strive	strove, strived	striven, strived
swear	swore	sworn
sweep	swept	swept
swell	swelled	swelled, swollen
swim	swam	swum
swing	swung	swung
take	took	taken
teach	taught	taught
tear	tore	torn
tell	told	told
think	thought	thought
thrive	throve, thrived	thrived, thriven
throw	threw	thrown
thrust	thrust	thrust
tread	trod, treaded	trodden, trod
unbend	unbent	unbent
undergo	underwent	undergone
understand	understood	understood
undertake	undertook	undertaken
undo	undid	undone
unwind	unwound	unwound
uphold	upheld	upheld
upset	upset	upset
wake	woke, waked	woken, waked, woke
wear	wore	worn
weave	wove	woven
wed	wedded, wed	wedded, wed
weep	wept	wept
wet	wet, wetted	wet
win	won	won
wind	wound	wound
withdraw	withdrew	withdrawn
withhold	withheld	withheld
withstand	withstood	withstood
wring	wrung	wrung
write	wrote	written

Word Beginnings

Afro- /af rō/ **1** of Africa: *an Afro-American* **2** African and: *Afro-Asian peoples*

Anglo- /ang glō/ **1** of England or Britain: *an Anglophile* (someone who loves Britain) **2** English or British and: *an Anglo-American treaty*

ante- /ant ē/ before: *antedate* — compare POST-

anti- /an tī or ant ē/ against; not in favor of; trying to prevent or destroy: *an anticancer drug* | *an antitank gun* | *He's very antiwar.* — compare PRO-

arch- /ärch/ chief; main: *our archenemy*

astro- /as trō/ of or about the stars and space: *astrophysics*

audio- /ô dē ō/ of, for, or using sound, esp. recorded sound: *audiovisual teaching aids* — compare VIDEO

Austro- /ôs trō/ **1** Australian and: *Austro-Malayan* **2** Austrian and: *the Austro-Italian border*

be- /bē/ *(makes verbs and adjectives)* cause to be or have: *a bedazzling light* | *She befriended me.*

bi- /bī/ two; twice: *a bicameral legislature* (= two chamber | house)

bio- /bī ō/ connected with (the study of) living things: *biochemistry*

centi- /sen tə/ hundredth part: *a centimeter* (= a hundredth of a meter)

co- /kō/ with; together: *my co-author, who wrote the book with me*

counter- /koun tə/ done in return or so as to have an opposite effect or make ineffective: *a counter-attack* | *counterespionage operations*

cross- /krôs/ going between the stated things: *cross-cultural influences*

de- /dē/ **1** (showing an opposite): *a depopulated area* (= which all or most of the population has left) **2** to remove: *to dethrone a king* | *to debug a computer program* **3** to make less: *devalue the currency*

deci- /desə/ tenth part: *a deciliter* (= a tenth of a liter)

dis- /dis/ not; the opposite of: *I disagree.* | *He is dishonest.* **2** removal: *nuclear disarmament*

em- /em/ (*before* b, m, *or* p) EN-: *emboldened*

en- /en/ *(makes verbs)* cause to be (more): *Enlarge the hole.*

equi- /ekwə *or* ēkwə/ equally: *two points equidistant from a third*

Euro- /ū rō/ of Europe, esp. the EEC: *the Europarliament*

ex- /eks/ former: *ex-president*

extra- /eks trə/ not (usu.) included; beyond; outside: *extracurricular lessons* | *extravehicular activity by astronauts*

fore- /fôr/ **1** before; in advance: *I was forewarned of their visit.* **2** in or at the front: *a boat's foresail*

Franco- /fran kō/ **1** of France: *a Francophile* (= someone who loves France) **2** French and: *the Franco-Prussian war*

geo- /gē ō/ connected with the study of the earth or its surface: *geophysics*

hecto- /hek tō/ hundred: *a hectoliter* (= a hundred liters) — compare CENTI-

hydro- /hī drō/ concerning or using water: *hydroelectricity*

hyper- /hī per/ very or too much: *hyperactive* | *hypercritical*

hypo- /hī pō/ under or beneath: *hypoactive* | *hypodermic*

il- /il/ not: *illiberal*

im- /im/ (*before* b, m, *or* p) IN-: impossible

in- /in/ **1** not: *indecisive* | *insane* **2** inward: *a sudden inrush of water*

inter- /in tər/ between or including both or all: *the intercity train service* | *an interdenominational marriage ceremony*

intra- /in trə/ within: *intramural basketball program*

ir- /ir/ (*before* r) not: *irrational*

kilo- /kē lō/ thousand: *a kilogram* (= a thousand grams) — compare MILLI-

mal- /mal/ bad(ly); wrong(ly): *a malformed body* | *maladministration*

maxi- /maks ē/ unusually large or long — compare MINI-

mega- /meg ə/ **1** million: *a ten-megaton nuclear bomb* **2** *sl* very great: *a movie megastar*

micro- /mī krō/ **1** (esp. with scientific words) extremely small: *a microcomputer* **2** using a microscope: *microsurgery* **3** millionth part: *a microsecond* (= a millionth of a second)

mid- /mid/ middle; in the middle of: *midwinter* | *in mid-Atlantic* | *She's in her mid-20's* (= is about 25 years old).

milli- /mil lə/ thousandth part: *a milliliter* (= a thousandth of a liter) — compare KILO-

mini- /min ē/ unusually small or short: *a miniskirt* | *a TV miniseries*

mis- **1** bad(ly); wrong(ly): *He mistreats his dog terribly.* | *I misheard what you said.* **2** lack of; opposite of: *mistrust* | *misfortune*

mono- one; single; UNI-: *monosyllabic* | *a monoplane* (with one wing on each side) compare POLY-

multi- /mul tə/ many: *a multi-purpose tool*

non- /non/ not: *nonaddictive* | *nonprofitmaking*

over- /ō vər/ **1** too much: *an over-indulgent parent* | *an overcooked dish* — compare UNDER- **2** above; across: *We took the overland route.*

poly- /pol ē/ many: *polysyllabic* — compare MONO-

post- /pōst/ after; later than: *the postwar years* — compare PRE-

pre- /prē/ before; earlier than: *the prewar years* | *a prelunch walk* — compare POST-

pro- /prō/ in favor of; supporting: *She's pro-life.* — compare ANTI-

pseudo- /so͞o dō/ only pretending to be; false: *pseudointellectuals*

psycho- /sī kō/ connected with (illness of) the mind: *psychotherapy* | *psychosomatic*

quasi- /kwə zē/ seeming to be; almost like: *a quasijudicial function*

re- /rē/ again: *The body was dug up and then reburied.*

self- /self/ of or by oneself or itself: *a self-charging battery* | *self-deception* | *She's completely self-taught.*

semi- /sem ē/ half: *a semicircle* **2** partly; incomplete(ly): *semi-permanent* | *in the semidarkness*

step- /step/ related through a parent who has remarried

sub- /sub/ **1** under; below: *subsoil* | *subzero temperatures* **2** smaller part of: *a subcategory* **3** less than; worse than: *subhuman intelligence* **4** next in rank below: *a subordinate* — compare SUPER-

super- /so͞o pə/ greater or more than: *superhuman strength* | *supertankers* (= very large ships) *carrying oil* — compare SUB-

trans- /trans/ across; on or to the other side of: *a transatlantic flight*

tri- /trī/ three: *trilingual* (= speaking three languages)

ultra- /ul trə/ very, esp. too: *ultramodern* | *ultracautious*

un- /un/ **1** *(makes adjectives and adverbs)* not: *uncomfortable* | *unfairly* | *unwashed* **2** *(makes verbs)* make or do the opposite of: *She tied a knot, and then untied it.*

under- /un dər/ **1** too little: *undercooked potatoes* | *under-production* **2** below: *an undersea cable* — compare OVER-

uni- /ū nə/ one; single; MONO-: *unicellular*

vice- /vīs/ next in rank below: *the vice-chairman of the committee*

video- /vid ē ō/ of, for, or using recorded pictures, esp. as produced by a VIDEO (2): *a videocassette*

Word Endings

-able /ə bəl/ also **-ible** *(in adjectives)* that can have the stated thing done to it: *a washable fabric*

-age /ij/ *(in nouns)* **1** the action or result of doing the stated thing: *to allow for shrinkage* (= getting smaller) | *several breakages* (= things broken) **2** the cost of doing the stated thing: *Postage is extra.* **3** the state or rank of: *in bondage*

-al /əl/ **1** *(in adjectives)* of; connected with: *autumnal mists* | *a musical performance (in nouns)* (an) act of doing something: *the arrival of the bus* | *several rehearsals*

-an /ən/ IAN: *the Elizabethan Age*

-ance /əns/ *(in nouns)* (an example of) the action, state or quality of doing or being the stated thing: *his sudden appearance* (= he appeared suddenly) | *her brilliance* (= she is BRILLIANT)

-ant /ənt/ *(in adjectives and nouns)* (person or thing) that does the stated thing: *in the resultant confusion* | *a bottle of disinfectant*

-ar /ər/ **1** *(in adjectives)* of; connected with; being: *the Polar regions* **2** *(in nouns)* -ER[2]: *a liar*

-arian /â rē ən/ *(in nouns)* person who supports and believes in: *a libertarian* (= person who supports freedom)

-ary /â rē/ *(in adjectives)* being: *with his customary* (= usual) *caution* | *her legendary* (= very famous) *courage*

-ate /ət/ **1** *(in verbs)* (cause to) become or have: *a hyphenated word* **2** *(in adjectives)* having: *a fortunate* (= lucky) *woman*

-ation /ā shən/ *(in nouns)* (an) act or result of doing the stated thing: *the continuation of the story*

-ative /ə tiv/ *(in adjectives)* **1** liking or tending to have or do: *argumentative* | *talkative* **2** for the purpose of the stated thing: *a consultative meeting*

-bound /bound/ *(in adjectives)* limited, kept in, or controlled in the stated way: *a fogbound aircraft*

-cy /sē/ *(makes nouns from adjectives ending in /t/ or /tik/)* - ITY: *several inaccuracies in the report*

-d /d/ *(after* e) -ED: *a wide-eyed stare*

-dom /dum/ *(in nouns)* **1** condition of being the stated thing: *freedom* | *boredom* **2** country or area ruled by: *a kingdom* **3** people of the stated sort: *despite the opposition of officialdom*

-ean /ē ən/ -IAN

-ed /ed/ **1** *(makes regular past t. and p. of verbs): We landed safely.* **2** *(in adjectives)* having or wearing the stated thing; with: *a long-tailed dog*

-ee /ē/ *(in nouns)* **1** person to whom the stated thing is done: *an employee* | *a trainee* **2** person who is or does the stated thing: *an absentee*

-eer /ēr/ *(in nouns)* person who does or is connected with the stated thing: *a mountaineer* | *The auctioneer asked for bids.*

-en /ən/ **1** *(in adjectives)* made of: *a wooden box* **2** *(in verbs)* make or become (more): *unsweetened tea* | *The sky darkened.*

-ence /əns/ *(in nouns)* -ANCE: *its existence* | *reference* | *occurrence*

-ent /ənt/ -ANT: *nonexistent*

-er[1] /ər/ *(in comparative of short adjectives and adverbs)* more: *faster* | *colder*

-er[2] /ər/ *(in nouns)* **1** person or thing that does the stated thing: *a singer* | *a trainer* (= person who trains others) | *an electric water heater* **2** person who comes from or lives in the stated place: *a New Yorker*

-ery /ərē/ *(in nouns)* **1** the stated condition; -NESS: bravery **2** the stated art or practice; -ING (2): *cookery* **3** place where the stated thing is done: *a brewery*

-es /əz/ *(after /s, z/)* -s: *bosses* | *matches*

-ese /ēz/ *(in nouns and adjectives)* (language) of the stated country: *Do you speak Japanese?* | *Portuguese food*

-esque /esk/ *(in adjectives)* in the manner or style of; like: *statuesque beauty* | *Kafkaesque*

-ess /es/ *(in nouns)* female: *an actress* (= a female actor) | *a lioness*

-est /est/ *(in superlative of short adjectives and adverbs)* most: *slowest* | *loveliest*

-eth /eth/ -TH: *the twentieth time*

-ette /et/ *(in nouns)* small: *a kitchenette*

-ey /ē/ *(esp. after* y*)* -Y: *clayey soil*

-fold /fōld/ *(in adjectives and adverbs)* multiplied by the stated number: *a fourfold increase*

-free /frē/ **1** *(in adjectives)* -LESS (1): *a troublefree journey*

-friendly /frend le/ *(in adjectives)* not difficult for the stated people to use: *a user-friendly computer*

-ful /fəl/ **1** *(in adjectives)* having or giving: *a sinful man* | *a restful day* **2** /fəl/ *(in nouns)* amount contained by: *a handful of coins* | *two spoonfuls of sugar*

-hood /ho͝od/ *(in nouns)* condition or period of being the stated thing: *falsehood* | *during her childhood*

-ial /ē əl/ -AL (1): *a commercial transaction* | *the presidential car*

-ian /ē ən *or* ən/ **1** *(in adjectives and nouns)* of or connected with the stated place or person: *Parisian restaurants* | *I speak Russian.* **2** *(in nouns)* person who studies the stated subject; EXPERT: *an historian* | *a theologian*

-ible /ə bəl/ -ABLE: *deductible*

-ic /ik/ also **ical** /ikəl/ *(in adjectives)* connected with; having or showing: *The design is completely symmetric/symmetrical.* | *an historic occasion* | *an historical novel*

-icide /ə sīd/ *(in nouns)* killing of: *suicide*

-ics /iks/ *(in nouns)* science or skill: *linguistics* | *aeronautics*

-ie /ē/ -Y (2)

-ify /əfī/ *(in verbs)* make or become: *purify* | *simplify*

-ine /īn/ **1** of or concerning: *equine* (= of horses) **2** made of; like: *crystalline*

-ing /ing/ **1** *(makes pres. p. of verbs): I'm coming.* | *a sleeping child* **2** *(makes nouns from verbs): Eating candy makes you fat.* | *a fine painting*

-ish /ish/ **1** *(in nouns and adjectives)* (language) of the stated country: *I speak Swedish.* | *British customs* **2** *(in adjectives)* **a** typical of: *a foolish man* | *girlish giggles* **b** rather: *a reddish glow* **c** about the stated number: *He's fortyish.* | *Come at sixish.*

-ism /iz əm/ *(in nouns)* **1** set of beliefs: *Buddhism* | *socialism* **2** quality or way of behaving: *heroism* | *male chauvinism* **3** way of speaking: *Britishisms*

-ist /ist/ **1** *(in nouns)* person who works with or does the stated thing: *A violinist plays the violin.* | *A machinist works machines.* **2** *(in adjectives and nouns)* (follower) of a set of beliefs: *a Buddhist* **3** making unfair differences between people because of the stated thing: *racist*

-ite /īt/ -IST (2): *a Trotskyite*

-itude /ə to͞od/ *(in nouns)* the state or degree of being: *exactitude* | *certitude* (= being certain)

-ity /ə tē/ *(in nouns)* the stated condition or quality; -NESS: *stupidity* | *sublimity*

-ive /iv/ *(in adjectives)* tending to do the stated thing: *a creative child* | *a supportive partner*

-ize /īz/ *(in verbs)* make or become: *popularizing a new brand of soap* | *to modernize our procedures*

-less /les/ *(in adjectives)* **1** without: *a windless day* | *We are powerless to act.* **2** that never does the stated thing: *a tireless worker*

-let /let/ *(in nouns)* small: *sailing on an inlet*

-like /līk/ *(in adjectives)* typical of: *childlike innocence*

-ly /lē/ **1** *(in adverbs)* in the stated way: *Drive carefully!* **2** *(in adjectives and adverbs)* every: *an hourly report* | *I see him daily.* **3** *(in adjectives)* typical of: *brotherly love* **4** *(in adverbs)* from the stated point of view: *Musically she's very gifted.*

-man /mən/ man who comes from the stated place: *a Frenchman*

-manship /mən ship/ *(in nouns)* the art or skill of a person of the stated type: *seamanship* | *horsemanship*

-ment /mənt/ *(in nouns)* act or result of doing the stated thing; ING (2): *enjoyment* | *encouragement*

-most /mōst/ -EST: *the northernmost parts of the country*

-ness /nes/ *(in nouns)* the stated condition or quality: *loudness*| *gentleness*

-ology /ol ə jī/ *(in nouns)* science or study of: *toxicology* (= the study of poisons) | *musicology*

-or /ər/ -ER[2]: *a sailor*

-ory[1] /ôr e/ *(in nouns)* place or thing used for doing the stated thing: *an observatory*

-ory[2] *(in adjectives)* that does the stated thing: *a congratulatory telegram*

-ous /ůs/ *(in adjectives)* having; full of: *a dangerous place* | *a spacious room*

-phile /fīl/ *(in nouns)* person who likes the stated thing or place very much: *an Anglophile* (= who likes England)

-phobe /fōb/ *(in nouns)* person who dislikes or fears the stated thing very much: *an Anglophobe* (= who dislikes England)

-phobia /fob ī ə/ *(in nouns)* great fear: *acrophobia*

-proof /pro͞of/ **1** *(in adjectives)* treated or made so as not to be harmed by the stated thing: *a bulletproof car* | *an ovenproof dish* **2** *(in verbs)* to treat or make in this way: *to soundproof a room*

-r /r/ *(after* e) -ER

-ridden /rid ən/ *(in adjectives)* **1** suffering from the effects of: *guilt-ridden* **2** too full of: *mosquito-ridden*

-ry /rē/ *(in nouns)* -ERY: *sheer wizardry*

-s /s *or* z/ **1** *(makes the pl. of nouns): one cat and two dogs* **2** *(makes the 3rd person pres. sing. of verbs): She laughs too much.*

-'s *(forms the possessive case of sing. nouns and of plural nouns that do not end in -s): my sister's husband* | *yesterday's lesson* | *the sheep's heads*

-s' *(forms the possessive case of plural nouns): the girls' dresses*

-scape /skāp/ *(in nouns)* a wide view of the stated area: *some old Dutch seascapes*

-ship /ship/ *(in nouns)* **1** condition of having or being the stated thing: *a business in partnership with his brother* | *kingship* **2** the stated skill: *her masterly musicianship*

-some /səm/ **1** *(in adjectives)* causing; producing: *a troublesome problem* **2** *(in nouns)* group of the stated number of people or things: *a twosome*

-speak /spēk/ *often derogatory (in nouns)* the special language, esp. slang words, used in the stated business or activity: *computerspeak*

-st /est/ *(after* e) -EST

-th /th/ *(makes adjectives from numbers, except those ending in 1, 2, or 3): the seventh day*

-tion /shən/ *(in nouns)* -ION

-tude /to͞od/ *(in nouns)* -ITUDE: *disquietude*

-ty /tē/ ITY: *cruelty*

-ure /zhər/ *(in nouns)* act or result of doing the stated thing: -ING (2): *the closure of the factory*

-ward /wəd/ also **-wards** /wədz/ *(in adjectives and adverbs)* in the stated direction: *the homeward journey* | *traveling northwards*

-ware /wâr/ *(in nouns)* containers, tools, etc., made of the stated material or for the stated purpose: *pewterware* | *kitchenware* (= for cooking)

-ways /wāz/ -WISE: *sideways*

-wise /wīz/ *(in adverbs)* **1** in the stated way or direction: *walked crabwise* **2** with regard to: *very inexperienced businesswise*

-y /ē/ **1** *(in adjectives)* of; like; having: *a lemony smell* | *a noisy room* **2** *(makes nouns more informal; used esp. when speaking to children): my granny* | *a nice little doggy* **3** *(in nouns)* -ITY: *jealousy*

Weights and Measures

The words in **dark type** are the ones most commonly used in general speech.

Metric

Units of Length

	1 millimeter	= 0.03937 inch
10 mm	= **1 centimeter**	= 0.3937 inch
10 cm	= 1 decimeter	= 3.937 inches
10 dm	= **1 meter**	= 39.37 inches
10 m	= 1 dekameter	= 10.94 yards
10 dam	= 1 hectometer	= 109.4 yards
10 hm	= **1 kilometer**	= 0.6214 mile

Units of Weight

	1 milligram	= 0.015 grain
10 mg	= 1 centigram	= 0.154 grain
10 cg	= 1 decigram	= 1.543 grains
10 dg	= **1 gram**	= 15.43 grains
		= 0.035 ounces
10 g	= 1 dekagram	= 0.353 ounce
10 dag	= 1 hectogram	= 3.527 ounces
10 hg	= **1 kilogram**	= 2.205 pounds
1000 kg	= **1 ton**	= 1.102 short tons
	(metric ton)	= 2204.62 pounds

Units of Capacity

	1 milliter	= 0.00176 pint
10 ml	= 1 centiliter	= 0.0176 pint
10 cl	= 1 dekaliter	= 0.176 pint
10 dl	= **1 liter**	= 1.76 pints
10 l	= 1 dekaliter	= 2.20 gallons
10 dal	= 1 hectoliter	= 22.0 gallons
10 hl	= 1 kiloliter	= 220.0 gallons

Units of Area

1 square millimeter		= 0.00155 square inch
100 mm^2	= 1 square centimeter	= 0.1550 in^2
100 cm^2	= 1 square meter	= 1.196 yd^2
100 m^2	= 1 are	= 119.6 yd^2
100 ares	= **1 hectare**	= 2.471 acres
100 ha	= 1 square kilometer	= 247.1 acres

Units of Volume

	1 cubic centimeter	= 0.06102 cubic inch
1000 cm^3	= 1 cubic decimeter	= 0.03532 cubic foot
100 dm^3	= 1 cubic meter	= 1.308 cubic yards

U.S. Customary

Units of Length

	1 inch	= 2.54 cm
12 inches	= **1 foot**	= 0.3048 m
3 feet	= **1 yard**	= 0.9144 m
5½ yards	= 1 rod	= 5.029 m
5,280 feet	= 1 mile	= 1.609 km

Units of Weight

	1 grain	= 64.8 mg
	1 dram	= 1.772 g
16 drams	= **1 ounce**	= 28.35 g
16 ounces	= **1 pound**	= 0.4536 kg
100 pounds	= **short hundredweight**	= 50.80 kg
112 pounds	= **long hundredweight**	= 45.36 kg
20 hundredweight	= 1 (short) **ton**	= 1.016 ton
2000 pounds	= 1 (short) **ton**	= 0.9072 ton

Units of Capacity (Liquid)

	1 fluid ounce	= 29.573 ml
4 fluid ounces	= 1 gill	= 118.294 ml
4 gills	= **1 pint**	= 0.473 ℓ
2 pints	= **1 quart**	= 0.946 ℓ
4 quarts	= **1 gallon**	= 3.785 ℓ

Units of Area

	1 square inch	= 6.452 cm^2
144 square inches	= 1 square foot	= 0.093 m^2
9 square feet	= 1 square yard	= 0.836 m^2
4840 square yards	= 1 acre	= 4047 m^2
640 acres	= 1 square mile	= 2.590 km^2

Units of Volume

	1 cubic inch	= 16.39 cm^3
1728 cubic inches	= 1 cubic foot	= 0.02832 m^3
		= 28.32 dm^3
27 cubic feet	= 1 cubic yard	= 0.7646 m^3
		= 764.6 dm^3

Units of Capacity (Dry)

1 pint	= ½ quart	= 0.551 ℓ
2 pints	= 1 quart	= 1.101 ℓ
8 quarts	= 1 peck	= 8.810 ℓ
4 pecks	= 1 bushel	= 35.239 ℓ

Temperature Conversions

° *Fahrenheit* $= \left(\frac{9}{5} \, ^\circ C \right) + 32$

° *Celsius* $= \left(\frac{5}{9} \, ^\circ F \right) - 32$